THE UNRELENTING GOD

David Bourgeen

2013

THE UNRELENTING GOD

God's Action in Scripture

ESSAYS IN HONOR OF
BEVERLY ROBERTS GAVENTA

Edited by

David J. Downs *&* Matthew L. Skinner

WILLIAM B. EERDMANS PUBLISHING COMPANY
GRAND RAPIDS, MICHIGAN / CAMBRIDGE, U.K.

Published 2013 by
Wm. B. Eerdmans Publishing Co.
2140 Oak Industrial Drive N.E., Grand Rapids, Michigan 49505 /
P.O. Box 163, Cambridge CB3 9PU U.K.

Printed in the United States of America

19 18 17 16 15 14 13   7 6 5 4 3 2 1

Library of Congress Cataloging-in-Publication Data

The unrelenting God: God's action in scripture. Essays in honor of
     Beverly Roberts Gaventa / edited by David J. Downs & Matthew L. Skinner.
          pages   cm
     Includes bibliographical references and index.
     ISBN 978-0-8028-6767-4 (pbk.: alk. paper)
     1. Bible. New Testament — Criticism, interpretation, etc.
     I. Gaventa, Beverly Roberts.   II. Downs, David J., 1977 — editor of compilation.

     BS2361.3.U57   2013
     225.6 — dc23

                                                  2013020948

www.eerdmans.com

Contents

Preface

David J. Downs and Matthew L. Skinner

Those who study the New Testament's Pauline and Lukan writings know Beverly Roberts Gaventa as a thorough and thoughtful voice encouraging others to attend to the theological deliberations taking place in the pages of Scripture. Those who have sat in her classes at Princeton Theological Seminary (and at Columbia Theological Seminary, at Colgate Rochester Crozer Divinity School, and elsewhere) know her as an erudite, careful, and insightful exegete. Her brand-new colleagues and students at Baylor University are coming to know this in full measure, even as this book goes to print during her first semester there. She is an exemplary teacher and a first-rate scholar. Her influence extends far and wide, propelled by her writings, students, and colleagues in New Testament and theological scholarship.

There is an eclectic quality to this celebration of Gaventa, in that the essays in the volume address various biblical texts — mostly the Pauline tradition, Luke-Acts, and even Ezekiel — as well as theological reflections on Jesus Christ. What holds the collection together, however, is stated in its subtitle: a focus on God's action as different scriptural authors attempt to identify and describe such a thing. The various contributors and the breadth of their essays' subject matter find their cohesion in the energy that Gaventa's teaching, scholarship, and publications have generated over the decades. Her work has been consistently theological. This is not to call it preachy or limited by confessional constraints; that is hardly the case. Rather, the theological character of her work stems from its recognition that in the New Testament we find authors and communities trying to give voice to who God is and how God operates in and for the sake of human existence. To miss this basic truth is to risk letting our reading and study of the Bible devolve into a limited exploration of ancient cultures or into self-absorbed anthropology. Gaventa has been interested in what the canonical authors have to say about God, and this interest has inspired her friends and fellow scholars. Accordingly, there are essays in this volume by her faculty colleagues, collaborators, and former students — plus a word from her onetime seminary professor — who have been motivated to contribute, not because of their friendship with Gaventa (although those friendships exist and are strong), but because her work has borne fruit in their own ways of thinking about the Bible, theology, and the character of God.

The editors extend their sincere thanks to Martha Schwehn Bardwell, Benjamin Lappenga, Brian Robinson, and Susan Wood for their careful and dedicated assistance in preparing this collection. Our gratitude goes to Linda Bieze, Jenny Hoffman, Jon Pott, and their team at Eerdmans. We are also grateful for the support and resources provided by our institutions, Fuller Theological Seminary and Luther Seminary. We could not have completed this project alone. We celebrate the work of our contributors and thank them for their enthusiastic desire to offer their talents and wisdom in honor of Beverly Roberts Gaventa.

We, the editors, fervently hope that this volume will indeed honor Beverly and her work, as an expression of how she and her contributions have already honored us and our pursuit of knowledge. May the book likewise encourage others to explore the theological questions raised by biblical texts, and may those explorations result in worship and praise of the God whose unrelenting love for humanity and for the entire cosmos knows no bounds.

A Personal Word

J. Louis Martyn

A venerable piece of wisdom has it that the true gift to the teacher is the genuine student whose learning process reaches out and engages the teacher, thereby causing both parties to emerge changed, enriched in ways anticipated by neither. Student becomes teacher and teacher student, as both are surprised by new vistas opened up precisely in their instructive comradeship. It is an event of grace; and so it was to be a teacher to Beverly Gaventa.

J. Louis Martyn is Edward Robinson Professor of Biblical Theology Emeritus at Union Theological Seminary in the City of New York.

Contributors

SHANE BERG, Vice President, Macedonian Ministry Foundation

ALEXANDRA R. BROWN, Jessie Ball duPont Professor of Religion, Washington and Lee University

WILLIAM SANGER CAMPBELL, Associate Professor of Theology and Religious Studies, the College of St. Scholastica

MARTINUS C. DE BOER, Professor of New Testament, Vrije Universiteit Amsterdam

DAVID J. DOWNS, Associate Professor of New Testament Studies, Fuller Theological Seminary

SUSAN GROVE EASTMAN, Associate Professor of the Practice of Bible and Christian Formation, the Divinity School, Duke University

JOEL B. GREEN, Associate Dean for the Center for Advanced Theological Studies and Professor of New Testament Interpretation, Fuller Theological Seminary

DOUGLAS HARINK, Professor of Theology, the King's University College

RICHARD B. HAYS, Dean and George Washington Ivey Professor of New Testament, the Divinity School, Duke University

L. ANN JERVIS, Professor of New Testament and Advanced Degree Director, Wycliffe College

JACQUELINE E. LAPSLEY, Associate Professor of Old Testament, Princeton Theological Seminary

JOHN B. F. MILLER, Associate Professor of Religion, McMurry University

MATTHEW L. SKINNER, Associate Professor of New Testament, Luther Seminary

KATHERINE SONDEREGGER, Professor of Theology, Virginia Theological Seminary

FRANCIS WATSON, Research Chair of Biblical Interpretation, Durham University

MICHAEL WELKER, Professor of Systematic Theology, University of Heidelberg

Abbreviations

AB	Anchor Bible
ABR	*Australian Biblical Review*
AnBib	Analecta biblica
ANE	Ancient Near Eastern
ANTC	Abingdon New Testament Commentaries
AOTC	Abingdon Old Testament Commentaries
BA	*Biblical Archaeologist*
BAG	Bauer, Walter, William F. Arndt, and F. Wilbur Gingrich. *A Greek-English Lexicon of the New Testament and Other Early Christian Literature.* Chicago: University of Chicago Press, 1957.
BAGD	Bauer, Walter, William F. Arndt, F. Wilbur Gingrich, and Frederick W. Danker. *A Greek-English Lexicon of the New Testament and Other Early Christian Literature.* 2nd ed. Chicago: University of Chicago Press, 1977.
BDAG	Bauer, Walter, Frederick W. Danker, William F. Arndt, and F. Wilbur Gingrich. *A Greek-English Lexicon of the New Testament and Other Early Christian Literature.* 3rd ed. Chicago: University of Chicago Press, 1999.
BDF	Blass, Friedrich A., F. Albert Debrunner, and Robert W. Funk. *A Greek Grammar of the New Testament and Other Early Christian Literature.* Chicago: University of Chicago Press, 1961.
Bib	*Biblica*
BJRL	*Bulletin of the John Rylands University Library of Manchester*
BZ	*Biblische Zeitschrift*
BZNW	Beihefte zur Zeitschrift für die neutestamentliche Wissenschaft
CBQ	*Catholic Biblical Quarterly*

CBQMS	Catholic Biblical Quarterly Monograph Series
CEB	Common English Bible
Chm	*Churchman*
CQ	*Classical Quarterly*
CTJ	*Calvin Theological Journal*
CTR	*Criswell Theological Review*
DSD	*Dead Sea Discoveries*
EDNT	*Exegetical Dictionary of the New Testament.* Edited by Horst Balz and Gerhard Schneider. 3 vols. Grand Rapids: Eerdmans, 1990-1993.
EKKNT	Evangelisch-katholischer Kommentar zum Neuen Testament
ETR	*Etudes théologiques et religieuses*
ExpTim	*Expository Times*
FAT	Forschungen zum Alten Testament
FRLANT	Forschungen zur Religion und Literatur des Alten und Neuen Testaments
HALOT	Koehler, Ludwig, Walter Baumgartner, and Johann Jakob Stamm. *The Hebrew and Aramaic Lexicon of the Old Testament.* Translated and edited under the supervision of M. E. J. Richardson. 4 vols. Leiden: Brill, 1994-1999.
HSM	Harvard Semitic Monographs
HR	*History of Religions*
HTKNT	Herders theologischer Kommentar zum Neuen Testament
ICC	International Critical Commentary
Int	*Interpretation*
JAAR	*Journal of the American Academy of Religion*
JBL	*Journal of Biblical Literature*
JECS	*Journal of Early Christian Studies*
JPTSup	Journal of Pentecostal Theology: Supplement Series
JQR	*Jewish Quarterly Review*
JSNT	*Journal for the Study of the New Testament*
JSNTSup	Journal for the Study of the New Testament: Supplement Series
JSOTSup	Journal for the Study of the Old Testament: Supplement Series
JTI	*Journal of Theological Interpretation*
JTS	*Journal of Theological Studies*
KJV	King James Version
LCL	Loeb Classical Library
LHBOTS	Library of Hebrew Bible/Old Testament Studies
LNTS	Library of New Testament Studies

LSJ	Liddell, Henry George, Robert Scott, and Henry Stuart Jones. *A Greek-English Lexicon*. 9th ed. Oxford: Clarendon, 1996.
LXX	Septuagint
MHT	Moulton, James Hope, Wilbert Francis Howard, and Nigel Turner. *A Grammar of New Testament Greek*. 4 vols. Edinburgh: T. & T. Clark, 1908-1976.
NA^{27}	*Novum Testamentum Graece*. Nestle Aland 27th ed.
NAB	New American Bible
NCB	New Century Bible
NEB	New English Bible
NETS	New English Translation of the Septuagint
NIBC	New International Biblical Commentary
NICNT	New International Commentary on the New Testament
NIDB	*The New Interpreter's Dictionary of the Bible*. Edited by Katharine Doob Sakenfeld et al. 5 vols. Nashville: Abingdon, 2006-2009.
NIDOTTE	*New International Dictionary of Old Testament Theology and Exegesis*. Edited by Willem A. VanGemeren. 5 vols. Grand Rapids: Zondervan, 1997.
NIGTC	New International Greek Testament Commentary
NIV	New International Version
NovT	*Novum Testamentum*
NovTSup	Novum Testamentum Supplements
NRSV	New Revised Standard Version
NTD	Das Neue Testament Deutsch
NTL	New Testament Library
NTS	*New Testament Studies*
OBT	Overtures to Biblical Theology
OTL	Old Testament Library
RB	*Revue biblique*
REB	Revised English Bible
RelArts	*Religion and the Arts*
RevExp	*Review and Expositor*
RGG	*Die Religion in Geschichte und Gegenwart: Handwörterbuch für Theologie und Religionswissenschaft*. Edited by Hans Dieter Betz et al. 8 vols. 4th ed. Tübingen: Mohr Siebeck, 1998-2005.
RSV	Revised Standard Version
SBLAB	Society of Biblical Literature Academia Biblica
SBLAIL	Society of Biblical Literature Ancient Israel and Its Literature
SBLDS	Society of Biblical Literature Dissertation Series

SBT	Studies in Biblical Theology
SJT	*Scottish Journal of Theology*
SNTS	Society for New Testament Studies
SNTSMS	Society for New Testament Studies Monograph Series
SNTW	Studies of the New Testament and Its World
SP	Sacra pagina
SPhilo	*Studia Philonica*
TDOT	*Theological Dictionary of the Old Testament.* Edited by G. Johannes Botterweck and Helmer Ringgren. Translated by John T. Willis, Geoffrey W. Bromiley, and David E. Green. 15 vols. Grand Rapids: Eerdmans, 1977-.
THKNT	Theologischer Handkommentar zum Neuen Testament
TLNT	Spicq, Ceslas. *Theological Lexicon of the New Testament.* Translated and edited by James D. Ernest. 3 vols. Peabody, MA: Hendrickson, 1994.
TOTC	Tyndale Old Testament Commentaries
TynBul	*Tyndale Bulletin*
WBC	Word Biblical Commentary
WUNT	Wissenschaftliche Untersuchungen zum Neuen Testament
WW	*Word and World*
ZAW	*Zeitschrift für die alttestamentliche Wissenschaft*
ZNW	*Zeitschrift für die neutestamentliche Wissenschaft und die Kunde der älteren Kirche*

Body Piercings Revisited:
Piercings and Profanations of "Bodies"
and the Character of God in Ezekiel

Jacqueline E. Lapsley

Classical and Grotesque Bodies in Ezekiel

How does this chapter on Ezekiel fit into a volume dedicated to celebrating the work of Beverly Roberts Gaventa, a Pauline scholar? Well, it is the odd-ball, in one sense, of course. But I have discovered after years of reading Ezekiel that the God to be found in his book is no less unrelenting than the God of the Apostle, so in that sense this chapter fits right into this volume. Indeed, it is Beverly Gaventa, my departmental colleague and dear friend, who has helped me to see that Ezekiel and Paul are kindred spirits in many ways, each struggling to articulate a compelling theological vision to an audience not all that willing or interested or even capable of hearing it; each overwhelmed by the stunning magnitude of human sin; but each also convinced that God's desire and will to overcome that sin are more than equal to it, powerful as it is.

In a previous article, I argue that one may observe some of Ezekiel's theological creativity in the interplay between grotesque bodies (briefly: protruding, bulging, and, in Ezekiel, "pierced," dead bodies) and classical bodies (whole, smooth, complete bodies).[1] In Ezekiel's world, a world flying

---

1. Jacqueline E. Lapsley, "Body Piercings: The Priestly Body and the 'Body' of the Temple in Ezekiel," *Hebrew Bible and Ancient Israel* 1 (2012): 231-45. Mikhail Bakhtin provides his now-famous definition of the classical body as one that "presents an entirely finished, completed, strictly limited body, which is shown from the outside as something individual. That which protrudes, bulges, sprouts, or branches off . . . is eliminated, hidden, or moderated. All orifices of the body are closed. The basis of the image is the individual, strictly limited mass, the impenetrable facade" (*Rabelais and His World,* trans. H. Iswolsky [Bloomington: Indiana University Press, 1984], p. 320).

apart into chaos and confusion in the years following the first Babylonian incursion of 597 BCE, the grotesque is a peculiarly appropriate literary form for the prophet to take up, as Wolfgang Kayser's definition makes clear: in the grotesque, "our world . . . ceases to be reliable, and we feel that we would be unable to live in this changed world. The grotesque instills fear of life rather than fear of death. Structurally, it presupposes that the categories which apply to our world view become inapplicable."[2] One has the sense reading Ezekiel that it is worse to *live* in the world that the prophet describes, the world of imminent invasion, with the bodies piling up, and a temple abandoned by God, than it is to *die* in it. The violations of Ezekiel's own priestly body in Ezekiel 4 and 5 share certain features with the violations of the "body" of the temple in chapter 8, shared features that point to a certain common identity between the classical body of the priest and the classical "body" of the temple. The sanctity of both these "classical" bodies is violated until the temple is destroyed and the classical body of the priest so closely associated with it also recedes. Thus, the classical body disappears in the book until it reappears at the very end in the vision of chapters 40–48. In the intervening chapters, the question of whether there can be any future for Israel, whose classical body has also been sullied, is in doubt, for as the classical bodies of temple and priest recede, other grotesque bodies pile up (chapters 6, 7, 16, 23, 29, 31, 32, and especially 38, 39), revealing Ezekiel's deep ambivalence about bodies — the classical bodies being the site of holiness and deliverance, the grotesque ones the site of disobedience and destruction.

To Profane חלל I and to Pierce חלל II

My attention in that earlier article focuses particularly on the body of Ezekiel as priest in chapters 4 and 5, and the "body" of the temple in chapter 8. I argue there that the sanctity of Ezekiel's body (and Israel's "body" insofar as Ezekiel represents Israel) and the sanctity of the temple body are pierced and profaned in parallel fashion, and that their classical bodies give way to a plethora of grotesque, dead bodies as the book progresses. But I only mention in passing what happens to the "bodies" in chapters 6 and 7.[3]

---

2. There are a number of different ways of approaching the grotesque, but for my purposes in looking at Ezekiel, Kayser's approach is particularly useful because it gets at the terrifying nature of the grotesque (Wolfgang Kayser, *The Grotesque in Art and Literature*, trans. U. Weisstein [Bloomington: Indiana University Press, 1963], p. 185).

3. Garber sees Ezekiel's use of חלל I as an articulation of his priestly worldview and

Here I want to address that lacuna because it is a piece of the larger puzzle of what Ezekiel is doing with bodies in his book, and an obvious link between chapters 4, 5, and 8. Picking up on the work of David G. Garber Jr., in this essay I will argue that a play on words between חלל I [*chalal;* to profane] and חלל II [*chalal;* to pierce] is present in chapters 6 and 7. It is also at work in other parts of Ezekiel as well because the occurrences of the roots are plentiful throughout the book (see footnotes 5 and 8 below), but there will not be space here to pursue other texts. The pun on the pierced bodies in chapter 6 and the profaned body of the temple in chapter 7 echoes throughout Ezekiel's book. I have in fact already suggested the presence of the pun in the second sentence of this paragraph: ". . . the sanctity of Ezekiel's body . . . and the sanctity of the temple body are *pierced and profaned* in parallel fashion. . . ."

Apart from Malachi, Ezekiel has by far the highest concentration of the root חלל [*chalal*] with a base meaning of "profane" in the Hebrew Bible.[4] It occurs thirty times in Ezekiel, usually in the *pi'el*.[5] The prophet uses it to speak on multiple occasions of the profaning of the temple, the divine name and person, and the Sabbath.[6] Likewise, apart from Lamentations, Ezekiel has by far the highest concentration of the root חלל [*chalal*] with a base meaning of "pierced," and therefore "slain" or "dead" bodies, in the Hebrew Bible.[7] It occurs thirty-four times in Ezekiel.[8] It is perhaps his fa-

---

חלל II as an expression of victimization; his interweaving of the two is part of the vocabulary of trauma (David G. Garber Jr., "A Vocabulary of Trauma in the Exilic Writings," in *Interpreting Exile: Displacement and Deportation in Biblical and Modern Contexts,* SBLAIL 10, ed. Brad E. Kelle, Frank Ritchel Ames, and Jacob L. Wright [Atlanta: Society of Biblical Literature, 2011], pp. 309-22).

4. It occurs three times in Malachi, which is relatively frequent for such a short book.

5. It occurs only rarely in Ezekiel with the meaning "to begin," e.g., 9:6. For the base meaning of "profane," see Ezek. 7:21, 22 (2x), 24; 13:19; 20:9, 13, 14, 16, 21, 22, 24, 39; 22:8, 16, 26 (2x); 23:38, 39; 24:21; 25:3; 28:7, 16, 18; 36:20, 21, 22, 23; 39:7; 44:7.

6. Occasionally "holy objects" are profaned (e.g., 22:26; קָדְשַׁי), and in an interesting case, the prince of Tyre's splendor is profaned in chapter 28. The latter case is interesting because the pun on חלל seems to be at work concerning the prince of Tyre within three verses: the nations will "profane" his splendor (וְחִלְּלוּ יִפְעָתֶךָ, 28:7); in the next verse he will die a "piercing" death in the heart of the seas (מְמוֹתֵי חָלָל בְּלֵב יַמִּים, v. 8); the text then asks whether he will claim to be a god when he is in the hand of one who "pierces" him (בְּיַד מְחַלְלֶיךָ, v. 9).

7. Lamentations has three occurrences of the root with this meaning, a slightly higher concentration per thousand words (1:24) than Ezekiel (1:16).

8. It occurs thirty-four times according to *HALOT*. See 6:4, 7, 13; 9:7; 11:6 (2x), 7; 21:19 (2x), 30, 34; 26:15; 28:8, 23; 30:4, 11, 24; 31:17, 18; 32:20, 21, 22, 23, 24, 25 (3x), 28, 29, 30 (2x), 31, 32; 35:8; plus a pol. form in 28:9. Mostly the *chalalim* ("pierced") ones are dead, but occa-

vorite word for speaking about dead bodies. Together, then, these homo-
phones of "profaned" and "pierced," "defiled" and "dead," resound markedly throughout the book.

Before turning to chapters 6 and 7 and the way in which חלל [*chalal*]
appears in those chapters, it is worth looking back briefly at chapters 4 and
5 for immediate context. There, Ezekiel's priestly body was "grotesqued," as
it were, by the sign-acts that he was required to perform, and chapter 5
ended with the inauguration of a terrifying world, as YHWH announces in
5:10 that he will do that which he has never done before: parents will eat
children, and children will eat parents. This is a grotesque image in every
sense of the word: all boundaries of the classical body are violated, and the
known world is turned upside down. All order and established values are
transgressed; it is the world of the terrifying grotesque (the kind
Hieronymus Bosch would evoke much later in his paintings).

To Profane חלל I and to Pierce חלל II in Ezekiel 6 and 7

Chapter 6 then begins with an oracle against the mountains. The mountains serve as the ostensible addressee because they are the location of the
"high places," which stand in for all the Judahites' idolatrous religious
practices in this chapter, and which are the focus of the divine judgment
in this chapter. But it is of course the people who engage in those practices who are the real object of the divine wrath here: wherever they live,
they shall be struck down by the sword (of the invading Babylonian
army) and will lie slain, or more literally, "pierced," among the ruins of
their idols.[9] In Ezekiel 6:4, "Your altars shall become desolate, and your
incense stands shall be broken; and I will cast down your pierced ones
[חַלְלֵיכֶם] in front of your idols/dung balls [גִּלּוּלֵיכֶם]."[10] The prophet de-

---

sionally the "pierced" ones are not quite dead, but rather only fatally wounded, as in 26:15
and 30:24, where they are still groaning, which evokes for readers of a certain age the "Bring
out your dead!" scene from *Monty Python and the Holy Grail*.

9. It is true a few will survive, to account for the exiles themselves (6:8-9). I have long
thought, a remnant notwithstanding, that Ezekiel 5 and 6 are two of the most terrifying
chapters in Scripture.

10. Unless indicated otherwise, all translations of biblical texts are my own. גִּלְּלִים
[*gillulim*] artfully conjures both idols and dung balls for the hearer, in that the word literally
means "dung balls" (Paul M. Joyce, *Ezekiel: A Commentary*, LHBOTS 482 [New York and
London: T. & T. Clark, 2007], p. 91).

scribes the dead with חלל [*chalal*] again in 6:7 and 6:13.[11] Like Ezekiel's priestly body itself, which had been violated in chapters 4 and 5 by the performance of the sign-acts, the classical body of Israel as a people is here literally "pierced."

In a bizarre scene in chapter 8, Ezekiel is commanded to dig a hole in the wall of the temple. As I argued in my earlier article, "Body Piercings," in doing so he violates the classical body of the temple in much the same way his own priestly body had been violated in chapters 4 and 5. Now the repeated language of חלל I [*chalal;* to profane] in chapter 7 will show that the prophet is not only announcing the profanation of the temple to come in the next chapter, but that there is a play on חלל I [*chalal;* to profane] and חלל II [*chalal;* to pierce] in chapters 6 and 7: bodies, both human and architectural, are pierced and profaned.

Chapter 7 is a series of almost stuttered poetic judgments announcing that the day of the end has come: "An end! The end has come upon the four corners of the land" (7:2).[12] Toward the end of the passage the focus turns to silver and gold, upon which everything seemed to depend during the good times, and which now, ironically, are worthless. The people will cast their silver and gold into the streets; these sources of wealth will now seem as unclean to them as a menstruant's blood (*niddah,* 7:19). What they once treasured will now disgust them. The people had put their trust in the same silver and gold to fill their stomachs. That misplaced trust is now ironically overturned by YHWH, whom the people had abandoned, as the value of the silver and gold is utterly voided due to collapse brought on by invasion. In this passage Ezekiel's concern to highlight the people's economic injustice is most apparent in verses 11-13 and 19-20, but it is a concern that appears in many places in the book. (It is especially pronounced in chapters 18, 22, 26–28, 34, as well as in 45:8-12; 46:18.)

Verse 20 is difficult, but it seems to continue implicitly the topic of silver and gold, now as the substance of idols in the temple:

---

11. In 6:5, he uses פֶּגֶר [*peger*, corpse] to describe the dead bodies, but this is not common in Ezekiel, occurring only twice more (Ezek. 43:7, 9).

12. The repetitions and stylistic "infelicities" in the chapter, and the relative shortness of the Greek text, led Walther Zimmerli to believe the Greek was witness to an earlier "original" text (*Ezekiel 1: A Commentary on the Book of the Prophet Ezekiel, Chapters 1–24,* Hermeneia, trans. Ronald E. Clements [Philadelphia: Fortress, 1979], pp. 193-94), but others are correct to see here Ezekiel's style at work (see Steven Tuell, *Ezekiel,* NIBC 15 [Peabody, MA: Hendrickson, 2009], pp. 41-42).

וּצְבִי עֶדְיוֹ לְגָאוֹן שָׂמָהוּ וְצַלְמֵי תוֹעֲבֹתָם שִׁקּוּצֵיהֶם עָשׂוּ בוֹ
עַל־כֵּן נְתַתִּיו לָהֶם לְנִדָּה

"In its beautiful ornament [presumably the beautiful ornamentation of the silver and gold; the temple sancta] they took pride; they fashioned of it images of abominable idols [i.e., they made images out of the gold and silver]. Therefore I will make it [the gold and silver] an unclean thing to them." (7:20)

The meaning of "beautiful ornament" is difficult, and there is little consensus. But the overall sense seems clear enough: the silver and gold are understood implicitly to be not only the source of misplaced economic trust but also the very substance of the idols in the temple — the ultimate source of misplaced trust. Ezekiel 16:17, which falls in the midst of the judgment of Jerusalem metaphorized as a sexually wayward orphan, supports the idea that the idols are crafted of silver and gold: "You also took your beautiful jewels of my gold and my silver that I had given you, and made for yourself male images, and with them played the whore" (NRSV).[13] So in 7:19-20, Ezekiel ties together his dual concerns for economic justice and idolatry in a wonderfully artful manner: YHWH will now make utterly repugnant and unclean the gold and silver by which the people had demonstrated their utter faithlessness, both by trusting gold and silver in the economic realm and by literally worshiping it in the idols they had made.

YHWH's intention to allow the temple to be profaned is then explicitly expressed in the verses that follow, and it is in these verses that חלל I [chalal; to profane] appears four times (vv. 21, 22 [2x], 24).

וּנְתַתִּיו בְּיַד־הַזָּרִים לָבַז וּלְרִשְׁעֵי הָאָרֶץ לְשָׁלָל וְחִלְּלָהוּ
וַהֲסִבּוֹתִי פָנַי מֵהֶם וְחִלְּלוּ אֶת־צְפוּנִי וּבָאוּ־בָהּ פָּרִיצִים וְחִלְּלוּהָ

"I will give it [the idols of silver and gold? the temple?] into the hand of foreigners as plunder, and to the wicked of the land as spoil, and they will profane [וְחִלְּלָהוּ] it. I will avert my face from them, and they will profane [וְחִלְּלוּ] my hidden place. The violent will enter it, and they will profane [וְחִלְּלוּהָ] it." (vv. 21-22)

What is being given over to be profaned here? To what does the "it" in the first clause refer? It might be the gold and silver of the temple that have

---

13. Zimmerli, too, believes Ezekiel means that the people have fashioned "gods" from their silver and gold (Ezekiel 1, p. 211).

been turned into idols, understood collectively, or it might be the temple itself.[14] But if the former, they are profaned already, by virtue of having been turned into idols. For this reason, I propose that the "it" in the first clause of verse 21 refers to the temple itself.[15]

Commentators have sometimes puzzled over what it means for the divine face to be averted, or rather, why it is happening here when YHWH is otherwise so actively present in judgment; but as Odell notes, YHWH's turning the divine face away is in keeping with the deity's distancing that is taking place throughout these chapters.[16] It seems, in fact, an appropriate way of signaling the imminent divine departure from the temple, to begin in chapter 10 (a turning away of the divine presence). In any case, of particular interest for the purposes of the present discussion is the fact that here *profaning* the temple is equated with *entering* it; in other words, to *profane* is to *pierce*. Of course it matters that it is violent, wicked foreigners who are doing the entering/piercing of the temple — their character as foreign alone makes it profanation.

So to profane the temple "body" is to enter it, to "pierce" it. This may help explain the gender of the suffixes that refer to the temple in these two verses. At the end of verse 21, we are confronted with a *Ketiv/Qere* in the form וְחִלְּלָה ("they will profane it"), reflecting ambivalence or uncertainty about the gender of the temple (וְחִלְּלָהּ is the *Ketiv*, וְחִלְּלוּהוּ is the *Qere*). The feminine singular here of the *Ketiv* marks a shift from referring to the temple as masculine (in vv. 20-21 to this point) to the feminine here. But the *Ketiv* is in keeping with all the other feminine singular forms that refer to the temple in the rest of these two verses: ". . . they will profane it (fem. sing.). I will avert my face from them, and they will profane my hidden place (צְפוּנִי).[17] The violent will enter it (fem. sing.), and they will profane it (fem. sing.)" (vv. 21c-22). In considering the female gender of the temple, the temple as female

14. Julie Galambush carefully acknowledges the ambiguities (*Jerusalem in the Book of Ezekiel: The City as Yahweh's Wife*, SBLDS 130 [Atlanta: Scholars Press, 1992], p. 133).

15. The temple may have been the referent back in verse 20 also, in which case an alternate reading of that verse would be: "In its [the temple's] beautiful ornament they took pride; they fashioned in it images of abominable idols [i.e., they made images out of the gold and silver *in* the temple]. Therefore I will make it [the temple] an unclean thing to them." This reading is supported by Ezek. 24:21: "I will profane my sanctuary, the pride of your power." It may be that part of the art of the passage is the impossibility of fixing the referent.

16. Margaret S. Odell, *Ezekiel,* Smyth & Helwys Bible Commentary 16 (Macon, GA: Smyth & Helwys, 2005), p. 94.

17. True, the *qal* passive participle "my hidden place" is masculine in form here.

"body," it is helpful to keep in mind that the temple is not infrequently understood as feminine, as F. W. Dobbs-Allsopp and Tod Linafelt have shown with respect to Lamentations, and Julie Galambush has argued in Ezekiel.[18]

And finally, in verse 23, the prophet again makes the case that the city deserves this fate, this penetration and profanation, on account of its injustice and violence: "the land is full of blood-smeared injustice, and the city is full of violence" (הָאָרֶץ מָלְאָה מִשְׁפַּט דָּמִים וְהָעִיר מָלְאָה חָמָס).[19] As a result, in verse 24, YHWH is sending the "wicked of the nations" to "take possession of their houses" and put an end to their arrogance; then "their holy places shall be profaned" (וְנִחֲלוּ מִקְדְּשֵׁיהֶם).[20] Paul M. Joyce rightly suggests that this refers to illicit sanctuaries (as in the focus of the judgments of chapter 6), not the temple, as in verses 21-22.[21] In this passage the "holy places" have been profaned, and also entered, pierced by invading foreign bodies.

Let us return to the temple body in verses 21-22, and the temple body as metaphorically female. Galambush understands the "hidden place" — which in our passage will be entered, penetrated by foreigners — to be the holy of holies, the inner sanctum of the temple, which according to her argument functions symbolically as the womb of the city of Jerusalem, also understood to be female.[22] Thus the imminent profanation of the temple by foreigners, punishment for the dual sins of economic injustice and idolatry, is expressed as a kind of rape.

The classical body of the temple is thus both profaned, as the language repeatedly actually declares (חלל I [chalal]), and penetrated, or pierced

---

18. Dobbs-Allsopp and Linafelt demonstrate this with reference to Lamentations 1 and 2, with the wider understanding of ANE temple bodies metaphorized as female in the background, and Galambush demonstrates the way Ezekiel assumes a female body for the temple especially in Ezekiel 23. See F. W. Dobbs-Allsopp and Tod Linafelt, "The Rape of Zion in Thr 1,10," *ZAW* 113 (2001): 77-81; Galambush, *Jerusalem*.

19. Odell, following Moshe Greenberg, understands the "blood-smeared injustice" to be "'judicial murder,' a reference to legally sanctioned abuses of power that harm the weaker members of the community. Those responsible for such crimes are the political elite who use the legal system to their advantage (cf. 9:9; 11:1-3; 22:6, 12a, 27)" (Odell, *Ezekiel*, p. 95).

20. Not only the temple, but other "holy places" will also be polluted — presumably the sanctuaries beyond Jerusalem.

21. Joyce, *Ezekiel*, p. 95.

22. Galambush points out that this view was widely accepted among ancient interpreters (e.g., Jerome, Theodoret), as well. She notes that the city itself may also be the object being profaned (it also being grammatically feminine; Joyce also observes this in *Ezekiel*, p. 95). "Whether city or temple, however, the image strongly suggests the feminine sexuality of Yahweh's 'private place'" (Galambush, *Jerusalem*, p. 134).

(חלל II [*chalal*]). Though the root is not present with the meaning of "pierced," readers of the book (and auditors, too) have just encountered the root with its "pierced" meaning three times in chapter 6, and may well hear the tones of "pierced" scuttling over the top of "profaned" each time it appears in this chapter (although the forms are different, obviously).[23] Such that one may see/hear:

> "I will give it into the hand of foreigners as plunder, and to the wicked of the land as spoil, and they will profane/*pierce* [וְחִלְּלֻהָ] it. I will avert my face from them, and they will profane/*pierce* [וְחִלְּלוּ] my hidden place. The violent will enter it, and they will profane/*pierce* [וְחִלְּלוּהָ] it." (vv. 21-22)[24]

The threat of divine judgment — to profane the temple body, with the echoed threat to pierce the temple body — has set up the events in the very next chapter.

Piercing and Profaning in Ezekiel 8, 9, and Beyond

The prophet, whose classical body had been profaned back in chapters 4 and 5 by the divinely required sign-acts, now must engage in another sign-act: his own body pierced, he will dig through the temple wall in chapter 8, piercing its walls, and touring its desecrated innards.

> And he brought me to the entrance [פֶּתַח] of the court; I looked, and there was a hole [חֹר] in the wall. Then he said to me, "Mortal, dig through the wall"; and when I dug through the wall, there was an entrance [פֶּתַח]. (8:7-8 NRSV)

---

23. David M. Carr points out that Ezekiel's prophecy "contains vivid imagery of the oral-written matrix," by which he means that writing and oral performance were not at opposite ends of a spectrum, as has often been argued in the past, but went hand-in-hand in the transmission of texts and traditions. Carr notes that in Ezekiel both written forms of prophecy appear (the prophet ingests the written scroll in ch. 2) and oral/aural aspects, insofar as the prophet is to tell all these words to the people (Ezek. 3:4-11; 33:30-33). See David M. Carr, *Writing on the Tablet of the Heart: Origins of Scripture and Literature* (New York: Oxford University Press, 2005), p. 149.

24. I put "pierce" in italics to reflect its echoing character. These *pi'el* forms that mean "profane" could not of course be mistaken for חלל II [*chalal*] that mean "pierce."

This scene prefigures a scene in chapter 12 where Ezekiel exits through the temple wall as a sign to the people of how they will leave in haste when the Babylonian invaders arrive. Yet that foreshadowing function alone does not explain the bizarre imagery in this passage.

The hole in the wall of the temple is baffling in some ways. (There is already a hole in the wall, and the prophet is to dig further, or is he to dig another hole? It is not clear.) Yet the hole is symbolically perfect: it epitomizes the end of the classical body of the temple, the reign of order that it represents, and the beginning of the era of the grotesque, when the pierced, distorted bodies that symbolize disorder and disequilibrium will reign. The "creeping and loathsome animals" that Ezekiel sees on the walls in the very next verse (8:10) after going through the hole in the wall of the temple are the harbingers of that reign, and the fact that they now appear on the walls of the temple itself signifies the end.

In the very next chapter, divine executioners are given instructions: "Defile the house, and fill the courts with pierced [חֲלָלִים] bodies" (9:7). These are pierced bodies for a pierced, profaned temple. At this point, the images and language of pierced and profaned bodies have now been intermingling, playing off one another, since chapter 6, thus creating an overall impression that the time of classical bodies — of the prophet (and of Israel), of the temple — is at an end. Exile means that a time of grotesque, disordered, pierced bodies is at hand, and with such grotesquing comes the profaning of the temple body as well, a piercing and profaning subtly marked by the wordplay on חלל [chalal] in these chapters. While there is not space here to pursue how the wordplays may continue in the rest of the book, as noted in footnotes 5 and 8 above, each root occurs more than thirty times in the book.

YHWH departs, leaving the pierced and profaned temple and people behind (11:23). But it is not the end of Ezekiel's story, of course. Although more grotesque bodies pile up throughout the course of the book, notably in chapters 16 and 23 with the sexually metaphorized women, with terrific bursts in the oracles against foreign nations (see especially chapters 31–32) and culminating in the apocalyptic pile-up of corpses in chapters 38 and 39, the book ends with a vision of YHWH in a restored temple. All along, Ezekiel's task has been to persuade his audience that YHWH is active in the chaos of events the exiles are experiencing. The disorder was set in motion by the people's failure to obey the covenantal requirements, but it is all nonetheless under the ultimate control of YHWH, and not the apparently powerful Babylonians or their gods.

Ezekiel's audience had difficulty believing such a claim, of course. Their classical world of order, the world of the temple, the covenant, has disappeared. In the context of exile only the world of the grotesque is visible; Kayser's definition that I cited earlier seems apt: "Structurally, it [the grotesque] presupposes that the categories which apply to our world view become inapplicable."[25] Even the great sacrificial banquet of chapter 39, which is meant to be a moment of deliverance for Israel, is worthy of Hieronymus Bosch in its grotesque imagery: "You shall eat the flesh of the mighty, and drink the blood of the princes of the earth — of rams, of lambs, and of goats, of bulls, all of them fatlings of Bashan" (39:18 NRSV).

The Unrelenting God in Ezekiel

God for Ezekiel is indeed unrelenting, as the title of this book suggests, but one has to read the whole book to understand the character of God in Ezekiel; he is not amenable to browsing, nor the "Quotable Ezekiel." To read only the first half of the book is to believe that God has abandoned the people, as indeed Ezekiel's audience seems to believe. Recently a doctoral student, in discussing God's stripping away of Israel's very identity — that is, it is stripped away unto death — asked me, in horror, how Israel's experience in Ezekiel is any different from the experience of the Jews in the Holocaust. This is a question that should be taken very seriously. Ezekiel is the hardest prophetic book — perhaps the hardest biblical book, in a tight race with Lamentations? — to read in a post-Holocaust world. It seems on the face of it that God punishes Israel for its sins by erasing the people. The key difference, of course, is that in Ezekiel God then makes Israel anew out of the very same raw material — this is Israel made even better than before. It does not answer the theological questions raised by those early chapters, but the book is no Nazi program.

We know that God creates Israel anew, even better than before, from the creation language in chapter 36. There all creation is made anew upon which a new Israel will dwell. The imagery echoes the imagery in Genesis 1–3, as the bracketed texts indicate:

"But you, O mountains of Israel, *shall shoot out your branches, and yield your fruit* [cf. Gen. 1:11, 12, 29] to my people Israel when they draw near

25. Kayser, *Grotesque*, p. 185.

to enter. See now, I am for you; I will turn to you, and *you shall be tilled* [cf. Gen. 2:5, 15; 3:23] and *sown* [cf. Gen. 1:11, 12, 29]; and *I will multiply human beings* [cf. Gen. 1:22, 26, 27, 28] upon you, the whole house of Israel, all of it; the towns shall be inhabited and the waste places rebuilt; and *I will multiply human beings and animals upon you* [cf. Gen. 1:24-26; 2:20]. *They shall increase and be fruitful* [cf. Gen. 1:22, 28; 9:1, 7] and I will cause you to be inhabited as in your former times, and will do more *good* [cf. Gen. 1:4, 10, 12, 18, 25, 31] to you than ever before. Then you shall know that I am YHWH." (Ezek. 36:8-11)

The Genesis accounts of creation also contain the italicized words — these reflect phrases common to both texts. "I will cause you [i.e., the mountains] to be inhabited as in your former times and will do more good to you than ever before" (36:11). The language of the goodness of creation is echoed here, but with the twist that this *new creation will be better than the first one,* which, as Genesis 1 was careful to claim, was not only good, but *very good* (Gen. 1:31). For Ezekiel, the new creation really must be better than the first one if all the dismal history of failure, idolatry, and torah violation are not to be repeated. The new creation envisioned here has to be better than "very good."

So one must read Ezekiel as a whole. To read only the second half of Ezekiel, or to leap into chapter 37, the valley of the dry bones, as many Christian preachers do, is to skip the valley of death that has gone before, and thereby to undervalue or misunderstand the nature of the promise. And what of the grotesque and the classical with which I began this essay? Grotesque bodies seem to articulate the disordered, chaotic flying-apart world especially well for Ezekiel, which makes the image of the scattered dry bones (grotesque!) coming together, bone to bone, sinew to sinew, into an army of the living, a perfect metaphor for the reassembly of the classical vision. Out of the grotesque, the classical form is reborn.

So Ezekiel does not leave his audience in the grotesque; rather, he makes a turn back to the classical in his final vision. As I have argued more extensively elsewhere, at the end of Ezekiel's book, in his final vision in chapters 40–48, Ezekiel offers a twofold hope, a paradoxical hope.[26] There is, on one hand, the hope embedded in the controlled measurements of the

26. Jacqueline E. Lapsley, "Doors Thrown Open and Waters Gushing Forth: Mark, Ezekiel, and the Architecture of Hope," in *The Ending of Mark and the Ends of God: Essays in Honor of Donald Harrisville Juel,* ed. Beverly Roberts Gaventa and Patrick D. Miller (Louisville: Westminster John Knox, 2005), pp. 139-54.

temple: where the chaos of exile has reigned, an obsessive mania for order and detail offers hope. But then, on the other hand, there is the water that bursts from the temple in chapter 47: the salvific action of divine water that cannot be measured. The imprecision of its description indexes the power of God in much the same way that the imprecise language of Ezekiel's vision of God in the first chapter of the book discloses the divine power and transcendence. The book ends much as it began, with God's wild power on the loose.

Recently Ezekiel scholars have been increasingly interested in how trauma theory can inform our understanding of the book.[27] In terms of grotesque and classical forms, in particular, I find the way that artists and sculptors responded to the trauma of World War I to be illuminating in thinking about Ezekiel.[28] After World War I, European artists and especially sculptors, in a return to classicism, resisted the fragmentation of the human body that had characterized modernist movements and instead sought to emphasize the clean lines and beauty of the human form. This classical impulse was a response to the searing trauma of the war and an affirmation of meaning where meaning had been stripped away. Sculpture, in particular, took on new importance after the First World War, perhaps as a way of affirming the integrity of the human body after the mutilation and fragmentation of so many bodies in the war. This is an impulse that Ezekiel would understand.

Unfortunately, the fascists of the 1930s warped classicism to suit their own murderous fantasies. The beauty and balance of classicism may not *inherently* lend itself to fanaticism, but even in Ezekiel's final vision one can see a tendency toward an obsessive mania for detail, at the very least.[29] Ezekiel seems to acknowledge the problem by including that wild, uncontrollable, immeasurable river in chapter 47. The classical body of the temple *is* restated and reasserted in all the rules and regulations of the temple — the architecture of the temple is reassuring after all the grotesqueries of the exile. But Ezekiel does not fall prey to the mistake of pursuing the classical lines of perfection to the exclusion of all else (see Nazi kitsch art). No,

27. See especially Nancy Bowen, *Ezekiel,* AOTC (Nashville: Abingdon, 2010); Daniel Smith-Christopher, *A Biblical Theology of Exile* (Minneapolis: Fortress, 2002).

28. Kenneth E. Silver, *Chaos & Classicism: Art in France, Italy, and Germany, 1918-1936* (New York: Guggenheim Museum, 2010).

29. Jon D. Levenson observes that Ezekiel's fondness for detail seems like an "indulgence in pedantry" (*Theology of the Program of Restoration of Ezekiel 40–48,* HSM 10 [Missoula, MT: Scholars, 1976], p. 1).

he leaves room for the wild element that cannot be measured. It probably makes him nervous, but he does it anyway.

The boundlessness of the water that begins as a trickle (47:1) and ends by healing all the land (47:12) makes a clear contrast with the otherwise restricted space and movement in this precise structure. The opening seems to mirror the one that Ezekiel encountered in the temple back in chapter 8; like it, this one is divinely made, but with restorative water pouring through it. What kind of "hole-in-the-temple" is this? At first just a trickle, then spewing from the temple to revivify the land, this symbol of God's power to give life is simply too powerful to be appraised by a yardstick. It is the only element of the temple vision that cannot be measured, standing in bold relief to the sips of water that Ezekiel had to measure out for himself as siege rations back in chapter 4 (4:11).[30]

In this way, Ezekiel's ending discloses some of the same tensions roiling under the surface in the rest of the book: hope for the future is apparent in the clean, controlled environment of the temple — there is hope in the reassertion of the classical architecture of the temple, with the order of its temple laws. And there is hope in the power of God to shatter the temple wall and heal both land and people with an immeasurable flow of life-giving water. Ezekiel expresses himself through bodies, and the categories of classical and grotesque express what he is up to with those bodies. But in the end, he moves beyond those categories, bursting their confines so that God can flow from the temple to all creation, bringing life to the land and the people alike.

---

30. My thanks to Jeremy Schipper for this observation.

Conversion in Luke-Acts:
God's Prevenience, Human Embodiment

Joel B. Green

As a number of scholars have recognized, conversion is ubiquitous in the Lukan narrative. With reference to Luke's second volume, for example, Thomas Finn has detected twenty-one conversion accounts in the Acts of the Apostles and claimed, "Conversion is the major theme in Luke's second volume."[1] Charles Talbert identified only ten such accounts in Acts, but refines Finn's overarching judgment only slightly: "Conversion is a central focus of Acts, maybe *the* central focus."[2] Earlier, Beverly Gaventa devoted just over half of her important study of "aspects of conversion in the New Testament" to the Lukan narrative.[3] For Guy Nave, repentance is "a keynote of the message in Luke-Acts," and the book of Acts is "full of conversion stories."[4] The importance of conversion for Luke's soteriology has led to the publication of several recent studies, examination of which reveals a series of fault lines in how best to understand Luke's emphasis.[5]

---

1. Thomas M. Finn, *From Death to Rebirth: Ritual and Conversion in Antiquity* (New York: Paulist, 1997), p. 27.

2. Charles H. Talbert, "Conversion in the Acts of the Apostles: Ancient Auditors' Perceptions," in *Reading Luke-Acts in Its Mediterranean Milieu,* NovTSup 107 (Leiden: Brill, 2003), p. 135.

3. Beverly Roberts Gaventa, *From Darkness to Light: Aspects of Conversion in the New Testament,* OBT 20 (Philadelphia: Fortress, 1986), pp. 52-129.

4. Guy D. Nave Jr., *The Role and Function of Repentance in Luke-Acts,* SBLAB 4 (Atlanta: Society of Biblical Literature, 2002), p. 3; Guy D. Nave, "Conversion," in *NIDB* 1:729.

5. In addition to those already mentioned, see Babu Immanuel, *Repent and Turn to God: Recounting Acts* (Perth, Australia: HIM International Ministries, 2004); Fernando Méndez-Moratalla, *The Paradigm of Conversion in Luke,* JSNTSup 252 (London: T. & T. Clark, 2004); Robert C. Tannehill, "Repentance in the Context of Lukan Soteriology," in *God's Word for Our World,* vol. 2: *Theological and Cultural Studies in Honor of Simon John De Vries,* ed. J. Harold

Among these controverted issues are the following: Is conversion a cognitive category, a moral category, or both? Is conversion a crossing of religious boundaries and rejection of one manner of life, embracing more fully the life one has chosen, or both? What is the relationship between conversion as a "change of mind" and behavioral transformation? Is conversion an event or a process? Does Luke's narrative support a "pattern" of conversion? What catalyzes conversion in Luke-Acts?

Although we cannot hope to put all of these questions to rest in this essay, we can make a beginning by means of an analysis of Luke 3:1-14, which serves as an important staging point for any exploration of Luke's perspective on conversion. What we see here anticipates much of the larger development of this motif in the Lukan narrative, namely, the dynamic action of God that opens the way and calls for people to embody in their lives "the way of the Lord."

Conversion and the Turn of the Ages

With its prominent geopolitical and chronological markers, Luke 3:1-2 signals a fresh beginning in the Lukan narrative. After recounting the births and summarizing the childhoods of John and Jesus, Luke moves John onto center stage, sketching the character of his prophetic ministry in preparation of Jesus' public ministry (3:1-20). John's ministry of renewal and transformation comes into focus in the précis Luke provides: "He went throughout the region of the Jordan, declaring a repentance-baptism for the forgiveness of sins" (3:3);[6] in words descriptive of John's work, borrowed from Isaiah: "Prepare the way for the Lord; straighten his paths . . ." (3:4; cf. Isa. 40:3); in John's words to the crowds, "produce fruit that demonstrates repentance" (3:8); and in John's spelling out for the crowds behaviors that would in fact demonstrate repentance (3:10-14).

Key to grasping the significance of Luke's introduction to John's mission is the structure of 3:1-6, and particularly the juxtaposition of sociopolitical (vv. 1-2) and redemptive-historical (vv. 4-6) contexts. These

---

Ellens et al., JSOTSup 389 (London: T. & T. Clark, 2004), pp. 199-215; Mihamm Kim-Rauchholz, *Umkehr bei Lukas: Zu Wesen und Bedeutung der Metanoia in der Theologie des dritten Evangelisten* (Neukirchen-Vluyn: Neukirchener, 2008).

6. Unless otherwise noted, translations of the Lukan material are my own and other biblical citations follow the NRSV.

are mutually interpretive, and together they provide the frame for our viewing of Luke's summary depiction of John's ministry in verse 3.

Verses 1-2 provide geopolitical markers reminiscent of Greco-Roman historiographers (e.g., Thucydides 2.2; Polybius 1.3; Josephus, *Ant.* 18.106), as well as OT figures — national leaders (Isa. 1:1; Amos 1:1) and especially prophets (Jer. 1:1-4; Ezek. 1:1-3; Hos. 1:1; Joel 1:1; Jonah 1:1; Mic. 1:1; Zeph. 1:1; Hag. 1:1; Zech. 1:1). If Luke's primary agenda in verses 1-2 had been to provide us with a precise dating for the onset of John's ministry, then he has not been very successful. The collocation of rulers he mentions supports only a rough estimation for dating the beginning of John's ministry: from 27 to 29 CE. This raises suspicions against the view that 3:1-2 was written primarily to locate John's ministry on the calendar. Rather, Luke uses this synchrony to situate John's prophetic appearance in a particular sociopolitical setting.[7]

Whatever else it is, then, the list of rulers in verse 1 is a stark reminder of the situation in which Israel finds itself: under foreign rule. And given the judgment on the powerful and wealthy portended in Mary's Song (1:52-53), it is surely damning that the temple dynasty represented by Annas and Caiaphas (v. 2a) is mentioned in the same breath with Rome's rulers. This narrative assessment coheres with the political power exercised historically by the high priesthood until the Roman era and, during the Roman era, with the twin facts that the Romans appointed and dismissed high priests (who, then, served at the behest of the Romans) and that high priests continued to preside over the nation's civil affairs.[8] The scene John enters is thus characterized as oppressive, top-heavy. Nevertheless, he enters as God's representative, God's prophet. It is to him — not rulers, nor even ruling priests — that God's word comes. And he is in the wilderness, not the urban centers of the civilized world where an emperor or a governor might make his home.

Intimations of what is to come are found in Luke's reference in verse 2b to John's presence "in the wilderness." Luke thus recalls John's wilderness location in 1:80 — a geographical note that might suggest that, with

---

7. The emphasis here is on "prophetic setting"; that is, although, like Greek and Roman historiographers, Luke situates his story in world history, he is closer to Israel's Scriptures in his emphasis on what God is doing in this world. Cf. Daniel Marguerat, *The First Christian Historian: Writing the 'Acts of the Apostles,'* SNTSMS 121 (Cambridge: Cambridge University Press, 2002), pp. 1-25; Kazuhiko Yamazaki-Ransom, *The Roman Empire in Luke's Narrative,* LNTS 404 (London: T. & T. Clark, 2010), pp. 74-78.

8. See Emil Schürer, *The History of the Jewish People in the Age of Jesus Christ,* vol. 2, rev. and ed. Geza Vermes, Fergus Millar, and Matthew Black (Edinburgh: T. & T. Clark, 1979), pp. 227-28, 230.

the onset of his ministry, John would have *departed* the wilderness. Thus it reads in the NRSV, "he was in the wilderness until the day he appeared publicly to Israel." Similarly, one might imagine that, in 3:3a, John departed "the wilderness" before going throughout the region of the Jordan River. This reading seems pivotal to Michael Fuller's thesis that, for Luke, "wilderness" is a metaphor for Israel's sinful and exilic situation, requiring that John exit the wilderness at the outset of his ministry.[9] But this reading is problematic in that it actually seems important to Luke that John exercised his prophetic commission "in the wilderness" (3:4); moreover, when people came out to see the prophet John, they did so by going "into the wilderness" (7:24). The preposition ἕως in 1:80 could signify that John was in the wilderness "until" his public ministry (i.e., and not thereafter), but it need not do so. Indeed, 1:80 need not be read as saying anything about John's whereabouts after he appeared publicly to Israel. Similarly, the phrase "he went" in verse 3 does not signify John's departure from the wilderness, but his traffic in the vicinity of the Jordan River. Throughout his ministry, then, he is located in a space, the wilderness, symbolically related to Israel's formative experience of exodus.

This persistent connection of John with the wilderness is important for the association of this prophet with earlier, exuberant visions of God's intervention *in* the wilderness to lead a second exodus *through* the wilderness. Consider, for example, these words from Isaiah, which explicitly tie expectations of deliverance from Babylon into memories of Israel's formation as a people and liberation from Egypt:

> Thus says the LORD,
>   your Redeemer, the Holy One of Israel:
> For your sake I will send to Babylon
>   and break down all the bars,
>   and the shouting of the Chaldeans will be turned to lamentation.
> I am the LORD, your Holy One,
>   the Creator of Israel, your King.
> Thus says the LORD,
>   who makes a way in the sea,

---

9. Michael E. Fuller, *The Restoration of Israel: Israel's Re-gathering and the Fate of the Nations in Early Jewish Literature and Luke-Acts*, BZNW 138 (Berlin: De Gruyter, 2006), esp. pp. 222-23. "Luke's most important means of describing Israel's continual exile is his characterization of Israel as a 'wilderness' (ἔρημος)," he writes (p. 211), but where in Luke-Acts is Israel thus designated?

a path in the mighty waters,
who brings out chariot and horse, army and warrior;
    they lie down, they cannot rise,
    they are extinguished, quenched like a wick:
Do not remember the former things,
    or consider the things of old.
I am about to do a new thing;
    now it springs forth, do you not perceive it?
I will make a way in the wilderness
    and rivers in the desert.
The wild animals will honor me,
    the jackals and the ostriches;
for I give water in the wilderness,
    rivers in the desert,
to give drink to my chosen people,
    the people whom I formed for myself
so that they might declare my praise. (Isa. 43:14-21)

God may be about "to do a new thing," as Isaiah puts it, but at key points, this new thing resembles the old — including making Israel a people, Israel's sea-crossing, and divine provision in the wilderness (cf. Exodus 15; 17; 19). Similarly, imagining the return from exile as a new exodus, Isaiah has it that God provides for his people in the wilderness just as before (e.g., Isa. 48:20-21; cf. Exod. 17:1-7). Restoration from exile thus recapitulates exodus from Egyptian slavery. The wilderness was to become the site of rejoicing, the land would be fertile and the people safe from wild animals, and God's people restored would see the LORD's glory (e.g., Isaiah 35; Ezek. 20:33-44; Hos. 2:14-23). These and related texts ground *wilderness* thematically in expectations of restoration from exile.[10]

"Wilderness" could signify rebellion, danger, testing, and punishment, to be sure (e.g., Num. 14:32-33; 27:14; Sir. 8:8-16; 13:19; 1QM 1:3; Heb. 3:7-11), but this is hardly the only interpretive option available to us. Philo clearly states what may be implicit in Luke, namely, that "wilderness" is the antithesis of "city," the latter characterized by distractions and corrup-

---

10. Cf. Ulrich W. Mauser, *Christ in the Wilderness: The Wilderness Theme in the Second Gospel and Its Basis in the Biblical Tradition*, SBT 39 (London: SCM, 1963), pp. 44-58; Shemaryahu Talmon, "The 'Desert Motif' in the Bible and in Qumran Literature," in *Biblical Motifs: Origins and Transformation*, ed. Alexander Altmann (Cambridge, MA: Harvard University Press, 1966), pp. 31-63.

tion that make withdrawal to the wilderness a prerequisite to purification and new life (see Philo, *Decal.* 10-13). John is made a prophet in the wilderness, and he conducts his ministry in the wilderness; the crowds encounter him in the wilderness and in the wilderness hear his message of transformation. As in Philo, might it be in Luke that cleansing and purification are unimaginable unless people first remove themselves from the ways of their hometowns? "Wilderness" could also be understood as the venue of divine revelation — the locus of God's past deliverance as well as the space within which God would reveal and enact liberation.[11] So profoundly was this the case that the Qumran sectarians made their home in the wilderness.[12] This space allowed them to pursue a lifestyle marked by religious purity (cf. 1QS 8:12-16) and thus to cultivate among themselves a community that embodied the Isaianic call to prepare the way of the LORD.[13] A similar correlation of a theologically charged notion of "wilderness" with geophysical space occurs in both Josephus and Luke in references to failed efforts at the prophetic restoration of God's people in the wilderness (see Josephus, *Ant.* 20.97-99, 167-72; *J. W.* 2.258-63; 7:438-39; Acts 21:38).

Verses 1-2 locate John on a map, in a place conducive to John's asceticism (cf. 1:15) and growth in the Spirit (1:80).[14] It is a place conducive to his formation as one who, having been "filled with the Holy Spirit even before his birth" (1:15), would "go before the Lord to prepare his ways" (1:76). Moreover, his wilderness venue participates in a wider discourse regarding Israel's hoped-for liberation. This underscores the theological potency of Luke's geographical markers in verses 1-2.

---

11. On these three uses of "wilderness" in Second Temple Judaism, see Hindy Najman, "Towards a Study of the Uses of the Concept of Wilderness in Ancient Judaism," *DSD* 13 (2006): 99-113; cf. Alison Schofield, "Wilderness," in *The Eerdmans Dictionary of Early Judaism,* ed. John J. Collins and Daniel C. Harlow (Grand Rapids: Eerdmans, 2010), pp. 1337-38.

12. This self-understanding depends on the Hebrew text of Isa. 40:3, in which a voice announces that the way of the Lord is to be prepared "in the wilderness"; compare the LXX, which has it instead that the wilderness marks the location of the voice crying out.

13. See James C. VanderKam, "The Judean Desert and the Community of the Dead Sea Scrolls," in *Antikes Judentum und Frühes Christentum: Festschrift für Hartmut Stegemann zum 65. Geburtstag,* ed. Bernd Kollmann et al., BZNW 97 (Berlin: De Gruyter, 1999), pp. 159-71; cf. Carl Judson Davis, *The Name and Way of the Lord: Old Testament Themes, New Testament Christology,* JSNTSup 129 (Sheffield: Sheffield Academic Press, 1996), pp. 78-82.

14. François Bovon, *Luke 1: A Commentary on the Gospel of Luke 1:1–9:50,* Hermeneia (Minneapolis: Fortress, 2002), p. 77: "Πνεύματι ('in spirit') is perhaps intentionally ambiguous, i.e., in his human spirit and in God's Spirit."

These hints regarding the significance of John's wilderness location are like sparks that, when tended, erupt into a blaze in verses 4-6. This means that Luke introduces his citation from Isaiah 40 not as a counter to but as an interpretive correlate of the synchrony of Luke 3:1-2a. John's prophetic ministry is thus contextualized with reference to the exilic situation of God's people. Or, to be more specific, John's prophetic ministry marks the conclusion of exile and so introduces the anticipated restoration. What is more, the introduction of Isaiah 40:3-5 in Luke 3:4-6 certifies that the shape of the events Luke will relate is determined by the outworking of God's saving purpose.[15]

Although the use of Isaiah 40 with reference to John's ministry is witnessed in the four canonical Gospels (Matt. 3:3; Mark 1:1-3; Luke 3:4-6; John 1:23), Luke's citation is the most extensive of the four. The Isaianic material on which he draws is found in the prologue of this new section of the prophet, in which God announces a new era for his people — the cessation of exile and, then, restoration, forgiveness, salvation, the coming of the Lord in strength. Issues concerning the authorship of this section of Isaiah aside, recent scholarship has underscored the thematic coherence of Isaiah 40–55, particularly vis-à-vis a constellation of images drawn from Israel's memory of exodus now recast in anticipation of new exodus.[16] Max Turner summarizes this pattern with reference to the following motifs in Isaiah 40–55:

a. God calls for a "way" for the Lord to be prepared in the wilderness for his saving activity (40.3-5; 43.19).
b. His advent "with might" as the divine warrior will defeat Israel's oppressors and release the oppressed (40.10-11; 42.13; 51.9-16; 49.9, 24-25).
c. The Lord will lead the glorious procession out of captivity along "the way" through the wilderness, his presence before and after them (52.11-12), through water and fire (43.1-3), and he will shepherd them along the way (40.11).
d. He will sustain them in the wilderness more fully than in the Exodus, ensuring they do not hunger, and providing streams in the desert (41.17-20; 43.19-21; 49.9-10). The very wilderness will be transformed to celebrate the release of God's people (43.19; 49.10-11; 55.12-13).

---

15. Cf. Bovon, *Luke 1*, p. 121; Yamazaki-Ransom, *Empire*, pp. 77-78.

16. See the brief summary of historical-critical study of Isaianic unity in Brevard S. Childs, *Isaiah*, OTL (Louisville: Westminster John Knox, 2001), pp. 289-91.

e. God will pour out his refreshing and restoring Spirit on his people (44.3) so that they own him as their Lord (44.5); he himself will teach them and lead them in "the way" (54.13; 48.17), so opening the eyes of the blind and the ears of the deaf.

f. The final goal of this New Exodus is God's enthronement in a restored Zion/Jerusalem (44.26; 45.13; 54.11-12). The announcement of this "good news" to her is her "comfort," the occasion for her bursting into song to celebrate her salvation (40.1, 9-10; 52.1-10).

g. These things will be accomplished at least in part through a somewhat enigmatic servant figure with "Israel," kingly and prophet-liberator traits.[17]

This constellation of images, most of which are anticipated already in Isaiah 40:1-11, serves as the backdrop by which Luke orients John's ministry in Luke 3.

Compared with the quotation of Isaiah 40 in the other three NT Gospels, the inclusion of additional material in Luke's extended citation highlights three emphases. First, it sketches what takes place in the wilderness in terms of reversal:

> Every ravine shall be filled up,
>   and every mountain and hill be made low,
> and all the crooked ways shall become straight,
>   and the rough place shall become plains. (Isa. 40:4, NETS)

Elsewhere, Luke will interpret such images in terms of status transformation and ethical comportment (see already 1:52-53; 2:34), and this is how he develops those images in the present context as he shines the spotlight on what a "people prepared" (1:17) looks like. Second, the Isaianic citation names the consequence of these preparations as salvation. Third, it extends the scope of this salvation universally.[18]

17. Max Turner, *Power from on High: The Spirit in Israel's Restoration and Witness in Luke-Acts*, JPTSup 9 (Sheffield: Sheffield Academic Press, 1996), p. 247. Presumably, the obscurity surrounding the servant-figure rests at least in part in the postponement of new exodus, with the servant replacing Cyrus as YHWH's agent of liberation; cf. Rikki Watts, "Consolation or Confrontation? Isaiah 40–55 and the Delay of the New Exodus," *TynBul* 41 (1990): 31-59.

18. Compared to the present version of the LXX, Luke's citation appears sans Isa. 40:5a and Isa. 40:5c ("Then the glory of the Lord shall appear," "because the Lord has spoken," NETS), presumably in order to highlight all the more the climactic phrase in Isa. 40:5b ("and all flesh shall see the salvation of God," NETS).

Luke's dependence on Isaiah is programmatic for his portrayal of John. This is established primarily by the formulaic phrase "as it was written in the book of the words of the prophet Isaiah" (Luke 3:4a). For Luke, John's mission as it is spelled out in 3:3 must be understood within the framework of Isaiah's pronouncement of restoration. We easily identify the correlations between John's repentance-baptism (v. 3) and the messenger's summons to "prepare the way of the Lord" (v. 4), and between John's proclamation of the forgiveness of sins (v. 3) and the messenger's promise of salvation (v. 4). A case could be made, too, that the prologue of Isaiah 40:1-11 shapes the broad contours of the whole of Luke's précis of John's ministry — with Isaiah 40:3-5 used explicitly to introduce the nature of John's call for conversion (Luke 3:1-14), and with the proclamation of good news (εὐαγγελίζω; Isa. 40:9) and the coming of God in strength in Isaiah 40:6-11 standing behind both John's words regarding the coming, powerful one (Luke 3:15-18)[19] and Luke's summary of John's mission as one of "proclaiming good news" (εὐαγγελίζω; Luke 3:18).

Against this backdrop, it remains to discuss more fully the metaphor of "the way" Luke introduces with his dependence on Isaiah 40 and the nature of John's ministry. Before turning to these issues, however, we should underscore what we have seen thus far, namely, that Luke has situated John's ministry, including his conversionist rhetoric, in a world of earthly expectation and divine restoration.

Conversion as Journey

Luke's understanding of John's baptism comes through the collocation of baptism with "repentance" or "conversion" (μετάνοια). John's is a repentance-baptism. Etymologically, μετανοέω refers to "knowing after" and, early on, took its significance from a change of mind that resulted

---

19. This way of construing the potential influence of Isa. 40:1-11 on Luke 3:1-18 turns on Luke's christological reading of the Isaianic text in which the LXX phrase εὐθείας ποιεῖτε τὰς τρίβους τοῦ θεοῦ ἡμῶν ("make straight the paths of our God"; Isa. 40:3) is transformed in Luke as εὐθείας ποιεῖτε τὰς τρίβους αὐτοῦ ("make straight his paths"; Luke 3:4), so that the antecedent of αὐτοῦ ("his") is the ambiguous κύριος ("lord"), which identifies the way of the Lord (Jesus) with the way of the Lord (YHWH). For incontrovertible references to Jesus as κύριος ("lord") thus far in the Lukan narrative, see Luke 1:43; 2:11. Similarly, then, the identity of "the Lord [who] comes with strength" (κύριος μετὰ ἰσχύος ἔρχεται; Isa. 40:10) would for Luke embrace the one more powerful than John who is coming (ἔρχεται . . . ὁ ἰσχυρότερος; Luke 3:16).

from this afterthought.[20] This might lead one to think of μετάνοια primarily in terms of a change-of-mind, an abstract, cognitive act. Such a move would be shortsighted, however. On one hand, more generally, a conversion between philosophies was not simply a change in worldview or "internal realignment of the intellect," as C. Kavin Rowe has recently reminded us, but rather a transformation of life patterns.[21] On the other hand, Luke's own concept of conversion as it has thus far been developed in his narrative refuses this sort of reductive approach.

The first time Luke presents John's mission, he invokes a journey frame.[22] The journey frame encompasses the entire process of movement from one place to another, and includes a range of constituent features — e.g., a path, a traveler, an itinerary, fellow travelers, mode of transportation, obstacles encountered, starting point and destination, and traveling paraphernalia. The journey frame is integral to a range of common metaphors, such as LOVE IS A JOURNEY, which capitalize on the primary metaphor, LIFE IS A JOURNEY.[23] The metaphor LIFE IS A JOURNEY invites correspondences such as the following:

Source Domain: Journey		Target Domain: Patterns of Life
Traveler	→	Person living a life
Destination	→	Purpose
Road, way	→	Means for achieving purpose
Obstacles	→	Impediments to achieving purpose
Landmark	→	Metric for measuring progress toward purpose
Crossroad	→	Choice in life

This chart exemplifies mapping between two conceptual domains on the basis of conceptual metaphor theory, for which metaphor is characteristic

---

20. Cf. MHT 2:318; *TLNT* 2:472.

21. C. Kavin Rowe, "The Grammar of Life: The Areopagus Speech and Pagan Tradition," *NTS* 57 (2011): 45; see also pp. 44-49.

22. "Frame" refers to "a schematisation of experience (a knowledge structure), which is represented at the conceptual level and held in long-term memory. The frame relates the elements and entities associated with a particular culturally embedded scene from human experience" (Vyvyan Evans and Melanie Green, *Cognitive Linguistics: An Introduction* [Edinburgh: Edinburgh University Press, 2006], p. 222).

23. Cf. George Lakoff and Mark Turner, *More Than Cool Reason: A Field Guide to Poetic Metaphor* (Chicago: University of Chicago Press, 1989), pp. 3-6.

of thought itself. Semantic structure mirrors conceptual structure as we conceive the world around us by projecting patterns from one domain of experience in order to structure another domain. The one is a source domain, the other a target domain, and studies have shown that where these two domains are active simultaneously, the two areas of the brain for each are active. Indeed, brain imaging has shown that when we use auditory-related words we experience increased blood flow to the areas of our brains implicated in auditory processing, and the same is true of sight-related terms or words related to speech, and so on.[24] Borrowing a principle from the neuropsychologist Donald Hebb, known as Hebb's Rule, we know that *neurons that fire together wire together* — with the result that conceptual metaphor theory is actually grounded in the embodiment of the patterns by which we conceptualize and respond to the world around us.[25] Essentially all of our abstract and theoretical concepts draw their meaning by mapping to embodied, experiential concepts hardwired in our brains. In this case, I am claiming that Luke portrays conversion in a way that triggers the journey frame and then conceptualizes conversion in terms of the metaphor LIFE IS A JOURNEY.

In Luke 1, John's mission and its anticipated outcomes were articulated above all in terms of movement. Thus, in 1:16 the key verb is ἐπιστρέφω, "to turn back" or "to return," with the extended sense "to change belief or course of conduct, with focus on the thing to which one turns" (in this case, "to the Lord their God").[26] Thus, "*He will turn* many of the people of Israel to the Lord their God." Luke 1:17 then functions epexegetically, sketching with three clauses how John will effect the commission summarized in verse 16:

- he will *go before* [προέρχομαι] him, endowed with the spirit and power of Elijah,
- *to turn* [ἐπιστρέφω] the hearts of fathers to their children, and the disobedient to the wisdom of the righteous,
- *to make ready* [ἑτοιμάζω] a people prepared for the Lord.

24. Cf. Michael J. Posner and Marcus E. Raichle, *Images of Mind* (New York: W. H. Freeman, 1997), p. 115. On this point more generally, see, e.g., Jerome A. Feldman, *From Molecule to Metaphor: A Neural Theory of Language* (Cambridge, MA: MIT Press, 2006).

25. Cf. Ning Yu, "Metaphor from Body and Culture," in *The Cambridge Handbook of Metaphor and Thought*, ed. Raymond W. Gibbs Jr. (Cambridge: Cambridge University Press, 2010), pp. 247-61.

26. BDAG, 382.

Of these three, the first articulates John's purpose in terms of a journey: "to go before." Since the third is related intertextually to Isaiah 40:3-5, cited in Luke 3:4-6, we will return to it shortly; it too is tied to the journey frame: people prepare for travel. The second is central in terms of identifying the anticipated outcome of John's mission in journey-related terms: ἐπιστρέφω, "to turn back," with reference first to the hearts of fathers returned to their children and then to the "disobedient" returned "to righteous patterns of thinking." Here, change is cast in directional terms that assume motion toward an objective. It is worth noting that ἐπιστρέφω is explicitly collocated with patterns of thought, thus denying in Lukan usage an easy distinction between conversion-as-motion and conversion-as-change-of-mind.

A similar move is found in Luke 3:3-6, where a noticeable consequence of Luke's use of Isaiah 40 is that the language of repentance or conversion (μετάνοια) is parsed with reference to "the way of the Lord" (v. 4) and developed in terms of "paths" (v. 4) and "roads" (v. 5). On one hand, then, we have the frame *change of direction,* which assumes a turn, a new direction, and continued travel in this new direction. On the other hand, Luke's language engages the frame of *the traveler* — someone on a journey, typically planned in advance with a purpose in mind, perhaps accompanied by fellow travelers, and so on. This leads to a consideration of "conversion" in relation to the metaphor CHANGE IS MOTION and the metaphor system LIFE IS A JOURNEY.

An outstanding question is how Luke's dependence on Israel's story and especially Isaiah's vision of restoration thickens his description of repentance in Luke 3:3-6. In Israel's story we find both a basic image for portraying the ongoing character of one's life (traveling or journeying, or simply walking) and a strong paradigm identifying the destination of God's people in terms of liberation from oppression and taking up residence in the promised land.

First, with regard to the conventional metaphor LIVING IS WALKING, we may observe frequent references in Israel's Scriptures to life itself as a "journey" or a "walk." "Way" (דרך) is the most common term for lexicalizing the concept of "life," and "walk" (הלך, rendered in the LXX by πορεύομαι ["to walk"] in about two-thirds of its 1,500 occurrences in the OT) is the most common term for "the act or process of living" in Israel's Scriptures.[27] This usage is hardly surprising among a nomadic people: "They live 'on the move.'"[28] Human life is a journey.

27. Eugene H. Merrill, "הלך," in *NIDOTTE,* 1:1032.
28. F. J. Helfmeyer, "הלך," in *TDOT,* 3:389.

What is more, since the outcome of the journey depends on the manner of the travelers' conduct, "to walk" can refer more broadly to "the process of living according to behavioral norms congruent with a particular goal." Several hundred of the more than 1,500 occurrences of the verb carry this metaphorical sense — famously with reference to lives of obedience and disobedience vis-à-vis YHWH (e.g., Lev. 18:3; 1 Kings 3:3). What does the Lord require, "but to do justice, and to love kindness, and to walk [MT: הלך; LXX: πορεύομαι] humbly with your God" (Mic. 6:8)? This metaphor is not limited to Israel's Scriptures but is also pervasive in early Christianity. For example, Paul articulates the Christian life as a step-by-step affair — that is, as walking (περιπατέω) "by the Spirit" (Gal. 5:16; cf. Rom. 8:4). In Luke's birth account, the evangelist echoes biblical usage when he writes of Zechariah and Elizabeth: "They were both righteous before God, walking (πορεύομαι) blamelessly according to all the commandments and regulations of the Lord" (1:6).

Second, exodus is ubiquitous as a paradigm of salvation for God's people in Israel's Scriptures.[29] In the Scriptures, exodus is alive in the memory of God's people, not only as historic event but also as a lens through which to make sense of present experience and as the matrix within which to shape future hopes. In the Psalms, for example, hymns of praise celebrate exodus (e.g., Psalms 66, 68, 105), and psalms of lament appeal to God's mighty act of deliverance (e.g., Psalms 74, 77, 80). The prophets paint Israel's infidelity with patterns taken either from Egypt or from Israel's rebellion in the wilderness, while portraying YHWH as the liberating God who would restore Israel.

Efforts at casting Israel's hope as a new exodus reach their zenith in Isaiah. In Isaiah 40 we find a message centered on the imagery of the highway: "prepare the way," "make straight a highway" for the coming of "our God." Appropriating the language of the exodus from Egypt (e.g., 11:16; 51:9-11; 52:3-15), the prophet envisions a road for the return of the exiles. The return of YHWH marks the return of his people. Earlier, the prophet had imagined a road through the wilderness:

> A pure way shall be there,
> and it shall be called a holy way;

---

29. Cf., e.g., Göran Larsson, *Bound for Freedom: The Book of Exodus in Jewish and Christian Traditions* (Peabody, MA: Hendrickson, 1999); Rikki E. Watts, "Exodus," in *New Dictionary of Biblical Theology*, ed. T. D. Alexander and Brian S. Rosner (Downers Grove, IL: InterVarsity, 2000), pp. 478-87.

and the unclean shall not pass by there,
  nor shall be there an unclean way,
but those who have been dispersed shall walk on it,
  and they shall not go astray.
And no lion shall be there,
  nor shall any of the evil beasts come up on it
or be found there,
  but the redeemed shall walk on it. (Isa. 35:8-9, NETS)

Five times in these two verses the adverb "there" (ἐκεῖ) designates the wilderness as the place where God saves.[30] This coheres with our earlier observation concerning the transformation of *wilderness* in a number of texts, from a place of judgment to one of blessing. Note that these verses are closely tied intratextually to, and anticipate, the material on which Luke explicitly draws in Isaiah 40:3-5. Note, too, how Isaiah draws on the hoary image LIVING IS WALKING to portray God's people as walking in God's holy way.[31]

One might imagine a certain tension between Isaiah 35 and Isaiah 40 since, in the former, the "way" (ὁδός) is simply "there," whereas in the latter the "way" (ὁδός) requires preparation. Although there are differences of emphasis, to be sure, in the end the distinction is not dramatic. Isaiah 40 also assumes the presence of a "way" or a "road"; however, this road is an obstructed one. It is uneven and crooked, when what is needed is a road that is smooth and straight (cf. Isa. 26:7; 33:15; 40:3, 4; 42:16; 45:13; 59:14). Roadwork is needed, and this is the significance of the call for preparations to be made. What form might this road construction take? It is none other than repentance, following the pattern of sin leading to exile, and repentance leading to restoration.[32] Accordingly, Isaiah's reference to the Lord's way can signal simultaneously God's restoration of his people and the way of life embraced by those people whom God restores. The same is assumed in the case of Isaiah 35, however, where we are told that the road in question is for those who return from the dispersion and a holy way on which only the "clean" shall walk.[33] In both instances, the road is not for everyone

---

30. Cf. John D. W. Watts, *Isaiah 34–66*, rev. ed., WBC 25 (Waco, TX: Thomas Nelson, 2005), p. 541.

31. Childs, *Isaiah*, pp. 298-99.

32. On this pattern, cf. Fuller, *Restoration*.

33. It is hard to understand why it would be necessary, with Øystein Lund, to choose between these two options (*Way Metaphors and Way Topics in Isaiah 40–55*, FAT 2/28 [Tübingen: Mohr Siebeck, 2007]).

but only for those who have adopted God's ways as their pattern of life and continue to live according to God's ways.[34] Accordingly, conversion refers to an ongoing journey on an obstructed path requiring ongoing roadwork: CONVERSION IS A JOURNEY.

Building on Isaiah, Luke's portrait is not simple; it can be understood in terms of walking the wrong path, or of walking on a path that needs reconstruction, or of walking in the wrong direction. However the problem is conceived, the point is that a change is required, and this change is not simply from one state to another, but from one kind of journey to another. That is, conversion signifies a continued journey in the right direction down a road under reconstruction. Borrowing from and building on Isaiah's portrait, repentance entails roadwork (that is, engaging in transformed patterns of life) as well as journeying along the road (that is, ongoing life oriented toward God's ways). Conversion thus exemplifies the metaphor LIFE IS A JOURNEY. We can provide a partial map of this metaphor:[35]

Source Domain: Journey		Target Domain: Patterns of Life
Journey, path, way	→	Pattern of life
Straight, level path	→	Path of conversion
Crooked, uneven path	→	Path refusing conversion
Traveler	→	People (or community of people)
Movement	→	Purposeful action toward a destination
Destination	→	For the repentant, salvation; for the unrepentant, divine wrath

According to Luke's presentation, the current path on which God's people are walking is uneven and crooked, and they are moving in the wrong direction — which is to say, they are pursuing ways of life and life-goals antithetical to the life purposed for them by God.

If Luke presents conversion as a journey, then we might expect the ensuing Lukan narrative to underscore this journey motif. In fact, the impor-

34. Cf. J. Alec Motyer, *Isaiah: An Introduction and Commentary,* TOTC 18 (Downers Grove, IL: InterVarsity, 1999), pp. 219-20. Cf. the further development of these images in Isa. 57:14-21.

35. The map is partial because I am excluding features that are less relevant to Luke's portrait.

tance of journeying for Luke is incontrovertible. Statistically, this is illustrated by the prominent use of such terms as πορεύομαι ("to walk" — 88 of 153 uses in the NT) and ὁδός ("way" — 40 of 101 uses in the NT) in Luke-Acts.[36] Even more compelling are:

- the thematic use of ὁδός ("way") in Luke 3:4 (cf. 7:27) to identify obedience as a "going" and God's will as a "path";
- the identification of God's purpose as "the way" (Luke 20:21; Acts 18:25, 26);
- the language of traveling with reference to Jesus' journey to Jerusalem in the service of God's saving agenda (Luke 9:52; 10:38; 13:22, 33; 17:11; 19:4; cf. Acts 20:22), including Jesus' assessment of his journey through rejection and death to his exaltation as an ἔξοδος ("departure," Luke 9:31);
- the use of ἡ ὁδός ("the way") as a means by which Luke identifies the community of Jesus' followers: "The Way" (Acts 9:2; 19:9, 23; 22:4; 24:14, 22); and
- the identification of the gospel as "way of salvation" (ὁδὸς σωτηρίας) in Acts 16:17, and related references to "the way of the Lord" in Acts 18:25 (ἡ ὁδὸς τοῦ κυρίου) and to "the way of God" in Acts 18:26 (ἡ ὁδὸς τοῦ θεοῦ).

If Jesus' life and mission constituted a journey, so also would that of his followers. Indeed, the coming of a powerful savior is to this end: "to guide our feet in the way of peace" (Luke 1:79). As Robert Maddox rightly observed, for Luke "the story of Jesus and of the church is a story full of purposeful movement."[37]

Although our survey has taken us beyond the boundaries of Luke's presentation of John's mission, we have seen that "the way," programmatically introduced with reference to John's ministry and tied to his mission of proclaiming repentance, is paradigmatic for the narrative as a whole. Luke's understanding of conversion is thus framed in terms of travel and builds on metaphors grounded in common, embodied human experience. Conversion entails movement, so it is conceptualized as a journey. What is

36. Since Luke constitutes some 27 percent of the NT, in terms of word counts, these statistics are telling. Luke is responsible for 58 percent of the uses of πορεύομαι and 40 percent of the uses of ὁδός.

37. Robert Maddox, *The Purpose of Luke-Acts*, FRLANT 126 (Göttingen: Vandenhoeck & Ruprecht, 1982), p. 11.

more, Luke roots his presentation in Isaiah's anticipation of new exodus, which is itself rooted in pervasive scriptural portraits of exodus and of walking in God's ways. The way of conversion follows in the well-worn pattern from sin to exile, from exile to repentance, and thus to restoration. Luke thus imaginatively shapes his readers' understanding of conversion so as to participate in the identity-forming history and hope of God's deliverance from exile and promised restoration.

Baptism, Conversion, Forgiveness

John is known throughout the Lukan narrative as one who baptizes. This conclusion takes seriously John's moniker, "John the Baptizer" (Luke 7:20, 33; 9:19); the identification of John with his baptism (Luke 20:4; Acts 1:22; 10:37; 18:25; 19:4); and the contrast between John and Jesus articulated in terms of their respective baptisms (Luke 3:16; Acts 1:5; 11:16; cf. 19:4-5). This emphasis coheres with Luke's observation in 3:7 that it was in order to be baptized by John that the crowds journeyed out to him.

Recognition of baptism as John's characteristic activity has led to ongoing discussion concerning the particular historical antecedent(s) of John's baptism, an inquiry stymied by the lack of any clear parallel in contemporary Jewish practice. The significance of this general lack of definitive, precursory practice should not be overdrawn, however, since one might justifiably postulate a common experience underlying all such practices. I refer to embodied cognition, and particularly to the grounding of relatively abstract concepts like morality in concrete experiences of physical cleanliness. In fact, in recent years, a growing literature has highlighted the embodiment of the moral-purity metaphor in expressions of physical cleanliness. For example: (1) A series of experiments conducted by Simone Schnall and her colleagues has demonstrated that surreptitiously activated cognitive concepts related to purity influenced moral decisions, that exposure to physical dirtiness shaped moral evaluations, and that physically cleansing oneself after experiencing disgust modulated the severity of moral judgments.[38] (2) Reporting in 2010 on two related experiments con-

---

38. E.g., Simone Schnall, Jennifer Benton, and Sophie Harvey, "With a Clean Conscience: Cleanliness Reduces the Severity of Moral Judgments," *Psychological Science* 19 (2008): 1219-22; Simone Schnall, Jonathan Haidt, Gerald L. Clore, and Alexander H. Jordan, "Disgust as Embodied Moral Judgment," *Personality and Social Psychology Bulletin* 34 (2008): 1096-1109.

cerned with how embodiment shapes cognition, Katie Liljenquist, Chen-Bo Zhong, and Adam D. Galinsky demonstrated that clean smells motivated virtuous behavior.[39] (3) Zhong and Liljenquist collaborated in other studies that demonstrated that the simple act of copying an immoral story increased the participants' desire for cleaning products, that those who thought about moral transgressions were more likely than those who thought about morally upright behavior to request an antiseptic cloth, and that using an antiseptic cloth after recollecting one's own past immoral behavior resulted in the apparent alleviation of guilt. They concluded that exposure to one's own or another's moral failure posed a moral threat and stimulated the need for physical cleansing.[40] (4) Spike W. S. Lee and Norbert Schwarz have taken a step further, demonstrating that physical cleansing removes traces of past decisions, reduces the need to justify those decisions, and can have the effect of wiping the slate clean.[41] In their analytical inventory of their own and others' recent work, Lee and Schwarz concluded:

> These findings show that the psychological impact of cleansing goes beyond the conceptual metaphor of moral cleanliness. The metaphoric notion of washing away one's sins seems to have generalized to a broader conceptualization of "wiping the slate clean." This allows people to remove unwanted residues of the past, from threats to a moral self-view to doubts about recent decisions and worries about bad luck. ... *In sum, physical cleansing removes not only physical contaminants but also moral taints and mental residues.*[42]

Given these basic observations concerning embodied cognition, we should not be surprised to find in Israel's literature the correlation of

---

39. Katie Liljenquist, Chen-Bo Zhong, and Adam D. Galinsky, "The Smell of Virtue: Clean Scents Promote Reciprocity and Charity," *Psychological Science* 21 (2010): 381-83.

40. Chen-Bo Zhong and Katie Liljenquist, "Washing Away Your Sins: Threatened Morality and Physical Cleansing," *Science* 313 (2006): 1451-52. Cf. Spike W. S. Lee and Norbert Schwarz, "Dirty Hands and Dirty Mouths: Embodiment of the Moral-Purity Metaphor Is Specific to the Motor Modality Involved in Moral Transgression," *Psychological Science* 21 (2010): 1423-25.

41. Spike W. S. Lee and Norbert Schwarz, "Washing Away Postdecisional Dissonance," *Science* 328 (2010): 709.

42. Spike W. S. Lee and Norbert Schwarz, "Wiping the Slate Clean: Psychological Consequences of Physical Cleansing," *Current Directions in Psychological Science* 20 (2011): 309-10, emphasis added.

washing with ethical comportment. In the opening chapter of Isaiah, for example, we read, "Wash yourselves; make yourselves clean; remove the evil of your doings from before my eyes; cease to do evil, learn to do good; seek justice, rescue the oppressed, defend the orphan, plead for the widow" (1:16-17). External cleansing is internally efficacious and leads to new behaviors — a reformation not only for individuals but for Israel as a people. Ezekiel envisions the regathering of God's people with these words:

> I will sprinkle clean water upon you, and you shall be clean from all your uncleannesses, and from all your idols I will cleanse you. A new heart I will give you, and a new spirit I will put within you; and I will remove from your body the heart of stone and give you a heart of flesh. I will put my spirit within you, and make you follow my statutes and be careful to observe my ordinances. Then you shall live in the land that I gave to your ancestors; and you shall be my people, and I will be your God. (36:25-28)

External cleansing is collocated with a religious-ethical new beginning, completing the pattern: sin-exile-conversion-restoration. The clearest evidence for this phenomenon in Luke-Acts comes in Ananias's words following Paul's visionary experience on the road to Damascus: "Why delay? Get up! Have yourself baptized and your sins washed away, as you call on his name!" (Acts 22:16).[43]

This emphasis on moral cleansing is precisely what we might have anticipated from our reading of Luke 3, where John's proclamation serves to specify the nature of the "washing" he practices. His is a repentance-baptism whose aim is forgiveness of sins (3:3). In Luke's presentation, this purpose is juxtaposed to the closing phrase of the Isaianic citation that follows in verses 4-6 — "All humanity will see God's salvation" — so that "forgiveness of sins" and "salvation" stand in parallel. Interestingly, the only reference to "forgiveness of sins" found earlier in the Lukan narrative is likewise collocated with "salvation" (1:77). Importantly, Zechariah's song (1:68-79) and the introduction to Luke 3 call for an eschatological reading

---

43. The verbs βάπτισαι ("to baptize") and ἀπόλουσαι ("to wash") stand in parallel: middle imperative verbs with a causative or permissive force; cf. 1 Corinthians 6:11; F. F. Bruce, *The Acts of the Apostles: Greek Text with Introduction and Commentary,* 3rd ed. (Grand Rapids: Eerdmans, 1990), pp. 457-58; BDF §317; A. T. Robertson, *A Grammar of Greek New Testament in the Light of Historical Research,* 4th ed. (New York: Hodder & Stoughton, 1923), p. 808.

centered on the restoration of God's people. The new era of salvation is dependent on, and inaugurated by, God's forgiving the people's sins, and this is the object of John's baptism.

That "forgiveness of sins" ought to be understood in such a wholistic way and, indeed, as a virtual stand-in for "God's act by which Israel is restored" has been documented by N. T. Wright. For him, *"[f]orgiveness of sins is another way of saying 'return from exile.'"*[44] This conclusion takes seriously the widespread view among the exilic prophets that Israel's exile was divine punishment for its sins — a state of affairs, then, that could be overturned only by God's forgiveness of Israel's sins. In support of these associations, Wright refers to Lamentations 4:22 ("The punishment of your iniquity, O daughter Zion, is accomplished, he will keep you in exile no longer . . .") and Jeremiah 31:31-34:

> The days are surely coming, says the LORD, when I will make a new covenant with the house of Israel and the house of Judah. It will not be like the covenant that I made with their ancestors when I took them by the hand to bring them out of the land of Egypt — a covenant that they broke, though I was their husband, says the LORD. But this is the covenant that I will make with the house of Israel after those days, says the LORD: I will put my law within them, and I will write it on their hearts; and I will be their God, and they shall be my people. No longer shall they teach one another, or say to each other, "Know the LORD," for they shall all know me, from the least of them to the greatest, says the LORD; *for I will forgive their iniquity, and remember their sin no more.* (Emphasis added)

Wright concludes, "Since covenant renewal means the reversal of exile, and since exile was the punishment for sin, covenant renewal/return from exile *means* that Israel's sins have been forgiven — and vice versa."[45] For our present purposes, this identification of forgiveness and restoration is secured above all by the intertextual frame within which Luke has sketched John's appearance and mission. As we have seen, in myriad ways Luke has underscored the significance of John's prophetic aims in terms of Israel's restoration. The words Luke borrows from Isaiah 40 to describe John follow and are predicated on God's announcement that the time of Israel's

---

44. N. T. Wright, *Jesus and the Victory of God,* Christian Origins and the Question of God 2 (Minneapolis: Fortress, 1996), p. 268, emphasis original; see pp. 268-71.

45. Wright, *Jesus,* p. 269, emphasis original. Cf. Jer. 33:4-11; Ezek. 36:24-26, 33; 37:21-23; Isa. 40:1-2; 43:25–44:3.

punishment is over and that Israel's sins are forgiven (Isa. 40:2; cf. 51:17). And, although "salvation" can refer to a range of benefactions, for Isaiah, as for Luke 1–2, the focus is above all on Israel's restoration from exile.[46]

One more line of evidence points in the direction of understanding "forgiveness of sins" and its correlate "salvation" in terms of Israel's restoration. Luke's citation of Isaiah 40 extends to 40:5: "all flesh shall see the salvation of God, because the Lord has spoken" (40:5 NETS). Read against the backdrop of Isaiah 35:4-5, this reference to "seeing" actually signifies a return of vision, since God's judgment was experienced as blindness. As quickly becomes evident, in Luke's understanding the "all" who will "see salvation" is parsed in two interrelated ways. First, as in Isaiah so in Luke, "all" refers to a faithful remnant (cf., e.g., Isaiah 12–13; 56) — or, perhaps better in Luke, the remnant that displays faithfulness through undergoing a repentance-baptism and living conversionary lives. Although Isaianic influence is self-evident in this presentation, it should not be overlooked that Luke's portrait actually inverts the Isaianic pattern. For Isaiah, judgment gives way to salvation, whereas for Luke the advent of salvation occasions judgment.[47] John addresses all Israel (cf. Luke 3:3, 15, 18, 21), even if his doing so segregates the repentant from those who fail to flee "the coming wrath" (3:7; cf. 3:9). Second, as in Isaiah so in Luke, "all" includes Gentiles (e.g., Isa. 49:6; 51:5; 60; 62; Luke 2:14, 31-32; Acts 11:18; 13:47). John's mission is more narrowly directed toward God's people, Israel, but it is integral to God's larger salvific agenda for all humanity.

Accordingly, the central emphasis in John's ministry on conversion cannot be segregated from its twofold embodiment — in the physical act of baptism and in the sociopolitical ramifications of God's restoration of his people. Regarding the former, Luke's epitome of John's ministry participates in a universal exemplar of embodied cognition: the embodiment of the moral-purity metaphor in expressions of physical cleanliness. Regarding the latter, "forgiveness of sin" and its correlate "salvation" cannot be reduced to an interior, subjective experience, but must be understood eschatologically and in terms of God's faithfulness to Israel.

---

46. Cf. Horst Dietrich Preuss, *Old Testament Theology,* vol. 2, trans. Leo G. Perdue, OTL (Louisville: Westminster John Knox, 1996), pp. 274-77; J. Richard Middleton and Michael J. Gorman, "Salvation," in *NIDB* 5:45-61: "Beneath the OT's use of explicit salvation language lies a coherent worldview in which the exodus from Egyptian bondage, followed by entry into the promised land, forms the most important paradigm or model" (p. 45).

47. This is also observed in David W. Pao, *Acts and the Isaianic New Exodus,* WUNT 2/130 (Tübingen: Mohr Siebeck, 2000; repr.: Grand Rapids: Baker Academic, 2002), p. 108.

Conversion Embodied

In Luke 3, Luke expends far more energy disclosing the character of John's proclamation than sketching the nature of the baptismal act or experience itself. This highlights John's identity as the Isaianic harbinger of good news (cf. Isa. 40:1-9; Luke 3:18). From the standpoint of ritual studies, it is easy to find in Luke's presentation a portrait of baptism as an initiatory rite of passage.[48] Thus, people (1) temporarily withdrew into the wilderness, away from their life routines and habitations, in order to participate in John's ministry through baptism (i.e., *separation*); (2) underwent a repentance-baptism signifying their (re)new(ed) devotion to God's aims (i.e., *transition*); and (3) returned to their everyday lives as pilgrims together on a conversionary journey (i.e., *incorporation*). This locates conversion in human practices that are more than activities arising from covenant relationship but that themselves comprise the very character of that relationship. Accordingly, the practices Luke describes in 3:7-14 are means by which God's restorative aims are brought to expression within human community. One's status (baptized or not) is inseparable from one's practices, with covenantal membership constituted by conversionary behaviors. And, according to John's proclamation, conversionary lives provide the basis on which judgment will be executed.

Klaus Berger's work represents one path into this decidedly non-Cartesian way of seeing the world.[49] His investigation of the historical psychology of the NT texts repeatedly underscores the problem of anachronistic assumptions about the nature of humanity, particularly the ease with which modern people assume of these ancient texts a conventional, but modernist, separation between being and doing, identity and behavior, internal and external. It will not do, then, to think of the behaviors John countenances as though they were supplementary to conversion or conversion's accessories. Behavior is not an add-on to conversion. Rather, conversionary practices are constitutive of conversion; this is because conversion refers to transformed patterns of human life. Practices serve not only as the window through which one's deepest commitments are on display, therefore, but also as the per se embodiment of those commitments.

---

48. The classic study, written in 1909, is Arnold van Gennep, *The Rites of Passage,* trans. Monika B. Vizedom and Gabrielle L. Caffee (Chicago: University of Chicago Press, 1960).

49. Klaus Berger, *Identity and Experience in the New Testament,* trans. Charles Muenchow (Minneapolis: Fortress, 2003).

In the present case of the Lukan narrative, perhaps this is no more transparent than in the reality that judgment is tied to conversion's fecundity: "Every tree that fails to produce good fruit will be chopped down and thrown into the fire" (3:9).

John's message turns on an *organic* metaphor, not a mechanical one. The resulting frame has no room for prioritizing inner (e.g., "soul" or "mind" or "heart") over outer (e.g., "body" or "behavior"), nor of fitting disparate pieces together to manufacture a "product," nor of correlating status and activity as cause and effect. An organic metaphor conjures no images of hierarchical systems but invites images of integration, interrelation, and interdependence. Practices do not occupy a space outside the system of change, but are themselves part and parcel of the system. Accordingly, John's agricultural metaphor inseparably binds "is" and "does" together.

What is more, we find here no hint of keeping an account of who has or has not been baptized. The act of baptism is thus integral to the ritual of status transformation, but not its sum.

The shape of conversionary life as this is related to John's mission takes multiple forms, two of which we will develop here. The first is only implicit in Luke 3 but becomes increasingly visible later in the Lukan narrative: the community that forms in relation to John's baptism. The second is more explicit, grounded as it is in the words of the crowds, toll collectors, and soldiers — all variations on the question, "What should we do?" (vv. 10, 12, 14).

Conversion and Community

Lars Hartman observes that the NT evidence presupposes a community of John's followers.[50] This is certainly true with regard to Luke's narrative, which refers to John's disciples (e.g., Luke 7:18); recognizes that John's disciples engage in characteristic behaviors by which they are identified (fasting, for example, and prayer [5:33; 11:1]); assumes of John's disciples that they share, or ought to share, a hopeful expectation of the coming of a Messiah who will baptize with the Holy Spirit and with fire, and, so, that John's followers ought to become members of the community of Jesus' dis-

50. Lars Hartman, *'Into the Name of the Lord Jesus': Baptism in the Early Church*, SNTW (Edinburgh: T. & T. Clark, 1997), p. 15.

ciples (3:15-16; 7:18-20; Acts 1:5; 11:16; 13:25; 19:3-4); and presupposes a geo-graphically expansive Baptist movement (Acts 18:24-25; 19:1-4).

The present importance of this Baptist community is grounded in two related observations. First, it points to a communal context for identity and moral formation. As conversionary practices are communally based, a community's common practices help to give it its identity and identify those associated with that community as its members. Even if the general practices of prayer and fasting characteristic of John's disciples are hardly unique to this apparently loosely organized cadre, they nonetheless serve as identity markers. How such practices might actually distinguish these persons as John's (as opposed, say, to the Pharisees') disciples is unclear; according to Luke 5:33, for example, both sets of disciples are unlike Jesus' followers in that followers of the Baptist and of the Pharisees "fast frequently" and "pray often." At the same time, Luke 11:1 at least opens the possibility of prayer patterns peculiar to John's community. That John's mission expresses itself communally gains significance, second, insofar as this is congruent with the accent in recent work on the sociology of conversion, which identifies conversion in part as *incorporation into a new community,* including adopting the rituals and practices peculiar to or definitive of that new community.[51] In this case, *incorporation* is marked by the initiatory act of undergoing John's baptism. These observations are fully at home with the emphasis thus far in our discussion of conversion relative to the eschatological restoration of a people whose common life puts into practice the aims of YHWH.

A Conversionary Life

In Luke 3:7-9, 15-17, the need for readiness is set against the backdrop of impending judgment. Abraham's children will escape the coming wrath, so the critical question is: Who are Abraham's children? Familial status in this instance is determined, not by genealogical record, but by how one responds to God's gracious initiative in bringing salvation. We recognize Abraham's children by means of their family resemblance measured in terms of embodied character.

---

51. Cf., e.g., Nicholas H. Taylor, "The Social Nature of Conversion in the Early Christian World," in *Modelling Early Christianity: Social-Scientific Studies of the New Testament in Its Context,* ed. Philip F. Esler (London: Routledge, 1995), pp. 128-36.

"Good fruit" (3:9) in this context is fruit that has a conversionary quality about it (3:8).[52] Eschewing any possibility that "conversion" might remain an abstraction (or be reduced to an interior decision), Luke's account elucidates conversion in terms of performance. The result is a focus on life at the local level in which one's routine network of relationships is touched by an ethical vision that makes conversion visible in the everydayness of human existence.

"What should we do, then?" The question posed by the crowds to John (3:10) is repeated by toll collectors in 3:12, soldiers in 3:14, a legal expert in 10:25, a rich ruler in 18:18, a Jerusalem audience in Acts 2:37, a jailor in Acts 16:30, and a zealous Jew in Acts 22:10. With one possible exception (Luke 18:18), the question arises as a response to proclamation or to a miracle, underscoring the importance of human performative response to divine initiative. In the present context, John has made clear the pivotal significance of conversionary performance over against any other attempt to define oneself as Abraham's child. John thus articulates the character of that performance with his charge that the converted, all of them, share what they have with those who lack the basic necessities of life. The apparently conventional character of John's directive (conventional, that is, among the converted) becomes clear elsewhere in Luke's Gospel, where we discover that care for the hungry and naked is nothing more or less than heeding Moses and the prophets (e.g., 16:19-31). Should anyone imagine that John has thus singled out these behaviors as the basis of membership among God's restored people, this would be due to a fundamental misunderstanding of a psychology, such as we find in Luke 3, that refuses to drive a wedge between one's character and commitments, on one hand, and one's practices, on the other. A life oriented toward the way of the Lord is one in which the way of the Lord — in this case, care for the have-nots — is in play.

From the general counsel directed to the crowds (3:10-11), the focus moves more narrowly to toll collectors who have come out to be baptized (3:12-13). This scene is an amplification of the first — one that presents a further, concrete instantiation of the words directed to the crowds and that turns attention to a particularly offensive subgroup of those who have journeyed out to participate in John's ministry, toll collectors. "Collect no more than you are authorized to collect" (3:13). How much is this? What

---

52. That is, καρπὸς ἄξιος τῆς μετανοίας, "fruit 'corresponding to' or 'worthy of' conversion" (see BDAG, 94).

percentage? We are told only that, for them, conversion is on display when they do not exceed the amount set by those in authority over them.[53] Apparently, a conversionary life is possible for toll collectors *qua* toll collectors. Emphasis falls on day-to-day life as the venue within which conversion is performed.

In 3:14, soldiers are similarly cast as an assemblage of surprising participants in John's mission, and their inquiry sets the stage for another concrete instantiation of John's call to bear fruit characteristic of a conversionary life. As with the toll-collecting system, so here John's response is not directed against the military complex per se. Instead, he calls for the cessation of behaviors by which soldiers manipulate the local populace to their advantage. Routine interactions provide the setting for an exegesis of conversion.

It is worth repeating that the behaviors John urges among his audience are not themselves the basis for covenantal restoration; it is better to say that they enact the covenant whose restoration God has initiated. Nor should we imagine that John's directives constitute the grand sum of conversionary behavior as this will be developed in the Lukan narrative. What Luke records here are nothing more than exemplars. If crowds and toll collectors and soldiers, what of synagogue leaders and jailors and dealers in purple dye? If John does not specifically address such persons in their day-to-day circumstances, this does not mean that they are left without guidance. John has begun to map the patterns of life that deserve the label "conversionary." Such patterns reflect the way of the Lord who brings salvation, who restores his people. Such patterns reach into the day-to-day interactions and affairs of life. Conversion is "the way of the Lord" embodied.

Conclusion

In this essay, I have urged that Luke presents conversion as integral to the grand mural of God's redemption of Israel and concomitant extension of salvation to all people. In doing so, I have targeted attempts to read conversion in Luke 3:1-14 in ways that reduce conversion to an interior decision, to individualistic decision making, or, indeed, to a (single) event. In their place, I have attempted to grapple with Luke's theology of conversion in

---

53. Elsewhere, Luke uses διατάσσω for activity performed under the authority of another (cf. Luke 8:55; 17:9-10; Acts 18:2; 23:31).

ways that take seriously the plotline according to which God initiates his restoration of his people through the forgiveness of sins. Conversion is first the story of God's prevenience, God's gracious visitation that provides the basis for and opens the way for human responses of repentance. Moreover, I have urged that the language by which Luke sketches the character of conversion highlights human embodiment, an emphasis further underscored by the human, bodily experience of washing, the windows Luke provides into the community of those being converted, the nature of conversion as a journey, and the importance of conversionary practices constitutive of covenant renewal. In the end, Luke emphasizes the dynamic action of God that opens the way and calls for people to embody in their lives "the way of the Lord."

"Not Knowing What Will Happen to Me There": Experiences of the Holy Spirit in Luke-Acts

John B. F. Miller

Ever since my initial reading of *From Darkness to Light* as a first-year seminary student, Beverly Gaventa has been challenging me to explore God's actions and the theological implications of those actions in Luke-Acts.[1] The present study is a response to that challenge, albeit a brief one, focusing on the role of the Holy Spirit in the Lukan narrative. More specifically, I wish to ask what seems like a simple question: What does the Holy Spirit *do* in Luke-Acts? For anyone familiar with Lukan scholarship, of course, it would be ridiculous to call this question "simple." The secondary literature on the role(s) of the Holy Spirit in Luke-Acts is vast and full of contention.[2] After a brief survey of some of the more recent studies, I will clarify that I am interested in engaging this question from a slightly different perspective than many whose works have dominated this scholarly landscape. In particular, attempts to develop consistent and coherent theories about Luke's portrayal of the Holy Spirit have tended to obscure, or otherwise ignore, passages that may resist consistency.[3] I am more interested, therefore, in examining pas-

1. Gaventa, *From Darkness to Light: Aspects of Conversion in the New Testament*, OBT 20 (Philadelphia: Fortress, 1986). I began studying with Professor Gaventa in 1994. Her work has always claimed my utmost respect; her mentoring and guidance have meant more to me than words can express. It is an honor to dedicate this essay to her, and I do so with deep and abiding gratitude.

2. One example is the extended debate between Max Turner and Robert Menzies over whether the Spirit should be linked with demonstrations of God's power (see bibliographical references below).

3. I will follow the common convention of referring to the author of Luke-Acts as "Luke." By doing so, I do not intend any necessary connection to the figure mentioned in other NT texts (e.g., Philem. 24).

sages that highlight tensions in Luke's portrayal of the Spirit. Two of these passages feature characters said to be "filled with the Holy Spirit" (Luke 1:15, 67), and two feature contradictory guidance from the same Spirit (Acts 19:21; 20:22-23; cf. Acts 21:4, 10-14).[4] I will argue that these passages encourage a more fluid and varied understanding of what the Spirit *does* in Luke's story — an understanding informed by the ways in which Luke's characters manifest their experience of the Holy Spirit's actions.

The Holy Spirit is mentioned more in the Gospel of Luke than in any of the other canonical Gospels and appears in Acts more frequently than in Matthew, Mark, and John combined.[5] Throughout the history of Christian tradition, in fact, Acts has received appellations such as "The Gospel of the Holy Spirit" and "The Acts of the Holy Spirit."[6] The prominence of the Spirit throughout Luke-Acts is rendered poignantly in Paul Minear's encapsulation: "Surely the whole sequence of events from the conception of John to the arrival of Paul in Rome belongs within the orbit of Luke's testimony to the ways in which God is pouring out his Spirit 'on all flesh.'"[7] It is not surprising, therefore, that scholars have focused a considerable amount of attention on the Holy Spirit in Luke-Acts. The questions and agendas that drive these studies are quite varied, however, as are the conclusions they render.

Most scholars find the primary background for Luke's conceptions of the Spirit in the traditions of Israelite religion and early Judaism.[8] Yet, there are some who argue for extensive connections with non-Jewish Greco-Roman religions.[9] Some argue that the Holy Spirit fulfills a pri-

---

4. Unless otherwise noted, all translations in this study are my own.

5. Although precise numbers are difficult (a few uses of the word πνεῦμα in these texts are ambiguous [e.g., Luke 1:17], and a few others are debated [e.g., Acts 19:21]), see the comparison in Max Turner, "The Work of the Holy Spirit in Luke-Acts," *WW* 23 (2003): 146.

6. See the discussion in F. F. Bruce, "Luke's Presentation of the Spirit in Acts," *CTR* 5 (1990): 18-19.

7. Paul S. Minear, "Luke's Use of the Birth Stories," in *Studies in Luke-Acts: Essays Presented in Honor of Paul Schubert*, ed. Leander E. Keck and J. Louis Martyn (Philadelphia: Fortress, 1980), p. 120.

8. This is the prevailing consensus in contemporary scholarship. See, for example, Joseph A. Fitzmyer, *The Gospel according to Luke I–IX*, AB 28 (New York: Doubleday, 1970), p. 228; G. W. H. Lampe, "The Holy Spirit in the Writings of St. Luke," in *Studies in the Gospels: Essays in Memory of R. H. Lightfoot*, ed. D. E. Nineham (Oxford: Blackwell, 1955), p. 163.

9. It would be misleading to suggest that any contemporary Lukan scholars connect Luke's conceptions of the Spirit solely to Greco-Roman religious traditions. For such an idea, one must look back to the days of the *religionsgeschichtliche Schule*; see, for example,

mary, or even singular, purpose in Luke-Acts.[10] Still others outline multifaceted roles of the Spirit in Luke's narrative.[11] Many treatments of the
Holy Spirit, both older and more recent, focus primarily behind Luke's
narrative, attempting to recover conceptions of the Spirit within early
Christian communities.[12] Some go so far as to abandon Luke's narrative in
its present form, arguing that meaningful answers can be found only in
speculation about Luke's sources.[13] Theological conclusions form a spectrum. It has become commonplace, however, to observe that Luke connects the Holy Spirit inextricably with God.[14] This point is foundational
for understanding Lukan theology. Although Luke refers to "God" (θεός)
well over two hundred times in Luke-Acts, he depicts God acting directly

---

the summary of H. Leisegang's *Pneuma Hagion: Der Ursprung des Geistesbegriffs der
synoptischen Evangelien aus der grieschen Mystik* (Leipzig: Hinrichs, 1922) in Max Turner,
Power from on High: The Spirit in Israel's Restoration and Witness in Luke-Acts, JPTSup 9
(Sheffield: Sheffield Academic Press, 1996), pp. 27-29. In more recent years, the trend has
been to argue that Luke's work blends Jewish and non-Jewish Greco-Roman conceptions of
"spirit"; see, for example, John R. Levison, *Filled with the Spirit* (Grand Rapids: Eerdmans,
2009), pp. 317-65.

10. The most prominent example is Robert Menzies, who argues that the Spirit is the
source of prophetic inspiration in Luke-Acts and argues against associating the Lukan Spirit
with concepts of soteriology or miraculous displays of divine power. See his *Empowered for
Witness: The Spirit in Luke-Acts*, JPTSup 6 (Sheffield: Sheffield Academic Press, 1994); originally published as *The Development of Early Christian Pneumatology: With Special Reference
to Luke-Acts*, JSNTSup 54 (Sheffield: Sheffield Academic Press, 1991); also his "Spirit and
Power in Luke-Acts: A Response to Max Turner," *JSNT* 49 (1993): 11-20. There are in the
scholarship on Luke-Acts few points of consensus about the role(s) of the Spirit. There is
widespread agreement, however, that the Holy Spirit inspires prophetic speech. For bibliographical details, see William H. Shepherd Jr., *The Narrative Function of the Holy Spirit as a
Character in Luke-Acts*, SBLDS 147 (Atlanta: Scholars Press, 1994), pp. 11-12.

11. See F. F. Bruce, "The Holy Spirit in the Acts of the Apostles," *Int* 27 (1973): 166-83;
Bruce, "Presentation," pp. 15-29. For one of the most comprehensive treatments of the Holy
Spirit in Luke-Acts, see Turner, *Power*.

12. See, for example, James D. G. Dunn, *Jesus and the Spirit: A Study of the Religious and
Charismatic Experience of Jesus and the First Christians as Reflected in the New Testament*
(Philadelphia: Westminster, 1975).

13. See, for example, J. C. O'Neill, "The Connection between Baptism and the Gift of
the Spirit in Acts," *JSNT* 63 (1996): 87.

14. Lampe, for example, argues that the Spirit "is the mode of God's activity in dealing
with man and the power in which he is active among his people" (Lampe, "Spirit," p. 163). As
Beverly Roberts Gaventa observes: "With respect to God, Jesus, and the Spirit, then, they are
so identified with one another in Acts that explicitly Trinitarian language seems an inevita-
ble development" (*Acts*, ANTC [Nashville: Abingdon, 2003], p. 39).

in the narrative only infrequently.[15] The actions of the Holy Spirit, which are necessarily linked to God, thus become all the more important.

My goal here is not a speculative reconstruction of the early Christian practices Luke's work may reflect, nor am I interested in exploring overarching questions about the Lukan Spirit. Although I appreciate the contributions made by those who have attempted comprehensive and categorical studies of the Spirit, I find that they frequently impose degrees of consistency and coherence that are not always compatible with the Lukan narrative. As a student of my teacher and fellow practitioner of narrative criticism, I am interested in the story Luke tells and in the way he tells it. In asking the question, What does the Spirit *do* in Luke-Acts?, I am particularly interested in the diverse ways in which the Spirit interacts with other characters in Luke-Acts.[16] I am interested in what it means for the Spirit to "fill" characters in the Lukan narrative and in depictions of characters acting "in" the Spirit or "through the Spirit." Understanding the relationship between the Spirit and other characters in Luke-Acts from a narrative perspective, I would argue, requires an examination of the ways in which characters respond to their experiences of the Holy Spirit.

I suggest Luke's presentation of such experiences and responses is diverse. Some of the passages in Luke's narrative offer what appear to be straightforward connections between various characters and the Holy Spirit. In Acts 11:28, for example, Agabus "indicated through the Spirit" (ἐσήμανεν διὰ τοῦ πνεύματος) that a "great famine" would take place. In the same verse, Luke's narrator then tells readers this famine occurred during the reign of Claudius. What Agabus said "through the Spirit" came to pass. In Acts 13:9-11, Paul is "filled with the Holy Spirit" (πλησθεὶς πνεύματος ἁγίου) just before he tells Bar-Jesus / Elymas that he will be blind. Immediately, "mist and darkness fall" upon Bar-Jesus. What Paul says when "filled" with the Spirit comes to pass. Not all Luke's descriptions, however, are so straightforward.

In Luke 1:15, Gabriel tells Zechariah that his son "will be filled with the Holy Spirit, even from his mother's womb." This statement is followed by a description of John's prophetic calling, but the precise significance of the Spirit's filling for John remains unclear. Later in the same chapter, Zechariah is "filled with the Spirit" and "prophesies" about his son (Luke 1:67-79). How and in what ways does this Spirit-filled prophecy find fulfillment

---

15. See, for example, Joel B. Green's discussion of the exceptional nature of the transfiguration scene (*The Gospel of Luke,* NICNT [Grand Rapids: Eerdmans, 1997], p. 383).

16. On the Holy Spirit as a character in Luke-Acts, see Shepherd, *Function,* pp. 90-97.

in Luke's narrative? In Acts 20:22-23, Paul declares to the Ephesian elders that he is on his way to Jerusalem, "bound to the Spirit." He does not know "what will happen to [him] there," but he declares that "the Holy Spirit testifies [to him] that chains and suffering await [him]." In the next chapter, however, one finds the enigmatic description of the Tyrian disciples who tell Paul "through the Spirit" not to go to Jerusalem (Acts 21:4). A few verses later, Agabus claims to relate the very words of the Holy Spirit ("the Holy Spirit says this" [Acts 21:11]). All those who hear Agabus accept this declaration — a declaration that does not reflect the course of events later in the narrative (Acts 21:27-34). How is Luke's reader to understand conflicting guidance from the same Spirit, and Spirit-inspired declarations that do not reflect the subsequent narrative? These passages stand in tension with what one might consider more straightforward depictions of the Holy Spirit in Luke-Acts. In the examination that follows, I will suggest that one arrives at a better understanding of Luke's portrayal of the Spirit only by engaging the complications in that portrayal.

The Holy Spirit and John

In Luke 1:15, the angel Gabriel announces to Zechariah that his son John "will be filled with the Holy Spirit, even from his mother's womb" (πνεύματος ἁγίου πλησθήσεται ἔτι ἐκ κοιλίας μητρὸς αὐτοῦ).[17] As many have noted, Gabriel's annunciation raises an immediate connection between John's filling of the Spirit and his prophetic work of "turning" and "preparing" people for the Lord (1:16-17).[18] Precisely how the "filling" of

17. Turner notes that the idea of someone being filled with the Spirit while still in the womb is unparalleled both in the OT and Judaism (Turner, *Power*, p. 151). Menzies suggests an interesting connection with Luke 7:26: the filling of the Spirit John experiences while still in the womb renders him "more than a prophet" (Menzies, *Empowered*, p. 108).

I concur with the many Lukan scholars who view the infancy stories, not as a roughly attached appendage to Luke's Gospel, but as an integral part of the Lukan narrative (see John B. F. Miller, *Convinced That God Had Called Us: Dreams, Visions, and the Perception of God's Will in Luke-Acts*, Biblical Interpretation Series 85 [Leiden: Brill, 2007], pp. 133-46). See also, for example, Minear, "Stories," pp. 111-30; Robert C. Tannehill, *The Narrative Unity of Luke-Acts: A Literary Interpretation*, 2 vols. (Philadelphia and Minneapolis: Fortress, 1986-1990), 1:20-44.

18. See, for example, John Michael Penney, *The Missionary Emphasis of Lukan Pneumatology*, JPTSup 12 (Sheffield: Sheffield Academic Press, 1997), p. 27; Green, *Luke*, pp. 75-78; and Tannehill, *Unity*, 1:23-24.

the Spirit will facilitate this turning and preparation may become clearer in Luke 3. In Luke 1, however, the reader is left with other questions, notably: What is the connection between John's "filling" of the Spirit and the other child described in Luke's infancy narrative?[19] Gabriel does not connect the work of John explicitly to Jesus, but the immediate narrative context hints at such a connection.

When she visits Elizabeth, Mary's greeting causes a surprising reaction: as the narrator explains (1:41), and as is later emphasized in Elizabeth's description (1:44), the "child" in Elizabeth's womb "leaps" (σκιρτάω) at Mary's greeting.[20] Elizabeth is then "filled with the Holy Spirit" (ἐπλήσθη πνεύματος ἁγίου [1:41]), just as Gabriel promised her unborn son would be (1:15). The narrative implication is that the filling of the Spirit led the unborn child to recognize what Elizabeth recognizes when filled with the Spirit: "How has this happened to me that the mother of my lord has come to me?" (1:43).[21] This Spirit-filled moment of recognition, however, highlights John's puzzling uncertainty about Jesus later in the narrative.

The implicit connection between the filling of the Spirit and prophetic speech ("the spirit and power of Elijah" [1:17]) in Gabriel's annunciation becomes more explicit in Luke 3:2 ("the word of God came to John" [ἐγένετο ῥῆμα θεοῦ ἐπὶ Ἰωάννην][22]) and in John's proclamation (3:7-17). Part of that proclamation includes John's reaction to speculation that he himself could be the Messiah. As in the other Synoptic Gospels, John does not identify himself as the Messiah but describes the "one coming" who "will baptize" the people "with the Holy Spirit and with fire" (3:16).[23] John's role of proclaiming the "one coming" is important for all of the Gospel writers. Similarities in the portrayal of John, especially in the Synoptic Gospels, thus come as little surprise. Far more intriguing are the points at which Luke's portrayal differs from the other Gospel accounts.

19. Tannehill (*Unity*, 1:15-20) and Green (*Luke*, pp. 82-85) offer thorough explorations of the interconnections between the story of John and the story of Jesus in the infancy narrative. Fitzmyer argues that the infancy narrative is structured so that it not only describes these interconnections but does so in a way that ensures the reader will understand that Jesus is superior to John (Fitzmyer, *Luke*, pp. 313-16).

20. Luke uses σκιρτάω only three times. Aside from the occurrence here and in verse 44, it is connected with the verb χαίρω in the context of "leaping for joy" (Luke 6:23).

21. Just as the reader finds a parallel in the recognition of Elizabeth and the unborn John, Turner observes that Elizabeth's Spirit-filled utterance (1:41-45) parallels Zechariah's proclamation in 1:67-79 (Turner, *Power*, p. 148).

22. This statement about John is a clear allusion to LXX Jer. 1:1.

23. Mark 1:7-8; Matt. 3:1-12.

Given the emphasis on John in the infancy narrative, it may not be surprising that Luke devotes more narrative description to John than the other Synoptic writers.[24] Because of the parallels between John and Jesus in Luke 1, however, it is surprising to find that Luke is careful to keep John separate from Jesus in the remainder of the narrative. In Mark, John baptizes Jesus (Mark 1:9). In Matthew, John not only baptizes Jesus but even offers some commentary on Jesus (Matt. 3:13-16).[25] In Luke, John is not specified as the one who baptizes Jesus.[26] In fact, Luke places his commentary about John's imprisonment immediately before Jesus' baptism (Luke 3:19-20). Although the unborn John recognizes the unborn Jesus (1:41), and although John later prophesies the coming of the Messiah (3:16-17), he never has an explicit encounter with Jesus in Luke's Gospel. This distance allows the puzzling passage in Luke 7 to flow a bit more naturally than its Matthean counterpart.

In Luke 7:19, John asks his disciples to inquire of Jesus, "Are you the one who is coming, or should we wait for another?"[27] This passage is not uniquely Lukan. Presumably from Q, the story is also in Matthew 11:2-6. Luke places more emphasis on this episode, however, by narrating both John's question and his disciples' repetition of the question in immediate succession (7:19, 20; cf. Matt. 11:3). The Matthean version is at odds with Matthew's earlier description of Jesus' baptism (Matt. 3:14), at which John appears to understand fully who Jesus is: "I need to be baptized by you, and you are coming to me?" In Luke, the tension is not with the baptism scene but with the earlier description of Mary and Elizabeth (1:41-44). Gabriel's announcement that John "will be filled with the Holy Spirit, even from his mother's womb" (1:15), is confirmed when the unborn John "leaps" at the recognition of Mary's greeting. Yet, in Luke 7, John must send disciples to ask Jesus whether he is "the one who is coming."

The narrative tension between these passages rests on a central ques-

---

24. Compare, for example, Mark 1:2-8; 6:14-16; Matt. 3:1-12; 11:2-19; 14:1-2; Luke 3:1-20; 7:18-35; 9:7-9. The pericope describing the circumstances surrounding John's execution is the only exception to this pattern (Mark 6:17-29; Matt. 14:3-12).

25. John's comments about Jesus are even more extensive in the Fourth Gospel (John 1:25-36).

26. Because John is an important part of the baptism scenes in the other canonical Gospels, this is an easy nuance to miss; see, for example, Bruce, "Holy Spirit," p. 167.

27. As Tannehill observes, the repeated use of προσδοκάω in verses 19-20 connects this scene to Luke 3:15 and to the messianic expectations to which John responded (*Unity*, 1:80 n. 8). Fitzmyer offers a summary of the ways in which various commentators throughout Christian tradition have understood "John's doubts" (*Luke*, p. 664).

tion: What does it mean that John "will be filled with the Holy Spirit, even from his mother's womb"? What does the Spirit *do* in this context? The Spirit apparently enables the unborn John to recognize Mary and the unborn Jesus. The same Spirit apparently inspires both John's call to repentance and his proclamation about the "one coming." The Spirit does not, however, enable John to recognize Jesus later as the "one coming" with any certainty. Scholarship on this passage has tended sometimes to gloss over the problem of uncertainty.[28] At other times it focuses instead on reading Luke 7:18-23 as a recapitulation of Jesus' ministry as a fulfillment of the proclamation in Nazareth (Luke 4:16-21).[29] Rather than succumbing to oversimplified and overly convenient answers, one may argue that this passage invites us to linger over the questions it raises about the Spirit's actions. The filling of the Spirit empowers John, but there are surprising limitations to that empowerment — surprising limitations that include the empowerment to proclaim, but not the empowerment to identify the fulfillment of that proclamation.

The preceding discussion focused on a general question: How is one to understand the filling of the Holy Spirit as it relates to John? Since this filling is characterized by Gabriel as an overarching reality for John's ministry, one must seek answers in John's response to the filling of the Spirit. John's uncertainty about Jesus in Luke 7 raises interesting questions about what it means to be "filled with the Spirit" and the perplexingly limited awareness that results. The discussion that follows focuses attention on a narrower

---

28. Turner, for example, argues that John is exceptional among those who have contact with the Holy Spirit in Luke 1–2 (i.e., Elizabeth, Mary, Zechariah, and Simeon); only John possesses the filling of the Spirit for more than brief prophetic moments, and only he fits the title of "eschatological prophet" (*Power,* p. 164). About John's uncertainty toward Jesus in 7:18, however, Turner says merely, "Luke is aware of some limitations on his understanding" (*Power,* p. 187). Others perhaps follow tacitly the reasoning offered by I. Howard Marshall: since John is in prison (Luke 3:19-20), and since Judea does not seem to be experiencing eschatological upheaval, John understandably wonders whether Jesus is really the "one who is coming" (*The Gospel of Luke: A Commentary on the Greek Text,* NIGTC [Grand Rapids: Eerdmans, 1978], p. 288). Robert C. Tannehill takes a different approach entirely. Although he notes the "prophetic" significance of Elizabeth's unborn child "leaping" at Mary's greeting, Tannehill's comments on 7:18 emphasize the distance between John and Jesus in the Lukan narrative discussed above: "There has been no indication in Luke that John recognized Jesus as the fulfillment of John's prophecies. . . . John's question does not represent the weakening of previous belief but the hopeful exploration of a possibility" (*Luke,* ANTC [Nashville: Abingdon, 1996], pp. 52, 129).

29. Green, *Luke,* pp. 295-96; Tannehill, *Unity,* 1:105.

question: How does Zechariah's prophecy, uttered under the filling of the Spirit, find fulfillment in the Lukan narrative?

The Holy Spirit and Zechariah

Following his encounter with Gabriel in Luke 1:11-20, Zechariah is mute until he confirms the name Elizabeth has given their newborn son (1:63-64). Although there is some question about the story time covered in the sequence of events described in 1:64-66, the narrative itself moves quickly from the "opening" of Zechariah's mouth and tongue (v. 64) to the point at which Zechariah "was filled with the Holy Spirit and prophesied" (v. 67).[30] Zechariah's song of praise that follows in verses 68-79, however, creates a problem for the reader. Specifically, some of what Zechariah prophesies does not come to pass in the remainder of Luke's story. These words, uttered under the filling of the Spirit, raise a number of questions about narrative expectations and fulfillment.[31] A thorough treatment of Zechariah's Benedictus is beyond the scope of the present study. For the purposes of this discussion, a summary of the salient issues will suffice.

Replete with echoes and allusions to promises from the OT, Zechariah's Benedictus proclaims God's "redemption" (λύτρωσις [Luke 1:68]) and "salvation" (σωτηρία [Luke 1:69, 71, 77]) of God's people.[32] Specifically, it proclaims God's salvation from the "enemies" (ἐχθρός [Luke 1:71, 74]) of, and "from the hand of all who hate" (ἐκ χειρὸς πάντων τῶν μισούντων [Luke 1:71]), Israel. This redemption and salvation mean that God will now allow God's people to "worship" or "serve" (λατρεύω) God "without fear" (ἀφόβως [Luke 1:74]). In short, Zechariah prophesies a "salvation" that will be manifested, at least partly, in political, social, and reli-

---

30. In narrative criticism, "story time" refers to the duration of described events (in this case, the indeterminate time it takes "all of these matters" to be discussed in all the hill country of Judea [1:65]), whereas "narrative time" refers to the number of words devoted to such a description in the narrative (Gérard Genette, *Narrative Discourse: An Essay in Method*, trans. Jane E. Lewin [Ithaca: Cornell University Press, 1980], p. 33).

31. For my own exploration of this problem, see Miller, *Convinced*, pp. 133-46.

32. For good discussions of the connections to the OT, see Green, *Luke*, pp. 115-20; Marshall, *Luke*, pp. 90-95. As Tannehill has observed, the use of λύτρωσις in the Benedictus provides an excellent example of unfulfilled expectation when compared with the use of λυτρόω in the Emmaus story (Luke 24:21). The events that transpire in Jesus' ministry do not bring the kind of redemption his disciples were expecting (Tannehill, *Unity*, 1:35, 281).

gious freedom.[33] Clearly, this kind of salvation does not come about in Luke-Acts.

Two pressing questions arise. First, how is the reader to understand Zechariah's words within the context of Luke's narrative? Second, how is the reader to reconcile this unfulfilled proclamation with the assertion that it is uttered under the filling of the Holy Spirit? Answers to the first question for much of the twentieth century focused on source-critical arguments: the Benedictus does not reflect the outcome of the Lukan narrative because it was not a part of the original Lukan narrative.[34] Scholarship in recent decades has offered far more compelling answers — answers found within the framework of the Lukan narrative itself. Four outstanding examples invite attention. Each features an examination of the way Luke's use of language redirects or reshapes the reader's expectations in the broader scope of the narrative.

Focusing especially on Luke's description of God's "visitation" (ἐπισκέπτομαι [Luke 1:68, 78; 7:16] and ἐπισκοπή [Luke 19:44]), Robert Tannehill has argued that Zechariah's unfulfilled prophecy is part of Luke's depiction of a tragedy: Zechariah proclaimed what would have happened if Jesus had not been rejected as God's Messiah.[35] Max Turner explores ways in which concepts of "salvation" from Luke 1–2 find unexpected forms of fulfillment in the ministry of Jesus.[36] Joel Green suggests that Jesus' identification of Satan as the true "enemy" (Luke 10:18-19) provides the necessary "interpretive" key to understand Zechariah's references in Luke 1:71, 74.[37] Finally, Mark Coleridge has argued that the Benedictus serves the purpose of allowing Luke to redefine messianic expectations, especially with regard to conceptions of salvation.[38] Each of these studies provides a way of reconciling the expectations created by Zechariah's prophecy with the rest of Luke-Acts.

The second question is perhaps more difficult. The arguments that Luke

---

33. See Tannehill, *Unity,* 1:32-38; Green, *Luke,* pp. 113-15.

34. See, for example, Raymond E. Brown, *The Birth of the Messiah: A Commentary on the Infancy Narratives in the Gospels of Matthew and Luke,* rev. ed. (New York: Doubleday, 1993), p. 347. There are even theories that the Benedictus itself was taken from a variety of sources (Marshall, *Luke,* p. 87).

35. Tannehill, *Unity,* 1:32-38; Tannehill, *Luke,* pp. 59-62.

36. Turner, *Power,* pp. 319-33.

37. Green, *Luke,* p. 419.

38. Mark Coleridge, *The Birth of the Lukan Narrative: Narrative as Christology in Luke 1–2,* JSNTSup 88 (Sheffield: Sheffield Academic Press, 1993), pp. 119-23.

reshapes expectations created by Zechariah's Benedictus, compelling as they may be, do not address adequately the fact that Zechariah's words are spoken while he is "filled with the Holy Spirit." In fact, such arguments underscore the central question of this study: What does the Holy Spirit *do* in Luke's narrative? In this case, perhaps the question can be phrased more narrowly: What is the relationship between the "filling of the Holy Spirit" and Zechariah "prophesying"? Were it not for the emphatic presence of the Spirit, narrative critics could more easily argue that Zechariah merely functions as an "unreliable character" or "fallible filter" (i.e., a character whom the reader should not necessarily assume is trustworthy).[39] Tannehill, in fact, offers just such an argument.[40] His argument has not met with widespread acceptance, however.[41] I would suggest that those who have balked at Tannehill's idea have done so based on certain presumptions about the nature of the "filling of the Holy Spirit." That is, they seem to presume that evaluating Zechariah as an "unreliable interpreter" is tantamount to evaluating the Spirit as unreliable. I would argue that such presumptions are not necessary.

What does it mean for someone to be "filled with the Holy Spirit"? In his comments on Luke 1:67, Joel Green offers the following:

> In Israel's past as well as in the early church of Acts, the filling of the Holy Spirit was often for the purpose of prophecy, so that the prophet would be recognized as providing God's perspective on events. Under the direction of the Spirit, Zechariah communicates from the divine point of view the significance of the extraordinary events narrated thus far. . . . Hence, from Luke's perspective, it is not a question of what Zechariah could or could not have possibly known. Endowed with the Spirit he now shares, however, temporarily, in the all-knowing perspective of the narrator and of God.[42]

39. On these terms, see Wayne C. Booth, *The Rhetoric of Fiction*, 2nd ed. (Chicago: University of Chicago Press, 1983), p. 175; Seymour Chatman, *Coming to Terms: The Rhetoric of Narrative in Fiction and Film* (Ithaca: Cornell University Press, 1990), p. 149.

40. Specifically, Tannehill argues that the filling of the Spirit (1:67) does not exempt Zechariah's words (1:68-79) from scrutiny: one must determine whether his words fit within the outcome of the narrative in order to determine his reliability as a character (*Unity*, 1:22). To the degree that Zechariah's words do not reflect the outcome of Luke's story, Zechariah becomes an "unreliable interpreter" (*Unity*, 1:35 n. 46).

41. See, for example, Green, *Luke*, p. 114. Tannehill himself did not continue to pursue this line of thought in his later commentary, part of which suggests a move away from the idea that Zechariah is an "unreliable interpreter" (Tannehill, *Luke*, pp. 59-62).

42. Green, *Luke*, p. 115, including n. 31.

In a discussion of the Magnificat, the Benedictus, and the Nunc Dimittis, Turner argues similarly: these passages "are all spoken by human characters, but this does not significantly lessen their reliability, as the real speaker (from the narrator's point of view) is the Spirit of prophecy, and this is regularly indicated by such introductory formulae as . . . 'Zechariah was filled with the Holy Spirit and prophesied.'"[43] These comments are helpful because they illuminate the presumptions that many interpreters bring to the text of Luke-Acts. In fact, they are helpful precisely because they force one to realize that *Luke* never offers any such explanation. Luke never suggests that an experience of the Holy Spirit allows someone to "share in the all-knowing perspective . . . of God." Luke also does not explicitly equate the filling of the Holy Spirit with the idea that the Spirit is then speaking through someone. On the contrary, Luke does the opposite.

All of the Synoptic Gospels feature an exhortation to the followers of Jesus not to fear being brought to trial for their faith. In Mark, one finds it phrased: "do not be anxious about what you are to say . . . for you are not the ones speaking, but the Holy Spirit" (μὴ προμεριμνᾶτε τί λαλήσητε . . . οὐ γάρ ἐστε ὑμεῖς οἱ λαλοῦντες ἀλλὰ τὸ πνεῦμα τὸ ἅγιον [Mark 13:11]). Matthew is similar: "for you are not the ones speaking, but the Spirit of the Father speaks in you" (οὐ γὰρ ὑμεῖς ἐστε οἱ λαλοῦντες ἀλλὰ τὸ πνεῦμα τοῦ πατρὸς ὑμῶν τὸ λαλοῦν ἐν ὑμῖν [Matt. 10:20]). Luke's version is different: "for the Holy Spirit will teach you in that hour the things which you must say" (τὸ γὰρ ἅγιον πνεῦμα διδάξει ὑμᾶς ἐν αὐτῇ τῇ ὥρᾳ ἃ δεῖ εἰπεῖν [Luke 12:12]). However one understands the source relationship between the Synoptic Gospels, it would appear that Luke is adjusting his source material here. Luke could easily have concurred with the idea that sometimes the Spirit takes over an individual and speaks through that individual. Instead, Luke suggests that the Spirit "will teach" believers. Given this evidence, the argument that the Spirit speaks through characters in Luke-Acts is difficult to accept.

I have argued elsewhere that Zechariah offers in the Benedictus an interpretation of his encounter with Gabriel earlier in Luke 1.[44] Perhaps "interpretation" is also the best way to understand the relationship between Zechariah's words and the filling of the Holy Spirit. That is, perhaps the best way to understand the Benedictus as a Spirit-inspired utterance is to think of the Spirit's filling as something that *may* require interpretation.

43. Turner, *Power,* p. 143.
44. Miller, *Convinced,* pp. 118-23.

This suggestion runs contrary to arguments that presume the "filling of the Spirit" is tantamount to sharing God's perspective or being taken over by the Spirit.[45] Nevertheless, this suggestion is more in keeping with what one actually finds in the Lukan narrative. That expectations raised by the Benedictus need to be reshaped in the remainder of the text makes more sense if the filling of the Spirit is something Zechariah has to interpret. Such an understanding may also help clarify the issues with John discussed above. If John ever shares the "all-knowing perspective of God," his question in Luke 7:19 makes little sense. If the filling of the Spirit is something John has to interpret, one can much more easily reconcile Luke 7:19 with the "filling of the Spirit" that Gabriel announces in 1:15. The reader is left to ask, therefore, whether there are any other passages in Luke-Acts that provide a basis for arguing that Luke understood the Spirit's filling, direction, or guidance, as something requiring interpretation. I will argue that the passages treated in the following section do exactly that.

The Holy Spirit, Paul, and the Believers in Tyre

In Acts 19:21, the narrator provides a glimpse of the travels that will occupy Paul for the remainder of the narrative: "Paul resolved in the Spirit to go to Jerusalem, passing through Macedonia and Achaea. 'After that,' he said, 'it is necessary that I also see Rome.'"[46] Paul's journey to Jerusalem offers interesting and varied portrayals of the Spirit's guidance. In Ephesus, Paul tells the gathered elders: "Now, bound to the Spirit, I am going to Jerusalem, not knowing the things I will encounter there. In every city, however, the Holy Spirit testifies to me saying that chains and suffering await me" (20:22-23). The language in these verses is striking.

First, Paul claims to be "bound to the Spirit" (δεδεμένος . . . τῷ πνεύματι), a phrase found nowhere else in the New Testament or Jewish Scripture. Paul's second reference to the Spirit in as many verses attributes action: the Spirit "testifies" (διαμαρτύρομαι). This verb is found three

45. Levison, for example, connects the Pentecost scene in Acts 2 with descriptions of spirits taking over individuals in non-Jewish Greco-Roman texts (Levison, *Filled*, pp. 326-35).

46. The phrase ἔθετο ὁ Παῦλος ἐν τῷ πνεύματι here can also be translated "Paul decided." The question is whether the πνεῦμα here is Paul's "spirit" or the Holy Spirit. For a discussion of the arguments interpreters have adduced for both translations, see Miller, *Convinced*, p. 225 n. 197.

times in verses 21-24. Paul says that he "testified" about repentance and faith "to both Jews and Gentiles" (20:21). The Spirit "testifies" to Paul that "chains and suffering await" him (20:23). Paul dismisses the threat of such tribulation, valuing only the opportunity to complete his "course" and "ministry" by "testifying" to the "gospel of God's grace" (20:24). Luke uses the verb διαμαρτύρομαι only two more times in Acts. In a dream, the Lord commends Paul for "testifying" in Jerusalem, and commands him to do the same in Rome (23:11). In Acts 28:23, Paul does just that.

More striking, however, is the subtle language wedged in between Paul's two references to the Spirit in Acts 20:22-23: "not knowing what will happen to me there" (τὰ ἐν αὐτῇ συναντήσοντά μοι μὴ εἰδώς [v. 22]). Paul's description of the Spirit in these verses is dramatic. He is "bound" to the Spirit, who "testifies" to him continually, in every city. That testimony, however, is vague. The Spirit's testimony leaves Paul with an awareness that chains and suffering await him — an awareness that apparently lacks any detail. Paul's certainty that he understands the direction in which the Spirit leads is offset by an amorphous image of what he will find when he gets there. There is no sense here in which Paul "shares in the all-knowing perspective of God."

Following their departure from Miletus, the narrative quickly brings Paul and his companions to Tyre. Stops at Rhodes and Patara elicit no comment from the narrator. Paul's interaction with believers in Tyre, however, is intriguing: ἀνευρόντες δὲ τοὺς μαθητὰς ἐπεμείναμεν αὐτοῦ ἡμέρας ἑπτά, οἵτινες τῷ Παύλῳ ἔλεγον διὰ τοῦ πνεύματος μὴ ἐπιβαίνειν εἰς Ἱεροσόλυμα (21:4). Changing verb tenses and the placement of the relative clause in this verse have challenged translators. The KJV is a nice illustration: "And finding disciples, we tarried there seven days: who said to Paul through the Spirit, that he should not go up to Jerusalem." The difficulty is rendering the shift from the aorist participle and verb (ἀνευρόντες . . . ἐπεμείναμεν) to the imperfect (ἔλεγον) in the relative clause: "We found the disciples and remained there for seven days. During that time, they were telling Paul through the Spirit not to go to Jerusalem."

As with the "testimony" to Paul in Acts 20:23, the Spirit's direction here is vague. There are no details offered as to why Paul should stay away from Jerusalem.[47] Luke's use of the imperfect ἔλεγον, however, suggests that this

---

47. Shepherd argues, "[T]he reader will fill in the gaps in light of Acts 20:22-23 and 21:11, and conclude that the prophets wish Paul to avoid the danger he will face" (*Function*, p. 236). There is no reason given, however, why readers should necessarily come to this con-

Spirit-directed message was given repeatedly. It is interesting that Luke offers no further commentary on these circumstances. Unlike his address to the Ephesian elders immediately preceding this passage (20:17-38), and unlike the discourse that follows Agabus's prophecy in the passage that follows (21:7-14), these verses simply feature characters telling Paul "through the Spirit" not to go to Jerusalem. The passage would be rather unremarkable if it did not indicate a dramatic tension between characters who express two very different understandings of direction from the same Spirit.[48]

In Caesarea, conflicting understandings of the Spirit's guidance result in conflicted discourse between Paul and his companions. Although the Holy Spirit is not mentioned until 21:11, cues earlier in the passage direct the reader's attention toward the Spirit. Paul and his companions stay in the house of Philip (21:8), who has not been mentioned in the narrative since his encounter with the Ethiopian — an encounter that begins with the Spirit's command to join the Ethiopian's chariot and ends when the Spirit "snatches" (ἁρπάζω) Philip away (8:39). Verses 9-10 mention Philip's four daughters who "prophesy" and the "prophet" Agabus, evoking the strong connection between prophecy and the Spirit in Luke's narrative.[49] After binding his own hands and feet with Paul's belt, Agabus states: "The Holy Spirit says this: 'So will the Jews in Jerusalem bind the man whose belt this is and betray him into the hands of the Gentiles'" (τάδε λέγει τὸ πνεῦμα τὸ ἅγιον· τὸν ἄνδρα οὗ ἐστιν ἡ ζώνη αὕτη, οὕτως δήσουσιν ἐν Ἰερουσαλὴμ οἱ Ἰουδαῖοι καὶ παραδώσουσιν εἰς χεῖρας ἐθνῶν [21:11]). This pronouncement leads both Paul's companions and the others present to "urge" Paul not to go up to Jerusalem (21:12). Paul, however, will not be swayed: he is ready "even to die" in Jerusalem (21:13). The contention is not resolved, nor does it continue.[50] Since Paul will not be persuaded, those with him say, "Let the will of the Lord be done" (21:14).

---

clusion. Much more satisfying is Tannehill's suggestion: "it is seldom easy to separate divine revelation from human interpretation" (Tannehill, *Unity,* 2:263). John Penney also observes that Acts 21:4, 11-14 seems to suggest an element of interpretation, but he does not explore the point further (Penney, *Emphasis,* p. 117).

48. One certainly wants to avoid conflations that remove the Tyrian believers from the scene altogether: "Paul is told by the Spirit not to go to Jerusalem" (Luke Timothy Johnson, *Scripture and Discernment: Decision Making in the Church* [Nashville: Abingdon, 1996], p. 82; see also his *The Acts of the Apostles,* SP 5 [Collegeville, MN: Liturgical Press, 1992], p. 372).

49. See Luke 1:67; Acts 2:17-18; 11:28; 19:6.

50. There is no textual basis for Bruce's claim that those with Paul acquiesced when they "recognized that [Paul] might be more sensitive to the Spirit's guidance than any of his

It is interesting that this passage features no disagreement about the meaning of the Spirit's message delivered by Agabus. Those with Paul accept the message and urge Paul to avoid the predicted situation. Paul accepts the message and emphasizes that he is willing to suffer a worse end. More peculiar for the present study is the simple fact that Agabus's prophecy, his declaration of what the Spirit says, does not turn out to be accurate. The Jews in Jerusalem "put their hands upon" Paul (ἐπέβαλον ἐπ' αὐτὸν τὰς χεῖρας [21:27]), and "grab" him (ἐπιλαμβάνω [21:30]), but it is the Roman soldiers who "bind" Paul (δέω [21:33]).[51]

These passages feature anything but straightforward experiences of the Spirit. Different characters are guided by the same Spirit in different directions, with little or no explanation. Even the explanation offered by Paul emphasizes how little detail the Spirit's "testimony" provides. Details, when they are given, do not necessarily clarify the situation: Agabus's prophecy, depicted as the very words of the Spirit, does not reflect accurately the events described later in the story. Placed alongside questions raised about the filling of the Spirit in relation to John and Zechariah, these passages invite further reflection on the role(s) of the Spirit in Luke-Acts.

Reconsidering the Role(s) of the Spirit

As noted above, there is a longstanding tradition in scholarship that recognizes the importance of the Holy Spirit for inspiring prophetic speech in Luke-Acts. Some scholars would add that the Holy Spirit also facilitates demonstrations of divine power. Without denying the importance of these observations, the present study explores a different aspect of the Spirit's role in Luke-Acts. In pursuing the question, What does the Spirit *do* in Luke-Acts?, a more specific question has emerged: How do characters respond to their experiences of the Spirit, and how do those responses help the reader understand the actions of the Spirit?

---

well-wishers" ("Holy Spirit," p. 182). Shepherd's conclusion borders on the absurd: "Luke thus pictures the Spirit working on both sides of this intercommunity conflict, bringing the community together once again through the powerful example of the prophetic pattern" (Shepherd, *Function*, p. 238).

51. Scholars note this discrepancy but frequently follow the point by mentioning that the Romans arrest Paul in response to the actions of the Jewish mob (e.g., Luke Timothy Johnson, *The Acts of the Apostles*, SP 5 [Collegeville, MN: Liturgical Press, 1992], p. 372). I prefer, instead, to linger on the significance of the discrepancy.

Observing the relationship between the Spirit and other characters requires sensitivity to the contours of Luke's story. As Gaventa has argued, Luke-Acts is a narrative, and any serious theological engagement of this text must engage it as a narrative.[52] Luke does not offer a systematic doctrine of the Holy Spirit. Instead, Luke tells a story in which the Holy Spirit figures prominently. The Spirit fills, guides, directs, speaks, and acts in this narrative. Any answer to questions about what the Spirit does or how the Spirit acts must take the narrative as a whole into account. At some points in the narrative, a character's encounter with the Spirit is straightforward: there is a clear connection between the Spirit's filling, guidance, or direction; the character's action; and some sense of verification that the character has understood the experience of the Spirit correctly. At other points, such a clear connection is elusive. That Luke includes descriptions of such varied experiences of the Spirit leads to a few important observations.

When the Spirit "fills" someone in Luke-Acts, the result is sometimes only a limited awareness or insight. More important, characters may or may not interpret that awareness correctly. John's experience of the Spirit allows recognition of Jesus before his birth, but not after. Paul and his companions experience the same Spirit but understand that experience in ways that are diametrically opposed. Both Zechariah and Agabus interpret their experience of the Spirit in ways that do not reflect events as they unfold in the narrative. By including these aspects of experience in the narrative, Luke provides a remarkably nuanced understanding of the Holy Spirit and of the experiences characters have with that Spirit. The passages examined in this discussion emphasize that contact with the Holy Spirit could be an experience that required significant interpretation. What the Spirit *does* in Luke-Acts resists generalization. Understanding the roles of the Spirit in the narrative requires the reader to accept what the Spirit does, or does not do, at various points in the story. As a great Lukan scholar has observed: "attempting to categorize the activity of the Holy Spirit in Acts is futile both theologically and narratively."[53]

---

52. Beverly Roberts Gaventa, "Toward a Theology of Acts: Reading and Rereading," *Int* 42 (1988): 146-57.

53. Gaventa, *Acts*, pp. 38-39.

Conclusion

Examinations of the Holy Spirit in Luke-Acts abound, both in older and more recent scholarship. While acknowledging the important contributions of these studies, the present discussion has attempted to highlight some underexplored aspects of Luke's portrayal of the Spirit. The suggestion made here is that understanding the Spirit's action from a narrative-critical perspective requires a close reading of the experience a character has with the Holy Spirit. Offering a corrective to studies that may overemphasize the positive, or seemingly straightforward descriptions of such character experiences in Luke-Acts, this examination focuses on those passages that feature more problematic descriptions of characters experiencing the Spirit.

John, one who "will be filled with the Holy Spirit, even from his mother's womb," is empowered by the Spirit to proclaim the coming Messiah. His relationship with the Spirit, however, does not result in a certain awareness that Jesus is that Messiah. Filled with the Spirit and responding to Gabriel's annunciation, Zechariah proclaims God's fulfillment of promises to Israel. The filling of the Spirit, however, does not guarantee that Zechariah will accurately predict the outcome of the events in Luke's story. Given these descriptions of the relationship between characters and the Holy Spirit early in the narrative, it should perhaps come as little surprise that Paul may understand the "testimony" of the Spirit differently than other believers he encounters. Indeed, Paul himself states that his experience of the Spirit is limited to an awareness that "chains and suffering" await him. Finally, the prophet Agabus, like Zechariah, offers confident proclamation based on his experience of the Spirit. Also like Zechariah, Agabus and his proclamation are a vital part of the narrative precisely because they demonstrate that the experience of the Spirit does not lead to a perfect knowledge of the future.

Because the Holy Spirit is inextricably connected to God in Luke's narrative, an understanding of the ways in which the Spirit functions in the narrative is crucial for understanding Luke's theology. Understanding Luke's presentation of the Spirit, however, is complicated. Any reading that engages seriously the whole of Luke-Acts will recognize that Luke's varied depiction of the Spirit thwarts attempts to define narrowly or impose coherence on what the Spirit *does* in this narrative. The willingness to engage Luke-Acts as a narrative requires that one be open to the theological complications that result.

The Word of God and the Church:
On the Theological Implications of Three
Summary Statements in the Acts of the Apostles

Matthew L. Skinner

[T]he church [in Acts] exists as evidence of God's plan and God's ac-
tivity in the world. The church draws its existence from God's inter-
vention, rather than from its own initiative.[1]

When it comes to its theology — its depiction of God and how God is
known and operates — the book of Acts can hardly be credited with providing precision. While certain theological themes, terms, and assertions
recur and figure prominently in the book, they usually resist easy categori-
zation or systematization. The most charitable and probably accurate explanation for this involves acknowledging that Luke, the name we ascribe
to the book's author, was not driven by the same impulses at work in modern readers who seek such conceptual clarity in their theology. The narrative of Acts seems more determined to convey a conviction *that* God has
been active or present within the world than to chart the precise means by
which divine activity manifests itself.[2]

---

1. Beverly Roberts Gaventa, *The Acts of the Apostles*, ANTC (Nashville: Abingdon, 2003),
p. 39.

2. For a prime example, consider the variety of ways the Holy Spirit works throughout
Acts. See Eric Franklin, *Christ the Lord: A Study in the Purpose and Theology of Luke-Acts*
(Philadelphia: Westminster, 1975), pp. 133-34. As Daniel Marguerat puts it, with regard to the
Holy Spirit, Luke "offers his readers *a pragmatic of the Spirit,*" in contrast to a discursive the-
ology of the Spirit, insofar as Acts devotes itself to "telling the work of the Spirit, rather than
talking about him" (*The First Christian Historian: Writing the 'Acts of the Apostles,'* trans. Ken
McKinney, Gregory J. Laughery, and Richard Bauckham, SNTSMS 121 [Cambridge: Cambridge University Press, 2002], p. 128, emphasis original; see also p. 125). The same holds true

We might easily chalk this up to the nature of the biblical documents; their character as testimony, passed along to us across generations, means we continually encounter in them assertions, remembrances, and persuasive methods that do not always align with how we were taught to do theology. But the narrative character of Acts also plays a part, and opacity always accompanies narrativity. Narratives can suggest a wide variety of possible connections and causalities at work among characters and events, but never can readers either definitively map all of these or expect utter consistency.[3] Just as real life usually resists thematic coherence, narrative follows suit. A narrative's power thus resides in its ability to draw audiences into imagining the possibilities giving shape to the world it narrates. When a story like Acts purports to say, or even faintly implies, something about God's influence upon the action involving other characters, it encourages readers to consider the nature of God's activity — to engage in conversations about what this activity is like and how they might apprehend it in their own lives.

Beverly Roberts Gaventa's scholarship on Acts contributes to these kinds of conversations. Her writings take the narrative character of Acts seriously and discover God's prominence throughout the story Luke narrates. Acts may make or imply theological claims that remain ambiguous, but it is itself unrelenting in advancing a perspective that God plays a part in the history of the church and the world.

Some of Gaventa's early writings about Acts attempt to cut through methodological confusion about what it means even to speak about "the theology of Acts"; in an often-cited article she proposes that narrative analysis must be a necessary piece of describing the theological contributions of Luke's second volume.[4] Her article's purpose goes far beyond endorsing narrative criticism's value for theologically oriented exegesis; it reiterates earlier scholars' insistence that the complexity of Acts as a whole defies reductionistic theological proposals. Accordingly, Gaventa takes aim at the hypothesis, associated most prominently with Hans Conzelmann, that the "theology" of Acts is essentially a theology of glory meant to buttress a church faced with the daunting task of surviving in the Roman

for most if not all of the theological topics in Acts, whether God, the church, conversion, and so on.

3. Frank Kermode, *The Genesis of Secrecy: On the Interpretation of Narrative* (Cambridge, MA: Harvard University Press, 1979), pp. 23-47; Marguerat, *Historian*, p. 46.

4. Beverly Roberts Gaventa, "Toward a Theology of Acts: Reading and Rereading," *Int* 42 (1988): 146-57.

world with decreased if not disappointed eschatological expectations.[5] Luke's interest in writing Acts, so the hypothesis went, was to provide ancient Christians with an upbuilding account of the church's history, not with much of a theology. This hypothesis tended to find little in Acts that addresses who God is or how God operates. In focusing on the narrative character of Acts, Gaventa points out other possibilities; she finds complexity and articulates a way of reading Acts as a story about God, and not primarily about the church, its people, its successes, or its struggles.[6]

The current essay examines a facet of the theological ecclesiology in Acts — or, to put it in a way that better respects the narrative character of Acts, a facet of the book's depiction of the church and God's role in the church's existence and activity. The essay emerges from my ongoing ruminations about how the portrayal of the church in Acts stems from an understanding of God, a God whose activity does more than *affect* or *guide* the church.[7] I embark on this investigation attentive to the narrative dynamics of Acts and appreciative of Gaventa's characterization of Acts as a theological story, a story as much about God as about the people or events in which God takes interest. I will explore three relatively obscure verses: Acts 6:7; 12:24; and 19:20. In each of these, the narrator offers a summary and describes "the word of God" or "the word of the Lord" increasing or growing (αὐξάνω). These verses appear at important junctures in the story, and the choice of words is peculiar enough to demand special attention. While many commentators take these verses as simple statements of the church's expansion in geographical and numerical terms, I will argue that Luke's statements also allow us to inquire after deeper theological implications, relevant for understanding the God made manifest through this

---

5. See, most notably, Hans Conzelmann, *The Theology of St. Luke,* trans. Geoffrey Buswell (Philadelphia: Fortress, 1961); *Acts of the Apostles: A Commentary on the Acts of the Apostles,* trans. James Limburg, A. Thomas Kraabel, and Donald H. Juel, Hermeneia (Philadelphia: Fortress, 1987). Conzelmann's views represented a larger constellation of opinion about Luke-Acts given momentum especially by Rudolf Bultmann and Ernst Käsemann.

6. She advances this perspective most forcefully in her commentary, *Acts.* Perhaps most important, Gaventa avoids the temptation to assume that Acts must advance *either* a theological depiction of God *or* a historical account of the church and its people.

7. In speaking about "the church," I do not imply that Acts operates with a sense of a universal, fully unified, or institutionalized church. I use the term as a shorthand expression to describe various yet kindred communities composed of Jesus' followers, or "Christians" (Acts 11:26). Of course Acts recognizes vital affinities and connections among these communities, but I do not want my use of the term to distract attention from the communities' discrete identities.

church, as well as for understanding the church itself. Although Luke does not provide much to support a precise definition of the relationship between "the word of God" and "the church," the repetition of language in the three summaries and their surrounding narrative contexts together encourage us to put the summaries in conversation with the rest of Acts and this book's depiction of a God whose activity connects to human affairs.

"The Word" That "Grows"

Summary statements appear frequently in Acts.[8] They lend a hand where the narrative takes stock of developments or turns in new directions, providing positive reports about the church's continuing and enlarging influence. Three of these statements, those on which this essay focuses, attract particular attention because of their similar use of peculiar language:

> Acts 6:7
> Καὶ ὁ λόγος τοῦ θεοῦ ηὔξανεν καὶ ἐπληθύνετο ὁ ἀριθμὸς τῶν μαθητῶν ἐν Ἰερουσαλὴμ σφόδρα, πολύς τε ὄχλος τῶν ἱερέων ὑπήκουον τῇ πίστει.
> The word of God kept on growing, the number of disciples in Jerusalem kept on increasing greatly, and a large group of the priests became obedient to the faith.[9]

> Acts 12:24
> Ὁ δὲ λόγος τοῦ θεοῦ ηὔξανεν καὶ ἐπληθύνετο.
> But the word of God kept on growing and increasing in number.

> Acts 19:20
> Οὕτως κατὰ κράτος τοῦ κυρίου ὁ λόγος ηὔξανεν καὶ ἴσχυεν.
> In such a manner, forcefully the word of the Lord kept on growing and demonstrating strength.[10]

8. Most interpreters agree on this list of the summary statements: Acts 6:7; 9:31; 12:24; 16:5; 19:20; 28:30-31. Some include Acts 2:47; 4:4; 5:16; 11:24; 18:11 (Brian S. Rosner, "The Progress of the Word," in *Witness to the Gospel: The Theology of Acts,* ed. I. Howard Marshall and David Peterson [Grand Rapids: Eerdmans, 1998], p. 222 n. 32).

9. All translations in this essay are my own.

10. Some commentators connect τοῦ κυρίου to κράτος instead of to ὁ λόγος, thus rendering the verse: ". . . with the power of the Lord, the word . . ." (e.g., Joseph A. Fitzmyer, *The Acts of the Apostles,* AB 31 [New York: Doubleday, 1998], p. 652). Such a translation

In addition to their language, which I will discuss shortly, these three verses, as summaries, attract attention because of how they interact with their wider narrative contexts. These contexts imply that vitality, resilience, and perseverance are part of what it means for "the word" to keep on growing. In each case, these statements of growth defuse a sense of imminent crisis, for they follow closely on the heels of events threatening to weaken the church's influence: the controversy concerning the neglect of Hellenist widows (Acts 6:1-6), vain Herod Agrippa I's execution of James and near-execution of Peter (12:1-23), and widespread use of magic and hypocritical exorcism techniques in Ephesus (19:13-19). The growth that Luke announces in these settings has an effect of one-upmanship in the face of danger, even as the growth makes a statement about perseverance.[11] Threats will not ultimately weaken "the word"; the community of the faithful will survive and even find greater stability, thanks to God.[12] Part of this stability, as these three one-verse summaries tell the story, involves new members joining a community of believers.

What Is the Word of God?

Each of these verses speaks about "the word of God" or "the word of the Lord."[13] Each uses the verb αὐξάνω and an additional verb to describe

might be more warranted if κατὰ κράτος was not such a common adverbial expression (Richard I. Pervo, *Acts: A Commentary*, Hermeneia [Minneapolis: Fortress, 2009], p. 481), the argument of Richard P. Thompson notwithstanding (*Keeping the Church in Its Place: The Church as Narrative Character in Acts* [New York: T. & T. Clark, 2006], p. 215 n. 278). The debate finally does not affect the argument put forward in this essay.

11. The God of Acts appears determined to have the word permeate all pockets of human society, whether or not conversions occur. See Matthew L. Skinner, "Acts," in *Theological Bible Commentary*, ed. Gail R. O'Day and David L. Petersen (Louisville: Westminster John Knox, 2009), p. 363.

12. With regard to the community's reinforced stability, note John B. Weaver's comments about Acts 12:24 and the importance Acts places on preserving the community of faith in Jerusalem (*Plots of Epiphany: Prison-Escape in Acts of the Apostles*, BZNW 131 [Berlin: De Gruyter, 2004], p. 213). Likewise, display of "strength" accompanies the growth in Acts 19:20, echoing the same verb (ἰσχύω) used in 19:16 to describe a demon-possessed man's power to overwhelm, injure, and shame seven would-be exorcists.

13. Obviously the language in the three summaries is not identical, only similar. These similarities are strong, however, as explained below in my discussion of the verses' salient terms. The point is that each of the three expresses a sense of "the word" expanding in terms of its membership or population. (And I take "the word of God" as essentially equivalent to

the word's growth or expansion. What does it mean that "the word of God" grows? I begin by considering what ὁ λόγος might indicate in these instances.

I will argue that in these verses Acts suggests a very close association between "the word of God" / "the word of the Lord" and the church or the company of Jesus' followers; yet, the book never explicitly identifies them with one another, as if "church" and "word" become plainly synonymous. Complicating the issue, throughout Luke's writings there is no univocal understanding of what "the word of God" (ὁ λόγος τοῦ θεοῦ) is. This is not to deny a clearly dominant use of this expression in Luke-Acts: in most cases it refers to the message the apostles (and others) preach (e.g., Acts 4:31; 11:1; 13:5, 7, 46; 17:13; 18:11).[14] Likewise, "the word of the Lord" (ὁ λόγος τοῦ κυρίου) usually means exactly the same thing (e.g., Acts 8:25; 13:44; 15:35-36; 16:32; 19:10), as do numerous instances of "the word" (ὁ λόγος) used either alone or paired with other genitive nouns (e.g., Acts 11:19; 13:26; 14:3; 15:7; 17:11; 18:5; 20:32).[15]

Luke-Acts also includes, however, noteworthy exceptions to this dominant usage — or, rather, Luke-Acts intimates an expanded significance about this usage — indicating a broader reservoir of meaning for λόγος. At least three additional Lukan texts speak about "the word" in ways that point attention beyond just a message from God or about Jesus. In these texts, "the word" takes on a more dynamic sense as something made manifest. First, when the Twelve state in Acts 6:4 their intention to persist in prayer and in "service" or "ministry" of the λόγος, they bring into view more than preaching alone. The rest of their apostolic activity showcased up to this point in Acts at least implies that their διακονία τοῦ λόγου also consists of performing signs and wonders. In that case, "ministry of the word" acknowledges a participation in the power or potential that God makes available alongside or through preaching, a dynamic very much on display thus far in the story, throughout Acts 2–5. Second, in Acts 8:21,

---

"the word of the Lord"; see, e.g., their use in Acts 13:44, 46.) This numerical increase is different from saying that *preaching activity* increases in frequency or geographic extent.

14. This list and the ones in the following sentence (concerning "the word of the Lord" and other appearances of "the word") are not exhaustive; they include only the clearest instances of λόγος as the "message" of/about Jesus. Note, too, that the expression "the word of God" appears more frequently in Acts than in Luke, but the consistent usage in the Third Gospel indicates a proclaimed message as well. See, e.g., Luke 5:1; 8:11-15, 21; 11:28.

15. In addition, twice Luke speaks of a (or the) ῥῆμα "of God" or "of the Lord," in Luke 3:2; Acts 11:16. See also Luke 2:29; Acts 10:37.

when Peter scolds Simon the magician and tells him he has "no share in this word," the apostle bars him from more than opportunities to proclaim a message. The context of their confrontation suggests that "this word" connects to the ability to impart the Holy Spirit through the laying on of hands, the phenomenon that gets Simon so excited in the first place (8:18-19).[16] Simon disqualifies himself from a "word" that appears to promise the ability to be part of an activity, the giving of the Spirit, ascribed ultimately to God.[17] Third, in the Gospel's prologue, Luke refers to "eyewitnesses and servants of the word" (Luke 1:2). The syntax suggests this phrase refers to a single group, namely, the apostles, who were original *witnesses* of the word and later became its *servants*.[18] "The word" they witnessed in the Gospel and now serve in Acts subtly suggests itself with more nuance than merely a message; it *is* a message, but it was rooted or originally manifested in the actual presence and activity of Jesus, the one who was the means by which God's "word" came to be known (cf. Acts 10:36, which refers to the word God sent, announced through Jesus Christ).[19] The Jesus of Luke-Acts is not the incarnate word as he is in the christology of John's Gospel. Nevertheless, Luke-Acts occasionally alludes to the word as something connected to the flesh-and-blood Jesus and his (and God's) ongoing activity. This word was expressed in Jesus' activity as much as in his speech, and likewise as something articulated in the actions of Jesus' apostles, who themselves continue Jesus' own ministry in the book of Acts as they preach and perform signs.[20]

16. I grant that "this word" in 8:21 may point to a different notion of λόγος than the other verses discussed thus far. The translations "this enterprise" (Pervo, *Acts*, p. 215 n. 23) or "this matter" (Fitzmyer, *Acts*, pp. 406-7) are plausible in 8:21 and may caution against ascribing too much theological significance to this ambiguous occurrence of λόγος (but cf. C. K. Barrett, *A Critical and Exegetical Commentary on the Acts of the Apostles*, 2 vols., ICC [Edinburgh: T. & T. Clark, 1994-1998], 1:414-15). Regardless of questions about the possible terminological relevance of this verse, the larger point still stands: Acts occasionally describes apostolic ministry in ways acknowledging the integral connections among people's proclamation of the gospel, performance of signs and powers, and participation in work animated by God.

17. See Acts 5:32; 15:8. In Acts 2:33, Peter names Jesus as the one who pours out the Holy Spirit (cf. Luke 24:49).

18. Joseph A. Fitzmyer, *The Gospel according to Luke I–IX*, AB 28 (New York: Doubleday, 1970), p. 294.

19. See Joel B. Green, *The Gospel of Luke*, NICNT (Grand Rapids: Eerdmans, 1997), p. 42.

20. Or, in François Bovon's words, "For Luke, the word of God was made flesh in Jesus, but not in John's manner: it is the word of God, in the past addressed *to the prophets* and not

These three examples are subtle, although their implications remain suggestive: "the word of God" in Luke-Acts, or "the word of the Lord" or "the word," may at times indicate or include more than a disembodied message or report. The word, in Luke's outlook, points sometimes to more than content, propositions, or an announcement. It has theological valence, in terms of the report it communicates to potential converts and also the effective performance or manifestation of that report. Some usage reminds readers to consider this "message's" origin — not simply communication *from* God or *from* Jesus, but actually an expression of God's activity through Jesus and the ongoing presence of the Holy Spirit. Although the term λόγος may never be utterly identical with "the church," or rarely suggestive of it, in Acts it can evoke the church's raison d'être and activity. It occasionally invites readers to notice the theological dimensions of God's own presence at work when the Christian message is preached and heard. When Acts 6:7; 12:24; and 19:20 speak of the word *growing,* then, we should inquire after what this means for our understanding of both the word and the people who are added to its membership.

What Does It Mean to Grow?

The recurrence of the verb αὐξάνω, along with the noun λόγος, invites us to consider Acts 6:7; 12:24; and 19:20 as a trio. The semantic range of this verb resembles that of "to grow" in English; on its own, it can indicate an increase in something's extension, significance, or membership. In Luke 1:80 and 2:40, for example, it describes the childhood development of both John and Jesus: they grow more mature, capable, and — we assume — taller. Later in the Gospel it expresses the notable growth of lilies and a "tree" produced by a mustard seed (Luke 12:27; 13:19). When Stephen addresses the hostile mob in Acts 7:17, the word describes the increase, in population and

---

preexistent in heaven, which took a body in Jesus (Acts 10.36f.)" (*Luke the Theologian: Thirty-three Years of Research [1950-1983],* trans. Ken McKinney, Princeton Theological Monograph Series 12 [Allison Park, PA: Pickwick, 1987], p. 197, emphasis original; quoted in Marguerat, *Historian,* p. 37). Bovon's description of a prophetic word of God may render the idea of that word as something fixed in the past; I suggest, however, that Jesus in Luke-Acts does not reanimate an old word but brings the word of God first expressed through the prophets into a fulfillment (see Luke 4:21) in which Jesus' speech and activity express something old and new. That is, God continues to speak and act through Jesus and his delegates, bringing old promises to new realizations.

prominence, of the Hebrew people during their time in Egypt after the famine.[21] While it may refer to something other than a gain in numbers or membership alone, nevertheless a sense of a numerical increase is common when the verb's subject is a collection of people (and perhaps also lilies). When a sentence includes both αὐξάνω and the verb πληθύνω, as in Acts 7:17 (and also in two of the three summaries being examined: 6:7; 12:24), a sense of numerical increase is undeniable. This pairing also makes it difficult to miss an echo of the "be fruitful and multiply" theme from Genesis and Jeremiah, a theme sustained by those same two verbs in the Septuagint.[22] It is possible, then, that the three summary statements about "the word of God"/"the word of the Lord" indicate the word's membership growing more numerous. This new phenomenon — the gospel, the word, this movement centered in Jesus himself — is gaining adherents.

Taken as a whole, the book of Acts describes the gradual movement and occasional increase of the church as a spreading out across lands, a theme of spatial and cultural expansion much in line with the geographical tenor of Acts. When Acts highlights this kind of extensive growth, Luke employs varied vocabulary. In 13:49, for example, "the word of the Lord" continued to *spread* (διαφέρω) throughout a region.[23] Also, in Acts 6:1 "*the disciples*" in Jerusalem increase in number (πληθύνω), and in Acts 9:31 "*the church* throughout Judea, Galilee, and Samaria" does the same thing (again, πληθύνω).[24] It is, therefore, striking to encounter verses that state (as in Acts 6:7; 12:24) or imply (as in Acts 19:20) that *the word of God* "grows" (αὐξάνω) as it increases its membership.[25] I say striking, because

21. The language of Acts 7:17 recalls Exod. 1:7, which also employs αὐξάνω and πληθύνω as a compound predicate (as does the summary verse Acts 12:24).

22. Septuagint readers find αὐξάνω and πληθύνω paired in Gen. 1:22, 28; 8:17; 9:1, 7; 17:20; 28:3; 35:11; 47:27; 48:4; Jer. 3:16; 23:3. See also Lev. 26:9. All these instances refer to numerical increases of groups of people or animals.

23. Acts can also describe numerical increase in ways less ambiguous and perhaps less theologically charged than what we encounter in 6:7; 12:24; and 19:20. In 16:5, for example, "the churches" (αἱ ἐκκλησίαι) "grow in number" (περισσεύω τῷ ἀριθμῷ).

24. Indeed, nearly all of the verses identified as summaries in note 8, above, make explicit mention of an increase in the number of believers (except Acts 5:16; 18:11; 28:30-31). It is significant to note the absence of growth reports after Paul announces his plans to return to Jerusalem in Acts 19:21. At the same time, Luke hardly presents Paul's return to Jerusalem and his resultant custody and legal travails as failures or insurmountable setbacks.

25. I do not claim that the verb αὐξάνω on its own *requires* a sense of numerical increase. Its pairing with πληθύνω in 6:7 and 12:24 (and elsewhere) encourages that interpretation. Since πληθύνω does not appear in 19:20, the sense of numerical growth in that verse

Luke-Acts does not otherwise indicate that "the word" is something that has membership. Even if Luke imagines the gospel message in such a way, its growth in membership obviously indicates growth of the community of believers. And Luke certainly understands the church as an entity capable of growing in number. These summaries invite readers to consider a close association implied between the church and the word of God as Luke speaks of a word that expands geographically, in terms of its influence and significance, and also *numerically*.[26] So deeply rooted is the church in this message of good news, that to join one is to join the other. The growth of one means the growth of the other. The word is not inert.

We thus encounter in these summaries a close, almost confused, and unexplained association between the word and the group of people elsewhere called the church, an association formed by the idea of the word expanding and adding new members. What theological implications arise from this evocative association? What connections might these verses imagine for the relationship between, on one hand, the word of God as a message embedded in the life, activity, words, and accomplishments of Jesus and, on the other hand, the church's existence, vitality, membership, and work in connection to this message?

Perspectives on the Three Summaries

Other interpreters have likewise considered the syntax of these summaries, taken seriously the association I have identified, and inquired after the association's theological implications.[27] Considering three different propos-

---

owes to Luke's use of αὐξάνω in the previous two summaries about "the word." It is doubtful that, were it not for 6:7 and 12:24, we would see a focus on numerical growth, as distinct from geographical extension, in 19:20.

26. The geographical expansion refers to more than drawing lines on a map. The word enters new regions and also new cultural pockets, such as the priestly class named in Acts 6:7. This verse's mention of "a large group of the priests" creates a bit of a surprise, in light of how the priests have been characterized in Acts 4–5. These new disciples need not come from the elite ranks of the Jerusalem priesthood, however, for the priestly rank-and-file held relatively low status, not at all near the echelons of power occupied by the chief priests. See Luke Timothy Johnson, *The Acts of the Apostles*, SP 5 (Collegeville, MN: Liturgical Press, 1992), p. 107; Robert W. Wall, "The Acts of the Apostles: Introduction, Commentary, and Reflections," *The New Interpreter's Bible*, vol. 10 (Nashville: Abingdon, 2002), p. 114.

27. Not all have pursued the theological implications. Michael W. Pahl, for example, recognizes that Acts 6:7; 12:24; and 19:20 describe the word's growth "as if it is a living thing,"

als will demonstrate the difficulties posed by these verses and set a foundation for expanding my own inquiry. The first two proposals attempt to describe the connection Luke intimates between the word of God and the church that proclaims it.

The Association between the Word and the Church

In 1974, Jerome Kodell published an article expounding what he calls "the ecclesial tendency" of ὁ λόγος at work in Acts 6:7; 12:24; and 19:20.[28] Quickly dismissing assumptions that the verb αὐξάνω means only that the gospel message *migrated* into new regions, Kodell takes seriously the idea of the word itself *gaining* new members, based mostly on passages in the Septuagint where αὐξάνω and πληθύνω appear together in a "be fruitful and multiply" sense.[29] He notes that Luke might have written about "the church" or "the people," instead of "the word," gaining members. Kodell proposes, then, that these verses reflect "a materialization of λόγος," in which the covenant community manifests or becomes the word of God.[30] The community exists as both the bearers and the expression of the word, the message about Jesus.

Kodell describes well the terminological evidence that provokes his — and my — investigation of these three summaries, rightly refusing to read over the verses too quickly as insignificant peculiarities. Yet his discussion of their theological ramifications leaves questions unanswered, and his notion of "a materialization of λόγος" finally overemphasizes ecclesiology at the ex-

---

but he does not delve into the significance of this observation, blunting it instead with a blanket statement that Luke's notion of λόγος consistently is essentially synonymous with the notion of εὐαγγέλιον in Paul's writings (*Discerning the 'Word of the Lord': The 'Word of the Lord' in 1 Thessalonians 4:15*, LNTS 389 [London: T. & T. Clark, 2009], pp. 134, 128-29).

28. Jerome Kodell, "'The Word of God Grew': The Ecclesial Tendency of Λόγος in Acts 6,7; 12,24; 19,20," *Bib* 55 (1974): 505-19.

29. For these passages, see my note 22, above. Kodell also calls attention to Luke 8:4-15, the Parable of the Sower, in which "the word of God" promises to bear much fruit in certain soil. Other interpreters read Acts 6:7; 12:24; and 19:20 in light of this parable and take the word of God to signify more than a message but "an active force in the world" (Robert C. Tannehill, *The Narrative Unity of Luke-Acts: A Literary Interpretation*, vol. 2: *The Acts of the Apostles* [Minneapolis: Fortress, 1990], p. 82; see also Rosner, "Progress," p. 223). A significant problem with appealing to Luke 8 in this way, however, is the absence of the verb αὐξάνω in Luke's version of the parable, a verb the author might have been expected to retain, since it appears in Mark's version (Mark 4:8).

30. Kodell, "Word," p. 509.

pense of a deeper understanding of the λόγος. The word of God is "ecclesial," claims Kodell, because salvation in the book of Acts means coming to belong to the community of the saved, a community possessing authority in itself as the company of those who bear witness to Jesus. "The life of believers" in Acts "is now bound up with the progress of the word, so much so that it can become a part of the preaching itself."[31] Witnesses, Kodell continues, are not fully separable from the message nor from the Christ about whom their message testifies; to accept the word requires accepting the community, for the word itself "is embedded in the Christian community."[32]

The problem with Kodell's proposal is that, while it respects Luke's efforts to associate "the word" and "the community," it cannot fully make sense of how or why it is *the word* that increases in number. Something "embedded" retains a distinction and remains separate; it is unclear how an embedded word might affect or participate in the thing or setting in which it is embedded, namely, the Christian community. Luke's wording in the summaries could imply a more dynamic understanding of the λόγος. For Kodell, "the word of God" remains a message, but a message whose validity or credibility becomes couched within a body of people.[33] Why Luke would then speak of the message *itself* growing in membership is not entirely clear. Thus Kodell's conclusions concerning these verses say more about the church than about the word. He privileges the church, as a collection of powerful witnesses who organically manifest the truth or fulfillment of God's word, over any sense that the message itself — or the God whose activity the message expresses and exhibits — exercises agency or actualizes God's own presence. Such a move is not fully consonant with the language in the three summaries, which subtly ascribes an organic, collective character to the word of God itself.

A second interpreter, David W. Pao, likewise finds the peculiar expression ὁ λόγος ηὔξανεν worthy of investigation. The three verses under consideration lead him to describe a "hypostatization" of the word of God and

31. Kodell, "Word," p. 516.

32. Kodell, "Word," p. 518.

33. Leo O'Reilly advances a similar argument, that these verses show the community of faith to have "a word dimension," because in the church "the word of God reaches down through the ages from one generation to the next" (*Word and Sign in the Acts of the Apostles: A Study in Lucan Theology*, Analecta Gregoriana 243, Series Facultatis Theologiae, Sectio B, 82 [Rome: Editrice Pontificia Università Gregoriana, 1987], p. 83). O'Reilly's understanding of the nature of the relationship among the word, the church, and Jesus himself never comes to a clear expression, however.

the power it possesses.[34] For him, the pairing of ὁ λόγος with αὐξάνω means Acts regards the word as a living being. This explains why Acts 13:48 can speak about Gentiles in Pisidian Antioch praising (δοξάζω) the word of the Lord, for in Luke-Acts nothing but God or Jesus deserves to receive praise.[35] The λόγος is not a synonym for God; it is God's "agent," which "accomplishes" or "represents" God's "will." The hypostatized word is a force, not a report or message, recalling to Pao the claim in Isaiah 55:11 that God's "word" (which the LXX renders as ῥῆμα, not λόγος!) will complete the task God desires, because God remains present in it, acting through it.

Pao's discussion comes as part of a larger argument devoted to establishing Luke's reliance on Isaianic themes for expressing the theology conveyed in Acts. Pao's proposal about hypostatization stems more from dynamics he sees in Isaiah than from a philosophical conception of hypostasis. His analysis makes a strong case for seeing divine activity implied in the three summaries' references to "the word," reaffirming that Acts tells the story of a God who operates in the midst of — or, in the form of — the church's efforts. He explains the theological significance of instances where ὁ λόγος serves as the subject of an active verb. Yet, for all his attention to the subject (ὁ λόγος), the relevant verbs used in the summaries (αὐξάνω and πληθύνω) receive little attention. The question remains: How does this hypostatic, living "word" increase in population? What exactly does this hypostasis indicate about the nature of the church, as servants of this active God, who somehow manifest or participate in God's will? Pao appears to imply that God, with the word as the medium, adds to the church's membership as the church preaches the message of the gospel. But it remains unclear how or why this must be a reasonable conclusion drawn from Acts 6:7; 12:24; and 19:20. Pao's theological claims contribute much, insofar as he recognizes in these verses the organic character, the living and growing character, of the word of God. Yet it remains unclear how his theological assertions connect to the enlarging community of faith in Acts or become actualized or even glimpsed in the community's particular endeavors.[36] How do God and the community

34. David W. Pao, *Acts and the Isaianic New Exodus*, WUNT 2/130 (Tübingen: Mohr Siebeck, 2000; repr.: Grand Rapids: Baker Academic, 2002), pp. 160-67.

35. Pao, *Exodus*, p. 161.

36. By my assessment, Pao too greatly reduces the significance of the community of faith and its own growth when he claims God and the word's shared "goal is to create a new community" and the word serves as "a tool" to identify this community's "true identity" (*Exodus*, p. 167).

interact? Or, is Luke depicting a church whose own agency is fully subsumed by God's?

Kodell and Pao, then, each in his own way, illustrate the challenge of making theological sense of Acts 6:7; 12:24; and 19:20. These verses invite investigation into their theological significance, but neither syntactical analysis nor comparisons to other biblical texts finally provide enough to support reasonable, adequately substantive conclusions about what these summaries indicate concerning the connection between the word of God and the church. While Kodell and Pao offer valuable insights, they also demonstrate that Luke gives little material to assist us in moving beyond an ambiguous notion of an integrally related church and divine agent. Attempts to describe the nature of this relationship appear to ask questions Acts will not answer. This leaves room for interpreters to speculate, of course, but questions about the proper scope of that speculation remain. I will revisit this topic later, and offer some speculation of my own, in the essay's concluding section.

Does Growth Mean Conquest?

A third interpreter deserves attention at this point; for not only do Acts 6:7; 12:24; and 19:20 prompt questions about the nature of the word and the church, they also invite us to consider the purpose or the meaning of the growth that occurs at three points in the plot of Acts. Alan J. Thompson, in a relatively recent study of the church in Acts, offers such an analysis, although he treats these three summary verses in a much less concentrated manner than Kodell or Pao.[37] Thompson considers the dynamics of "the word" in the summaries as part of his survey exploring how this word conquers opposition throughout all of Acts.[38] His analysis reiterates a basic claim: expressions of the church's unity in Acts regularly serve to indicate triumph over forces threatening to harm or undo the church. For example, the proximity of Acts 6:7 to the account of unity rescued from the jaws of disunity in 6:1-6 leads Thompson to regard the word's subsequent growth as an announcement of the word's conquest of Jerusalem.[39] Likewise,

---

37. Alan J. Thompson, *One Lord, One People: The Unity of the Church in Acts in Its Literary Setting*, LNTS 359 (London: T. & T. Clark, 2008).

38. The word's conquest is also a major focus of Pao's reading of Acts in his *Exodus.* Thompson picks up and advances his teacher's understanding of this theme.

39. Thompson, *One Lord,* p. 140.

Thompson finds themes of unity and disunity in the tale of Herod's downfall in Acts 12, making the summary in 12:24 a statement of progress specifically to declare victory over opposition that threatened to inflict turmoil upon the church.[40] Similarly, Acts 19:20 intimates the word's ongoing conquest within "the Gentile world."[41]

Thompson's theological inquiries differ from mine, given that his focus is on establishing unity as one of the church's chief, defining characteristics in Acts. I cite his book mostly to raise the issue of what we may learn from the surrounding narrative contexts when we consider Acts 6:7; 12:24; and 19:20. As mentioned previously, these three summary verses all follow descriptions of threats to the church and its ability to preserve a reliable, strong witness to Jesus Christ. In each case, those threats are neutralized, and Luke immediately announces that the word kept on growing. No doubt, then, the summaries strike a doxological tone, announcing, "Crisis averted." But they also have a competitive sound to them. To be more specific, Acts 6:7 speaks a word of provocation, for it mentions the priests who become obedient to the faith just after the heightened antagonism from the chief priests in Acts 4–5 and just prior to Stephen's so-called trial before the high priest, his council, and a mob.[42] The juxtaposition between the celebration of "the word of God" in Acts 12:24 and the preceding verse, in which Herod fails to give glory to God and dies gruesomely, is humorous in its stark contrast between the word's perseverance and a blasphemous king's demise. In Acts 19:20, the doxology has violent overtones, given the sense of κατὰ κράτος as "forcefully" or "with violence."[43] Richard Pervo sees a sharp display of power in that statement, wherein "Paul crushes the opposition" embodied in the sons of Sceva.[44]

Later I will return briefly to the question of whether conquest or triumphalism plays a part in the summaries, but for now two observations suffice. First, it is possible these passages are not especially interested in describing a God who consistently out-muscles any development or any person that stands in the church's way. They appear more interested in cele-

40. Thompson, *One Lord*, pp. 141-43.

41. Thompson, *One Lord*, p. 151.

42. Gaventa, *Acts*, p. 116.

43. See Barrett, *Acts*, 2:914.

44. Pervo, *Acts*, p. 482. It is not clear to me, however, that Acts implies *Paul's* agency in the humiliation and beating of Sceva's sons. More defensible is Pervo's more general assertion concerning the expression ὁ λόγος ηὔξανεν: "The phrase describes the conquest of the world by the Gospel" (p. 163 n. 93).

brating the ongoing survival and increased influence of communities of faith and their witness.[45] We should not split the difference between these possibilities too neatly, of course, since the latter appears to require the former, at least when legitimate threats (particularly Herod!) are involved. Still, the question is, How much does the word's growth in the face of adversity accentuate God's unmatched power, and how much does it point to God's protective presence among, or enfleshed within, an otherwise vulnerable community?

Second, one of the theological implications of Luke's descriptions of the word of God increasing in number may be a focus on the theological nature of what dwells *outside* the church — the true character of the things that threaten God's people and their witness. For God to side with and preserve the church says more than "God is stronger than whatever would inhibit the church." It also says, "The church's antagonists are also God's antagonists, and God's chief antagonist stands behind the things that threaten the church's vitality. In obstructing God's people, that antagonist opposes God." A satanic impulse imbues opposition to the gospel throughout Luke-Acts, even in places where the narrative does not give explicit attention to the diabolical.[46] What may look like political struggle, or conflict among differing groups within a society, is often to Luke a showdown between God and Satan. The growth of the word of God may therefore imply a defeat of Satan; but also, to put it another way, the summaries make statements about the preservation of the church threatened by an enemy its members cannot defeat alone. And this enemy targets the vulnerable church as a means of targeting God. The summaries therefore connect to narrative contexts that raise questions about how the people of this church, especially its leaders, will be able to secure its vitality and continuing existence. It is therefore worthwhile to ask, What more can we learn about the summaries by exploring their surrounding narrative contexts? What more can we glimpse, in particular, about the people who make up the church and who seek to be responsive to God?

45. Cf. again Weaver's interpretation of Acts 12:24 (*Plots,* p. 213).

46. Joel B. Green, *The Theology of the Gospel of Luke,* New Testament Theology (Cambridge: Cambridge University Press, 1995), p. 34.

Acts 6, 12, and 19 in Light of the Wider Narrative

It is not enough to examine the language of Acts 6:7; 12:24; and 19:20. Exploring these summaries' theological implications and pondering the nature of their subtle association of the word and the church also benefit from our considering the surrounding narrative contexts. Attending to narrative development is not methodological garnish; it allows us to respect the character of Acts and Luke's manner of giving voice to theology through storytelling.

As I have mentioned, the three verses in question follow some description of circumstances that threaten to undermine or disempower the church's work, but this is not the whole story. All three also appear in contexts that raise questions about what should be expected from key, visible figures in the church's leadership.[47]

The first summary, Acts 6:7, appears just after complaints about food distribution threaten the harmony of the community in Jerusalem. A large part of the concern, too, is whether the twelve apostles will be able to continue devoting themselves to prayer and "serving the word"; this leads them to appoint others to oversee the food distribution. The apostles' centrality to proclaiming the gospel appears imperiled by the crisis; the summary then reaffirms the importance and the influence of their preaching. Immediately following this, however, Stephen, one of the seven chosen to wait on tables, distinguishes himself through his performance of signs and wonders, his wisdom, and his speaking (6:8-10) — very "apostolic" activities, based on what Acts has shown up to this point. Do the apostles correctly discern what they should be doing, in serving the word rather than tables?[48] It matters little, once the narrative brings Stephen's deeds to light; the continuation of the word's growth hardly depends on the Twelve alone. Stephen comes across as just as capable.

---

47. As others have noted, there is also a geographical dimension to these verses' placement in the narrative (e.g., Meinert H. Grumm, "Another Look at Acts," *ExpTim* 96 [1985]: 335). Soon after 6:7, believers are propelled out of Jerusalem into wider Judea and Samaria. Almost immediately after 12:24, the narrator's focus turns to Barnabas and Saul when the Spirit sends them to Cyprus and beyond. In the verse following 19:20, Paul announces his Spirit-inspired intention to return to Jerusalem and eventually wind up in Rome, a trip that begins with the start of Acts 20.

48. The potential for irony is great, if the apostles actually misjudge their role and derogate table service, since Jesus describes himself in Luke 22:27 as "one who serves" his followers as they sit at a table.

Peter is the most central human figure in Acts 1–11; whoever comes in second place hardly approaches Peter in importance, as far as narrated action is concerned. His signs, wonders, preaching, and boldness in Acts 1–5, his importance in Cornelius's conversion — these make him a significant, strategic catch for Herod in Acts 12. But Peter's escape and Herod's death do not return Peter to the same kind of public ministry, according to what the narrator allows readers to see; instead, according to Acts 12:17, Peter "departed and went to another place." After chapter 12, Acts speaks of him only once again, when he makes his cameo appearance at the Jerusalem Council in Acts 15. He virtually vanishes from the narrative's spotlight. But, before that, Acts implies in 12:24 that the church grows after Peter gains his freedom from Herod. If readers are tempted to assume from this summary that the ongoing success or growth of the church depends upon Peter and his freedom, the following chapters quickly disabuse them of that assumption by turning attention to Barnabas and Saul right after the summary statement of Acts 12:24. Peter's removal from the stage and the narrative's turning toward new missionaries are, as Gaventa correctly observes, hardly a succession narrative, in which new people step into Peter's role.[49] But Peter's departure and the reintroduction of Barnabas and Saul do make for a relativization narrative, at once underscoring Peter's role in advancing the word of God even while diminishing any sense of his ongoing importance or indispensability.

The narrative context of Acts 19:20 differs significantly from the contexts of the other two summaries. The threats detailed in 19:13-19 seem directed not explicitly at a community of faith or its ability to perform effective ministry. Others who misuse magical or spiritual powers are exposed previously in Acts, without suggestion that their deeds pose unusual or unique peril to the wider church (see Simon in 8:9-24; Elymas in 13:6-12). Further, Paul does not disappear from the narrative after 19:20; rather, the locations and audiences for his witness to Christ change dramatically in Acts 21–28. Nevertheless, the summary does closely follow a description of Paul performing very impressive wonders (19:11-12), and it concludes a long series of public accusations against Paul, who comes across as impressive in all of them (Acts 16–19).[50] The narrative has dedicated much effort to establishing Paul's gifts and importance, yet immediately after Acts 19:20 Paul

---

49. Gaventa, *Acts,* p. 188.

50. See Tannehill's description of a "public accusation type-scene" recurring in Acts 16–19 (*Unity,* pp. 201-3).

begins his journey toward eventual martyrdom, a trek he undertakes mostly in isolation from other church leaders. It is correct to say, "The narrator is not simply glorifying Paul" in 19:20, because of Luke's explicit and overriding focus in this context on "the word of the Lord" (19:10, 20).[51] Yet Paul's contributions are undoubtedly celebrated by the summary and all that precedes it. Still, again, because it leans into the part of the story that will result in Paul being sequestered and later executed, the summary statement about "the word" participates in de-emphasizing a celebrated church leader's centrality, or the centrality of his dramatic, visible contributions.[52]

On one hand, these three summary verses, in connection with their wider narrative contexts, confirm the importance of various key figures: the Twelve as a whole, Peter, and Paul. These people's faithfulness and obedience contribute to the church's numerical growth and vitality. On the other hand, these verses serve as hinges into new narrative developments, reminding readers that the perseverance of the word hardly depends on these particular people. Narrative developments cause the summaries to say more than that God continues to increase the numbers of those touched by the gospel and brought into Christian communities. These passages, in context, also counter any expectations the narrative may otherwise promote about certain characters' irreplaceability. They call into question any putative centrality of these men and open the door to new developments, when others come forward in the narrative to fulfill God's purposes. The word in Acts is not a force entirely separate from the efforts of people. But it is always about more than specific individuals within the church, and it is hardly dependent on these persons.

The three summaries also redirect attention away from certain forms of ministry or ways of bearing witness to Christ. Stephen comes to prominence after Acts 6:7 as the Twelve fade; his ministry resembles theirs at first, but martyrdom will end his story. Peter disappears from the narrative spotlight after Acts 12, but readers assume his move to "another place" is not relocation to a retirement home; he will certainly contribute in other ways in other venues. Paul's ministry continues after his return to Jerusalem, but the mode and contexts of that ministry become very different once his incarceration begins. The word — or the ministry of the word —

---

51. Tannehill, *Unity*, p. 238.

52. Grumm notes that the second half of Acts 19 and the first half of Acts 20 together mention ten of Paul's companions ("Another," p. 335). This highlighting of Paul's associates further attenuates his centrality and erodes any presumption that he is an irreplaceable piece of God's plan concerning the spread of the gospel.

does not fit a single mold. These three summaries, again in connection to their narrative contexts, keep that reality in readers' eyes, simultaneously celebrating and undermining the particular leaders and forms of ministry that readers encounter in the narrative. The theological significance of this, and its importance for understanding the three summary statements, will become clearer in this essay's conclusion.

Conclusions

I have argued that the summary statements in Acts 6:7; 12:24; and 19:20 invite readers to consider a very close association between the word of God and the church, a close association forged by statements indicating the word's increase in membership, when the clear sense is that it is the community of believers that gains members. But the nature of this association remains frustratingly difficult to ascertain; Luke gives us little to work with, beyond these verses' repeated impetus to take the association seriously. Pao's notion of a hypostatized word offers a helpful way of imagining a "word" that is more than a message, something hardly inert.[53] But his explanation tells us little about what it means for communities of faith to embody or express this divine agency. I submit that it must mean something other than an assertion that the church and its people will always win or come through every threat somehow intact. What might we make of Luke's suggestion that the church is the dwelling place of God's word, the actual organic expression of God's purposes? I conclude with my modest proposals.

Expansion and infiltration occur throughout Acts. Witnesses travel from Jerusalem into much of the wider Roman world. The gospel is preached and lived out in diverse cultural settings. Members of the priesthood, a Roman proconsul, an Ethiopian official, former magicians, a jailer, soldiers, and other exceptional members of society respond positively to the word of God. People bear witness to Jesus before those occupying the highest echelons of political power as well as to slaves and prisoners. Luke portrays the word of God as something other than a message that finds creative expression in different social and physical places, and as some-

---

53. Cf. Graham H. Twelftree, who describes the increasing church membership in Acts as involving "the realization of the activity or presence of God" (*People of the Spirit: Exploring Luke's View of the Church* [London: SPCK, 2009; repr.: Grand Rapids: Baker Academic, 2009], p. 40).

thing other than a power that strong-arms its way through cultural boundaries to obliterate opposition and confront new audiences. Associated with a growing, nurturing community of people, the word operates as an activity that creates, inhabits, and energizes an arena where God's intentions become actualized in the existence and efforts of the church. The word grows, not simply because converts increase the church's rolls, but because they are brought into the arena of divine action, a place where they apprehend God and exist within God's purposes as those are expressed in the gospel message of and about Jesus Christ.

It is, then, incomplete to speak of God as the source of the church's vitality in Acts. The church is also more than "evidence" (to recall this essay's epigraph) of God's plan and activity; although the church *is* this evidence, and in Acts the church is certainly born of God's "intervention," in addition it is the lived reality of God's plan and activity, a living embodiment of God's own presence and agency. This means there can be no talk of "ecclesiology in Acts" without accounting for "theology in Acts." Patterns of living, religious practices, church organization, and similar topics cannot constitute the substance of Lukan ecclesiology. The church expresses the reality of the gospel, and God becomes present to the world through a real identification with the church's experiences and witness. Acts might sometimes acknowledge a God who exists separate from the church's existence, but Acts devotes much more attention to asserting an observable reality of this God's activity integrated with the witnessing church's life, successes, and failures.

Such a close connection between God and church cannot help but arouse concerns among theologically minded readers of Acts, especially those who themselves spend time in communities of faith and know well these communities' shortcomings and hubristic tendencies. Can this be a God worth following? Can any church live up to such a billing?

Those questions, as well as the risk of allowing ecclesiology to *replace* theology, underscore the importance of attending to the three summaries' surrounding narrative contexts, which I summarized in the preceding section. Even as Luke in the summaries brings the word and the church very close — perhaps uncomfortably close — in their identification and description, the broader narrative destabilizes any assumption that the church deserves confidence as the flawless expression of God's presence or the full array of God's activity. Bringing this essay now to its end, I explain how the wider Acts narrative helps qualify the close association the summaries posit between the word and the church.

First, just as Acts presents an idealized history of the church's early years, it also proposes in the summaries a highly idealized understanding of the church itself. Such an understanding exists in tension, however, with depictions of church members like Ananias and Sapphira (Acts 5:1-11) and those in Jerusalem who appear to leave Paul in the lurch after his arrest beginning in Acts 21.[54] The idealism must answer to the modulating criticisms found in the same narrative.

Second, Acts does not understand the church as constituting the exclusive setting where God's agency or purposes are actualized. To take the story of Cornelius and Peter (10:1–11:18) as an example, prompts toward accomplishing God's purposes come from outside the church's existing understanding, even *through* a person outside the church (namely, Cornelius). God occasionally reroutes the church and its work. The ability of those in the church to express in themselves the reality of the gospel does not mean they are beyond correction or unable to expand their grasp of their identity and roles. The church does not identify with God's word so closely that *on its own* it proposes or discovers new dimensions of God's intentions.

Finally, Luke's vision of who constitutes "the church" is wider than what some of his readers may realize. It is not merely a community (or communities) defined by the apostles or its most prominent leaders. Yet, this is easy to miss, given all the attention Acts pays to those who lead in ministry. In reality, Acts presents the entire church as a kind of tangible demonstration of God's presence and concern. One of Daniel Marguerat's observations is helpful here. He considers Acts 5:38-39, where Gamaliel warns his colleagues against opposing the "plan or activity" expressed in the apostles' ministry, lest the ministry succeed and thus validate its divine character. Marguerat proposes that, for Luke's readers, Acts itself performs a related function: *the narrative* of Acts allows readers to receive verification that "the work of the apostles is indeed 'of God,'" and so the act of reading becomes "the place to perceive the ways of God."[55] The book's story fulfills Gamaliel's criteria for latter-day observers, those in Luke's audience who wonder whether the Christian movement can be trusted as an expression of God's purposes. Still, to build on Marguerat's understand-

---

54. There is something appropriate about the fact that the word ἐκκλησία does not appear in Luke-Acts until Acts 5:11. "The church" does not receive its name until readers have seen both the best and the worst of its potential expressed side by side in Acts 4:32–5:10.

55. Marguerat, *Historian,* pp. 93, 94.

ing, the church might do a similar thing. For these ancient readers, who would easily perceive historical continuity between the church portrayed in the story of Acts and communities of faith in their midst, the narrative encourages them to look also beyond itself to those communities persevering in bearing witness to Jesus Christ. Those communities' existence, life, and work, according to Luke, provide additional means of verifying the ongoing presence of God's plan or activity.[56] But in Luke's time, of course, there were no apostles left guiding those communities. The narrative contexts surrounding the three summaries we have explored thus reveal their importance: for all of the church's significance as an embodiment of the word of God in Acts, its leaders and forms of ministry remain remarkably fluid and disposable. As the church — and the word — continues to grow, its members simultaneously see that its ability to manifest the ways of God depends less on inspired leadership or the heroic deeds of a few and more on its simple existence and its commitment to bear witness. The result is not a story promising ongoing victory and conquest over threats; it is a story more temperately celebrating both God's promise to be present and the church's stamina to persevere as a manifest expression of that presence.

---

56. These communities, Luke might say, also validate the presence of God's promises through their connections to the covenantal community of God's people in the Jewish Scriptures, connections that Acts asserts in its depiction of the church. See, e.g., Arie W. Zwiep, *Christ, the Spirit and the Community of God: Essays on the Acts of the Apostles*, WUNT 2/293 (Tübingen: Mohr Siebeck, 2010), p. 132.

Lost in Translation: A Reflection on Romans in the Common English Bible

Richard B. Hays

Omnis traductor traditor. The familiar maxim suggests that all acts of translation from one language into another are inevitably acts of betrayal, revisionary performances that twist the delicate nuances of a literary work into the alien contours of a target language different from the tongue of the original author. Even in the best of translations, there is always semantic leakage — or, more properly, semantic transformation. A translation is always a *reading*, an attempt to interpret and rearticulate what was said in a different linguistic matrix. And so, word by word and sentence by sentence, the translator is forced to make decisions about the reception and transmission of the text's meaning and about the shape and sense of the work as a whole.

If that is true for the translation of any text, it is so *a fortiori* for Paul's Letter to the Romans, an intricately wrought composition that has inspired countless commentaries, launched passionate debates, and (it is not too much to say) shaped the history of Christian culture. Thus, it was with a sense of chastened humility and, at the same time, hopeful excitement that Beverly Gaventa and I approached the challenge of translating Romans together during the spring of 2009.

We had been asked to work together on producing a draft translation for the new Common English Bible.[1] I was spending a semester in residence at the Center of Theological Inquiry in Princeton; consequently, the two of us had the opportunity to work closely together on this formidable task. Over several months we met periodically over lunch or coffee to review drafts of new sections and to debate the merits of different solutions

---

1. *The Common English Bible: New Testament* (Nashville: Common English Bible, 2010).

to translation problems. By the summer, we had a complete text. Neither of us thought the translation was perfect, but we were satisfied that we had hammered out an engaging and coherent rendering that sought to incorporate important recent advances in the study of Pauline theology. So we shipped our draft off to the editors of the CEB.

When the CEB New Testament appeared in print a year later, however, its translation of Romans bore only a slight resemblance to the text Beverly and I had labored over. Why? The goal of the CEB editorial team was to produce a translation into simple, idiomatic modern English that was deemed readily accessible to the average reader today. Consequently, the translation we had drafted was filtered through an editorial panel of "readability" experts, whose assignment was to produce a final version at a seventh-grade reading level. Of course, to turn a magisterial theological reflection such as Romans into an easy-reading text for the average American seventh-grader necessarily entails certain modifications, tradeoffs, and sacrifices — a point to which I shall return at the end of this essay. Most disappointing, however, was the fact that Beverly and I, as the authors of the draft translation, were given no opportunity to review and comment on the greatly altered text that was rushed into print by the publisher. I am therefore grateful that the editors wisely decided not to print a list of the names of the translators of individual books of the Bible in this new version. I will not presume to speak for my collaborator, but I myself would not want to claim this rendering as my work.

However, precisely because the printed CEB translation of Romans differs substantially from the version that Beverly and I produced, its publication does offer an opportunity for fresh critical reflection on the interpretation of Paul's weighty letter, on the hermeneutical consequences of the decisions made by the CEB editorial team, and on the perils and prospects of translating Scripture. That critical reflection is the task I will undertake in the present essay.

What I will not do is work painstakingly through a detailed list of the changes made by the editors (to do that would produce an essay much longer than Romans itself); rather, I shall single out a few of the most salient *theological* issues highlighted by the particular *Tendenzen* manifest in the CEB's inflection of Paul's text. I undertake this exercise as an offering of gratitude to my longtime friend and colleague Beverly Gaventa, συνεργὸς τῷ εὐαγγελίῳ, in hopes that this essay will provide some small stimulation for her in the much larger task in which she is engaged: the writing of a full-scale critical commentary on the Letter to the Romans.

Muting Paul's Apocalyptic Notes

One of the first impressions that struck me upon reading through Romans in the CEB was that this translation had muted the apocalyptic tones in Paul's message. Perhaps this impression is partly a consequence of the translation's casual informality. The repeated use of contractions and low-intensity everyday diction creates a relaxed conversational tone that lowers the temperature of the discourse. For example, in 16:19, ἐφ' ὑμῖν οὖν χαίρω ("Therefore, I rejoice over you") becomes, in the CEB, "so I'm happy for you."[2] But upon closer examination, one finds that the reader's impression of apocalyptic de-escalation is not merely a function of the translation's mundane diction. Rather, it is a function of several translational choices that seem to shy away deliberately from the language and imagery of a Jewish apocalyptic worldview.

This tendency is strikingly apparent in the benediction at the end of the letter (16:25-27). There Paul declares that his proclamation of the gospel of Jesus Christ is κατὰ ἀποκάλυψιν μυστηρίου χρόνοις αἰωνίοις σεσιγημένου ("according to the revelation of the mystery that was kept silent for long ages"). In the CEB, however, this portentous apocalyptic phrase is rendered blandly as "with the announcement of the secret that was kept quiet for a long time." The revelation (ἀποκάλυψιν) has become an "announcement," the mystery (μυστηρίου) has become a "secret,"[3] and the span of the world's ages has become "a long time." The CEB's language would be more fitting to describe, say, a delayed wedding announcement than to designate the apostolic unveiling of the hidden mystery of God's eternal design for saving the world. The softening of apocalyptic connotation here is evident.

Reading back through the letter after this tepid conclusion, we find a number of places where the CEB, whether intentionally or unintentionally, has opted for muting Paul's apocalyptic tone. For example, in 3:8, Paul refers to detractors who slander him by distorting his message and observes that "their condemnation is just" (τὸ κρίμα ἔνδικόν ἐστιν) — meaning that the just God who is to judge the world (3:5-6) will pronounce condemnation upon them at the eschatological judgment.[4] But the CEB's Paul, by contrast, remarks in a tone of evenhanded detachment that "these

---

2. "Happy *for* you," which would suggest a sort of mild congratulation to the Roman Christians for their religious achievements, is certainly *not* Paul's meaning in this sentence.

3. In a footnote, the CEB does offer "mystery" as an alternate translation.

4. See, for example, the use of κρίμα in Acts 24:25; Heb. 6:2; and Rev. 20:4.

people deserve criticism." Presumably they are to be criticized on talk shows or in letters to the editor?

A similar elision of judgment terminology appears in Paul's notoriously difficult discussion of governing authorities in chapter 13. There he counsels his readers to do good and to be subordinate to the divinely constituted authority, θεοῦ γὰρ διάκονός ἐστιν ἔκδικος εἰς ὀργὴν τῷ τὸ κακὸν πράσσοντι (13:4). I would translate this as follows: "for it is God's servant to execute vengeance, to bring wrath on those who do evil." But in the CEB, we find a tamer formulation: "It is God's servant put in place to carry out his punishment on those who do what is wrong." Here God's "vengeance" and "wrath" have been reduced to "punishment" — with the not insignificant consequence that the English reader loses the connection between 13:4 and Paul's earlier programmatic reference to God's wrath in 1:18. "Punishment" sounds much more like some form of historically immanent consequence for bad behavior; perhaps a fine or a jail sentence rather than death by sword as an enactment of God's eschatological judgment on human unrighteousness.

Another part of the problem is that the CEB seems in numerous places to have shifted the emphasis of the discourse subtly away from Paul's pronouncements about eschatological divine action towards an emphasis on present human action. As one indicator of this tendency, consider Romans 1:22: φάσκοντες εἶναι σοφοὶ ἐμωράνθησαν ("While claiming to be wise, they were made fools"). Here the passive verb points to the divine action: Paul is asserting that it is *God* who has made fools out of them, just as in 1 Corinthians 1:20b: "Has not God made foolish (ἐμώρανεν) the wisdom of this world?" But in place of Paul's emphasis on divine action, the CEB offers "they made fools of themselves." This translation sounds clever, and it is certainly idiomatic English; unfortunately, it obscures Paul's theological point.

A subtler — but more significant — illustration of the same difficulty may be seen in the CEB's translation of Paul's threefold repetition of παρέδωκεν αὐτοὺς ὁ θεός in Romans 1:24, 26, and 28 as "God abandoned them." The problem here is that the verb παραδίδωμι means *"hand over,"* not *"abandon."* What is the difference? It is the distinction between delivering a prisoner into the hands of an occupying power and, on the other hand, shrugging and walking away from a hapless person in a perilous circumstance. As Beverly Gaventa has compellingly argued, both the evidence of the LXX and Paul's usage elsewhere suggest strongly that when Paul writes παρέδωκεν, he is referring to a divine action of turning unfaithful human beings over into the custody of another power. And this interpretation of the text points in turn to a dramatic narrative that indicates "the cosmic apocalyptic character of Romans."[5] Within Paul's apocalyptic account, human beings are not simply "abandoned" to follow their own devices and desires but actively consigned by God into slavery under a cosmic power — that is, the power of Sin.

This observation leads us to a particularly crucial point at which the CEB has decisively rejected the Hays/Gaventa translation draft and thereby transposed our apocalyptic reading of the letter into a moral/forensic key. In the translation we submitted, there are twenty-six instances in which we translated ἁμαρτία as "Sin." The capitalization was meant to signify clearly that Paul — especially in the dense argument of chapters 6 and 7 — depicts Sin as a personified Power that actively enslaves humanity. I offer here just a few examples to illustrate the effect of this interpretation:

> This is what we know: our old human identity was crucified with him in order to abolish Sin's grip on our bodies,[6] so that we might no longer be slaves to Sin. (6:6)

> So then, don't let Sin reign in your mortal body, to make you obey its desires. And don't present your members to Sin as weapons[7] of unrighteousness, but present yourselves to God, as people brought to life from the dead, and present your members to God as weapons of righteousness. (6:12-13)

> Sin, seizing the opportunity through the commandment, deceived me and killed me. (7:11)

> But if the very thing I do is what I don't want, then I am no longer the one doing it; instead, it is Sin that dwells in me. (7:20)

In these texts, Sin is a malevolent power that possesses agency; it rules over its human slaves. It deceives human beings, takes control over their bodies, and acts in and through them, with or without their volitional cooperation. The interpreter of Romans will have to decide how to deal with Paul's

---

5. Beverly Roberts Gaventa, "God Handed Them Over: Reading Romans 1:18-32 Apocalyptically," *ABR* 53 (2005): 53. (Revised and republished in Beverly Roberts Gaventa, *Our Mother Saint Paul* [Louisville: Westminster John Knox, 2007], pp. 113-23.)

6. Lit. "the body of Sin," i.e., the body under the power of Sin.

7. I was pleased to see that the CEB did accept our translation of ὅπλα, a common military term, as "weapons," rather than the more nondescript "instruments." The term appears again with the same sense in 13:12.

depiction of Sin: is this merely an instance of poetic personification, or does Paul regard ἁμαρτία as an actual cosmic power?[8] No matter which of these hermeneutical options may be chosen, it seems incontrovertible that Paul's discourse portrays Sin as a *character* in the cosmic drama of God's redemption of the world. As Gaventa writes, "[I]n Romans in particular, sin is Sin — not a lowercase transgression, not even a human disposition or flaw in human nature, but an uppercase Power that enslaves humankind and stands over against God."[9]

The CEB, however, has consistently "corrected" all twenty-six instances in which our translation highlighted Paul's portrayal of Sin as a character, turning them all into lowercase references to "sin."[10] For the common English reader, this seemingly small change is likely to encourage a nonapocalyptic reading in which Paul's chief concern in Romans 5–8 is how human beings can gain control over their own worst impulses in order to live an upright moral life.

I want to emphasize that I am not merely complaining about the decision of the editors to make this change. Rather, I am drawing attention to this particular translational decision in order to illustrate how the process of translation entails judgments that are deeply *theological* in character. It is certainly possible that the editors of the CEB considered the theological question at stake here and decided to reject the apocalyptic interpretation presented by the Hays/Gaventa translation. On the other hand, it seems equally possible that the decision was simply made by a copyeditor who noticed that capitalizing the noun "sin" was inconsistent with the CEB's style guidelines. Which was it? Unfortunately, Beverly and I do not know, because we were not consulted about this or any of the other wide-ranging transmutations of our draft translation.

Two final examples may be offered to illustrate the way in which the CEB de-emphasizes the apocalyptic perspective. In Paul's pivotal exhortation in Romans 12:2, the CEB reads, "Don't be conformed to the patterns

8. For a spirited presentation of the latter interpretation, see Beverly Roberts Gaventa, "The Cosmic Power of Sin in Paul's Letter to the Romans: Toward a Widescreen Edition," *Int* 58 (2004): 229-40. (Revised and republished in Gaventa, *Mother*, pp. 125-36.)

9. Gaventa, "Cosmic," p. 231. See also Paul W. Meyer, "The Worm at the Core of the Apple: Exegetical Reflections on Romans 7," in *The Conversation Continues: Studies in Paul and John in Honor of J. Louis Martyn*, ed. Robert T. Fortna and Beverly R. Gaventa (Nashville: Abingdon, 1990), pp. 62-84.

10. The other instances are found in 5:21; 6:7, 12-23; 7:7-25; and 8:2-3. To this list I would also add 3:9 as another possible case in which Paul thinks of Sin as a power.

of this world. . . ." The translation of τῷ αἰῶνι τούτῳ as "this world" is very common in the broad tradition of English translations going back to the KJV. But such a rendering forfeits the temporal sense which is, after all, the primary connotation of the noun αἰών. A much better translation would be "Don't be conformed to the pattern of *this age*."[11] Such a rendering would make it clear that Paul is thinking in the two-age schema character-istic of Jewish apocalyptic thought. The reason why Paul's readers should not be "conformed" is *not* because they should live in light of some *other-worldly* standards; rather, it is because the new age inaugurated by Jesus Christ's death and resurrection has broken in to human time and space and rendered the former norms of the old age obsolete. But Paul's apoca-lyptic call to transformation is "de-eschatologized" when τῷ αἰῶνι τούτῳ is translated as "this world."

Finally, we return to chapter 16, where we started this brief tour through the nonapocalyptic tendencies of the CEB's Romans. One of the most puzzling translations anywhere in the letter appears in Romans 16:13: ἀσπάσασθε ῾Ροῦφον τὸν ἐκλεκτὸν ἐν κυρίῳ. The CEB unaccountably translates this as, "Say hello to Rufus, *who is an outstanding believer*" (em-phasis mine). The literal meaning, of course is "Greet Rufus, *the one chosen in the Lord*." What possible reason is there for the CEB's strange para-phrastic rewriting of this simple text? Could it be that the editors, drawing near the end of this long letter, finally were overcome by some nagging dis-comfort with the Jewish apocalyptic concept of God's special election of some? This qualm does not seem to have affected the CEB's translation of chapters 9–11, where the concept of God's election plays a central role, faithfully represented in the CEB. But then in 16:13, suddenly God's act of singling out Rufus as "elect in the Lord" is suppressed and creatively re-placed by Rufus's exemplary act of believing. Here I can only suspect the editorial hand of a readability consultant — perhaps a different one from the consultant(s) who processed chapters 9–11? But to delve into specula-tive hypotheses about the different redactional hands of different readabil-ity consultants would take me too far afield from the purposes of this es-say. It will suffice to observe that in Romans 16:13, the theocentric apocalyptic idea of election is supplanted by a cheerful commendation of one human's believing as an "outstanding" achievement deserving special commendation. I am afraid that if Paul could read the translation of this

11. I note with interest that Jerome's Latin Vulgate rendered the passage as "et nolite conformari huic *saeculo*."

verse, he might lament, as he does in the CEB's reading of Galatians 4:11, "Perhaps my hard work for you has been for nothing."

Faith, Faithfulness, and Trust

The curious characterization of Rufus as an "outstanding believer" — unsupported by anything in the Greek text — serves as a useful transition to an examination of the way in which the CEB treats the difficult problem of translating πίστις, πιστεύειν, and related terms in Romans. This new translation gets off to a promising start in 1:17: "God's righteousness is being revealed in the gospel, from faithfulness for faith . . . ," with footnotes offering the alternative possibilities of translating ἐκ πίστεως as "from faith" and/or translating εἰς πίστιν as "for faithfulness." Here the editorial board has made a clear and defensible exegetical choice while also alerting the reader that there is ambiguity in Paul's formulation. It is less clear, however, what the editors were doing in 3:3, where the CEB offers this: "What does it matter, then, if some weren't faithful (ἠπίστησάν τινες)? Their lack of faith (ἀπιστία) won't cancel God's faithfulness (πίστιν), will it?" The verb ἠπίστησάν most likely alludes to Israel's disobedience to God's commandments; in that case, "some weren't faithful" is the right translation, rather than "some did not have faith" or some such. And τὴν πίστιν τοῦ θεοῦ unquestionably refers to God's faithfulness — his unbreakable fidelity to his covenant promises.[12] But why then is ἀπιστία rendered as "lack of faith"? Surely, as the opposition to "God's faithfulness" would suggest, it should be translated simply as "unfaithfulness."

When we arrive at the much-discussed crux in 3:22, we find the editors apparently making a definite exegetical choice for the subjective-genitive interpretation of the phrase διὰ πίστεως ᾽Ιησοῦ Χριστοῦ: "God's righteousness comes through *the faithfulness of Jesus Christ* for all who have faith in him" (emphasis mine).[13] This reading corresponds nicely to the

---

12. This is a clear example of the subjective genitive case following the noun πίστις. It is clearly God's own faithfulness under discussion here. No one would translate this sentence as, "Their lack of faithfulness won't cancel their faith in God, will it?"

13. This translation accords, of course, with my own interpretation of the passage. See Richard B. Hays, *The Faith of Jesus Christ: The Narrative Substructure of Galatians 3:1–4:11,* 2nd ed. (Grand Rapids: Eerdmans, 2002). See especially my further reflections in the "Introduction to the Second Edition" (pp. xxi-lii) and "Appendix 2: Πίστις and Pauline Christology: What Is at Stake?" (pp. 272-97).

CEB's earlier treatment of ἐκ πίστεως εἰς πίστιν in 1:17: the *source* of righteousness is God's act in Christ, and this righteousness is offered for all who now place their trust in him. Unfortunately, however, the exegesis starts to wobble in 3:26, where τὸν ἐκ πίστεως Ἰησοῦ is rendered, inconsistently, as "the one who *has faith in Jesus.*" From this point onwards in the letter, the interpretation of Jesus Christ's own faithfulness as the means of humanity's redemption and rectification disappears from the CEB translation (with the single exception of 5:1, to which we shall return in a moment). In 3:27-31 and throughout chapter 4, "faith" is used consistently (in preference to "faithfulness" or "trust") for πίστις and its cognates.

At Romans 5:1, a key transitional moment in the argument, the translators of the CEB seem to suffer from a sudden attack of ambivalence, rendering the two Greek words ἐκ πίστεως with an extended English phrase: "Therefore, since we have been made righteous *through his faithfulness combined with our faith. . . .*" Combined with? What sort of synergistic soteriology is presupposed here? Presumably this translation attempts to encapsulate the message expressed in 1:17 and 3:22. If so, why not treat Romans 5:1 in the same way the editors handled 1:17, making a clear exegetical choice and placing the alternative interpretation in a footnote? But the translation actually given in the CEB combines two different interpretations by simple addition. Were there debates among the editors that were settled by this unsatisfying compromise?

A sidelong glance at the other key πίστις Χριστοῦ texts in the Pauline corpus strengthens the suspicion that the CEB editorial board could not make up its mind on this contested question. Their translation of Galatians emphatically sides with the Reformation's traditional objective genitive reading, in which Christ is the *object* of our faith:[14]

However, we know that a person isn't made righteous by the works of the Law[15] but rather *by faith in Jesus Christ* (διὰ πίστεως Ἰησοῦ

14. The translations of Gal. 2:16; 2:20; and 3:22 cited here appear in the 2010 edition of the CEB. This is the version that was sent by the publisher to contributors. After the completion of the present essay, the editors of this volume drew my attention to the fact that in 2011 CEB issued a revised translation in which the expression πίστις Ἰησοῦ Χριστοῦ is rendered as "faithfulness of Jesus Christ" in all three of these passages. Because the publishing house never issued any public announcement of a revision of the original publication, this important change had escaped my notice. I am pleased to note this decision to translate these passages in a way that is consistent with the CEB's rendering of Rom. 3:22 and Phil. 3:9.

15. Oddly, the expression "works of the Law" — used repeatedly in the CEB's transla-

Χριστοῦ). We ourselves believed in Christ Jesus so that we could be made righteous *by faith in Christ* (ἐκ πίστεως Χριστοῦ) and not by the works of the Law. . . . (Gal. 2:16)

And the life that I now live in my body, I live *by faith in the Son of God* (ἐν πίστει ζῶ τῇ τοῦ υἱοῦ τοῦ θεοῦ). . . . (Gal. 2:20)

But scripture locked up all things under sin, so that the promise *based on faith in Jesus Christ* (ἐκ πίστεως Ἰησοῦ Χριστοῦ) might be given to those who believe. (Gal. 3:22)

But when we turn to Philippians, we find this:

In Christ I have a righteousness that is not my own and that does not come from the Law but rather *from the faithfulness of Christ* (διὰ πίστεως Χριστοῦ). (Phil. 3:9)

Either the editors of the CEB could not make up their minds on this admittedly challenging exegetical question or, perhaps more likely, the left hand did not know what the right was doing.[16] The tension between these different construals is reflected in the CEB's odd fence-sitting translation of Romans 5:1.

There is, however, another issue about the translation of Paul's πίστις/ πιστεύειν terminology that may have still wider impact on the overall impression conveyed by the CEB's reading of Romans. The semantic range of these terms is fairly broad, but their root sense has to do with the placing of trust or confidence in someone or something, rather than with the granting of intellectual assent to ideas or propositions. The CEB has, accordingly, done a good job of minimizing references to "belief" or "believing" in Romans. Instead, they have opted fairly consistently for "faith" as the translation of the noun πίστις and "have faith" as the rendering of the verb πιστεύειν. It is difficult to argue that this translational decision is wrong in principle. But the cumulative effect of reading through the letter thus translated is (in the ears of this interpreter) to load a great deal of

---

tion of Galatians — is expunged from Romans, with various circumlocutions used at Rom. 2:15; 3:20; and 3:28, as well as all the other passages where the word ἔργα appears in the Greek.

16. This observation applies to the original 2010 edition of the CEB. Apparently, by 2011, the editorial committee recognized the inconsistency and corrected it in the relevant Galatians passages.

weight on the subjective disposition or experience of the individual subject who "has" the quality of faith.

The draft translation that Beverly Gaventa and I submitted sought to address this concern by frequently translating both noun and verb with the English word "trust."[17] This strategy has the advantage of clearly reproducing numerous verbal links and wordplays in the Greek text. More importantly, in our judgment, the use of "trust," particularly to translate the verb, has the effect of more securely anchoring the source of salvation in God rather than in the subjective state of individual consciousness.[18] Consider the following example, taken from Romans 10:9-10:

> Hays/Gaventa: Because if you confess with your mouth "Jesus is Lord" and trust in your heart that God raised him from the dead, you will be saved. For it is the heart that trusts, leading to righteousness, and it is the mouth that confesses, leading to salvation.

> CEB: Because if you confess with your mouth "Jesus is Lord" and in your heart *you have faith* that God raised him from the dead, you will be saved. It is the heart that *has faith* that leads to righteousness, and it is the mouth that confesses that leads to salvation. [Emphasis mine][19]

The difference may appear relatively small, but I would submit that the italicized phrases in the CEB translation tilt the emphasis ever so slightly in the direction of the subjective attitude of the individual believer as the crucial determinant of salvation.

This sort of alteration is repeated over and over again by the CEB. On a quick count, I have found about forty-five instances where our translation used "trust" to render forms of πίστις or πιστεύειν. In the great majority of cases, the CEB editorial team rejected this reading and replaced it with "faith" or "have faith." When one adds up the cumulative impact of these changes, the two versions of the letter read rather differently.

It is not clear why the CEB editors preferred "faith" to "trust." The latter is a simple, strong English word with a positive connotation for the com-

---

17. For a concise exposition of the message of Romans through the lens of "trust," see my essay "A Hermeneutics of Trust," in Richard B. Hays, *The Conversion of the Imagination: Paul as Interpreter of Israel's Scripture* (Grand Rapids: Eerdmans, 2005), pp. 190-201.

18. Consider, by way of illustrative comparison, the difference in German between *glauben* and *trauen*, or, in noun form, the distinction between *der Glaube* and *das Vertrauen*.

19. Once again, this translation is corrected in the 2011 edition: "Trusting with the heart leads to righteousness, and confessing with the mouth leads to salvation."

mon reader. One can only suppose that subtle theological concerns dictated the choice. The net effect of the CEB's preference for "faith" over "trust," along with its equivocal position on the πίστις Χριστοῦ question, is to slide the CEB more closely into alignment with the so-called "Lutheran" interpretation of Paul,[20] and subtly away from the narrative/apocalyptic reading that Beverly and I, among many others, have argued for in recent years.

Justification

A similar tendency towards equivocation can be observed in the CEB's handling of Paul's even more difficult use of δίκαιος, δικαιοσύνη, δικαιοῦν, and related terms. This is a perennial problem for English translators, because of the different semantic domains represented by "just/justice/justify," on one hand, and "righteous/righteousness," on the other, along with the absence in common English parlance of a verbal form corresponding to the latter.[21] The CEB opts, for the most part, against "just/justice/justify" and tends to prefer "righteous/righteousness" throughout the letter.[22]

This strategy has the virtue of enabling readers to recognize important linguistic connections in Paul's discourse, but it introduces new problems in the translation of the verbal forms derived from δικαιοῦν. The translators vacillate between "treat as righteous" and "make righteous" — i.e., between the idea that God's act is a forensic declaration and the idea that God's act is an efficacious moral transformation of his people. So, for example, in the crucial passage 3:23-24 we find this:

> All have sinned and fall short of God's glory, but all are *treated as righteous* (δικαιούμενοι) freely by his grace because of a ransom that was paid by Jesus Christ.[23]

20. Once again, this judgment applies more strongly to the 2010 edition than to its revision in 2011.

21. Of course, there have been proposals to address the problem of an appropriate verb by using the archaic form "to rightwise" or the verb "to rectify." The latter choice, adopted by J. Louis Martyn in his commentary on Galatians, is by far a better solution.

22. For exceptions, see 1:18, 29; 2:5; and 3:5-6.

23. The choice of the translators to refer to a "ransom" paid by Christ introduces another range of issues that I cannot pursue fully within the course of this essay. This reading is clearly tied to a notion of substitutionary atonement; it inevitably introduces the question of why "ransom" is necessary and to whom such a ransom was paid. The Hays/Gaventa translation of this passage read as follows: "all have sinned and fallen short of the glory of

This reading would appear to endorse the interpretation of justification as a forensic fiction, in which righteousness is imputed, rather than imparted, as a result of Christ's death as a form of substitutionary atonement. The translation "treated as righteous" also appears in 2:13; 3:20, 26, and 28.

But then, when we arrive at 3:30, we abruptly find this translation:

> Since God is one, then the one who *makes the circumcised righteous* by faith (δικαιώσει περιτομὴν ἐκ πίστεως) will also *make the one who isn't circumcised righteous* through faith.

After this point we find the translation "make righteous" or "made righteous" several more times in the letter (e.g., 4:2, 5; 5:1, 9, 19; 8:30), while "treat as righteous" disappears. This creates the impression that Paul has *shifted* at the end of Romans 3 from a focus on forensic declaration to a focus on actual transformation into a state of righteousness. This is potentially confusing to the common reader — particularly when in 8:33 the CEB reverts to forensic categories, translating θεὸς ὁ δικαιῶν as "It is God who acquits them." Interestingly, in the translation of Galatians, the CEB consistently opts for "made/make righteous" (see Gal. 2:16-17; 3:8, 11, 24; 5:4). This makes the decision to render δικαιοῦν as "treat as righteous" in the opening chapters of Romans all the more puzzling. It is hard to see what "justification" there is for shifting from one linguistic register to another between Romans 3:28 and 3:30. Here again, it seems that the CEB's handling of this translational issue results in an awkward compromise that may produce more confusion than clarity about the *theological* meaning of justification in Paul.

Any translator of Romans must recognize the great difficulty of these issues, and I suspect there really is no fully adequate solution for rendering these passages into English. But the CEB's particular resolution of the problem does leave this reader, at least, with the impression that a residual theological preference for the substitutionary "forensic fiction" interpretation of justification seems to have overdetermined its translation, particularly in Romans 3:20-28.

God, but all are justified freely by his grace through the redemption accomplished in Christ Jesus." This rendering leaves open the possibility of interpreting ἀπολύτρωσις in the more general sense of "release" or "deliverance," without tying it so closely to the imagery of the making of a payment for the manumission of a slave. See the discussion of ἀπολύτρωσις in BDAG, 117. With the wisdom of hindsight, I would now prefer the translation "through the deliverance accomplished in Christ Jesus."

How Does an Epistle Mean? Reflections on Translation Strategy

Having examined the treatment of selected major theological issues in the CEB's rendering of Romans, I turn in this final section to some observations and reflections about the strategy, or philosophy, of translation that is embodied in this fresh version of the letter.

The Use of Paraphrase

At a number of points, the CEB's aim of providing a translation that is "relevant" and "readable" results in decisions to employ language that broadly paraphrases the text, seeking to translate it into conceptualities accessible to readers who are unfamiliar with the social and religious categories of the first-century Mediterranean world and of Judaism in that era.[24] For example, "uncleanness" (ἀκαθαρσία) in 1:24 is translated as "moral corruption." Similarly, in 14:20, Paul's declaration that "all things are pure" (καθαρά) becomes "All food is acceptable." Here the categories of purity and impurity, grounded in the prescriptions of the Torah, are transposed into terminology that suggests the issues have to do either with moral/ethical concerns, or simply with social convention ("acceptable"). One could argue that the translation thereby achieves more general applicability for today's readers. But its historical specificity is diminished.

We may make a comparable observation about 9:21, where Paul remarks that a potter may make from one lump of clay "one vessel for honor (εἰς τιμὴν) and another for dishonor (εἰς ἀτιμίαν)." The CEB offers this broad paraphrase: "one pot for special purposes and another for garbage." The contemporary reader will have no trouble understanding this sentence, but the categories of understanding will not be Paul's. The language of honor and dishonor was resonant in the social world of Mediterranean antiquity. Paul evokes honor/shame categories precisely because his metaphor points to issues of prestige and acceptance among different social or ethnic groups. Again, this historical specificity is sacrificed by the CEB's translation.

Occasionally, the penchant for paraphrase results in the importation of conceptualities that differ dramatically from the simple sense of Paul's

24. The descriptions "relevant" and "readable" appear on the back cover of the 2010 paperback edition of the CEB New Testament.

words. A good example is found in 12:16, where Paul writes τὸ αὐτὸ εἰς ἀλλήλους φρονοῦντες. This means, "Come to agreement with one another," or possibly, as in both the NIV and the NRSV, "Live in harmony with one another." It certainly does not mean, however, what the CEB suggests: "Consider everyone as equal." This may be good counsel for the church today, but it is not quite what Paul wrote.

In a few cases, the CEB's Paul lapses into modern psychological jargon. In 5:11, he proclaims that through Christ "we now have *a restored relationship* with God." This paraphrase of τὴν καταλλαγὴν ἐλάβομεν is surprising in view of the fact that in the previous verse the translation has retained "we were reconciled to God" as the rendering of κατηλλάγημεν τῷ θεῷ. Surely, then, the cognate noun "reconciliation" would not be too overwhelming for the CEB's targeted seventh-grade readers. Apparently, however, the readability specialists must have thought so, because in Romans 11:15 the translation skirts the term again: "If their rejection has brought about *a close relationship between God and the world* . . . (καταλλαγὴ κόσμου)." This particular paraphrase strikes me as especially cloying and unnecessary. Much more forceful and theologically rich would be the simpler rendering, "For if their rejection brings the reconciliation of the world. . . ."

The preference for the semantic domain of modern psychology may also explain a few other translation choices made at various points in the letter that weaken Paul's portrayal of the gravity of the human predicament. For example, Adam's transgression (παράπτωμα) in 5:15-18 becomes his "failure." And in 4:25, Paul declares that Jesus our Lord was "handed over because of our *mistakes* (παραπτώματα)."[25]

The most pervasive and egregious case of this psychological paraphrasing, however, occurs in the CEB's systematic avoidance of "flesh" as a translation of Paul's term σάρξ. To be sure, this is a word that demands careful interpretation, for Paul uses it in a sense that goes far beyond literal reference to the skin on our bodies. In many contexts he uses it by metonymy to describe fallen human nature in its state of finitude, mortality, and alienation from God. It is nearly impossible to find a term in common modern English usage that conveys the connotative range of "flesh" in Paul's theological lexicon. Perhaps it is unwise even to try to find a para-

---

25. I would also take note of the CEB's rendering of Rom. 5:3, where ἀλλὰ καὶ καυχώμεθα ἐν ταῖς θλίψεσιν comes out as "We even take pride in our problems." Given the frequent use of θλίψις in Jewish apocalyptic texts to describe eschatological affliction, this passage might also have been cited earlier in this essay as an example of CEB's muting of Paul's apocalyptic tone.

phrase. Perhaps it would be better to translate the word that Paul actually uses, and to let its sense be unpacked contextually by readers of the letter.

The CEB's solution to this problem, however, is to render σάρξ repeatedly in Romans 7 and 8 as "selfishness" or "self-centered." Indeed, that captures some part of its meaning, but surely a dramatically reduced part. And it leads to a number of unfortunate translations. In Romans 8:3 we are told that the Law did not have the power to liberate us from sin and death, "since it was weak because of selfishness." Was that the whole problem? Again, in Romans 8:8 we are admonished, "People who are self-centered aren't able to please God." But then in the following sentence we are reassured: "But you aren't self-centered." Not only is this paraphrasing translation reductive, it also makes Paul sound like an elementary school teacher admonishing his class to be well-behaved and take turns with their classmates on the playground.

In the very same section of Romans, however, there are other sentences in which it would be nonsensical to translate σάρξ as "selfishness." In these cases the CEB adopts the even more catastrophic expedient of translating the term as "body." So we hear Paul saying, "I know that good doesn't live in me — that is, in my body" (7:18). And so, he is "a slave to sin's law in my body" (7:25). These translations fall into line with a long tradition of ascetic dualism in Christianity that locates the human predicament in the very fact of our embodied existence. But deprecation of the physical body is certainly *not* what Paul is talking about in Romans 7. He is, rather, deploring the way in which, apart from the transforming grace of Christ and the power of the Spirit, the human condition is enmeshed in a state of powerlessness and contradictory impulses.

The CEB has created this quagmire of anthropological confusion because its editors felt compelled to find some sort of circumlocution to paraphrase the term "flesh." I am suggesting that this strategy of translation is fundamentally mistaken, and that it inevitably leads to the sort of unfortunate theological outcomes I have sketched here. The simple and metaphorically potent image of "flesh" does literary and theological work that no paraphrase can adequately represent.

Stylistic Reductiveness

My foregoing comments addressed passages where the CEB's attempt to use paraphrase to update the language of Romans results in an actual reduction or distortion of Paul's message. I turn now to consider a few examples that may at first appear to concern matters of aesthetic taste rather than weighty theological import. But I want to suggest that style and substance cannot finally be separated. In seeking to simplify the rhetoric of Romans, the CEB has entered inevitably into a certain set of tradeoffs, perhaps gaining a reader-friendly directness that makes the letter accessible to readers who would otherwise not make the effort to understand it. In the bargain, however, something may also be lost. In the final paragraphs of this essay, I shall attempt to gesture towards what that "something" might be.

One of the most striking things about the CEB's version of Romans is its lack of internal discursive connectivity. The translation has severely reduced the numerous linking conjunctions, particles, and adverbs that Paul employs to join his clauses and sentences together. The conjunction γάρ, which appears well over a hundred times in the letter, has been banished to near-oblivion. Where Paul links clauses logically to one another with γάρ, the CEB generally places a full stop and starts a new sentence with no conjunction of any kind. Many dependent clauses and participial phrases receive the same treatment: they are broken off from the complex sentences in which they occur and converted into freestanding sentences. The result is a choppy series of short sentences that can be read more or less as sound bites, disconnected from one another. Thus, the translation reflects a diminished sense of the argument's complex continuity, as well as the way in which some of its statements are logically subordinate to or dependent upon others.

The subjunctive mood is similarly relegated to a minor speaking part in this translation. The use of the subjunctive has long receded in popular American speech. But there are instances in which it plays a necessary role; in a few cases, the sense of Paul's statements is lost through the CEB's submersion of the subjunctive. I offer two examples to illustrate the problem. First, in Romans 6:4, the CEB states that "we were buried together with him through baptism into his death, so that just as Christ was raised from the dead . . . , we too can walk in newness of life." Here the words "*can* walk" translate the aorist subjunctive verb περιπατήσωμεν. A better translation would be "might walk." By abandoning the subjunctive, the CEB converts a statement about purpose or possibility into an affirmation of power actually possessed now by Christians. Second, there is a parallel instance in 7:4, where Paul's purpose clause (ἵνα καρποφορήσωμεν τῷ θεῷ) is apparently changed by the CEB into a result clause celebrating what we actually *can* do: "You are united with the one who was raised from the dead *so that we can* bear fruit for God." "Yes we can" may be a good political slogan, but it falls short of conveying the logical nuance of Paul's writing in these cases.

Another feature of the CEB is its strong preference for constructing sentences in a word order that follows a predictable sequence of subject-verb-predicate, and for placing the independent clause of a complex sentence first, even where this entails reversing Paul's word order. So, for example, "through the Law comes knowledge of sin" is revised into "the knowledge of sin comes through the Law" (3:20). "Apart from Law, Sin is dead" is squeezed into the same format: "Sin is dead without the Law" (7:8). I have selected short sentences here to illustrate the translational technique, but the same thing is done on a larger scale in longer sentences (see, for example, 5:18-19). The result is a monotony of sentence rhythm that diminishes the artful impact of Paul's prose and sometimes subtly shifts the emphasis, which characteristically falls on the end of a sentence. By ending his short sentence with the word νεκρά in 7:8, Paul increases its impact. Recasting the sentence order changes the effect. This is even more striking in 3:20: "Through the Law comes. . . ." The devout Jewish reader, shaped by texts like Psalm 19:7-11, would expect the sentence to conclude with something like "life" or "righteousness." So when Paul concludes with ". . . knowledge of sin," the rhetorical effect is one of reversal, a figurative slap in the face. This effect is lost in a plodding, information-conveying translation that says "the knowledge of sin comes through the Law."

Perhaps the clearest example of this sort of deadening rhetorical anticlimax in the CEB's Romans is to be found at the end of chapter 8, one of the most sweeping and eloquent passages Paul ever composed. Here is what Paul wrote:

> For I am persuaded that neither death nor life, neither angels nor rulers, neither things present nor things to come, neither powers nor height nor depth, nor any other created being, can separate us from the love of God in Christ Jesus our Lord. (8:38-39)

And here is the CEB's allegedly more readable version, with subject and verb primly placed at the beginning of the sentence:

> I'm convinced that nothing can separate us from God's love in Christ Jesus our Lord: not death or life, not angels or rulers, not present things or future things, not powers or height or depth, or any other thing that is created.

Paul's sentence gathers and swells to a powerful climax that leaves "the love of God in Christ Jesus our Lord" ringing in the ears of the hearer or reader. The CEB's rendering trails off into a list that ends with the equivalent of "etc." This illustrates the way in which something terribly important can be lost in translation, even when the literal sense of the words is accurate.

In sum, with reluctance, I must judge the CEB's inflection of Romans to be disappointing. In the effort to achieve readability, it has not only sacrificed Paul's stylistic elegance but also subtly obscured the letter's theological coherence on key points. It has domesticated Paul's gospel by muting its apocalyptic notes, dulling its sharp emphasis on the priority of God's action in Christ to effect the justification of humanity, and reducing its rhetorical grandeur to a casual, plodding discourse. In this essay, I have attempted to show how these outcomes flow from a certain set of translational strategies and priorities that have unfortunate theological consequences. My critique is intended not just as a complaint that the translation Beverly and I developed was so largely painted over by the editorial board of the CEB; rather, it is intended as a contribution to the ongoing task of helping the church read Scripture more closely and faithfully. It has been an honor and pleasure to share in that task with Beverly Roberts Gaventa over many years. I look forward to her commentary on Romans, which will no doubt rectify our understanding in many ways and, in the spirit of Romans 1:11-12, enable the whole church to be mutually encouraged and strengthened — not just by our common wisdom, but by the power and faithfulness of God.

Is Paul a Covenantal Theologian?

Francis Watson

How might Paul or anyone else be understood as a *covenantal* theologian? What type of theology does the term "covenantal" represent, and how might it be differentiated from other kinds of theology?

These questions are concerned with the *concept* of "covenant" rather than with word usage.[1] Whether or not the word "covenant" is used, a covenantal theology is one that *(a)* differentiates Israel from the nations on the basis of its election by God; *(b)* understands certain scripturally attested events as foundational for the ongoing covenantal relationship; *(c)* emphasizes the continuity within that relationship, as this relationship is grounded in divine faithfulness; and *(d)* views this salvation-historical continuum as the comprehensive context of theological reflection. Thus a theology would *not* be "covenantal" in this sense if it *(a)* focused primarily on the individual rather than the elect community; *(b)* gave no special prominence to events such as the call of Abraham, the exodus from Egypt, or the revelation at Sinai over other scripturally narrated events; *(c)* emphasized the discontinuities created by human sinfulness, resulting perhaps in a divine redefinition of the covenant and its scope; *or (d)* viewed

---

1. As E. P. Sanders argues, "a firm belief in a covenant between God and Israel" can be presupposed even where the word itself is absent (*Paul and Palestinian Judaism: A Comparison of Patterns of Religion* [London: SCM, 1977], p. 82).

Unlike other essays in this volume, this one was actually commissioned by Beverly Roberts Gaventa, in her role as co-chair of the Theology of Romans and Galatians seminar of the SNTS, for presentation at the society's Vienna meeting in 2009. I am grateful to Beverly for the opportunity to prepare it, and I hope that its return in the present context will not be unwelcome to her.

covenantal salvation-history as one among a number of possible themes for theological reflection.

On this understanding of the covenant concept, the theology of Philo of Alexandria, for example, would not qualify as covenantal. In Philo's writings as a whole, the primary orientation is towards the individual in his or her relation to God, rather than towards the community. Thus Philo is more interested in the individual histories of Genesis than in the communal history of Exodus through Deuteronomy; and, within Genesis, he is as interested in the so-called "primeval history" of Genesis 1–11 as he is in the patriarchal narratives. While there are of course covenantal elements in his work, Philo practices an interpretation of Scripture in which major hermeneutical roles are assigned to other concepts. Evidently one can be a scriptural theologian without necessarily being a covenantal one. The question is whether this applies equally to Paul.

The assumption that Paul is a covenantal theologian has become widespread in the Pauline scholarship of the past few decades, especially in English-language contexts.[2] The aim is to show that — in spite of disagreement over the role of the Torah — Paul inhabits essentially the same covenantal frame of reference as most of his Jewish contemporaries. Almost all Jews, Paul included, are said to be committed to the divine election of Israel as the absolute, nonnegotiable foundation of God's relationship to the world, even if — as Paul believes — the covenant has been extended in Christ to embrace Gentiles as well as Jews. Paul is unusual in failing to promote covenantal *nomism,* but he remains a covenantal theologian. For him, the election of Israel is axiomatic and foundational. The *locus classicus* for this reading of Paul is Romans 11, seen now as the goal towards which the

---

2. Thus, according to N. T. Wright, Pauline theology is based on "the story of the covenant," which "reached its climax" in Christ (*The Climax of the Covenant: Christ and the Law in Pauline Theology* [Edinburgh: T. & T. Clark, 1991], p. 258). Paul provides a radical answer to the question posed by his Jewish contemporaries, "[H]ow is God fulfilling the covenant?" (p. 259). According to J. D. G. Dunn, "God's righteousness is . . . God's covenant faithfulness, his saving power and love for his people Israel," and justification is "God's acknowledgement that someone is in the covenant" ("The New Perspective on Paul" [1983], repr. in *The New Perspective on Paul,* WUNT 185 [Tübingen: Mohr Siebeck, 2005], p. 107). North American Pauline scholars are less likely to give special prominence to the term "covenant," but are at least equally concerned to show that the election of the Jewish people is fundamental for Paul; see, for example, Lloyd Gaston, *Paul and the Torah* (Vancouver: University of British Columbia, 1987); Mark D. Nanos, *The Mystery of Romans: The Jewish Context of Paul's Letter* (Minneapolis: Fortress, 1996); John G. Gager, *Reinventing Paul* (New York: Oxford University Press, 2000).

entire argument of his last and greatest letter is directed. While an earlier Pauline theology viewed the argument of Romans as grounded in the initial affirmation of "righteousness by faith," this more recent account sees the argument as moving towards the affirmation that all Israel will be saved (alongside the Gentiles) on the basis of the irrevocable divine promise to the patriarchs.[3] On this view, the single argument of Romans is determined not so much by its starting point as by its goal: the entire letter is to be read from the standpoint that finally comes to light in Romans 11. The purpose of the Pauline Gentile mission is not only the salvation of Gentiles but also the salvation of Israel; the apparent deviation from the covenant is in fact a detour whose goal is precisely the covenant's triumphant fulfillment. According to this interpretation, Paul himself emerges as a covenantal theologian, one for whom God's covenant with Israel is the most fundamental and comprehensive of all theological categories.

An alternative would be to see Paul as a *scriptural theologian* — placing equal emphasis on both of those terms in order to make it clear that God (θεός) is fundamental to Pauline discourse (λόγος), but also that his discourse about God is itself shaped by earlier prophetic texts in which God heralds his own powerful interventions on behalf of humankind (cf. Rom. 1:1-2).[4] While the covenant too is attested in Scripture, a covenant-centered reading of Scripture is only one interpretative possibility among many. It is characteristic of Pauline scriptural interpretation that the covenantal distinction between Israel and the nations is both acknowledged and transcended. Also characteristic is an understanding of Scripture as divine discourse containing first-person announcements and disclosures of imminent divine acts of judgment and mercy — judgment

---

3. Krister Stendahl has been followed by many in his claim that "the real center of gravity" in Romans is to be found in chapters 9–11 (*Paul among Jews and Gentiles* [Philadelphia: Fortress, 1976], p. 28).

4. For a detailed demonstration that Paul genuinely engages with Scripture, and does not merely use it to confirm views he holds anyway, see my *Paul and the Hermeneutics of Faith* (London & New York: T. & T. Clark, 2004) and, more briefly, "Scripture in Pauline Theology: How Far Down Does It Go?" *JTI* 2 (2008): 181-92. Since Paul's engagement is not with a text as such but with the God of whom the text speaks and who speaks in and through the text, my own scriptural emphasis is fully compatible with the theocentric, "apocalyptic" reading of Paul developed especially by J. Louis Martyn in his outstanding commentary on Galatians (*Galatians: A New Translation with Introduction and Commentary*, AB 33A [New York: Doubleday, 1997]). Martyn's insights will surely bear further fruit in Beverly Roberts Gaventa's commentary on Romans, the completion and publication of which I and many others eagerly await.

with a view to mercy. For Paul, God's action is anticipated, accompanied, and succeeded by God's scriptural *self*-interpretation. The apostle and his readers are themselves drawn into this inclusive revelatory dynamic.[5]

Scripture versus Covenant

Romans 9 opens with an unexplained juxtaposition. Paul emphasizes the "great grief and incessant pain" that he experiences (vv. 1-2) and reports his willingness to forfeit his own salvation for the sake of fellow Jews (v. 3). Instead of explaining why these fellow Jews cause him such intense grief, Paul proceeds to list their privileges: "They are Israelites, and theirs are the sonship and the glory and the covenants and the giving of the law and the worship and the promises . . ." (v. 4). Paul's unexplained grief must reflect his fear that fellow Israelites will not finally benefit from their privileged status, on account of their rejection of the gospel. Only at the end of the chapter is explicit reference made to this, by way of a composite Isaianic citation in which the "stone" established by God "in Zion" is the occasion of faith and salvation for some but of "stumbling" for others (vv. 32-33). At the outset, Paul can take it for granted that his readers will understand *why* he might be distressed on account of his fellow Israelites, emphasizing instead the sheer fact *that* he is distressed — as though his readers needed to be convinced of this.[6]

The privileges that Paul lists include "the covenants" as one among a number of items. The plural αἱ διαθῆκαι refers to particular occasions on which, according to Scripture, God made a covenant with the patriarchs or with the people of Israel as a whole (cf. Gen. 15:18; 17:2; Exod. 19:5; 24:7-8; 34:10, 27-28; Deut. 5:2; 28:69 [LXX]).[7] In another sense, the whole list of privileges can be described as "covenantal." The privileges are said to belong specifically to "Israelites": οἵτινές εἰσιν Ἰσραηλῖται, ὧν ἡ υἱοθεσία,

---

5. If divine acts are always also *speech*-acts, communicative in intent, then it is a mistake to highlight the apocalyptic nature of divine saving agency at the expense of Paul's engagement with Scripture, viewing the latter as occasioned merely by the polemical needs of the moment; for egregious examples of this tendency, see Douglas A. Campbell, *The Deliverance of God: An Apocalyptic Rereading of Justification in Paul* (Grand Rapids: Eerdmans, 2009).

6. On this point, see Leander E. Keck, *Romans,* ANTC (Nashville: Abingdon, 2005), pp. 224-25.

7. A plurality of covenants is recognized in Sir. 44:12, 18; Wis. 18:22; 2 Macc. 8:15 (so Ulrich Wilckens, *Der Brief an die Römer,* EKKNT, 3 vols. [Zurich/Neukirchen: Benziger, 1978-82], 2:188).

κτλ (Rom. 9:4). "Israelites" are the scriptural "children of Israel," who assume this identity as their God leads them out of Egypt, in fulfillment of the covenant made with their fathers (cf. Exod. 2:24; 6:4-5), and enters into covenant with them at Sinai (cf. Exod. 19:5; 24:3-8). To be an Israelite is to be a member of "the covenant," an addressee of the divine promise that "I shall be your God and you shall be my people" (Lev. 26:12). The privileges Paul lists are covenantal, and they are all rooted in Scripture. They presuppose a covenantal reading of Scripture. And it is precisely such a reading of Scripture that underlies the grief and distress that Paul reports. It would seem that the covenantal relationship is somehow in jeopardy.

It is remarkable, then, that the initial resolution of this crisis of the covenant takes the form of an appeal to the word of God: "It is not that the word of God [ὁ λόγος τοῦ θεοῦ] has failed, for not all who are of Israel are Israel" (Rom. 9:6). The word of God is the scriptural word that redefines the elect community as called "not only from Jews but also from Gentiles" (v. 24), although containing only "a remnant" of "the children of Israel" (v. 27). This "remnant" will later be compared with the seven thousand in Israel who did not bow the knee to Baal in the time of Elijah (11:4). It represents the moment of continuity within the great reversal in which the rest of Israel changes places with those called from among the Gentiles. The word of God is a word that addresses those who were not God's people as "my people," while it is a "word that concludes and cuts short" (λόγον συντελῶν καὶ συντέμνων [9:28]) for the majority of the "children of Israel." The word of God is thus a single divine word of mercy for some and judgment for others. This λόγος τοῦ θεοῦ is singular, in the sense that it represents a single divine electing purpose, but it is also plural, in the sense that it is instantiated in each of the scriptural passages from Genesis, Exodus, and the Prophets that make up the argument of Romans 9.[8] Thus these passages are mostly divine utterances, often in the first person singular. The first six of these are arranged in pairs (italics = Paul's citations in Romans 9):

(1a) And God said to Abraham, "Let there be no difficulty in the matter concerning the boy and the slave-girl, and obey Sarah's

8. This connection between "the word of God" and Paul's citations is preferable to generalizing interpretations for which the word of God is simply the promise (Ernst Käsemann, *Commentary on Romans,* trans. Geoffrey W. Bromiley [Grand Rapids: Eerdmans, 1980], p. 261), or "das Israel angehende und als 'Israel' begründende Wort im umfassenden Sinn" (Heinrich Schlier, *Der Römerbrief,* HTKNT 6 [Freiburg, Basel, and Wien: Herder, 1979], p. 290).

voice in everything she says to you, for *in Isaac shall your seed be called*" (Gen. 21:12 LXX; cf. Rom. 9:7).

(1b)   And he said to him, "Where is Sarah your wife?" He answering said, "Behold, in the tent." And he said: "Returning *I shall come to you at this time* for an hour, and Sarah your wife will bear a son. . . ." And the Lord said to Abraham, "Why did Sarah laugh in herself, saying, 'Shall I really bear a child, when I am old?' Is anything impossible for the Lord? At this time I shall return to you for an hour, *and Sarah shall have a son*" (Gen. 18:9-14; cf. Rom. 9:9).

(2a)   . . . And [Rebekah] went to enquire of the Lord, and the Lord said to her: "Two nations are in your womb, and two peoples from your belly will be separated. And one people will surpass the other, and *the greater will serve the lesser*" (Gen. 25:22-23; cf. Rom. 9:12).

(2b)   "I have loved you," says the Lord, and you say: "How have you loved us?" "Was not Esau Jacob's brother?" says the Lord. "And *I loved Jacob, and I hated Esau,* and I destroyed his hill country . . ." (Mal. 1:2-3; cf. Rom. 9:13).

(3a)   And [Moses] said: "Show me your own glory." And he said: "I will pass before you in my glory, and I will proclaim my name, 'Lord,' before you; and *I will have mercy on whom I have mercy, and I will show compassion to whom I show compassion.*" And he said: "You cannot see my face . . ." (Exod. 33:18-20; cf. Rom. 9:15).

(3b)   And the Lord said to Moses, "Rise up early and stand before Pharaoh and you shall say to him: 'Thus says the Lord God of the Hebrews: "Send forth my people, so that they may worship me. . . . For now, putting forth my hand, I shall smite you and your people with death, and you will be destroyed from the earth. And *for this reason* you were preserved, *so that I may reveal in you my* strength, *and so that my name may be proclaimed in all the earth*"'" (Exod. 9:13-16; cf. Rom. 9:17).

By selecting these passages and arranging them in pairs, Paul demonstrates a scriptural pattern in which one is chosen *at the expense of another.*[9] That is true also of the third pair, from which Paul draws the con-

9. According to E. Elizabeth Johnson, Romans 9 is concerned to show only that "God's redemptive word of election . . . has not collapsed with the inclusion of Gentiles because that

clusions that "it is not a matter of human willing or effort but of the God who has mercy," and that "he has mercy on whom he wills and hardens whom he wills" (Rom. 9:16, 18). The scriptural pattern is a typological fore-shadowing of the great reversal — more clearly announced in the Prophets — in which Gentiles who were "not my people" are called to be "my people," while "the children of Israel" are reduced to an elect remnant (9:25-29). Just as the divine mercy is grounded exclusively in God's will and is in no way responsive to any prior human initiative, so it is with the divine hardening. Isaac, Jacob, and Moses are "vessels of mercy" because the divine potter created them to be so, not in recognition of some special merit that precedes the divine electing purpose (cf. 9:23). The divine electing purpose has its ground *within* God and not *outside of* God. Again, Ishmael, Esau, and Pharaoh are "vessels of wrath" because that was what the divine potter willed them to be, not because there was anything inherently reprehensible about them. God hardens whom he wills; for Paul, God's hardening is *not* a divine confirmation of its objects' prior decision to oppose God, for the hardening of some is the logically necessary corollary of the free election of others.[10] In rejecting the majority of the children of Israel and in calling Gentiles, God does not recognize in Gentiles some quality that makes them the fit objects of his mercy, or in Jews some quality that makes them the fit objects of his wrath. On the contrary, the Gentiles who attained righteousness or salvation "did not pursue righteousness," unlike Israel, which practiced a law observance that displayed a genuine zeal for God (cf. 9:30-31; 10:2). If God's election rested on prior human merit, then the covenant with Israel would proceed in unbroken continuity. But since God's election is in reality grounded in the divine will and enacted in the divine word, there is nothing to hinder the divine turning towards the Gentiles.

Two additional points may be noted in passing. First, Paul's argument is totally at odds with what was to become the standard argument of Christian supersessionism, according to which God's rejection of Israel

---

inclusion has been accomplished on precisely the same terms as God's call of Israel" ("Romans 9–11: The Faithfulness and Impartiality of God," in *Pauline Theology*, vol. 3: *Romans*, ed. David M. Hay and E. Elizabeth Johnson [Minneapolis: Fortress, 1995], p. 227). That is to overlook the antithetical structuring that runs throughout the chapter.

10. In the context of Romans 9, mercy and hardening represent interrelated but mutually exclusive divine actions and are not "expressions of the same merciful will," as C. E. B. Cranfield argues (*Romans*, ICC, 2 vols. [Edinburgh: T. & T. Clark, 1975-79], 2:488). It is a mistake to read the conclusion of the argument (Rom. 11:30-32) back into this passage.

and turn to the Gentiles was occasioned by Israel's long history of rebellion against God, culminating in the murder of the Messiah. Second, Paul is also at odds here with other contemporary readers of Genesis, for whom it was important to supply Jacob with virtues and Esau with vices so as to establish a basis for the election of some at the expense of others.[11] For such readers, the Genesis narrative — which says little or nothing about any such virtues or vices — must be supplemented in order to show that God elects those worthy to be elected and rejects those who deserve to be rejected. For Paul, the Genesis narrative needs no such supplementation.

In Romans 9 as a whole, the logic of the free divine word of election and rejection eclipses the logic of the divine covenant with Israel. The covenantal logic is evident both in the listing of Israel's divinely given privileges (vv. 4-5) and in the corresponding practice of zealous law observance (v. 31). One might assume that covenant and Scripture are inseparable and that an anti-covenantal argument would also have to oppose Scripture to some degree — for example, by rejecting Scripture's "literal" sense while claiming to endorse a "spiritual" sense. But what actually takes place in Romans 9 is precisely the reverse of this. It is in Scripture that God announces his self-grounded electing purpose, thereby preparing and legitimating the reversal of the covenantal differentiation between Israel and the Gentiles, as the elect and the nonelect change places. The author of this remarkable argument shows himself to be a scriptural theologian rather than a covenantal one.

That Romans 9–10 constitutes a single, scripturally based argument is evident from the single scriptural sequence that runs through these chapters, from Genesis into Exodus and from the beginning to the end of the book of Isaiah.[12] The Isaianic sequence is interspersed with related prophetic material from the Book of the Twelve, Psalms, and Deuteronomy:

Hos. 2:23: "I will call . . ." (Rom. 9:25-26)
Isa. 10:22-23: "If the number of the children of Israel . . ." (Rom. 9:27-28)
Isa. 1:9: "If the Lord of hosts . . ." (Rom. 9:29)
Isa. 28:16; 8:14: "Behold, I lay in Zion . . ." (Rom. 9:33; cf. 10:11)

11. See John C. Endres, *Biblical Interpretation in the Book of Jubilees*, CBQMS 18 (Washington, DC: Catholic Biblical Association of America, 1987), pp. 22-24; Neil Richardson, *Paul's Language about God*, JSNTSup 99 (Sheffield: Sheffield Academic Press, 1994), pp. 44-52.

12. See my *Paul, Judaism, and the Gentiles: Beyond the New Perspective*, 2nd ed. (Grand Rapids: Eerdmans, 2007), pp. 301-33.

Joel 2:32: "Everyone who calls upon the name . . ." (Rom. 10:13)
Isa. 52:7: "How beautiful are the feet . . ." (Rom. 10:15)
Isa. 53:1: "Lord, who has believed . . . ?" (Rom. 10:16)
Ps. 19:4: "Their sound has gone out . . ." (Rom. 10:18)
Deut. 32:21: "I will make you jealous . . ." (Rom. 10:19)
Isa. 65:1, 2: "I was found . . ." (Rom. 10:20-21)

The single Isaianic sequence indicates there is no reason to find a sharp break in the argument at Romans 9:30 or 10:1. Paul actually notes the one deviation from the scriptural sequence in his reference to what "Isaiah had said before [προείρηκεν]," i.e., in an earlier chapter (Rom. 9:29).[13]

Paul's Isaianic material initially provides general confirmation for his claim that "the children of Israel" have been reduced to a remnant in the turning of God's electing purpose towards the Gentiles; subsequently, it is employed to articulate the concrete content of that turn in its negative and positive aspects. Both negative and positive are conflated in Paul's composite citation from Isaiah 28:16 and 8:14:

Behold, I place in Zion a stone of stumbling [λίθον προσκόμματος] and a rock of offense [πέτραν σκανδάλου], and the one who believes in it/ him [ὁ πιστεύων ἐπ' αὐτῷ] will not be put to shame. (Rom. 9:33)

While the first part of this citation deviates significantly from septuagintal wording, the second part corresponds closely:

Therefore hear the word of the Lord, O men who are in distress and rulers of this people in Jerusalem. Because you say, "We have made a covenant with Hades and an agreement with Death, that the driven storm — if it comes — will not fall upon us; we have made a lie our hope and in falsehood we shall be sheltered," therefore thus says the Lord, "*Behold, I* set down *in* the foundations of *Zion a stone* precious and select, a valuable cornerstone in her foundations, *and the one who believes in it will not be put to shame.*" (Isa. 28:14-16 LXX)

---

13. Citations of Isa. 10:22-23; 1:9; 53:1; 65:1-2 are introduced with references to the prophet's own speaking; citations of Isa. 28:16 and 52:7 are introduced with the conventional formula, καθὼς γέγραπται. Since the two types of introduction are evidently interchangeable, Richard Hays's distinction between Scripture as "inscribed text" and as "living word" seems questionable (*Echoes of Scripture in the Letters of Paul* [New Haven: Yale University Press, 1989], p. 168).

Sanctify the Lord himself, and he shall be your fear. And if you trust in him, he will be to you a sanctuary, and not as *a stone* for *stumbling* [λίθου προσκόμματι] shall you encounter him, nor as *a rock* for tripping [πέτρας πτώματι]. But the house of Jacob is in a trap, and those who dwell in Jerusalem are in a rut. (Isa. 8:13-14 LXX)

In both passages, the Lord is closely identified with a "stone" set in opposition to those who trust in falsehood.[14] The stone or cornerstone is the true, divinely established basis for security and well-being in the face of the coming storm; but if it is rejected as such, it will cause one to stumble and fall. For Paul, the stone is identified with Christ. In the repetition of the second half of the citation in Romans 10:11, the antecedent of "everyone who believes in *him* . . ." is Jesus, who is to be confessed as Lord and whom God raised from the dead (v. 9). He is the rock on which a new community is founded: "No other foundation can be laid than that which has been laid, that is, Jesus Christ" (1 Cor. 3:11). Yet Christ crucified is a σκάνδαλον to Jews (1 Cor. 1:23), a term that may derive from the πέτρα σκανδάλου of Paul's Isaiah citation. In the context of Romans, it is Israel's covenantal practice of law observance that makes of Christ a stone of stumbling and a rock of offense, leaving it to others to find in him a new and eternally secure foundation for their lives. Thus the content of the divine word of judgment pronounced over Israel (Rom. 9:28) is the rejection of the covenantal practice prescribed by Moses — "works," "the righteousness which is from the law" (9:32; 10:5) — in order to establish in Christ a new foundation for a new people that includes Gentiles. The rejection of Ishmael, Esau, Pharaoh, and all other "vessels of wrath" points not to some dire scene of eschatological judgment but to God's turning away from a community founded on law observance in order to establish a new community on the basis of faith in the crucified and risen Christ.[15] That is the decision announced already in the words of Isaiah; it is here that the concrete content of the decree of "double predestination" finally comes to light.

14. For detailed discussion of Paul's treatment of this Isaianic material, see J. Ross Wagner, *Heralds of the Good News: Isaiah and Paul "in Concert" in the Letter to the Romans,* NovTSup 101 (Leiden: Brill, 2002), pp. 120-57.

15. As Douglas Harink notes, "[T]here is no hint in 9:30–10:3 of 'Israel's failure,' but only of God's purpose of bringing righteousness to the Gentiles being worked out through God's own mysterious hardening and tripping-up of Israel, who remains ignorant of that purpose" (*Paul among the Postliberals: Pauline Theology beyond Christendom and Modernity* [Grand Rapids: Brazos, 2003], pp. 171-72).

Indeed, this double predestination is not only announced but is also *enacted* through the divine utterances recorded in prophetic Scripture. The notion of a hidden decree is irrelevant here. The enactment of the divine decree leaves the people of Israel continuing to observe the law of Moses, exactly as before. There are no visible signs of divine displeasure. It is simply that a new community has come into being, including many Gentiles, which finds the key to the Scriptures not in covenantal practice but in the risen Christ, and which will henceforth coexist with the synagogue as a radical and unwelcome alternative. Law-observant Israel, faithful to the covenant, is rejected in order that a new community should be established in the sphere of those to whom it had previously been said: "You are not my people" (cf. 9:26). The "supersession" of Jews by Gentiles is, more precisely, a reversal of the covenantal differentiation of one people from others. Here, elect and nonelect change places.

The Teleology of Election

God's covenant with Israel is founded on the divine decision that "you shall be my people," a decision that also constitutes others as "not my people." Paul argues on scriptural grounds that the divine decision has now been reversed, and the scriptural grounding indicates that this reversal does not reflect a sudden change of heart but was intended from the very beginning. In the covenant, an order is established in which one takes precedence over another; and yet, as Scripture discloses, God's electing purpose is actually that "the greater will serve the lesser" (Rom. 9:12). Israel is subordinated to the Gentiles, and the subordination occurs *for the sake of* the Gentiles. So long as Israel continues to benefit from covenantal privileges and displays a corresponding covenantal practice in the form of law observance, Gentiles remain permanently excluded. Under the terms of the covenant, the division of humanity into "my people" and "not my people" is a rigidly fixed structure. Where its scripturally anticipated reversal is disclosed, however, a more dynamic relationship between the newly excluded and the newly included comes to light. "My people" become "not my people" *in order that* those who were "not my people" should be called to be "my people." The divine decision not to recognize the covenantal practice of Torah as "righteousness" is the necessary precondition for the reconstitution of righteousness on the basis of the crucified and risen Christ, his universal proclamation as such in the gospel, and the "faith" in him that the gospel elicits. The apparent symmetry of Paul's claim that God has mercy on some and hardens others is in reality a *teleology:* God hardens some in order to have mercy on others. Scripture itself makes this unambiguously clear in the case of Pharaoh. God did not harden Pharaoh's heart because Pharaoh was a member of the eternally fixed category of the reprobate, destined for damnation. God or Scripture addresses Pharaoh as follows: "For this purpose I raised you up, *so that* I might reveal my power in you and *so that* my name might be proclaimed in all the earth" (Rom. 9:17; Exod. 9:16). There is an exact analogy here with the messengers of the gospel, of whom it is said: "Their sound has gone out into all the earth, and their words to the ends of the world" (Rom. 10:18; Ps. 18:5). Israel's unbelief leads to the proclamation to the Gentiles and was always intended to do so. The scriptural overturning of the covenant establishes a teleological relationship between rejection and election.[16]

This teleological relationship between rejection and election is repeatedly emphasized in Romans 11:

> I say, therefore, have they stumbled so as to fall? By no means! But by their trespass [τῷ αὐτῶν παραπτώματι] salvation has come to the Gentiles . . . (11:11)

> But if their trespass means riches for the world, and their loss [τὸ ἥττημα αὐτῶν] means riches for the Gentiles . . . (11:12)

> For if their rejection [ἡ ἀποβολὴ αὐτῶν] means the reconciliation of the world . . . (11:15)

---

16. Inability to account for this teleology is one of several crucial weaknesses of the Augustinian-Calvinist reading of Romans 9. According to Calvin, commenting on 9:23, the teleological statement (". . . *so that* he might make known the riches of his glory") teaches "that the infinite mercy of God towards the elect will gain our increasing praise, when we see how wretched are all those who do not escape His wrath" (*The Epistles of Paul to the Romans and Thessalonians,* trans. Ross Mackenzie, Calvin's New Testament Commentaries 8, ed. David W. Torrance and Thomas Forsyth Torrance [Grand Rapids: Eerdmans, 1995], p. 211). As Romans 11 will repeatedly show, however, the teleology has to do with salvation itself and not just its disclosure to its beneficiaries: Israel is cast off *so that* the world should be reconciled (11:15). Contrary to Calvin, Paul in Rom. 9:22-24 and elsewhere speaks not "of a content of God's will which is to be interpreted as an abstract duality, but of God's way on which in execution of his one purpose He wills and executes in a determined sequence and order this twofold operation" (Karl Barth, *Church Dogmatics* II/2: *The Election of the Community,* trans. Geoffrey W. Bromiley et al. [Edinburgh: T. & T. Clark, 1957], p. 225).

But if some of the branches were broken off, and you, a wild olive shoot, were grafted in among them and came to share in the rich root of the olive tree . . . (11:17)

You will say then, "Branches were broken off so that I might be grafted in." That is true. They were broken off because of their unbelief [τῇ ἀπιστίᾳ] . . . (11:19-20)

A partial hardening has come upon Israel until the fullness of the Gentiles enters in . . . (11:25)

As regards the gospel, they are enemies for your sake [δι' ὑμᾶς] . . . (11:28)

For just as you were once disobedient to God but now have received mercy on the grounds of their disobedience [τῇ τούτων ἀπειθείᾳ] . . . (11:30)

In these passages, "trespass" (vv. 11, 12), "loss" (v. 12), and "disobedience" (v. 30) are synonymous with "unbelief" (v. 20), the refusal of the gospel. While it might seem that the divine "rejection" (v. 15) is a contingent response to human unbelief, it is clear from Romans 9–10 that rejection is more the grounds of unbelief than its consequence, that the teleological relationship of rejection and reconciliation is divinely ordained, and that rejection and unbelief are consequent on the divine decision to bind the righteousness intended for humanity to faith in the risen Christ rather than to the practice of Torah. The overturning of the covenantal order by the scriptural and christological one is therefore a presupposition of Romans 11.

In this same chapter, however, covenantal conceptuality reappears as a positive factor for the first time since the listing of covenant privileges in 9:4-5:

If the firstfruit is holy, so is the lump; and if the root is holy, so are the branches. (11:16)

If you were cut from what is by nature [κατὰ φύσιν] a wild olive tree and grafted contrary to nature [παρὰ φύσιν] into a cultivated olive tree, how much more will the natural branches [οὗτοι οἱ κατὰ φύσιν] be grafted back into their own olive tree. (11:24)

As regards the gospel they are enemies for your sake, but as regards election they are beloved because of the fathers. For the gifts and the calling of God are irrevocable. (11:28-29)

In view of the replacement of covenantal logic with that of "the word of God" in Romans 9, these covenantal passages are unexpected. Having previously been identified with figures of rejection (Ishmael, Esau, and Pharaoh), Israel here is reconnected to the elect lineage of Abraham, Isaac, and Jacob. Does the scriptural argumentation of Romans 9–10 finally give way to the renewed covenantal logic of chapter 11, according to which "all Israel will be saved" (v. 26)?[17]

That would be a defensible conclusion, but it would not reach to the heart of Paul's argument. The renewed engagement with the covenant occurs in the context of Paul's concern to establish the coherence and symmetry of God's merciful electing purpose, and to do so on scriptural grounds. Repeatedly in 11:11-15, a teleological relationship between Israel's rejection and Gentile salvation is asserted to draw further conclusions about Israel's restoration:

> I say, therefore, have they stumbled so as to fall? By no means! But by their trespass salvation has come to the Gentiles, so as to make them jealous. But if their trespass means riches for the world, and their loss means riches for the Gentiles, how much more their fullness? I speak now to you who are Gentiles: since I am apostle of the Gentiles, I magnify my ministry, so that I may make my flesh jealous and save some of them. For if their rejection means the reconciliation of the world, what does their inclusion mean but life from the dead? (Rom. 11:11-15)

The double reference to the jealousy motif refers back to the citation in Romans 10:19, drawn from the song of Moses: "I will make you jealous of a non-nation; I will enrage you with a senseless nation" (Deut. 32:21). It is Paul's own ministry as apostle to the Gentiles that provokes this "jealousy" on the part of his fellow Jews, potentially leading some of them to salvation. The teleology that led from Jewish rejection to Gentile salvation is supplemented with a second, wholly positive teleology in which Gentile salvation leads to Jewish salvation — already in part, comprehensively in

---

17. According to Wilckens, the difference between the positions Paul develops in Romans 9 and 11 amounts to "nichts weniger als eine Wende in seinem heilsgeschichtlichen Denken" (*Römer,* 2:185). The discrepancy is all the more striking if one follows Klaus Haacker in tracing in these chapters an orderly progression from "die Anfänge der biblischen Geschichte" (Romans 9) to "die gegenwärtige Haltung Israels gegenüber Gott" (Romans 10) to "[die] Frage nach der Zukunft Israels" (Romans 11) (*Der Brief des Paulus an die Römer,* THKNT 6 [Leipzig: Evangelische Verlagsanstalt, 2006], p. 245).

the future. This is a remarkably positive and expansive interpretation of the scriptural jealousy theme.

Still more significant is Paul's reversion to the themes of divine mercy and hardening, stemming from his Exodus citations in Romans 9:15-18.[18] The divine words addressed to Moses and to Pharaoh show that God "has mercy upon whom he wills and hardens whom he wills" (9:18). When this language returns in chapter 11, however, the suggestion of equivalence has entirely disappeared: divine hardening is subordinated to divine mercy. Israel is hardened, partially and temporarily, until the fullness of the Gentiles has entered in, but thereafter Israel too will be saved. The salvation of all Israel is the fulfillment of the covenant, and yet this occurs within an economy not of covenant privilege but of divine mercy:

> . . . [A]s regards election, they are beloved because of the fathers. For the gifts and the calling of God are irrevocable. For just as you were once disobedient to God but now have received mercy on the grounds of their disobedience, so they have now been disobedient in order that by the mercy shown to you they may receive mercy. For God has consigned all people to disobedience, so that he might have mercy on all. (11:28-32)

What God said to Moses was not that he has mercy on whom he wills and hardens whom he wills. What God said was that he has mercy on whom he wills and compassion on whom he wills. Paul finally concludes from this scriptural text that the divine mercy and compassion are boundless. His renewed concern with the covenant theme is intended to secure Israel's participation in a salvation extended to all.

Postscript

In Romans 11, Paul reverts to the covenantal conceptuality that he has apparently rejected in the scriptural argumentation of chapters 9–10. Yet here too it is Scripture that constitutes the comprehensive framework within which the argument unfolds. Just as Paul's selected scriptural texts bear the weight of the argument about the reversal of the distinction between elect

18. For a fuller discussion of the ongoing biblical interpretation underlying Romans 11, see my *Paul*, pp. 334-43. To the five passages identified on p. 340 as influencing the argument of Romans 11, I would now add a fourth, namely, the citation of Isa. 65:2 in Rom. 10:21. As Keck rightly notes, the Isaianic reference to "God's outstretched hands toward disobedient Israel suggests that ultimately God's posture will not be in vain" (*Romans*, p. 262).

and nonelect, so also the same texts point beyond the reversal towards a future in which the distinction itself will be dissolved. The divine self-determination to be merciful to disobedient humanity, as attested in Scripture, is the basis and context of the covenant itself.

The covenant that distinguishes Israel from the Gentiles plays a limited and subordinate role within Paul's scriptural interpretation. The point is illustrated again by a passage in Romans 15 in which the application of the theological argumentation to the divided Roman Christian community comes to light. In this postscript to Romans 11, the covenantal differentiation is once again reasserted:

> So welcome one another, as Christ welcomed you to the glory of God. For I say that Christ became a servant to the circumcision because of the truthfulness of God, so as to confirm the promises made to the fathers, and so that the Gentiles might glorify God for his mercy. (Rom. 15:7-9a)

Initially, it appears that Christ embodies different things to Jewish and to Gentile believers: for one party he demonstrates that God is true to his covenantal promises, to the other he represents sheer uncovenanted mercy. Yet the differentiation serves, first, to give greater precision to the preceding point about Christ's inclusive welcome and the reciprocal welcome founded on it, and, second, to introduce the three citations that follow, which speak of the unity of Jews with Gentiles and Gentiles with Jews in the common worship of God (vv. 9b-12). If for Jews Christ confirms the promises made to the patriarchs, for Gentiles he fulfills the promise made through Isaiah: "A root shall come from Jesse, and the one who rises to rule the nations — in him shall Gentiles hope" (v. 12, citing Isa. 11:10). In this catena of citations from the Psalms, Deuteronomy, and Isaiah, the covenantal differentiation between Israel and the Gentiles is comprehended within the scriptural testimony to a common calling and a shared worship.

This continued engagement with Scripture is itself the theme of the summary statement in verse 4: "Whatever was written formerly was written for our instruction, so that by patience and the encouragement of the Scriptures we may have hope." This statement summarizes the letter to the Romans.[19] It is Scripture that provides Paul with the language of righ-

---

19. Martin Luther was right to claim that Paul in Romans sought "to prepare an introduction to the whole Old Testament" ("Preface to the Epistle of St. Paul to the Romans," ed. E. Theodore Bachmann, *Luther's Works: Word and Sacrament* 35 [Philadelphia: Fortress, 1960], p. 380).

teousness by faith, explored in the opening chapters, and it is Scripture that defines the context of God's righteousness as universal human guilt before God. On the basis of his key texts from Habakkuk and Genesis, Paul develops a scriptural soteriology in which the divine word of promise or gospel evokes an answering faith in Jews and Gentiles alike, in spite of covenantal differentiation. Later in the letter, Paul strives to show that the reversal of the covenantal categories of elect and nonelect is rooted in Scripture, as is the final transcending of the reversal itself in the disclosure of the universal divine mercy. The letter itself articulates the hope-filled instruction and encouragement that is Scripture's rationale.

Sin's Corruption of the Knowledge of God and the Law in Romans 1–8

Shane Berg

It has been my distinct honor to have been both a student in Beverly Gaventa's classes and her faculty colleague at Princeton Theological Seminary. In the spring semester of 1999, I enrolled in her Greek exegesis of Acts class and was spellbound by her clear and persuasive argument that divine agency played a central role in the narrative. Serving on the faculty with her, I had the opportunity to learn from Beverly's insights as she explored the theme of divine agency in Paul's letters in publications, in lectures, and, most dear to me, in our private conversations. Her typically lucid accounts of the complex relationship between divine and human agency in the New Testament, and especially in the Pauline Letters, have taught me a great deal and influenced my own work in my area of research, religious epistemology. This essay on religious epistemology in Romans is informed and inspired by her work and intended as a complement to it. It is a privilege to offer it as a modest token of my appreciation, admiration, and affection for her.

Like many of their Second Temple Jewish counterparts, the authors of the New Testament are deeply invested in questions of divine revelation and its function in the lives of individuals and communities. How is knowledge of God possible? How does God impart knowledge to human recipients? Is knowledge of God or from God universally available or restricted to particular communities or individuals? These kinds of questions achieve prominence in many Jewish circles in the Hellenistic and Roman periods.

Among New Testament writers, Paul in particular gives considerable attention to matters of religious epistemology.[1] In 1 Corinthians 2:6-16, for

---

1. For a comprehensive attempt to examine Paul's epistemology, see Ian W. Scott, *Paul's Way of Knowing: Story, Experience, and the Spirit* (Grand Rapids: Baker Academic, 2009). For

example, he offers what amounts to a mini-treatise on the logic and means of divine revelation. He explains that the mystery of Christ's death is comprehensible in the community of faith because of the presence and revelatory action of God's Spirit among its members. To those outside the church, Christ's death is an impenetrable event whose nature and significance cannot be grasped. Paul's religious epistemology as articulated in this passage contains a robust notion of divine agency — God's work in the Holy Spirit is necessary for a right knowledge of God's work in Christ.

While he emphasizes the role of divine agency in revelation in 1 Corinthians 2:6-16, in Romans 1–8 Paul explores the flip side of this coin — the tragic failure of human knowledge when it does not have the benefit of divine revelatory agency. He shows that merely human knowledge of God and of the law fails to lead to worshiping and obeying God. Instead, Paul contends, such knowledge leads to idolatry and other sinful acts.

The goal of this essay is to explore Paul's treatment of human knowledge of God and of the law in Romans 1–8, although a brief foray into 1 Corinthians 2 will be undertaken to illuminate some of the dark corners of Paul's argument in Romans. This study will attempt to demonstrate that Paul's account of human knowing is a function of his apocalyptic worldview. In Romans, Paul presents a cosmic conflict between God and hostile powers in which human beings are inextricably bound up. Ernst Käsemann, arguing that for Paul human nature and identity are so constituted by this dramatic struggle in the cosmos that it is impossible to speak of "the human" in Paul apart from it, famously wrote that "[a]nthropology is cosmology *in concreto*."[2] The truth of Käsemann's dictum is borne out by studying Paul's understanding in Romans of what human beings can know and what results from that knowledge, which in every case is closely linked to what is happening in the cosmic battle between God and the forces arrayed against God. That Paul's religious epistemology is intricately bound up with questions of theological anthropology, cosmology, and extra-human agency locates him comfortably within discourses about knowledge that can be found in other Second Temple apocalyptic Jewish groups.[3]

---

an important and more succinct discussion, see J. Louis Martyn, *Theological Issues in the Letters of Paul* (Nashville: Abingdon, 1997), pp. 89-110.

2. "On Paul's Anthropology," in *Perspectives on Paul,* trans. Margaret Kohl (London: SCM, 1971), p. 27.

3. The list of scholars who regard Paul's apocalyptic convictions as central to his theology is growing rapidly. Of particular influence for this study are the works of J. Louis Martyn and Beverly Roberts Gaventa; see references to their work *passim.*

The Failure of the Knowledge of God and of the Law in Romans

In Romans 1–8, Paul's ambitious theological agenda includes a pair of surprising claims about the failure of human knowledge of God or God's law to bear its proper fruit in the life of the knower. Paul readily concedes that it is possible for the human being to have some knowledge of God's being and nature and to comprehend the law. What Paul denies, however, is that such knowledge leads to the appropriate corresponding action in the life of the knower. Instead of worship and obedience, human knowledge of God and the law inevitably, for Paul, leads to the opposite of these intended results — idolatry and sinful acts.

Romans 1:18-32: The Failure of the Knowledge of God

As has been widely recognized, the way that Paul traces the rise of idolatry among human beings in Romans 1:18-32 is indebted to stock ways in Jewish literature of portraying Gentile idolatry. The account given in Wisdom of Solomon 13:1-9 is quite similar, in fact, in details and sequence to Paul's description in 1:18-32. Despite this similarity, however, Paul's version of the rise of idolatry is distinctly cast to make a particular point about human knowing and knowledge within his larger argument in Romans 1–3. Although Gentiles are clearly foregrounded here, an examination of Paul's overall religious epistemology in Romans 1–8 demonstrates that his assertions in Romans 1:18-32 apply universally to all human beings.[4]

The passage opens with the assertion that God's wrath is "revealed" against all human impiety and unrighteousness (1:18).[5] God's wrath is

---

4. See my section "Putting It All Together," below, for the argument for this point.

5. The verb ἀποκαλύπτεται here in 1:18 repeats the same verb that occurs in the immediately preceding verse (1:17), where Paul proclaims that God's righteousness is "revealed" in the gospel. In an important essay, Simon Gathercole takes a cue from this revelatory language to examine how sin relates to God's revelatory purposes in Romans ("Sin in God's Economy: Agencies in Romans 1 and 7," in *Divine and Human Agency in Paul and His Cultural Environment*, ed. John M. G. Barclay and Simon J. Gathercole [London: T. & T. Clark, 2008], pp. 158-72). He argues that Paul's accounts of sin in Romans 1 and 7 "both function as means of divine revelation, and therefore play a crucial role in God's economy" (p. 158). Gathercole convincingly shows how in Romans 1 and 7 God's revelatory purposes are accomplished in and through the agency of sin; in Romans 1, the idolatry of humanity is exposed, while in Romans 7, the nefarious power of sin is made patently clear. The result of this revelatory function of sin is that God's wrath against humanity and condemnation of

rightly revealed, Paul claims, because knowledge of God — at least knowledge of God's eternality and power and divinity — is possible through the observation of the created order (1:19-20). Paul here affirms that human beings are capable in some sense of knowing God. But the knowledge of God that is available to human beings from the created order goes terribly wrong. Human beings fail to act rightly in accord with this knowledge; they do not glorify and give thanks to God (1:21). The knowledge of God derived from creation should lead to praise and thanksgiving, in Paul's view, but instead leads to indifference to God.

This failure to acknowledge God initiates a tragic chain reaction in which human cognition is compromised and divine punishment is meted out. The first consequence of their failure to praise and worship God is that human beings "become futile" (ἐματαιώθησαν) in their "reasoning" (ἐν τοῖς διαλογισμοῖς), and their "unperceiving heart grows dark" (1:21: ἐσκοτίσθη ἡ ἀσύνετος αὐτῶν καρδία).[6] Human pretension to "wisdom" (φάσκοντες εἶναι σοφοί) is belied by the fact that their increasing "foolishness" (ἐμωράνθησαν) leads them to create idols in the forms of human beings and animals (1:22-23).

The voice of the verbs in 1:21-23 must be briefly considered, because deciding whether they are middle or passive will determine the agency that lies behind the action of the verb. The form of the verbs is ambiguous with respect to voice, for ἐματαιώθησαν, ἐσκοτίσθη, and ἐμωράνθησαν can all be analyzed as middles or passives.[7] If the voice is regarded as passive, then

---

sin sets the stage for the revelation of God's righteousness in Jesus Christ. This study is indebted to Gathercole's fine treatment of Romans 1 and 7 and attempts to build on his insights. But while Gathercole is primarily concerned to explore the relationship between God's divine agency and the revelatory nature of sin, in this examination Romans 1 and 7 (as well as Romans 3 and 8) will be viewed from a different angle of vision. The focus in this piece is on the human being and the question of the possibility of authentic knowledge of and from God.

6. All translations in this essay are my own.

7. Contrary to what one often encounters in Greek learning grammars, the -θ endings of the aorist tense are medial-passive, just as one finds shared medial-passive forms in the present, imperfect, and perfect tenses. Although the evolutionary development is complex, it suffices here simply to note that the aorist system has two sets of medial-passive endings — one with -σ endings and another with -θ endings. Recognizing this state of affairs releases one from the burden of trying to analyze a form like ἐγερθείς in Matt. 1:24 ("Joseph 'got up' from sleeping and . . .") as some kind of passive when it is so clearly a middle. So the verb ἐγέρθην can mean either "I got up" (middle) or "I was raised" (passive); as with all medial-passive forms, context will determine which is appropriate in any given occurrence. For a

God presumably is the one who makes human reasoning futile and darkens their hearts and renders them foolish. If the voice is regarded as middle, then the human beings themselves would be the agents of the verbs; their failure to acknowledge God leads to further confusion in their deliberative capabilities. Since Paul makes it clear in this passage when God's agency is operative (e.g., when he describes God's agency in "handing over" human beings to various misfortunes), it is probably best to refrain from reading divine agency into the verbs of 1:21-22 and instead analyze them as middle-voice verbs describing a gradual degradation of human cognition and decision making that does not have its origin in God's activity. On this reading, Paul in 1:21-23 details the failure of human knowledge to engender in the knower the worship that God rightly deserves. Quite tragically, human knowledge left to its own devices ends up befuddled and confused and unable to distinguish creator from creation.[8]

As a result of this descent into idolatry (1:25), God "handed over" (παρέδωκεν) humanity to unclean and dishonorable passions and actions (1:24, 26-27).[9] In 1:28, Paul encapsulates the reciprocal and fitting divine punishment that falls on human beings for their failure to acknowledge God: just as they "did not see fit to acknowledge God [οὐκ ἐδοκίμασαν τὸν θεὸν ἔχειν ἐν ἐπιγνώσει], God handed them over [παρέδωκεν] to an unfit mind." It is important to recognize that Paul here draws attention to the cognitive dimensions of God's punishment. A failure of the human being to respond correctly to basic knowledge of God available in creation leads to some kind of divine alienation of the human intellect that leads to all manner of sinful acts, which Paul lists at some length in 1:29-31.

Paul makes one final point in 1:32 concerning the knowledge of those whose failure to acknowledge God has led them down a path of self-delusion and divine punishment. He claims that although they "knew"

---

good example in close proximity in Romans 1, consider the verb ἐσεβάσθησαν ("they reverenced") in 1:25. It is clearly a middle ("they revered") and not a passive ("they were revered").

8. To argue that God's agency is not involved in the initial failure of human beings to acknowledge and worship God the creator does not necessarily mean that Paul regards that failure as a function of human agency alone. What kind of agency "sin" might have is explored in this study.

9. Beverly Roberts Gaventa argues that God "hands over" idolatrous human beings to the jurisdiction of anti-God powers within the context of the apocalyptic drama Paul sketches out in Romans. For her compelling case, see *Our Mother Saint Paul* (Louisville: Westminster John Knox, 2007), pp. 113-23.

(ἐπιγνόντες) the "precept" (δικαίωμα) of God that stipulates that doers of such sinful deeds (i.e., those listed in 1:29-31) are worthy of death, they not only committed such sinful acts but approved of others who did the same. Paul does not explain how this δικαίωμα is known to human beings but rather asserts it. What is striking here is that Paul once again highlights human knowledge and knowing.

To consider the question of human knowing and knowledge in Romans 1:18-32 is not to force an alien question on the passage. Paul's emphatic points frequently involve assertions about what human beings know or do not know and what actions follow from their knowledge or lack thereof. In this passage, Paul describes a tragic downward spiral in human cognition. Although possessing knowledge of God, human beings failed to worship God and subsequently experienced such a profound deterioration of their judgment and reasoning that they come in the end to idolatry. In response, God consigns them to live with the dire consequences of their failure in discernment — deluded idolatry and unchecked immorality.

But to what does Paul attribute the initial failure of the knowledge of God to lead to the worship of God? Unfortunately, we do not have much to go on here. Something goes terribly wrong with human knowledge of God, and although Paul gives us a good sense of the divine and human agencies in the chain reaction that stems from that event, he does not give us any insights into this initial failure to acknowledge God. We will have to bracket the question as we turn to yet another sobering account of the unexpected results of human knowledge, this time specifically related to the Jewish law.

Romans 3:9-20 and 7:7-13: The Failure of the Knowledge of Sin

Near the end of his long and stinging critique of Jewish assumptions about the law and his accusations that Jews neglect to practice and live by its mandates (2:1–3:21), Paul brings his argument to a pivotal rhetorical juncture in 3:9. Having condemned Gentile idolatry and Jewish hypocrisy and disobedience of the law, he bluntly states their common lot in the world: both Jew and Gentile are "under sin" (ὑφ' ἁμαρτίαν). So here is a promising candidate for Paul's answer to the question of why the knowledge of God failed to lead to its proper end among the Gentiles: they are "under sin," a state of affairs we will look at more closely in due course. But more immediately, does being "under sin," whatever that means, have any implications for knowledge among the Jews? Indeed it does, and in a most surprising way.

On the heels of this bold declaration that both Jew and Gentile are "under sin" in 3:9, Paul stitches together a series of biblical citations, mostly from the Psalms, to underscore the sinfulness of the whole human race (3:10-18). In 3:19, he quite abruptly asserts that the purpose of the law's "speaking" to those under the law is to "shut every mouth" and to render "the entire cosmos subject to God."[10] Paul concludes that "nobody will be justified before God through works of the law, for knowledge of sin (ἐπίγνωσις ἁμαρτίας) comes through the law" (3:20).

Here again knowledge assumes a prominent, and surprising, place in Paul's argument. Knowledge of sin is presented as an obstacle to justification by works of the law. If we only had this one verse, we would struggle to puzzle out exactly what Paul means. Thankfully, he picks up this idea — that the law brings knowledge of sin — again in chapter 7 and explicates it somewhat more clearly. Before turning to 7:7-13, however, it is necessary to pause briefly over Romans 5:12-21, where Paul provides crucial information about the entry of sin into the world. Paul's assertions about what sin is and what kind of evil it wreaks have a significant bearing on the question of the failure of human knowledge.

Romans 5:12-21: Sin's Entry into the World

Paul's treatment of Genesis 3 in Romans 5:12-21 is famously robust. Adam's primal disobedience is treated by Paul as the point at which sin and death commence their subjugation of the entire human race. Adam's singular role in opening the door to the reign of sin is contrasted with Christ's singular obedience in bringing about the dethroning of these powers and the inauguration of the reign of grace. Paul does not explore or exploit in this passage the rich narrative description of Adam's transgression in the garden in Genesis 3. For Paul, the salient feature of Adam's story is the singular fact of his disobedience.

10. For a careful discussion of the place of 3:10-18 in Paul's apocalyptic horizon in Romans, see Beverly Roberts Gaventa, "From Toxic Speech to the Redemption of Doxology in Paul's Letter to the Romans," in *The Word Leaps the Gap: Essays on Scripture and Theology in Honor of Richard B. Hays*, ed. J. Ross Wagner, C. Kavin Rowe, and A. Katherine Grieb (Grand Rapids: Eerdmans, 2008), pp. 392-408.

Paul clearly uses the word "sin" to refer to discrete acts of human disobedience in Romans 5:12-21, a point that can be discerned from his vocabulary for Adam's act in these verses. He makes reference to Adam's "sin"
(v. 12: ἁμαρτία), "transgression" (v. 14: παράβασις), "trespass" (vv. 15, 17, 18:
παράπτωμα), "sinning" (v. 16: ἁμαρτήσας), and "disobedience" (v. 19:
παρακοή).

But this is not the only sense in which Paul deploys the word "sin." He
speaks in 5:12 of sin (and death) "entering the world," and in 5:21 he asserts
that sin "reigns."[11] Elsewhere in Romans, Paul can describe human beings
as "enslaved" to sin and "liberated" from sin.[12] Also, as has been previously
mentioned, he can refer to humanity as being "under sin" (see 3:9: ὑφ'
ἁμαρτίαν). Paul regards "sin" as more than simply a way to refer to discrete
acts of human disobedience; he also speaks of it as some kind of cosmic
power that has agency in the realm of human affairs.[13] In attempting to
look closely at Paul's treatment of the knowledge of God and the law in
Romans, it is absolutely crucial that his distinctive cosmological picture, in
which sin is presented as an active malignant agent, is recognized and considered. While he does not address the question of knowledge in this passage, Paul will return to the Adam story in 7:7-13, and there the relationship between sin and knowledge occupies a central role.

Romans 7:7-13: The Failure of the Knowledge of the Law[14]

In 7:7-13, Paul picks up the point he so enigmatically made in 3:21 and explains the relationship between the knowledge of sin that the law provides
and the provocation to commit sinful acts. Knowledge of sin, he argues,

---

11. 5:12: δι' ἑνὸς ἀνθρώπου ἡ ἁμαρτία εἰς τὸν κόσμον εἰσῆλθεν; 5:21: ὥσπερ ἐβασίλευσεν
ἡ ἁμαρτία ἐν τῷ θανάτῳ; cf. 6:12: μὴ οὖν βασιλευέτω ἡ ἁμαρτία ἐν τῷ θνητῷ ὑμῶν σώματι;
6:14: ἁμαρτία γὰρ ὑμῶν οὐ κυριεύσει.

12. 6:6: ἵνα καταργηθῇ τὸ σῶμα τῆς ἁμαρτίας τοῦ μηκέτι δουλεύειν ἡμᾶς τῇ ἁμαρτίᾳ;
6:22: νυνὶ δὲ ἐλευθερωθέντες ἀπὸ τῆς ἁμαρτίας δουλωθέντες δὲ τῷ θεῷ. Note that "sin" in
6:22 is parallel to God.

13. For an excellent discussion of sin as a cosmic power, see Gaventa, *Mother*, pp. 125-36.

14. This section and the next are deeply indebted to Paul Meyer's groundbreaking essay
on the corrupting power of sin in relation to the law in Rom. 7:7-25 ("The Worm at the Core
of the Apple: Exegetical Reflections on Romans 7," in *The Word in This World: Essays in New
Testament Exegesis and Theology*, ed. John T. Carroll, NTL [Louisville: Westminster John
Knox, 2004], pp. 57-77). See also the succinct discussion of Meyer's work in Gaventa, *Mother*,
pp. 130-31.

comes through knowing the specific commands of the law (7:7).[15] The commandment to refrain from coveting, for example, provides to the one who hears it the knowledge of what covetousness is (7:7).[16] What is the result of this knowledge of sin the law produces? An "opportunity" (ἀφορμή) for sin to provoke the very act that the law prohibits (7:8). So the law brings a knowledge of sin that in turn causes sin, which leads to death (7:10-11).

For Paul, the significant point here is that the law is "holy," and the commandment is "holy and just and good" (7:12) and cannot be regarded as the source of deception and death. This is for Paul an important theological point because God is the one who gives the law. If the law itself were to bring death, then God would be responsible for death. Paul, however, is insistent that it is sin that brings death by hijacking the law and using it for nefarious purposes.[17] But in so manipulating that which is "good" (= the law), sin is caught out, and its destructive purposes are made manifest for all to see (7:13).[18]

This clever passage is making allusions to two biblical narratives simultaneously. On one level it is a creative retelling of the story of primal disobedience found in Genesis 3. Paul here speaks of the "commandment" that became the opportunity for "sin" to enter in and "deceive" and "kill" him. Each of these terms certainly evokes a key element of Adam and Eve's disobedience. God "commanded" Adam to refrain from eating the fruit of the tree of the knowledge of good and evil on the pain of "death."[19] But the serpent "deceived" Eve, and she ate of the apple and Adam subsequently did the same.[20]

---

15. 7:7: ἀλλὰ τὴν ἁμαρτίαν οὐκ ἔγνων εἰ μὴ διὰ νόμου.

16. 7:7: τήν τε γὰρ ἐπιθυμίαν οὐκ ᾔδειν εἰ μὴ ὁ νόμος ἔλεγεν οὐκ ἐπιθυμήσεις.

17. The idea that sin takes control of the law is persuasively argued by J. Louis Martyn, who takes Paul's references to νόμος plus a genitive modifier as his exegetical starting point. See his "*NOMOS* Plus Genitive Noun in Paul: The History of God's Law," in *Early Christianity and Classical Culture: Comparative Essays in Honor of Abraham J. Malherbe,* ed. John T. Fitzgerald, Thomas H. Olbricht, and L. Michael White, NovTSup 110 (Leiden: Brill, 2003), pp. 575-87. Martyn's essay builds on fundamental insights about Rom. 7:7-25 advanced by Meyer in "Worm."

18. For the way this exposure of sin for what it truly is fits into Paul's idea of God's larger purposes in Romans, see Gathercole, "Sin," esp. pp. 171-72.

19. On the command, see Gen. 2:16: καὶ ἐνετείλετο κύριος ὁ θεὸς τῷ Αδαμ . . . ; see also Gen. 3:17 and cf. Paul's repeated use (6x) of the noun ἐντολή in 7:7-13. On death, God tells Adam in Gen. 2:17 that if he eats of the fruit of the tree of the knowledge of good and evil, he will "surely die"; cf. Gen. 3:3, 4, 19.

20. See Gen. 3:13, in which Eve reports to God that the serpent "deceived" her (ὁ ὄφις ἠπάτησέν με); cf. Paul's claim that sin "deceived" him in Rom. 7:11 (ἡ γὰρ ἁμαρτία ἀφορμὴν λαβοῦσα διὰ τῆς ἐντολῆς ἐξηπάτησέν με).

So this is a more elaborate way of saying what Paul asserted in Romans 5:12 — that in this primal act of disobedience "sin" entered the world, and death along with it.

But 7:7-13 does not refer only to the Adam and Eve story; it also alludes to the giving of the Mosaic law. In his attempt to defend the law's integrity and goodness, Paul is arguing that "sin" takes control of the law, which intends life and good, and instead produces sin and death. So Paul's point is that "sin" works in the Mosaic law generally in the same way that it worked with God's very first commandment to Adam and Eve in the garden. Paul here is not merely commenting on the past but rather articulates a general observation about how sin operates in the world. It is perpetually taking advantage of the dictates of the law to provoke sinful acts in those who are under the law.

In 7:7-13, knowledge once again plays a central role in Paul's theological argumentation, and as was the case with the knowledge of God in Romans 1:18-32, so here also the knowledge of the law takes a tragic wrong turn and does not come to its intended destination. While in Romans 1 knowledge of God leads not to right worship but idolatry, in Romans 3 and 7 knowledge of sin that comes from the law leads to sin rather than to obedience to the law.

In these passages, Paul sets forth a provocative and novel view of human knowledge of God and the law that raises several pressing questions. One such question, already raised, is what causes the initial failure of humanity to acknowledge and worship God, despite the knowledge of God available to it from creation? Another is why do those under the law not suffer the same degradation of the intellect as those who descend into idolatry?

Addressing these and related questions will require some attention to Paul's theological anthropology and to his view of extrahuman agency. It is no accident that 7:7-13 is followed immediately by an extended discussion of how the human being under the law experiences the power of sin (7:14-25) and then by discussion of the role of the Spirit in combating the power of sin (8:1-11).

Knowledge and Theological Anthropology

One of the distinctive features of several prominent Second Temple Jewish apocalyptic texts is the way notions of divine revelation are closely related to the nature and constitution of the human recipient. In some texts, the possibility of divine revelation depends on whether one is "spiritual" or "fleshly." In others, all human beings are "fleshly," and revelation is made available to those to whom God grants the Spirit. What such texts demonstrate is that claims about knowledge of God or from God are quite often constructed in concert with claims about theological anthropology. This is precisely what one finds in Romans and elsewhere in Paul's letters.

Romans 7:14-25: Knowing Good, but Doing Evil

In this much-debated passage, Paul reflects, perhaps autobiographically, on the struggle with sin that characterizes the person under the Jewish law, which has just been described as hijacked by "sin" to accomplish destructive ends. For the purposes of the present investigation, it is important to note that what the speaker knows in his mind and discerns with his powers of judgment are central to the argument.

The speaker opens by contrasting the law, which is "spiritual," with himself, a "fleshly" person who has been "sold under sin" (7:14).[21] He goes on to detail a struggle between his mind and will, on one hand, and his body and actions, on the other. He desires to do the right thing but cannot accomplish it.[22] The implication of his desire to obey the law (i.e., that which is good) is that the law is itself good, even if he cannot obey the law.[23] The problem is that "sin" dwells in the "flesh" and prevents the doing of the law in which the mind takes delight.[24] This tension between "flesh" and "mind" leads the speaker to exclaim, "Who will rescue me from this body of death?" (7:24). After a thanksgiving, the speaker declares, "Therefore I serve the law of God in my mind but I serve the law of sin in my flesh" (7:25).

---

21. 7:14: ἐγὼ δὲ σάρκινός εἰμι πεπραμένος ὑπὸ τὴν ἁμαρτίαν. References to the "flesh" are particularly concentrated in 7:14-25 as well as in 8:1-17 (six occurrences of σάρξ in Rom. 1:1–7:13; fifteen occurrences of σάρξ and one occurrence of σάρκινος in 7:14–8:17).

22. 7:15: οὐ γὰρ ὃ θέλω τοῦτο πράσσω, ἀλλ᾽ ὃ μισῶ ποιῶ; 7:18: τὸ γὰρ θέλειν παράκειταί μοι, τὸ δὲ κατεργάζεσθαι τὸ καλὸν οὔ; 7:19: οὐ γὰρ ὃ θέλω ποιῶ ἀγαθόν, ἀλλὰ ὃ οὐ θέλω κακὸν τοῦτο πράσσω; cf. also 7:20, 21.

23. 7:16: εἰ δὲ ὃ οὐ θέλω τοῦτο ποιῶ, σύμφημι τῷ νόμῳ ὅτι καλός; cf. also 7:22, 25.

24. 7:17: νυνὶ δὲ οὐκέτι ἐγὼ κατεργάζομαι αὐτὸ ἀλλὰ ἡ οἰκοῦσα ἐν ἐμοὶ ἁμαρτία; 7:20: εἰ δὲ ὃ οὐ θέλω ἐγὼ τοῦτο ποιῶ, οὐκέτι ἐγὼ κατεργάζομαι αὐτὸ ἀλλὰ ἡ οἰκοῦσα ἐν ἐμοὶ ἁμαρτία; cf. also 7:23.

The anthropological categories and distinctions of this passage are quite closely linked to questions of religious epistemology. The human person here is conceived as comprising "flesh" and "mind," which is presumably the seat of, or linked in some way with, the "will."[25] The mind and will are apparently free in some sense from "sin" and can delight in the law and desire to obey it. The "flesh" in this passage is not described as bad in itself. Rather, it is the locus of sin's habitation and a base for its operations (7:17, 20). Sin comes to indwell the members of the body and works actively against the accomplishment of the mind and will (7:23).

In distinction from the idolaters in chapter 1, not only can the one under the law know and properly acknowledge God's existence, he or she is also able to know the content of the law and can affirm its goodness. The receipt of God's law is apparently sufficient to keep the "mind" from failing utterly when it comes to the knowledge of God; there is no corruption or degradation of the cognitive faculties such as we saw in chapter 1. The struggle for the one under the law, rather, is that the knowledge of the law becomes co-opted by "sin," which goes to work in the flesh and thwarts the intentions and desires of the mind. Instead of law obedience, the knowledge of the law becomes the very means by which sinful acts are induced.

Romans 8:1-11: Flesh and Spirit

The discourse in 7:7-25 centers on the failure of the knowledge of the law to lead to obedience. With 8:1-11, Paul shifts the discussion and begins to explain the means by which this failure is overcome. God's sending of Jesus Christ results in a dethroning (although not the destruction)[26] of sin, and the giving of the Spirit to believers in Christ that follows on this defeat goes to work to counteract the destructive power of sin working in the flesh. While the specific agency of the πνεῦμα in Paul's religious epistemology is most clearly explicated in 1 Corinthians 2:6-16, it is nonetheless evident in the opening sections of Romans 8.

Paul begins with the stirring assertion that there is no condemnation for those in Christ Jesus (8:1), because the "law in the power of the Spirit of life in Christ Jesus" has brought liberation from "the law in the power of

25. σαρκινός, 7:14; σάρξ, 7:18, 25; νοῦς, 7:23, 25; θέλω, 7:15, 16, 18, 19 (2x), 20, 21.
26. The ultimate victory and elimination of sin remain an eschatological event for Paul; see 1 Cor. 15:24-28.

sin and death" (8:2).[27] The law has thus been wrested from the control of sin and death, powers that manipulated the law to achieve evil purposes in human life, and comes under the control of the Spirit. This confiscation of the law was necessary because the law was not able to achieve its intended purpose because of the "weakness of the flesh" that allowed "sin" to seize control of it (8:3).[28] Control of the law by the Spirit is achieved when God sends the Son "in the likeness of sinful flesh" to condemn sin in the flesh.[29] One of the effects of God's sending the Son is the reception of the Holy Spirit by the community of believers (8:4).

It is initially tempting to conclude that God's defeat of sin in Christ and the subsequent sending of the Spirit result in law obedience for those who believe. Perhaps Paul is arguing that the law, which has been freed from sin's control, is now able to be obeyed without hindrance and with the assistance of the Spirit. But this is not at all the state of affairs that Paul envisions, as is clear not only from the present passage but from all his letters.[30] Although the law has been freed from sin's control, at the same time the age of "works of the law" has passed in Paul's view and a new age has begun in which obedience to God is understood in a radically new way. The means by which a God-pleasing life is achieved in the "new creation" is the guiding of the Spirit rather than obedience to the law.[31]

That the role and understanding of law obedience has been transformed is glimpsed in 8:4 and becomes clearer as Paul's argument unfolds in Romans 8. Paul in 8:4 is stating the purpose of God's sending the Son to defeat sin: "in order that the precept of the law might be fulfilled among us who walk not according to flesh but according to the Spirit." The language

27. 8:2: ὁ νόμος τοῦ πνεύματος τῆς ζωῆς ἐν Χριστῷ Ἰησοῦ, ὁ νόμος τῆς ἁμαρτίας καὶ τοῦ θανάτου.

28. 8:3a essentially summarizes 7:7-25.

29. 8:3: ἐν ὁμοιώματι σαρκὸς ἁμαρτίας, usually translated "in the likeness of sinful flesh." But taking a cue from Martyn's suggestion for translating νόμος ἁμαρτίας, we should perhaps consider translating this phrase "flesh in the grip of sin." This translation would provide a possible explanation for why Paul uses the term "likeness" here. The point might be that Jesus, although truly taking on human flesh, was in some way free from "the grip of sin" insofar as the command of God to him was not used by sin to provoke sinful acts.

30. Paul makes frequent reference and allusion to the fact that the law is not binding for believers, but see especially his sustained argument that law obedience is not necessary for believers in Galatians 1–4.

31. For a discussion of the "new creation" as naming for Paul the new age that is contrasted to the "present evil age" (Gal. 1:4), see J. Louis Martyn, *Galatians: A New Translation with Introduction and Commentary*, AB 33A (New York: Doubleday, 1997), pp. 570-74.

of "fulfillment" (8:4: πληρωθῇ) belongs to the semantic domain of purpose and intent. So while sin working in the flesh prevented the purpose of the law from being realized, those who walk according to the Spirit are able to realize that purpose. J. Louis Martyn argues that for Paul the ultimate purpose of the law is to bring life to people, a notion with a rich and deep heritage in Israel's Scriptures.[32] Paul's references in 8:2, 6, 10, and 11 to "life" lend considerable credence to Martyn's claim.

In Romans 8:5-7, the epistemological dimensions of life in the Spirit come into view. In fact, this discussion of the Spirit and flesh is cast in cognitive terms — "to think" (φρονεῖν) and "way of thinking" (φρόνημα). Paul asserts in 8:5 that "those who are according to flesh" set their minds on "things pertaining to the flesh," while "those who are according to the Spirit" set their minds on "thing pertaining to the Spirit." He adds an explanatory comment in 8:6: "flesh" and "Spirit" have divergent φρονήματα — death in the case of the flesh, life and peace in the case of the Spirit. Accordingly, he concludes in 8:7-8, those who are fleshly have minds set on death and are hostile to God because the φρόνημα of death is not (and, Paul adds, cannot be) subject to the law.

But what can it mean that those in whom the Spirit dwells "set their minds" on the things of the Spirit? Is this a result of the Spirit's activity, or is it a human act, or both? Paul does not address these points clearly here in Romans 8:1-11. In the Spirit, the power of sin to manipulate the law to provoke sin is broken, but how does Paul imagine that human knowledge of God and from God works in light of Christ's death and the reception of the Spirit? Paul's most substantial treatment of the logic of revelation in the Spirit comes in 1 Corinthians 2:6-16. A brief examination of this passage can shed light on Paul's thoughts about religious epistemology in Romans 1–8.

One cannot uncritically assume, of course, that all the authentic Pauline letters are theologically coherent. Important differences between them can be detected.[33] But neither is it the case that the Pauline letters need to be treated in hermetic isolation from one another. In Romans 1–8, Paul's negative case about human knowing and knowledge is tied up with his un-

---

32. Martyn, "*NOMOS*," pp. 583-87.

33. E.g., Edward Adams has shown that Paul uses the important term κόσμος quite differently in 1 Corinthians and Romans; in 1 Corinthians, Paul portrays the κόσμος as inherently hostile to God, while in Romans it is used in a more neutral sense. For this argument, see his important study *Constructing the World: A Study in Paul's Cosmological Language*, SNTW (Edinburgh: T. & T. Clark, 2000), esp. pp. 105-94.

derstanding of the constitution of the human being. He does not, however, spell out clearly his positive case for how human knowledge of God works, although it most certainly surfaces briefly in Romans 8:1-11. It is in 1 Corinthians that one finds Paul's discussion of God's means of revelation, which Paul explains with significant recourse to anthropology. If one assumes that Paul's theological anthropology is at least relatively stable as one moves from Romans to 1 Corinthians, the result is that Paul's positive understanding of revelation in 1 Corinthians 2:6-16 helps to fill some gaps in his account of the failure of human knowledge of God and the law in Romans 1–8.

1 Corinthians 2:6–3:4: A Mini-Treatise on Religious Epistemology

Paul's treatment of revelation in 1 Corinthians 2:6-16 comes on the heels of a carefully crafted and clever discourse on the futility of human wisdom and rhetoric in 1:18–2:5. Having claimed that he has no pretenses to worldly wisdom, Paul proceeds to describe a different sort of wisdom that is manifested in the community of faith. His description of this "spiritual" wisdom constitutes a mini-treatise on religious epistemology. He opens by asserting that the sort of wisdom he is talking about does not belong to "this age" or its "rulers who are being rendered ineffectual" (2:6: σοφίαν δὲ οὐ τοῦ αἰῶνος τούτου οὐδὲ τῶν ἀρχόντων τοῦ αἰῶνος τούτου τῶν καταργουμένων). Rather, he speaks of a wisdom that is "concealed in a mystery" that God established pretemporally and that remains unavailable to the rulers of this age (2:7-8).[34] Had they had access to this divinely ordained and concealed wisdom, they would not have crucified Jesus (2:8).

Not only does Paul claim that some form of divine wisdom has been revealed within the community of believers, he provides a brief sketch of how the mechanism of this revelation works in 2:9-16.[35] In verse 9, Paul

---

34. The best treatment of Paul's use of μυσήτριον remains Markus N. A. Bockmuehl, *Revelation and Mystery in Ancient Judaism and Pauline Christianity* (Grand Rapids: Eerdmans, 1997), pp. 157-65.

35. Bockmuehl concludes from Paul's reference to a wisdom discourse among the "mature" (2:6) that the mystery is not revealed "spiritually" to everyone in the community but rather only to the apostles and prophets, who then transmit its content to the rest of the believers (*Revelation*, pp. 163-65, esp. note 35). More compelling and coherent, however, is Ian Scott's argument that Paul has all believers in view when he speaks of the revelation of God's wisdom (*Knowing*, pp. 39-45).

cites Isaiah 64:4 to establish that God makes revelations to those who love God, presumably to underscore Paul's claim that God reveals the concealed divine wisdom within the community of believers. The means by which God makes such revelations is "through God's Spirit" (2:10: διὰ τοῦ πνεύματος). To explain why God's Spirit has revelatory effectiveness, Paul asserts that any given person's πνεῦμα possesses the most complete knowledge of that person (2:11). By analogy, then, God's Spirit possesses knowledge of even the "deep things" of God (2:10, 11). Since this Spirit of God that knows God intimately has been granted to those in the community of faith (rather than a spirit "of the world"), it follows that believers have received God's wisdom once they have received God's Spirit.

Paul in 2:13-16 elaborates further on the logic of revelation by the Spirit. Discourse within the community of faith is "spiritual" (πνευματικός) rather than merely "human" or "physical" (ψυχικός) because at the human level of discourse and judgment it is impossible to discern and appreciate that which is revealed by the Spirit. A familiarity with the Jewish apocalyptic tradition in general, and the community hymns of Qumran in particular, might lead us to expect that Paul would make a contrast between πνεῦμα and σάρξ here, but he does not. In the next section of the letter (3:1-4), however, he does seem to make a contrast between "spirit" and "flesh," but as we shall see, not in the way we might expect.

So Paul states the matter here quite simply: spiritual things must be spiritually discerned, and this is only possible for those who have received God's Spirit. It follows that those who do not enjoy the presence and activity of the Spirit — those who are merely "physical" — cannot receive nor comprehend this revelation. In a clever play on the verb ἀνακρίνω, he asserts that the "spiritual person" (πνευματικός), by which he clearly means one to whom the Spirit brings revelation, "discerns" all things and is "judged" by nobody (2:15).

Paul rounds out this treatise on religious epistemology with a citation of Isaiah 40:13, a rhetorical question that asks, "Who has known the mind of the Lord?" (2:16). In its context in Isaiah, the point of the question is clearly that nobody has known the "mind of the Lord." For Paul, however, the answer is presumably affirmative, because, he says, "we have the mind of Christ" (2:16). So in Paul's understanding of revelation, believers know the "deep things" of God and the "mind" of Christ through the revealing work of the Spirit.

Paul intends this little lesson in Christian epistemology to apply to the turf wars in Corinth. He tells the immature Corinthians who are engaged in petty infighting and the forming of cliques that in so acting they are σαρκικοῖ and acting in a "human" (3:4: κατὰ ἄνθρωπον) fashion. So Paul does here contrast "spirit" and "flesh," but not as a dichotomy between believers and outsiders; rather, he applies it to those in the community of believers who are acting in ways destructive of the Christian community.[36] The hard line Paul draws is between πνευματικός and ψυχικός, not πνεῦμα and σάρξ. Even though the Corinthians have received the πνεῦμα, they still possess σάρξ and can even act in ways consistent with σάρξ. What they are not any longer as believers, apparently, are mere ψυχικοί. The significance of this anthropological point will be seen as we turn to a final overview of Romans 1–8.

Putting It All Together: Human Knowledge of God and the Law in Romans

It is now time to pull together all of these passages and attempt a synthesis of Paul's religious epistemology in Romans 1–8, with an assist from 1 Corinthians 2:6-16. The starting point for such a synthesis is Paul's creative and provocative reading of Genesis 3.

Paul's account of Adam's primal disobedience in the garden places knowledge in a central role. In Romans 5:12, Paul plainly and without elaboration asserts that the disobedience of Adam is the precipitating event in the subjugation of humanity to the power of sin. In Romans 7:7-13, however, Paul provides some insight into how sin got this foothold in the cosmos. Based on Romans 5:12-21; 7:7-13; and 7:14-25, we can attempt to capture Paul's logic of how "sin" used the command to provoke the flesh to commit sin that the command prohibits.

The divine "command" to Adam and Eve in the garden gave them a certain kind of knowledge — namely, that eating of the tree of the fruit of good and evil is off-limits. But the very knowledge of what constitutes sin is able to be manipulated by Sin (with a capital S, construed as a power) indwelling the flesh and working in the body and its members to bring about

---

36. It is quite intriguing that Paul provides a lengthy lesson on the revelatory action of the Spirit in 2:6-16 in order to address the issue of *actions* carried out in a "fleshly" or "human" fashion. Paul seems to imply here that the revealing work of the Spirit has direct implications for actions and behavior. It is not the transformation of the flesh that is lifted up here by Paul but rather what he might call (as he does in Romans 12) the "renewal of the mind." This idea is worth exploring further.

the commission of that very act of sin. In so doing, Adam and Eve "died," in the sense that God had warned that the day they ate of the fruit of the tree of the knowledge of good and evil they would "surely die." And indeed they were expelled from the garden and consigned to a mortal life in which they would return to the dust from which they had been fashioned. Sin had entered the world in their disobedience and would henceforth be at work in the flesh of human beings.

It is in this context that we should imagine the scenario that Paul describes in Romans 1:18-32. Mortal human beings who have not received a command from God — in other words, Gentiles who do not have the law — possess knowledge of God's existence and attributes but fail to act rightly on that knowledge. They create idols for themselves rather than worshiping and glorifying God the creator. Within the context of Paul's anthropology, it seems reasonable to conclude that this failure of the knowledge of God to lead to its proper end in the praise of God is a result of Sin working in the flesh to the point that even the mind and will are compromised. Sin working in the flesh produces delusion and ignorance, which is then compounded by divine judgment and punishment.

For Jews, the situation is different because they have received the command of God — the law. In their lives the pattern of Adam and Eve is writ large. The command enters in, and Sin goes to work through it. The command brings knowledge of sin, and that knowledge of sin is used by Sin to provoke the very act that is prohibited by the command. So in Sin's nefarious purposes, the knowledge of what the law requires does not lead to obedience but to disobedience. As the speech in character in Romans 7:7-13 shows, the Jew under the law lives with this constant struggle of the flesh, occupied by sin, against the mind and the will, which delight in the law and desire to obey it. The Jewish mind is not portrayed by Paul as confused and deluded, as is the mind and thinking of the Gentiles. The Jews do not fall into idolatry, because the law acts as a sort of intellectual prophylactic against idolatry. God's revelation, even though manipulated to bad ends by Sin, at the very least has the benefit of preventing the abomination of idolatry.

So does Paul think that deficient or defective "flesh" is responsible for the failures of human knowledge of God and God's will in Romans 1–8? Flesh is portrayed as the locus where "sin" is at work, and in Romans "sin" is often portrayed like some kind of external, cosmic entity. But Paul can also say that the flesh was "weak" and thus susceptible to this penetration by "sin," so that is at least a hint that flesh is not without defect. In Romans 8 Paul seems to begin speaking of the "flesh" in ways that suggest it is inherently bad. Perhaps for Paul the corrupting nature of sin working in the flesh since the time of creation is so pervasive, persistent, and destructive that flesh can now be spoken of as inherently corrupt (i.e., it has its own mental predisposition, it can order human life, and so on). Thus there is a tension in Paul between materiality and external agency when it comes to the flesh and its problems.

Although it falls outside Romans 1–8, Paul's reference to the Jews and knowledge in Romans 10 should be mentioned here. Paul argues in Romans 10:2 that the Jews have a "zeal for God" but that it is not κατ' ἐπίγνωσιν. Because they did not seek God "knowledgeably," Paul argues, they sadly ended up seeking "their own righteousness" rather than God's (10:3). Paul will go on to say that righteousness comes from faith for everyone who believes in Christ, who is the τέλος of the law (10:4-5). So the Jews did not know that righteousness is based on faith, which is presumably part of what the Spirit reveals to the community of believers when it makes known to them "the gifts that have been given to them by God" (1 Cor. 2:12). Put simply, the Jews did not know Christ and so did not pursue righteousness κατ' ἐπίγνωσιν.

This charge of not seeking God "knowledgeably" has touch-points with Paul's discussion of the failure of the Gentiles to acknowledge God as God in Romans 1. Since the Jews did not seek God κατ' ἐπίγνωσιν, their seeking turned inward on themselves — they sought their own righteousness. Paul asserts a similar kind of inward turn in Romans 1. As we have already discussed, the knowledge of God that the Gentiles have from creation does not lead to worship of God but rather eventually leads to idolatry and then to penalties received in their own bodies. Paul sums all of this up in 1:28 with the phrase καὶ καθὼς οὐκ ἐδοκίμασαν τὸν θεὸν ἔχειν ἐν ἐπιγνώσει, "and just as they did not see fit to strive for God knowledgeably," God handed them over to an "unfit mind."[37] So it would seem that despite the differences in how knowledge goes astray for Jew and Gentile, in Paul's thinking they share the fate that their knowledge leads them to an inward focus rather than a proper orientation toward God.

As Paul intimates in Romans 8 and makes quite clear in 1 Corinthians 2:6-16, the failure of human knowledge to lead to its proper end is only overcome when Christ breaks the power of sin and God gives the Spirit to

---

37. The verb ἔχω can mean "to be eager for," "to be zealous for," "to cleave/cling to a thing." But it can also mean "to understand" (like Latin *teneo*), or perhaps the infinitive plus the adverbial prepositional phrase simply means "to acknowledge" (so the NRSV).

those who come to believe in him. Those outside the community of faith remain impaired in their knowing in the way Paul has described: Gentiles continue to fall into idolatry, and Jews are drawn into sin because their knowledge ultimately leads them astray. To take up the language Paul uses in 1 Corinthians 2, we might say that Jew and Gentile are alike in their status as ψυχικοί, but different in the particular way that their knowledge of God and God's will is compromised. The Gentile is a ψυχικός without the law, while the Jew is a ψυχικός with the law. But those who receive the Spirit — the πνευματικοι — are able to know "the gifts that have been given to them by God." These gifts would include a comprehension of the "mystery" of God and the significance of Jesus Christ within that divine plan.

Conclusion

This study has not attempted a comprehensive treatment of Paul's religious epistemology. It rather has had the basic goal of highlighting two interesting cases in Romans 1–8 in which Paul attends to the failure of human knowledge to lead to its proper end in human action — the failure of the knowledge of God discerned from creation to lead to the worship and praise of God, and the failure of the knowledge of the law to lead to obedience to the law. An examination of these two cases demonstrates that Paul's thoroughgoing apocalyptic worldview has shaped his understanding of how the human being can come to an authentic knowledge of God and God's will that can be expressed in appropriate and corresponding action. Humanity, afflicted by the power of Sin working in the flesh, is unable of its own accord to come to the right knowledge of God or to carry out the actions that the knowledge of God's will demands. It requires the intervention of God in breaking the power of Sin and sending the Spirit to make right knowledge and action possible within the community of faith.

This account of one facet of human life and experience in Romans — knowledge of God and the law — buttresses Beverly Gaventa's broader assertion that God plays the definitive role in the cosmic defeat of Sin and in breaking Sin's enslavement of human beings. It confirms her judgment that Sin is "a character who enslaves, who brings death, who ensnares even God's Torah, and whose demise is guaranteed by God's action in the death and resurrection of Jesus Christ."[38]

38. Gaventa, *Mother*, p. 127.

Time in Romans 5–8: From Life to Life

L. Ann Jervis

Beverly Roberts Gaventa's repeated and important claim that Paul understands God to be waging a cosmic battle against anti-God powers (and
that humanity is the object of this conflict) is, among other things, implicitly a claim about the kind of time in which we live.[1] Like many others, I
am immensely grateful for Dr. Gaventa's courageous and energetic exegesis, which never fails to open the widescreen on Paul's view of the drama of
this cosmic battle. Battles and dramas take place in time. I express my gratitude for Dr. Gaventa's work and friendship by offering some reflections
on Paul's view of time. I will base my reflections on Romans 5–8.[2]

Unlike the question of Gaventa's esteemed friend, J. Louis Martyn, my
question about time is not "What time is it?"[3] My question is, rather, "What
kind of time is it?" What is the character of the time that the saints live?[4]

---

1. See, recently, her "Neither Height nor Depth: Discerning the Cosmology of Romans,"
SJT 64 (2011): 270.

2. Even if Dr. Gaventa had not persuaded me to give a paper at a conference she recently organized on Romans 5–8 (that paper being the inspiration for this essay), I would
have turned first to these great chapters. Here Paul illuminates his understanding of the
saints' being (ontology), their possibilities for living, and the horizons of their reality. To ask
Paul a question about time, there is arguably no richer source for an answer than these four
chapters.

3. J. Louis Martyn, *Galatians: A New Translation with Introduction and Commentary,*
AB 33A (New York: Doubleday, 1997), p. 23.

4. It has become customary to avoid using the anachronistic word *Christians* for Paul's
addressees by using instead the word "believers." Since Paul's term "believers" may set off in
a reader's mind connections with "justification by grace through faith" as Paul's
soteriological center of gravity (an understanding I do not share), I will call Paul's addressees, as he does regularly, "the saints" ("the holy ones"), or those who are in Christ.

While it may be thought that that question is long settled — the saints live in a kind of time that is "already and not yet" — I wish to ask it again.[5] It will be for my readers to decide whether the proposal I offer here amounts to the same answer in other words. I hope that even if that proves to be so, my proposal will likewise prove to freshly reframe what has become taken for granted in this generation of Pauline scholarship.

I begin with the observation, based on both these four chapters of Romans and the rest of Paul's letters, that Paul thinks those who accept that Jesus is raised from the dead and now is Lord are those who are in Christ and have Christ in them. I am convinced that Paul's most profound and generative way of understanding the meaning of Christ for humanity is that, because of his life, death, resurrection, and exaltation, people may live in Christ and have Christ living in them. I begin my exploration of time in Romans 5–8, then, by following in the trail blazed by Adolf Deissmann, Albert Schweitzer, and E. P. Sanders.

In regard to the question of this essay — what *kind* of time do the saints live? — the simplest answer is that, since they live in Christ and Christ lives in them, they live the kind of time that Christ lives. Paul says as much in Romans 8:9, to give a paraphrase: "You are . . . in the spirit, since the Spirit of God (which is also the Spirit of Christ) *dwells* in you." I add the emphasis to draw attention to the word οἰκεῖ. To dwell is to live somewhere — in time. Since Paul thinks of the Spirit of God and Christ as dwelling in the saints, the time of those in whom the Spirit of God and Christ dwells must be the time of the greater being — the Spirit of God and Christ. Likewise, Paul's conviction that the holy ones are in Christ

---

5. The phrase "already and not yet" is regularly used as the shorthand label for the idea that salvation is inaugurated but not complete. See, for example, J. Paul Sampley, *Walking between the Times: Paul's Moral Reasoning* (Minneapolis: Fortress, 1991), pp. 17-24. Scholars who take this view do not always use this label, however. As J. Christiaan Beker puts it: "[T]he apocalyptic hope for Paul is an existential reality that is part and parcel of Christian life. . . . Neither a collapsing of the tension between present and future in realized eschatology, nor a diffusing of it by postponing the end to an indefinite future, accomplishes the hermeneutical task" (*Paul the Apostle: The Triumph of God in Life and Thought* [Philadelphia: Fortress, 1984], pp. 366-67). Martyn writes: "[T]he present evil age has not been simply followed by the new creation. Nor do the two exist in isolation . . . the evil age and the new creation are dynamically interrelated" (*Galatians*, p. 99). Gaventa says succinctly: "God's triumph is not yet complete" ("The Mission of God in Paul's Letter to the Romans," in *Paul as Missionary: Identity, Activity, Theology, and Practice,* ed. Trevor J. Burke and Brian S. Rosner, LNTS 420 [London: T. & T. Clark, 2011], p. 74); and again, "redemption [is] begun but not yet complete" ("Neither," p. 265).

surely suggests that their lives take place in the time of the one in whom they live — Christ.

I start, then, from the assumption that, for Paul, whatever time is in the life of Christ is also the kind of time lived by those who have Christ in them and who are "in Christ."[6] The purpose of this essay is not to prove that point but, on the basis of it, to explore the question of the character of time lived by the saints. I begin, then, with a description of what I find Paul saying about the nature of the time lived by Christ and then turn to what I hear him saying about the kind of time lived by those who are in Christ.

The Time That Christ Lives

The first thing to clarify is that I am not asking about the time that Christ lived during his human life, the time he lived when he was "in the likeness of humanity" (Phil. 2:7).[7] Rather, as should be clear, I am asking about the kind of time Christ now lives subsequent to his being "highly exalted" (Phil. 2:9).

The kind of time the crucified, risen, and exalted Christ lives has a radically different quality from the time into which Christ came. Death shaped the time into which Jesus Christ came. Paul states that death reigned from Adam to Moses (Rom. 5:14), and, when the law came, sin increased (Rom. 5:20). Paul thinks of sin as the agent of death (Rom. 5:12), as the source of what destroys (Rom. 1:29-31). The character of the time into which Christ was born in human form was, then, defined by loss and by endings. It was time that flowed away toward the past — a time of entropy. Fear was the mode of life in that kind of time (Rom. 8:15); for that kind of time was always slipping away, disappearing.

Critical to understanding the time Christ *now* lives is Paul's foundational conviction that God raised Christ from the dead and that death is something he will never again experience: "Christ, being raised from the

---

6. As is clear from Rom. 8:9, Paul is certain that the Spirit dwells in the saints and the saints in the Spirit; therefore, I might choose to explore what Paul thinks about the time the Spirit lives. However, given my already stated conviction that, to use E. P. Sanders's phrase, the "Christians' participation in Christ" is *"the theme, above all, to which Paul appeals both in parenesis and polemic"* (*Paul and Palestinian Judaism: A Comparison of Patterns of Religion* [Philadelphia: Fortress, 1977], p. 456, emphasis original), I focus rather on the time of Christ. Furthermore, as Rom. 8:9 makes plain, the Spirit is the Spirit of Christ.

7. Unless otherwise noted, biblical translations are my own.

dead, will never die again" (Rom. 6:9 NRSV). In the time Christ himself lives there is no death.

Subsequent to Christ's crucifixion, resurrection, and exaltation, then, a new kind of time has appeared: time without death, time without sin — the time that Christ now lives.[8] The absence of death and of sin in the time Christ lives means that the character of this kind of time is that it moves only forward. In Christ Jesus is the spirit of life; there is no sin and death (8:2). The time Christ lives moves from life toward life, rather than backward to death and destruction.[9] Paul says as much when he writes that the life Christ lives he lives to God (6:10).[10]

Paul highlights the absence of death in the kind of time that Christ lives by describing Christ's life as eternal. Eternal life is the life that Christ lives. Paul states this clearly at the end of chapter 6 where he speaks of eternal life being in Christ Jesus our Lord (6:23). Christ's time, then, is life-time: eternal life-time. By qualifying the kind of life Christ lives as "eternal," I take Paul to mean that such life keeps on going because there is nothing to make it stop. An analogy to Newton's first law of motion might help to clarify what I am suggesting. Given that for Christ there is now no force (i.e., death) that can compel time to change its forward motion, by either stopping it or making it go backward, the time that Christ lives just keeps on going.[11]

8. My essay raises the matter of whether Paul thinks that subsequent to Christ's resurrection the death-dominated time still exists. Clearly, Paul thinks that *aspects* of the non-Christ kind of time still exist. Sin is not dead; rather, the saints are to consider themselves dead to it. And even those who are in Christ still die. The continued existence of sin and death does not, however, mean that sin and death are, as they were before Christ, powerful enough to control or characterize a kind of time. Did Paul conceive of sin and death as illusions in the sense that, if granted no reality by the saints ("consider yourselves dead to sin and alive to God," Rom. 6:11 NRSV), for the saints they would be nonexistent? In regard to time, then, death-dominated time may actually not exist for the saints. Taking this line of thought does not need to lead either to a prosperity gospel or to a tight-lipped denial of life's pains, the power of evil, and the horror of physical death (or to a Stoic Paul). This should be clear from my discussions below of the afflictions of Christ and the saints.

9. In this thought I am close to that of T. F. Torrance, who writes that "the resurrection is the establishing of the creature in a reality that does not crumble away into the dust or degenerate into nothingness or slip into the oblivion of the past" (*Space, Time and Resurrection* [Edinburgh: Handsel Press, 1976], p. 79).

10. See also the phrase εἰς ζωὴν αἰώνιον in 5:21, where the preposition εἰς indicates that, by Christ's agency, grace reigning through righteousness occurs in a forward/toward movement.

11. Newton's first law of motion: "Every object persists in its state of rest or uniform motion in a straight line unless it is compelled to change that state by forces impressed on it." While there is much to disagree with in Oscar Cullmann's *Christ and Time: The Primitive*

As it is time without death, the time that Christ lives is life-time, time that lives from life and leans ahead to more and more life. Christ will never again know death (6:9); his life goes only on ahead. Since Christ is the exemplar of one who loves God, Romans 8:28 may be understood to say something not only about Christ's brothers and sisters (8:29) but also about him. In the time that Christ lives everything works together *toward* (εἰς) the good. Such forward motion is a feature of God's time; God knows ahead, God foreknows and chooses beforehand (8:29). God's time is lived forward. Christ, living in God's presence (8:34), shares this kind of time.

The forward movement of Christ's time — the movement to more and more life, which is the same thing as more and more time — involves suffering. While Christ's time does not include sin and death, it does include affliction. As Paul writes in Romans 8:18, there are sufferings in the "now time." Christ participates in these sufferings along with those who are in him (8:17).[12] These sufferings are intrinsic to eager expectation and straining forward in hope toward resurrection — an event that so far Christ alone has experienced. These sufferings will not go on endlessly, however. Subsequent to the coming redemption and liberation about which Paul speaks in Romans 8:21-23, suffering will cease, for the travail of intense longing will be over (8:19, 22).

The eternal life that Christ lives is lived toward and into the ever-ongoing life of a transformed creation at one with God. The eternal life that Christ lives will course through the events that will produce cosmic peace in God. The event of Christ's return, then, does not define Christ's time.[13] Rather, what defines Christ's time is life that will continue endlessly, having surged from his resurrection, through the future event of his return, into a liberated creation.

Christian Conception of Time and History, trans. Floyd V. Filson, rev. ed. (London: SCM, 1962) — much of which has been articulated by James Barr in *Biblical Words for Time,* SBT 33 (London: SCM, 1962) — his insight that "the forward direction" of the "time that extends beyond the end of the present age" is "unlimited, unending, and . . . in this sense it is eternal" (Cullmann, *Christ,* p. 48) is akin to what I understand as "eternal life." Eternity is a kind of time. I understand Paul to think of eternity as a kind of time that began at Christ's resurrection and will continue without end.

12. This understands συμπάσχομεν in 8:17 to mean that Christ suffers now with the saints who suffer now.

13. Paul does not mention Christ's return in Romans 5–8, but only its before and after (Rom. 8:18-23). I mention it here, however, because, given the context of Paul's writings as a whole, Christ's return is presumed in Romans 8; and, in regards to time, Christ's return is critical both to Paul's gospel and his interpreters.

The most common presentation of Paul's view of time is in the categories of eschatology and apocalyptic. While there is a discussion to be had about the distinctions and connections between these two ways of organizing Paul's thought, both understand the *eschaton* as definitive of the time lived by the saints. With eschatology and apocalyptic as frameworks for reading Paul, the time of the saints is defined by the End, either because the End is understood to loom over the present, or because the saints are viewed as living in the midst of it. As mentioned above, Pauline scholarship has come to a consensus that the time the saints live is "already and not yet." This view typically entails understanding time as characterized by the conflict between God's saving actions and sin's resistance. What is "already" is the inauguration of God's triumph. What is "not yet" is the continued presence of sin and death.

My focus on the kind of time that Christ lives (which, I propose, is at once the time lived by the saints) offers a different perspective. While Paul clearly believes there are events to come, and that in the time before these events there is physical death and all creation groans, it is not the *eschaton* (its eventual arrival nor its present manifestation) that characterizes Christ's time. What shapes utterly Christ's time is life — life now that will surge through the *eschaton* to what comes after.

Since there is only life in Christ, the present lived in him is complete. To step outside of Romans to corroborate my point, perhaps the reason Paul can call the saints τέλειοι, "those who are complete" (Phil. 3:15; 1 Cor. 2:6), is because he conceives of them living in time that is itself complete, even though there is more to come. Paul can say that he himself is not yet perfected/completed (Phil. 3:12) but that he strains forward as one who is perfect/complete (Phil. 3:15). From complete to more complete.

The present in Christ, being life without death, will produce only more and more of itself — life. The time of Christ is complete, even though there is unfinished business.[14]

---

14. Paul's words in 1 Cor. 13:10 have typically been understood in a way that would contradict this idea. Paul is understood to be saying that for the saints the present, being partial (ἐκ μέρους), is incomplete — this incompleteness being understood to be comprised of a mixture of God's saving actions and sin's designs. It should be noted, however, that in 1 Corinthians 13 Paul is extolling the presence of ἀγάπη. The presence of love is the presence of completeness, of what is perfect, for love will never fail. In context, it is our prophecy and our knowledge that are incomplete (1 Cor. 13:9). The presence of incompleteness — the prophecy and knowledge (and tongues, 1 Cor. 13:8) of Paul and the saints — is a mixture of what is good and will pass away with what is good and will never end (ἀγάπη). What is now

The Time Lived by Those in Christ

Paul believes that when people are baptized into Christ's death, they are in the one whose death was transformed into life with God. Consequently, those who are in Christ's death are also in his life with God. While Paul (or one or more of his heirs) makes this thought explicit in Colossians and Ephesians, it is barely less than explicit when Paul writes in Romans that those baptized into Christ's death might walk in newness of life (6:4).[15] Those who are baptized into Christ are, then, in the one who lives with God.

The kind of time in which those in Christ live is, then, completely and thoroughly different from the kind of time available before Christ came. This is nowhere clearer than in Paul's captivating words in Romans 7. While Romans 7:7-25 addresses many aspects of Paul's gospel, this passage can be heard also to depict the quality of time lived before Christ.[16] It was time dominated by sin and death, time in which even the best intentions and the best of instruments (God's law) produce death.

As Romans 8:1-2 explains, however, unlike that time, the "now" of those in Christ is fundamentally and totally different: "There is therefore no condemnation for those who are in Christ Jesus, for the law of the spirit of life in Christ Jesus has set you/me/us[17] free from the law of sin and death." The "now" is the time initiated by Christ's death (5:9, 11; 7:4-6). It is a present that is free of sin and death. The "now" is characterized by life and peace (8:3-6).

---

incomplete is so only in the sense that it is not all it will be. It is not incomplete in the sense that it is a mixture of the good with the bad. It is this sense that I find also in Romans 5–8, and that I have chosen to describe as the present in Christ being complete even though there are more events — some of them extremely challenging — to come.

15. Unlike Paul's words in the following verse about future resurrection, the aorist subjunctive περιπατήσωμεν does not indicate a future event. Rather, "newness of life stands in antithesis to pre-Christian life" (J. Baumgarten, "καινός κτλ," *EDNT* 2 [1991], p. 230). It describes what is now.

16. Particularly, as Paul Meyer famously argued, Paul's understanding that there is a cleavage in the law itself ("The Worm at the Core of the Apple: Exegetical Reflections on Romans 7," in *The Word in This World: Essays in New Testament Exegesis and Theology*, ed. John T. Carroll, NTL [Louisville: Westminster John Knox, 2004], p. 75). It will be seen that I have changed my mind about whether in Romans 7 Paul is speaking about life before or after Christ. See my earlier article, "'The Commandment Which Is for Life' (Romans 7.10): Sin's Use of the Obedience of Faith," *JSNT* 27 (2004): 193-216.

17. Depending on which manuscript one chooses.

When Paul says in Romans 8:10 that, if Christ is in people, the body is dead with reference to sin[18] and the spirit alive with respect to righteousness,[19] he is speaking of a present from which the past of sin and death is absent. Unlike many, I do not understand 8:10 to indicate an "already and not yet" kind of time. Martinus C. de Boer, for instance, understands Paul's words to describe the "dialectical interplay between the reality of the old age and the reality of the new age."[20] Rather, as should be clear from the translation I am sharing with Käsemann, I hear Paul declaring that the present for those "in Christ" is one of life and righteousness (righteousness being linked to life the way sin is to death). Time lived by those in Christ is lived not being pulled backward into destruction and death but from life forward to life.

The "now" time is a present separated from the death-dominated past. Paul makes plain this understanding of the distinctive quality of the "now" in Christ when he writes that those in Christ are glorified (using δοξάζω in the aorist; 8:30); they have eternal life (using ἔχω in the present indicative; 6:22).

Regularly in our four chapters, when describing the state of those in Christ, Paul starts with a passive participle and goes on to describe the present or the future on the basis of the state described by the participle. This pattern starts at the beginning of chapter 5: "Having been made righteous by faith we have [or: 'let us have'] peace toward God" (5:1); at 5:9, "Having now been made righteous . . . we shall be saved"; at 5:10, "Having been reconciled we shall be saved"; at 6:18, "Having been set free from sin, you have become enslaved to righteousness"; at 6:22, "Having been set free from sin, you have become enslaved to God."

At chapter 8 a semantically equivalent pattern emerges. Paul describes the state of those in Christ with present indicatives and, on the basis of the present, looks to the future. For instance, "you are not in the flesh, you are in the Spirit. . . . If the spirit of the one who raised Jesus from the dead

---

18. Using Ernst Käsemann's translation of διά with the accusative as "with reference to" (*Commentary on Romans,* trans. and ed. Geoffrey W. Bromiley [Grand Rapids: Eerdmans, 1980], p. 224).

19. While there is debate over the meaning of the phrase τὸ δὲ πνεῦμα ζωὴ διὰ δικαιοσύνην (see options for translation in Robert Jewett, *Romans: A Commentary,* Hermeneia [Minneapolis: Fortress, 2007], pp. 491-92), I follow Käsemann — "the Spirit who is given us makes alive so far as concerns righteousness" (*Romans,* p. 224).

20. *The Defeat of Death: Apocalyptic Eschatology in 1 Corinthians 15 and Romans 5,* JSNTSup 22 (Sheffield: Sheffield Academic Press, 1988), p. 175.

dwells in you, the one who raised Christ from the dead will make alive your mortal bodies also" (8:9, 11).

When Paul does look elsewhere than the present and the future, it is to describe a kind of time that is now gone for those who are in Christ. The time in which sin and death reigned (5:12-14) is a kind of time in which those in Christ do not live. The present, the "now," of those who are in Christ is a present without that past. Those who are "in Christ" are to recognize that they are dead to sin and living to God (6:11). They are to put themselves at God's disposal as if brought out of the dead (6:13) and so, although Paul does not state this explicitly, as if living as the resurrected Christ lives. They are to know themselves to have died to sin (6:2), to be united with Christ in his death (6:5), to no longer serve sin (6:6).

The characteristic of the time in which those in Christ live is that it is lived in a present from which the death-dominated past has been obliterated. The only past that matters is the moment that established the present — Christ's death, resurrection, and exaltation. The only past that matters is that Christ died, was raised, and was exalted.[21] But *this* past is not past but present. The past events of Christ's death and resurrection are part of the present, since the saints are those who are baptized into Christ's death (6:4) and are brought from death to life (6:13), and Christ (the one who is at God's right hand) now lives in them (8:10). The time in which those in Christ live is time with only a present that leans toward the future.[22] Paul puts it this way: "It was in hope that we were saved" (8:24).[23] The time of the saints is time that lives from a "now" without a past, a "now" that, from a state of hope, leans forward.

The time in which those in Christ live is time that looks toward: toward reigning in life (5:17), toward being united with Christ in his resurrection (6:5),[24] toward bodies being made alive (8:11), toward being glori-

---

21. Let me pause here and acknowledge that, if I were to continue this study outside these four chapters, I would need to do more thinking about how Paul's honoring of God's history with Israel, and his conviction about God's irrevocable call to Israel, fits into such a "now." I suspect it might be that Paul assumes that the present in Christ *includes* God's history with Israel. As he says to the saints at Rome, Israel is "the root that supports you" (Rom. 11:18 NRSV).

22. Might this reading contribute to an understanding of the curious lack of reference to the past in Rom. 8:38?

23. Using C. E. B. Cranfield's translation (*A Critical and Exegetical Commentary on the Epistle to the Romans*, ICC [Edinburgh: T. & T. Clark, 1975-1979], 1:404).

24. Taking this in context to be a reference to Christ's resurrection. See Jewett, *Romans*, p. 401.

fied with Christ (8:17), toward the glory that will be revealed (8:18), toward being given all things with Christ (8:32).

This living forward is done from a "now" based in hope. I understand ἐπί with the dative ἐλπίδι in 5:2 to denote the basis for a state of being.[25] The state of the "now" is hope. And, as the "now" does not include death or sin, those in the state of hope live only forward.

This does not mean that there is no struggle in the kind of time lived "in Christ." Until creation is liberated, there is indeed struggle. Paul writes that those who are children of God — that is, those who know Christ to be the firstborn of their family (8:29) — groan as they wait for the redemption of their bodies (8:23). In other words, they groan as they wait for their resurrection in a transformed creation. They groan in hope (8:20-21)[26] as they live toward resurrection and creation's liberation.[27]

What distinguishes struggle in Christ's time from that in the time dominated by sin and death is that in Christ's time the struggle is productive. Paul describes this productivity in Romans 5:2-5. From the secure present of standing in grace, as the REB puts it well, Paul speaks of rejoicing in "hope of the divine glory that is to be ours" (5:2). This rejoicing takes place at the same time as rejoicing in afflictions. Paul describes these afflictions as productive of endurance, character, and hope. From hope more hope is produced, by means of afflictions.

Paul also highlights the productive character of afflictions in the "now" time in his description of the groaning of creation and of the children of God (8:18-23). While Paul does not say that these afflictions will *produce* a transformed creation, they are part of the "now time" — the νῦν καιρός (8:18) — that leans toward that transformed creation. These sufferings are not, in other words, directed toward death and destruction.[28]

Certain kinds of afflictions — the afflictions that Christ knows, which produce life — are an intrinsic feature of a kind of time that leans toward resurrection and God's liberation of God's world. Clearly Paul thought that when creation is set free these afflictions will end. Like time on the

---

25. As BDF §235 explains, although not with reference to this verse, ἐπί with the dative "most frequently denotes the basis for a state of being."

26. Taking children of God to be part of creation in Rom. 8:19-20.

27. Paul exemplifies this struggle in his self-description in Phil. 3:8-13.

28. See my "Accepting Affliction: Paul's Preaching on Suffering," in *Character and Scripture: Moral Formation, Community, and Biblical Interpretation,* ed. William P. Brown (Grand Rapids: Eerdmans, 2002), pp. 290-316; also my *At the Heart of the Gospel: Suffering in the Earliest Christian Message* (Grand Rapids: Eerdmans, 2007).

other side of that liberation, time on this side is not, however, defined by afflictions but by Christ's resurrected life. The ethical consequence for the saints of this kind of time is that they participate in God's battle by acting from the life of Christ for the sake of life for all of God's creation.

Paul acknowledges that it is possible for those in Christ to be oblivious to the quality of the time in which they live. Consequently, he is constrained to exhort them to consider themselves dead to sin and living to God in Christ Jesus (6:11). Later in the letter he will direct them not to be conformed to "this age" (12:2). Paul's energy goes toward helping those in Christ recognize the kind of time they live. When they do so, they understand that sin and death inhabit a kind of time that for them no longer exists. Even the death of their bodies is undergone in the light of life (8:11). They live in a "now" in which they are saved in hope — a "now" in which they are glorified; they have eternal life — a now that is complete and will produce more of itself.

Paul did not have a realized eschatology, and he was convinced that God was waging a cosmic battle against sin. For human beings, who are the object of that conflict, God's battle is taking place in a time shaped utterly by Christ's resurrection. Christ's time is free of anything but life. Likewise, the kind of time lived by those in Christ — by those afflicted as they strain toward resurrection and the liberation of creation — is life-time in a state of hope for more and more life. To refashion one of Paul's more famous phrases: the kind of time that the saints live is "from life to life" (2 Cor. 2:16).

"Who Hopes for What Is Seen?": Political Theology through Romans

Douglas Harink

That Paul's letter to the Romans is intrinsically a political document, concerned throughout with issues of political sovereignty and loyalty, law and justice, and the purpose and destiny of nations, is, while not an undisputed conclusion, one that is increasingly shared among students of Paul. From earlier works by Dieter Georgi, Neil Elliott, and Richard Horsley, to more recent works by N. T. Wright, Neil Elliott (again), and others, the historical case for reading Paul's writings in general and Romans in particular as political theology is increasingly compelling.[1] From a wholly other angle, some recent European political philosophers, such as Jacob Taubes, Alain Badiou, Giorgio Agamben, and Slavoj Žižek, standing completely outside the sphere of New Testament scholarship, have also come more or less independently to the conclusion that Paul's letters were politically charged in

---

1. For a summary and argument by one of the key proponents of the political Paul, see N. T. Wright, "Paul and Empire" (and the attendant bibliography), in *The Blackwell Companion to Paul,* ed. Stephen Westerholm (Oxford and Malden, MA: Wiley-Blackwell, 2011), pp. 285-97. See also John M. G. Barclay, "Why the Roman Empire Was Insignificant for Paul," in *Pauline Churches and Diaspora Jews,* WUNT 275 (Tübingen: Mohr Siebeck, 2011), pp. 363-87, on which the present essay heavily depends. Barclay is critical of the way Wright and others construe Paul's political theology as being *in opposition to* the imperial rule of the Caesars and Rome. The most thoroughgoing (Marxist) political reading of Romans is now Neil Elliott, *The Arrogance of Nations: Reading Romans in the Shadow of Empire,* Paul in Critical Contexts (Minneapolis: Fortress, 2008).

An earlier version of this essay was presented to the Pauline Soteriology Group of the Society of Biblical Literature, San Francisco, November 2011. I am grateful for the comments I received on the paper in that setting. I am also grateful to Prof. John Barclay for carefully reading and commenting on the paper, which has resulted in a number of improvements.

the beginning and still hold largely untapped political potential.[2] It is not the purpose of this essay to make that case again, either historically-exegetically or by following the recent political philosophers. Rather, drawing on those materials, I will sketch an outline of what *kind* of political vision and practice the Letter to the Romans (and Paul's letters more generally) invites — or compels — Christians to adopt in our own time.[3] That vision and practice is summed up in a clumsy but, I think, helpful caption: *messianic-apocalyptic political universalism*. In what follows I will explicate each of those terms — in reverse order — as a way of getting at the character of the political theology of Romans.

Universalism

"Universalism" is usually used in addressing the issue of the "scope of salvation," that is, the question whether all or only some individuals are destined to be "saved." There are certainly texts in Romans and elsewhere in Paul's letters that are germane to that discussion, but it is not the question to be treated here. It is, rather, the question of *political* universalism that concerns us here: in other words, the claim (the "good news") of a universal political sovereignty that Paul announces in Romans and the corresponding political loyalty, mission, and practice evoked by that claim.

Universal claims in Romans are hard to miss. They come at every important juncture of the letter, and they regularly have to do with regimes of power. In Romans 1:16-17, Paul declares that God's power for salvation and justice is "apocalypsed" (ἀποκαλύπτεται) in the gospel for "all who believe." Simultaneously, this same gospel "apocalypses" the wrath of God against all human impiety and injustice (1:18), the regime of sin under which all are bound (ὑφ' ἁμαρτίαν — 3:9; cf. 3:23; 7:14), and the judgment

2. For an excellent discussion of Paul in recent philosophy see P. Travis Kroeker, "Recent Continental Philosophy" (and the attendant bibliography), in *Blackwell*, pp. 440-54. Philosophical appropriations of the political Paul are now also having an impact on contemporary theology, exemplified in the essays in Douglas Harink, ed., *Paul, Philosophy, and the Theopolitical Vision: Critical Engagements with Agamben, Badiou, Žižek and Others*, Theopolitical Visions 7 (Eugene, OR: Cascade, 2010) and in John Milbank, Slavoj Žižek, and Creston Davis, *Paul's New Moment: Continental Philosophy and the Future of Christian Theology* (Grand Rapids: Brazos, 2010).

3. I say "compels" for those who take Romans and the other Pauline letters as Christian Scripture and therefore seek therein normative direction for contemporary political witness.

of God under which "the whole world" is placed (3:19). Crucial in the early chapters of Romans is that divine and cosmic *regimes of power* are in play, claiming dominion over all peoples, whether Gentile or Jew. The gospel reveals that there are powers that war against God and enslave humankind. Indeed, in Romans 5 these powers are depicted as agents in their own right (Death — ὁ θάνατος ἐβασίλευσεν [5:17]; Sin — ἐβασίλευσεν ἡ ἁμαρτία [5:21]).[4] But the powers do not ultimately threaten God's eternal sovereign power (ἀΐδιος αὐτοῦ δύναμις καὶ θειότης — 1:20). Quite the contrary: even though these powers enter into the scene of history through human disobedience, they are made to serve God's purpose. When Gentiles refused to acknowledge the Creator as the true divine power and instead worshiped cosmic, creaturely powers, "God handed them over" (διὸ παρέδωκεν αὐτοὺς ὁ θεὸς) to those powers, as Paul declares three times (1:24, 26, 28), until the time of deliverance. Thus the powers (against their will) are made to play something like a providential role in God's purpose, which is finally to defeat those very same powers and to deliver humankind from bondage to them. As Beverly Roberts Gaventa writes, "God's handing over of humanity is not simply a response to human action but an event in God's conflict with the anti-God powers."[5]

Nevertheless, as the apostle describes in Romans 1:24-32, those cosmic/ historical, anti-God powers, to which all humankind is now in subjection, unleash a fury of disobedience, disorder, and destruction throughout personal, social, and political life, and these powers even conscript humankind into their attack on God (cf. 5:6-10: the "ungodly" and "sinners" become "enemies" of God). Enslavement to the powers and enmity with God are the actual condition of humankind. This condition is universal and, we might say, "absolute." Clearly, such a description of "the human condition" does not emerge from empirical investigation or relative moral judgments;

---

4. As Beverly Roberts Gaventa observes, "Especially in [Romans] chapters 5–7, Paul pairs sin and its partner death with active verbs: sin 'entered' (5:12), death 'spread' (5:12), death 'ruled' (5:14, 17; 6:9), sin 'increased' (5:20), sin 'ruled' (5:21; 6:12, 14), sin 'seized an opportunity' (7:8, 11), sin 'produced' (7:8), sin 'sprang to life' (7:9), sin 'deceived' and 'killed' me (7:11), sin 'lives in me' (7:17, 20)" ("Paul and the Roman Believers," in *Blackwell*, p. 105). Elsewhere, Gaventa writes: "*Brought together, these 'achievements' of Sin's résumé create the portrait of a cosmic terrorist. Sin not only entered the cosmos with Adam; it also enslaved, it unleashed Death itself, it even managed to take the law of God captive to its power*" (*Our Mother Saint Paul* [Louisville: Westminster John Knox, 2007], pp. 130-31, emphasis original). Beverly Gaventa's extensive work on Paul and Romans undergirds a good deal of the argument of this essay.

5. Gaventa, *Mother*, p. 118.

rather, it is apocalypsed simultaneously with the gospel (1:18). It is "the human condition" that the gospel reveals and upon which the gospel comes as God's interruptive, invasive act of grace and justice, the assertion of God's victory over the powers in a decisive act of liberation: "But now . . . the justice of God has been disclosed . . . , the justice of God through the faith of Jesus Messiah for all who believe" (3:21-22, author's translation).

In Romans 5:12-21, the universality of the gospel reaches all the way back to the beginning and encompasses all humankind. Jesus Messiah is here figured as the second Adam who himself (like all humankind) "was handed over" (παρεδόθη) to the regime of Death (4:25). Nevertheless, precisely under the reign of the powers of Sin and Death, and against them, he renders his total life to God as a single act of obedience and justice, and thereby fully and superabundantly overcomes the effect of the first Adam's disobedience and injustice. Here again the language of regimes of power plays a crucial role. Where the regime of Sin (ἐβασίλευσεν ἡ ἁμαρτία — 5:21) and the regime of Death (ὁ θάνατος ἐβασίλευσεν — 5:14, 17) invaded and imposed themselves on humankind through "the one man's trespass," through the other man's act of justice a new regime arrives, overcomes, and transcends the old powers. It is a regime of gift and grace (ἡ χάρις βασιλεύσῃ — 5:21) in which humankind itself is returned to its own rightful reign in creation (οἱ . . . ἐν ζωῇ βασιλεύσουσιν — 5:17). And this, again, for all! "Therefore just as one man's trespass led to judgment *for all* (εἰς πάντας ἀνθρώπους), so one man's act of justice leads to rectification of life *for all* (εἰς πάντας ἀνθρώπους)" (5:18).

In Romans 8 this gospel universalism ultimately stretches out, in hope, over the totality of creation (8:18-23), encompassing all potentially threatening historical and cosmic powers (8:31-39). As before, in this context we again encounter the hostile powers. Along with humankind, it seems, creation itself was given over ("subjected," ὑπετάγη — 8:20) to the enslaving power of "futility" (ματαιότης — 8:20) and corruption/decay (φθορά — 8:21), a condition in which creation waits eagerly and expectantly for the apocalypse of the glorious liberation of the "sons of God" — the redemption of our bodies — and simultaneously its own glorious liberation, all of this accomplished through the "Son" whom God "handed over" on behalf of all (ὑπὲρ ἡμῶν πάντων παρέδωκεν αὐτόν — 8:32). The liberation Paul envisages here is, no doubt, none other than that "reigning in life" of which he wrote in Romans 5:17, that proper "dominion" in creation (Gen. 1:26-28) that is restored again to humankind through the obedience and justice of the second Adam, and that bears with it the life and freedom of all things.

We cannot, finally, carry on with the universality theme in Romans without noting how, through all of the convoluted argument of chapters 9–11, Paul arrives at the great declaration of historical universalism in Romans 11:32. At one time or another, Paul writes, either the Gentiles or Israel have experienced a "hardening," have been "disobedient." But here again Paul is not making an empirical moral judgment on the history of either the nations or Israel. While the "disobedience" is itself inescapably culpable in some sense (cf. 1:18-23), the focus, as in Romans 1, lies elsewhere, that is, on the work of God in "consigning" or "imprisoning" all in disobedience (συνέκλεισεν γὰρ ὁ θεὸς τοὺς πάντας εἰς ἀπείθειαν — 11:32), the nations at one time, Israel at another. And God has done this toward a single, all-encompassing end: "that he may be merciful to all" (ἵνα τοὺς πάντας ἐλεήσῃ — 11:32). "For from him and through him and to him are all things" (11:36).

All of this, the ultimate universalism, we might say, is, however, hidden in hope: as Paul writes, "For in hope we were saved. Now hope that is seen is not hope. For who hopes for what is seen? But if we hope for what we do not see, we wait for it with patience" (8:24-25). Our confidence, full of hope, is that God is working in "all things" (πάντα) to bring about good for those whom he calls (8:28); that against every form of historical and political opposition (ἐν τούτοις πᾶσιν), including the "sword" (μάχαιρα — 8:35), we are "more than conquerors" through the Messiah who loves us (8:37); that no imaginable historical or cosmic power in all creation (οὔτε τις κτίσις ἑτέρα) "will be able to separate us from the love of God in Messiah Jesus our Lord" (8:39).

What are we to make of the unmistakable universalism that runs throughout Romans — indeed, that is at its very core — and elsewhere in Paul's letters? While there may be some things to criticize about Alain Badiou's construal of Pauline universalism, Badiou nevertheless rightly reminds us how central it is to Paul's message and mission. The gospel, in its absolute singularity, is about and for all, or it is about nothing at all. Badiou draws our attention to the startling strangeness of Pauline universalism:

> [W]hen one reads Paul, one is stupefied by the paucity of traces left in his prose by the era, genres, and circumstances. There is in this prose, under the imperative of the event, something solid and timeless, something that, precisely because it is a question of orienting a thought toward the universal *in its suddenly emerging singularity,* but indepen-

dently of all anecdote, is intelligible to us without having to resort to cumbersome historical mediations. . . .[6]

Badiou may overstate the matter here, but particularly with respect to Romans he puts his finger on one of the reasons why it has been so hard for scholars to specify "the reasons for Romans" and the various "historical mediations" of the message of Romans that depend on those reasons. There is an "absoluteness" about Paul's universalism in Romans that is not related as a response to any merely historical circumstance or as an outcome of any merely historical trajectory. Consider the claims: "all the nations," or "all have sinned," or "condemnation for all" and "justification and life for all," or "all in disobedience" and "mercy to all."[7] Where are the traceable lines of connection between those claims and the messy, complex, ambiguous, contested, so-called "empirical realities" of history, whether in Paul's time or our own? What is revealed in the gospel here, as Karl Barth recognized, is *another world,* one that does not "emerge" from any immanent desire, disaster, or potentiality in the world as we think we know it, but one that enters into, interrupts, and discloses for the first time the truth about the world we thought we knew. Indeed, precisely in relation to "era, genres, and circumstances," in relation to "all anecdote," the gospel is the explosive disaster that comes upon all, for the sake of all: "What is there, then, in Christ Jesus?" Barth asks in his commentary. "There is that which *horrifies:* the dissolution of history in history, the destruction of the structure of events within their known structure, the end of time in the order of time."[8]

Thinking politically, that is surely the reason why imperial Rome, in its historical existence as *the* universal empire and political authority in Paul's time, does not appear in this treatise of *political* universalism. As *imperium,* Rome is in fact *invisible* in the letter; or rather, Rome is only indirectly visible, insofar as (we must assume) it is included in and among the comprehensive "all's" of the letter, that is, among the generic "nations" and

6. Alain Badiou, *Saint Paul: The Foundation of Universalism,* trans. Ray Brassier (Stanford: Stanford University Press, 2003), p. 36, emphasis original.

7. Jacob Taubes's remark about 1 Corinthians applies equally, or even more truly, to Romans: the letter is "one great fugue around the single word *pan.* The whole text revolves, is constructed, around this word" (*The Political Theology of Paul,* trans. Dana Hollander [Stanford: Stanford University Press, 2004], p. 1).

8. Karl Barth, *The Epistle to the Romans,* 6th ed., trans. E. C. Hoskyns (Oxford: Oxford University Press, 1968), p. 103, emphasis added.

(in Rom. 13:1-7) the "governing authorities." As a specific historical empire and political authority Rome has no significant role to play in, and bears no remarkable relation, either negative or positive, to the universal divine sovereignty that Paul is declaring in Romans as the good news.[9] Rome is, rather, simply one among τὰ ἔθνη (καὶ ἐν ὑμῖν καθὼς καὶ ἐν τοῖς λοιποῖς ἔθνεσιν — 1:13; καὶ ὑμῖν τοῖς ἐν ᾽Ρώμῃ — 1:15) that owe faithful obedience to the true sovereign who is the subject of Paul's political good news.

Paul's disregard of the only so-called "real" political universal in play at the time does not mean, however, that the discourse of Romans merely floats above history as a kind of general political theory. On the contrary, the entirety of Paul's political vision hinges on the very real and particular historical figures that do show up constitutively in the letter: Jesus the Messiah, "descended from David κατὰ σάρκα" (1:3); the people Israel, from whom also the Messiah comes κατὰ σάρκα (9:5); and the messianic community (Romans 12–14), whom Paul addresses as ἀδελφοί ("comrades" — Badiou) and whose flesh-and-blood members he knows by name (Romans 16). This, by the way, is the critical aspect in Paul that Badiou misses, and that renders his version of Paul's universalism fundamentally flawed. For it is these three figures — Jesus, Israel, and the messianic community — that determine the particular shape of Paul's political universalism and the particular character of its historical practice. I shall return to this point later.

Political

God's universal sovereignty, understood in theological-providential terms as God directing the course of world occurrence, has frequently been proposed as the overarching theme of Romans (particularly in traditions influenced by Calvin). But that Romans declares a divinely wrought, universal *political* sovereignty has rarely been noticed in either traditional or most modern interpretation. For Calvin, for example — who is far from deaf to the political meaning of the gospel — the statement that Christ is the Messiah descended from David (ἐκ σπέρματος Δαυὶδ κατὰ σάρκα — 1:3) "recalls us to the *promise*, and removes any doubt which we may have

9. This is the persuasive argument made by John Barclay (over against N. T. Wright's claim that Roman imperial authority and theology are of signal importance for Paul in shaping his own political theology) in "Empire," pp. 363-87.

of His being the very One who was previously promised"; the phrase therefore serves "the confirmation of our faith" in God's promise that is providentially fulfilled in the coming of the Messiah.[10] There is no exploration in Calvin's comments of Jewish royal theology and its political significance. The thought that the phrase "seed of David" might be specifying the one in whom God's sovereignty over Israel and all nations is now being *politically* enacted is rarely entertained even in the latest commentaries on Romans.[11] The importance of political sovereignty in Romans, which should be almost immediately legible in the title "Messiah" and in the phrase "descended from David" (and other phrases), also continues to be missed (or avoided) when modern interpreters read Romans 1:3-4 as a pre-Pauline creedal formula that Paul borrows from a Jewish-Christian context, a formula that, as such, is thought to be an alien element in Paul's theology that has no particular significance for understanding the message of Romans.[12]

There are several important explanations for traditional and contemporary failures to see the whole of the letter to the Romans as political theology. We might note first the effect that the reversal of political fortunes for Christians and the church in the third and fourth centuries after Christ — represented in the label "Constantinianism" — had on the Christian political imagination. Prior to that shift, the scattered messianic communities had little reason to expect that their conviction that Jesus is the Sovereign of the cosmos and history would be affirmed, embraced, and promoted by the powers that be. That sovereignty had to be believed because

10. John Calvin, *The Epistles of Paul to the Romans and to the Thessalonians,* trans. Ross Mackenzie, Calvin's Commentaries 8 (Grand Rapids: Eerdmans, 1960), p. 16, emphasis added. Commentators on Rom. 1:3-4 in the early church tend to read the text as an important witness to the humanity and divinity of Christ; see J. Patout Burns with Constantine Newman, ed. and trans., *Romans: Interpreted by Early Christian Commentators* (Grand Rapids: Eerdmans, 2012), pp. 13-19. More recently, C. E. B. Cranfield, like Calvin, suggests that the phrase emphasizes the theme of promise and fulfillment (*A Critical and Exegetical Commentary on the Epistle to the Romans,* vol. 1, ICC 28 [Edinburgh: T. & T. Clark, 1975], pp. 58-59).

11. The Jewish philosopher Jacob Taubes recognized (in lectures from 1987) the political significance of Rom. 1:1-7 well before most Christian commentators did. Taubes took these verses to be "a *political* declaration of war on the Caesar" (*Political,* p. 16, emphasis original). One Christian interpreter, John Howard Yoder, was reading Paul politically already in the 1960s and 1970s; see *The Politics of Jesus: Vicit Agnus Noster,* 2nd ed. (Grand Rapids: Eerdmans, 1994).

12. See the discussion in Elliott, *Arrogance,* pp. 62-65.

it was not seen. Following the Constantinian reversal (i.e., cessation of persecution of Christians, imperial toleration, and later establishment of the Christian religion), Christian historical-political hopes were increasingly placed on the christianized political authority of earthly emperors, kings and princes, and governments.[13] From this point of view, Romans 13:1-7 moves to the center of attention for those seeking political direction from the letter. The obedient loyalty that Gentile believers (εἰς ὑπακοὴν πίστεως ἐν πᾶσιν τοῖς ἔθνεσιν — Rom. 1:5) are to give to the sovereign Messiah Jesus, which is the heart of the good news to the nations, is now turned toward the "governing authorities."

Equally important, and related in some measure to the "Constantinian shift," is the traditional assumption that the New Testament marks a turn from the obvious national and political concerns and hopes of Israel in the Old Testament to religious and spiritual concerns. Indeed, according to that assumption, the theological universalism of a text like Romans is precisely enabled by the "transcending" of those "Jewish," earthly, political-historical horizons through a more exalted, spiritual vision of the meaning of the church and history in which the categories of Israel and the nations are irrelevant. Whatever terms like "Messiah" and "descended from David" might have meant politically to "pre-Christian" Jews in the time of Jesus and Paul, they no longer bore such meaning after Christ. In this understanding, Romans as a whole is concerned with the Christian "doctrine of salvation" (understood individualistically) on one hand — even chapters 9–11 are read primarily as a treatise on the election and predestination of individual believers — and with "the Christian life" on the other. One aspect of "the Christian life" is what one "owes" to the earthly "governing authorities" according to Romans 13:1-7, and this is normally understood to be political loyalty and taxes, matters that of themselves are irrelevant to "salvation," and therefore not subject to serious theological critique.[14]

---

13. John Howard Yoder's essay, "The Constantinian Sources of Western Social Ethics," in *The Priestly Kingdom: Social Ethics as Gospel* (Notre Dame: University of Notre Dame Press, 1984), pp. 135-47, remains of fundamental importance. The essay is not a study of "the historical Constantine," nor a detailed historical account of the transition from the political situation of the early church to that of the medieval church. Instead, its aim is to delineate the effects of the Constantinian settlement on the Christian "social imaginary" in the early, medieval, and modern church.

14. This is clearly a deeply supersessionist reading of Romans, in which the spiritually more highly developed and universally valid life of Christians and the church replaces the

Finally, in the modern era, and for primarily political reasons, "religion" and "politics" have been portioned off into distinct and constitutionally separate spheres of life, the private and the public respectively. Since it is assumed that a document like the New Testament or a letter like Romans is at the foundation of "the Christian religion," it must be read as a "religious" text that "expresses" the religious experiences, beliefs, and practices of the early church and its founders. Even if New Testament texts might express political visions here and there, precisely as political those visions are taken to be incidental to the original religious meaning of the text and anachronistic to any political thoughts and practices we might have in our time. The instruction of Romans 13:1-7 to "submit" to governing authorities was expedient political advice in the era of emperors, kings, and despots, but in the age of liberal-democratic nation-states it is relatively meaningless — neither important for a vibrant personal "religious" life, nor significant for determining how to vote on election day.[15]

The pioneering works of Neil Elliott, Richard Horsley, N. T. Wright, and others are now challenging our apolitical understandings of Jesus and Paul. In the first place, they show that the neat modern separation of religion and politics is simply not applicable to the Jewish, Greek, and Roman worlds of the first century. Every political rule and authority was understood to be founded in and dependent upon divine authority and favor, and sustained by the cultic practices and sacrifices that garnered that divine favor. These works show, further, how a text such as Romans 1:3-7, when read alongside the Psalms and Prophets, and alongside such Roman texts as the Priene Inscription, reverberates with the rhetoric, propaganda, and slogans of the imperial theology of Rome and the royal messianic theology of Judaism.[16] "Good news about the all-powerful son of God who,

---

more earthly, ethnic, and national life of the Jews. For the serious and often destructive theological and political consequences of supersessionism, see Scott Bader-Saye, *Church and Israel after Christendom: The Politics of Election* (Boulder: Westview, 1999).

15. Crucial contributions to tracing the history, theology, and politics involved in the modern separation of religion and politics are made in the works of William T. Cavanaugh; see especially *Migrations of the Holy: God, State, and the Political Meaning of the Church* (Grand Rapids: Eerdmans, 2011). See also C. C. Pecknold, *Christianity and Politics: A Brief Guide to the History* (Eugene, OR: Cascade, 2010), which is far more than "a guide to the history"; the theopolitical vision presented there and by Cavanaugh are essential background to the political reading of Romans I am providing here.

16. For the Priene Inscription, see Neil Elliott and Mark Reasoner, eds., *Documents and Images for the Study of Paul* (Minneapolis: Fortress, 2011), pp. 35, 126-27. The inscription decrees that on the birthday of Augustus honor and worship should be given to him as divine,

coming from the ancient Israelite royal family, claims universal allegiance! The echoes of Psalm 2 and similar passages are matched by the echoes of Roman imperial rhetoric."[17] That those echoes might have been heard by the first hearers and readers of Romans seems likely, particularly for believers in Rome. Still, here we must enter a caveat against the more direct political readings of Paul offered by Elliott, Horsley, Wright, and others. Paul does not let Jewish and Roman political rhetoric set the framework for receiving, understanding, and acting upon those echoes.[18] The first few verses of Romans 1 immediately establish a theopolitical frame of reference in God, in "the spirit of holiness," and in the resurrected Jesus Messiah that simply eclipses, rather than directly opposes or subverts, the other political rhetorics of Paul's time.

When we encounter the phrase "descended from the seed of David," or the declaration that this one descended from David "was declared to be Son of God with power according to the spirit of holiness by resurrection from the dead," or the title Ἰησοῦς Χριστὸς τοῦ κυρίου ἡμῶν, or the expression "the obedience of faith among all the nations," we recognize in these statements that from the beginning of his letter Paul is making an emphatic and bold *theo*political declaration about a sovereignty that is without rival and establishes its own frame of reference: *Jesus the Messiah is the rightful Davidic sovereign, the divinely appointed and anointed agent of God's own universal sovereign rule and justice, to whom Israel and all nations owe loyal obedience.* All of this "good news" is announced without direct reference to any existing worldly rule or power.

As at the beginning of the letter, so also at the end: when in Romans 15:7-13 Paul exhorts Jews and Gentiles in Rome to "welcome one another . . . just as Messiah has welcomed you, for the glory of God," we see that the apostle discerns in that mutual welcome a concrete sign of the theopolitical destiny of all the Gentile peoples joining with Israel in joyful allegiance to and praise of the divine messianic Sovereign of all peoples. We see in Paul's description of his priestly service to the nations in 15:14-29 a commission to declare to all the nations — all the way to Spain, the end of the world — the good news that their true political destiny is to be found

---

as the Savior who brought peace and justice to all, as the one who has inaugurated an unsurpassable new age, as himself the divine "good news" for the whole world.

17. Wright, "Paul," p. 292.

18. In Elliott, especially, the directly political frame of reference, whether ancient (imperial) or modern (Marxist), sets the conditions within which the obviously theological ("kyriarchal") vision of Paul in Romans is to be received. See *Arrogance,* esp. pp. 157-66.

in offering faithful obedience to the one God and the Sovereign Jesus Messiah. Again, all these things are written to the Romans without referring to any existing worldly sovereignty that might form the background or frame of reference for the good news that Paul declares. Having had our eyes trained to see Romans in this light, that is, in the reality of the universal political sovereignty and justice of God now being enacted through Jesus the Messiah, we start discerning the unique political character of the letter as a whole. Matters of power, slavery and dominion, justice, injustice and judgment, fidelity, law and works, participation in the body of the Messiah, the destiny of the people Israel, the newly created messianic community, and so on require both a political and a theological reading. Or rather, the political and the theological are not two alternative possible readings, but they necessarily co-inhere as one, the political always being subsumed into and defined by the theological.

That is the case, however, not only in relation to the theopolitical meanings of such terms as υἱὸς θεοῦ, Χριστός, κύριος, εὐαγγέλιον, ὑπακοὴ πίστεως, but also in relation to the various powers warring against God, the Messiah, the Spirit, and the messianic community. Those powers, whether the great and comprehensive ones such as Sin and Death, or the multiplicity of powers that might threaten humanity, as Paul lists them in Romans 8:35-39, cannot be separated and portioned off — as "spiritual" — from the ordinary social and political realities of day-to-day life. It is impossible to draw any clear dividing line between the "spiritual" and the social, economic, political, and cosmic effects the powers have on history. As is abundantly clear in Romans 1:18-32, when "God handed [the peoples] over" to powers of their own choosing, the results for personal, social, and political life were devastating all the way up and all the way down. Conversely, the now-apocalypsed reign of God brought about in and by the second Adam, the Lord Jesus Messiah, and his Spirit likewise, but superabundantly, has its own concrete effects across the whole range of cosmic and human existence, all the way up and all the way down. "The challenge to which the proclamation of Christ's rule over the rebellious world speaks a word of grace is not a problem within the self but a split within the cosmos. . . . That Christ is Lord, a proclamation to which only individuals can respond, is nonetheless a social, political, *structural* fact which constitutes a challenge to the Powers."[19] Where the powers had enslaved and brought destruction to the political life of humankind, the Messiah, through the

---

19. Yoder, *Politics*, pp. 161, 156-57, emphasis original.

powerful Holy Spirit at work in the messianic community, brings about liberation, healing, and a new form of political existence.[20]

From this interpretive orientation the entire text of Romans (and not only Rom. 13:1-7, which becomes something of an aside) speaks as a document of political theology and begins to open up toward some of the most critical questions of Christian political witness in our own time: What is the true nature of sovereign rule, if it is singularly revealed in Jesus the Messiah? What is the meaning of the history of nations in light of that sovereignty? If God's justice is apocalyptically revealed in the death and resurrection of Jesus, where is worldly justice to be found; what does it look like; how is it done? If the Messiah is the τέλος of the νόμος, what are the purposes and limits of law? What is the character of life beyond the limits of the legal and the political? How are justice, reconciliation, and healing done among nations in view of their constitutive determination by Jesus the Messiah, the people Israel, and the messianic community? How can a Pauline political universalism be engaged to resist the horrors committed in the name of all kinds of political universalisms throughout the centuries and around the world?

We could go on with such questions, which are now especially being raised and explored by those European philosophers (Taubes, Badiou, Žižek, Agamben) who have found something of crucial importance in Paul, and pursued further by theologians awakened to such questions by Pauline scholars and philosophers. In the next two sections I will sketch an approach to some of these questions that homes in more closely on the uniqueness of the political vision of Romans.

Apocalyptic

I have already noted that the political universalism of Paul's gospel almost completely eclipses and occludes the specific historical fact of the Roman

---

20. Among those who have argued persuasively for eradicating any hard separation between the "spiritual" and the social and political dimensions of human life when thinking about "the principalities and powers," see especially Hendrikus Berkhof, *Christ and the Powers,* trans. John Howard Yoder, 2nd ed. (Scottdale, PA: Herald, 1977); Yoder, *Politics,* pp. 134-61; Walter Wink, *Naming the Powers: The Language of Power in the New Testament* (Philadelphia: Fortress, 1984); Wink, *Unmasking the Powers: The Invisible Forces That Determine Human Existence* (Philadelphia: Fortress, 1986); Wink, *Engaging the Powers: Discernment and Resistance in a World of Domination* (Minneapolis: Fortress, 1992).

imperial order, rendering almost invisible what might otherwise be its particular and overwhelmingly obvious political claim on the author and audience of the letter, and reducing it to a general truth: Rome is only one among the unnamed, enslaved ἔθνη that are confronted by the justice of God in the sovereign Messiah Jesus for their judgment and deliverance from bondage. Standing, as we might be, on the near side of the gospel's liberating power, and having been seized by its truth, it may take an effort of the imagination to see that, *from the other side* — from the view of imperial Rome and other such political entities — the coming political order that Paul proclaims is surely marked by an *even more profound invisibility.* Where, except in traces here and there — in a fabulous account of a resurrection, in a local disturbance over an exorcism or some unusual cultic practice, in news about some small gathering of messianic "believers" — would the newly proclaimed order have any purchase whatsoever in the "real" political world?[21] By what accounting, according to any ordinary measure of realistic political effectiveness, would this new political order, shaped around faithful loyalty to a crucified "χριστός," be reckoned as anything at all? Paul, an itinerant Jewish proclaimer of a new order, has himself claimed no territory, established no permanent base of operations, gathered neither a band of guerrillas nor an organized military, and explicitly rejected any revolutionary action (in the usual sense) against the existing powers. The people from which he comes, the Jews, seem to have no real political future of their own apart from subjection to the empire, and they have rejected the political "good news" he announces on their behalf. Paul seems to accept the most meager of results from his proclamation, counting mere handfuls of Gentile believers in the eastern provinces of the empire as sufficient for him to say, "there is no further place for me in these regions" (Rom. 15:23). Even as he writes the Letter to the Romans he seems divided in his plans, desiring, on one hand, to come to Rome and then press on toward Spain, and, on the other, heading in the opposite direction with contributions for the poor in Jerusalem. His vision of a new political order, already real and powerful and active in the world, seems confused, even delusional in the extreme.

Which is why Paul himself, and any who believe the proclamation,

---

21. Not that such traces were, politically, completely insignificant. The book of Acts records a number of events in which the social, economic, and/or political threat of the messianic movement was recognized and responded to at local levels. See especially the compelling apocalyptic-political reading of Acts by C. Kavin Rowe, *World Upside Down: Reading Acts in the Graeco-Roman Age* (Oxford: Oxford University Press, 2009).

must grasp this new, virtually invisible, political sovereignty only through apocalypse (ἀποκάλυψις) — the sudden, interruptive arrival upon the world stage of a *hidden* but politically *explosive* divine power. Hidden, because it is invisible from the vantage point of what normally counts as a "meaningful" political entity or force. Explosive, because it has the power, through a "renewing of the mind," to dissolve what counts as politically meaningful, to reduce it to another feature in the general situation, and to generate a new political logic, vision, and community formed around God and the Messiah Jesus.[22] It is not as if there is nothing that *appears* in this explosion, nothing that "breaks the surface" of ordinary political reality; but what does appear becomes visible as a new *political* sovereignty and order only through the ἀποκάλυψις μυστηρίου (16:25), the new frame of reference graciously given to those whose eyes are opened by the good news itself. Where the sovereignty of Messiah Jesus is claimed to be a thing immediately visible and recognizable to the normal political gaze of the "rulers of this age" (in, say, a "Christian" political party, nation, or empire, or in "Christian" kings, princes, and presidents), and not a matter of apocalypse, we must doubt whether it is the sovereignty that is declared as good news in Romans.[23]

The apocalypse of God's theopolitical sovereignty presents itself this way in Romans: in 1:1, Jesus the Messiah, the "gospel of God," is announced immediately, without preamble, even though it was "promised beforehand" by the prophets in the Scriptures. In 1:15-17, the letter itself becomes a sudden proclamation of good news in Rome, an unleashing of the "power of God," an apocalypse of the "justice of God." In 1:18–2:16, the apocalypse of God's justice immediately discloses the impiety, injustice, and idolatry of the nations, reducing to nothing their arrogant pretensions to be the bringers of *iustitia, clementia, pietas, virtus*.[24] Therefore, believers of this apocalypse immediately become *unbelievers in the political alternatives to the gospel*. In 3:21-26, the justice of God suddenly intrudes itself into the realm of the universal injustice among nations, manifesting itself, with no hint of preparation ("straight down from above," according to Barth), in the faithful, sacrificial death of the sovereign, the Messiah Jesus. In 5:12-

---

22. The terms "counts" and "situation" are here used in a way that borrows from Badiou.

23. Not only in Romans, of course. Paul's most explicit statement about this occurs in 1 Cor. 2:6-13.

24. On Rome's claim to embody and establish these politically, see Elliott, *Arrogance, passim*.

21, the sovereign himself enacts the faithful obedience and justice required of all humankind, for the sake of all humankind, and opens the way for bodily participation in the new order of justice and freedom established in his crucifixion and resurrection (Romans 6). In 8:18-39, we hear of the un-imaginable and presently invisible hope of the whole creation for its liber-ation and glorification, together with the children of God. In Romans 9–11, the hidden but glorious destiny of the suffering people Israel is disclosed, against all of the empirical evidence provided by their "unbelief," and against the arrogant boasting of the nations. In 15:7-13, the hidden destiny of the nations is disclosed in the life of the messianic community as Jews and Gentiles together praise the "one who rises to rule the nations."

None of this meets the faithless eye of worldly political realism. Through Romans we come to understand that God's apocalypse of his sovereignty and justice in Jesus Messiah creates its own evidence, its own visibility, in the messianic community of those who trust not in the vaunted words and swords of the powerful among the nations but who trust, like the founding father Abraham, in the promising God who raises from the dead and gives the powerful Holy Spirit. What was otherwise incontrovertibly the "real," visible, and potent political sovereignty prior to the proclamation of the gospel is now only acknowledged, along with all other sovereignties, in its shadowy bondage to idolatry, injustice, and corruption; in its conscripted service of executing "wrath" and reward in the cause of the one true sover-eign; and in its hope of redemption only through "the mercies of God." The political sovereignties of this age are subsumed into another sover-eignty and purpose and glory that they cannot see according to the usual calculus of political achievement. It is the sovereignty, purpose, and glory graciously apocalypsed in the death and resurrection of Jesus Messiah, al-ready being experienced and made visible in part by the suffering messi-anic community through the Holy Spirit, and eagerly anticipated by "all creation" as its promised destiny. It cannot be attained by the usual politi-cal striving, conflict, and triumph. Only God can graciously bestow it through the Messiah. It is bestowed only on those who have been given to participate in the reality of the Messiah.

Messianic

If we combine the three terms we have just parsed, *apocalyptic political uni-versalism,* and claim them as our political vision, we should not be surprised if we detect astonishment and horror in the eyes of our listeners or readers. Every war ever fought, every nation ever founded, every political sovereignty ever established is done under the sign of some kind of apocalypse, some revelation of a (supposedly) transcendent truth, justice, or glory that captures the imagination of a sovereign and its people (or the sovereign people).[25] Empires rise and conquer under the sign of a universal vision, with the thought that their truth, justice, and glory must be good for all peoples in all places. In the gospel, Paul declares the apocalypse of a universal sovereign and his empire. How can that be "good news"?

Here we have to attend to those figures "on the ground," in history, around which the Pauline political vision is concretely focused and from which it derives. Critical and determinative is the figure of Jesus Messiah. The body of the Letter to the Romans is framed at both ends (1:3-6; 15:7-13) by declarations of Jesus' exalted sovereign rule of the nations and the faithful obedience that they owe him. In the heart of the letter, however, Jesus is declared as himself the obedient, faithful, and just one: obedient and faithful precisely in his atoning *death* for the sake of Israel and the nations (3:21-26; 5:6-11) as the concrete form of God's justice, and obedient and just in his representative *life*, lived for all, and bestowed eternally upon all (5:12-21) who through baptism participate in his death and resurrection (Romans 6). Indeed, the political point of his death and resurrection is not only that he himself might rule among the nations, but also that those who participate in him through baptism might rule over the powers of Sin and Death that held them in bondage and be "more than conquerors" in the war against the powers that threaten to separate them from God's love in the Messiah. In other words, the life, death, and resurrection of the sovereign Messiah is given to others for their sake, that they might share fully in his victory and sovereignty.

But the sovereignty of Jesus Messiah, while apocalyptically revealed in

---

25. This is the theopolitical point of Rom. 1:18–2:16. The basic theological character of sovereignty is argued variously by Carl Schmitt, *Political Theology: Four Chapters on the Concept of Sovereignty,* trans. George Schwab (Chicago: University of Chicago Press, 2005); Paul W. Kahn, *Political Theology: Four New Chapters on the Concept of Sovereignty* (New York: Columbia University Press, 2011); Giorgio Agamben, *The Kingdom and the Glory: For a Theological Genealogy of Economy and Government,* trans. Lorenzo Chiesa with Matteo Mandarini (Stanford: Stanford University Press, 2011). Bringing a specifically Christian-apocalyptic voice and critique to this discussion is Stanley Hauerwas, most recently and pointedly in *War and the American Difference: Theological Reflections on Violence and National Identity* (Grand Rapids: Baker Academic, 2011).

his resurrection and exaltation, remains for the time being hidden from view to the eyes of political realism. The "hope of sharing the glory of God" exists now in the "sufferings" that "produce endurance" (5:2-3). The inheritance of the messianic kingdom comes to those who for the time being (τοῦ νῦν καιροῦ — 8:18) "suffer with him so that [they] may also be glorified with him" (8:17). The glory that is theirs remains hidden: it is "coming," about "to be revealed" (τὴν μέλλουσαν δόξαν ἀποκαλυφθῆναι — 8:18), together with the hidden glory of the still-suffering creation. By this understanding, then, the idea of an *apocalyptic political universalism* is both less frightening and more frightening than our worst fears about such a political vision. Less frightening, because it is in no sense whatsoever a repetition of the horrors of apocalyptic political universalisms enacted violently by rulers, nations, and empires. More frightening, because for those who share in *this* apocalyptic political universalism through participation in the Messiah and the Spirit there is only one mode of thus sharing — vulnerability, patience, suffering — that is, bearing the burden of its apocalypsed reality under the sign of the hidden power of its crucified sovereign — that is, as "weak messianic power" (Walter Benjamin).[26] Political agency in this messianic mode "disavows the use of narratives involving the mastery of risk and the conquest of contingency."[27] It refuses the quest for "glory" assumed and pursued by the "rulers of this age."

According to Romans 9–11, that disavowal is also the calling, for the time being, of the paradigmatic political reality of Israel, the elect and representative people of God.[28] For the sake of God's messianic justice being extended to all the nations, God has subjected Israel (in the form of its zeal for the law, which, Paul says, has been taken captive by Sin [Romans 7]) to the "disobedience" that was once the property of the Gentile nations. She thereby, unwittingly and unwillingly, finds herself sharing in her own form

---

26. See Walter Benjamin, "Theses on the Philosophy of History," in *Illuminations: Essays and Reflections,* trans. Harry Zohn, ed. Hannah Arendt (New York: Schocken Books, 1969), pp. 253-64.

27. J. Alexander Sider, *To See History Doxologically: History and Holiness in John Howard Yoder's Ecclesiology* (Grand Rapids: Eerdmans, 2011), p. 112. Sider is explicating Yoder's "non-Constantinian" vision of "being historical."

28. In what follows, "Israel" indicates the theological entity (the people created and defined by God's election) that Paul has in mind in Romans 9–11 (cf. also Gal. 6:16). By extension, it may also indicate the Jewish people throughout history from Abraham to the present time. "Israel's" relation to the current nation-state of Israel is fraught with ambiguity and problems.

of "weak messianic power." According to Paul, Israel in messianic time is
given to repeat in its political existence the destiny of the crucified Messiah. "He who did not withhold his own Son, but handed him over
(παρέδωκεν) for all of us, will he not with him (σὺν αὐτῷ) also graciously
give us all things?" (8:32). As the divinely elected, paradigmatic political
community, Israel, through God's own decision and act, displays before
the Gentile nations the mode in which the nations themselves might share
in the glory that is to come: vulnerability, patience, suffering. If the Gentile
peoples — even "Christian" ones — remain or become again arrogant and
boastful with respect to Israel, rather than finding themselves in messianic
solidarity with Israel, they risk forfeiting their own share in the coming
glory (11:17-24). Israel's weakness stands, not as a testimony to its own
"failure," but as a testimony to God's merciful decision to extend his grace
and salvation to the ungodly and unjust Gentile peoples. The political
good news to the Gentile peoples that comes in the story of Messiah Jesus
and his people Israel is this: live in the Messiah, follow the messianic pattern.[29] Watch that you are not "cut off" by God from this good news because of your pride, arrogance, and quest for glory. For Israel, however,
there remains a sure hope, represented already in the "remnant," that is,
the hope of deliverance (which is surely also political deliverance — "the
Deliverer will come ἐκ Σιὼν" — 11:26), "life from the dead" (11:15), and participation in the glory that is coming.

Finally, we turn to the third historical figure that "grounds" Paul's
apocalyptic political universalism: the messianic community. The members of this political body, drawn from the nations by the mercies of God,
are called to present their bodies — their visible, public selves — as "living
sacrifices," which is the form of their "reasonable public service" (λογικὴ
λατρεία — 12:1). The visible messianic political body formed by these
members is not conformed to the dominating *apocalyptic political
universalisms* that characterize the nations and empires of "this age";
rather, it embodies and displays a wholly new political rationality (νοῦς)
that eschews the arrogance of the ungodly and unjust nations and renders
within itself the kind of humble service that builds up the political body of
the Messiah, a body that lives to bless the nations rather than to curse
them. Paul describes at length in Romans 12:1–15:6 (and in other letters)

29. Does not the willing embrace of Diaspora by many Jews throughout the centuries
reflect such a messianic participation and existence? Are not Zionism and Israel as a modern
nation-state contradictions of it?

the contours of the internal life and the external relations of the messianic community. Internally, it is marked by mutual honoring, especially of those who are deemed the least honorable according to measures and standards of the present age. It is marked by sharing gifts that build up the whole. It is characterized by a unity of spirit and affection and purpose that disregards the boundaries that would normally separate members from one another along lines of ethnic belonging and social status. At any specific point of tension or conflict, for example, around such concrete matters as eating and drinking together, the pattern of the Messiah is brought to bear on the situation: "Each of us must please our neighbor for the good purpose of building up the neighbor. For Christ did not please himself; but, as it is written, 'The insults of those who insult you have fallen on me'" (Rom. 15:2-3; cf. 14:7-9).[30]

That same pattern fundamentally shapes not only the internal political life of the community but also its external relations. The messianic community is not closed in on itself or removed from society at large; it is a community, a political body, in *Rome* after all. Its boundaries are porous in both directions, and of course it is always welcoming refugees and migrants. While its purpose and calling is to "live peaceably with all" insofar as that depends on them, not all in the wider public are willing to live peaceably with it or its members. They may be met with enmity, evil intentions, and persecution. Here, too, the messianic pattern applies: "Extend hospitality to strangers." "Bless those who persecute you." "Do not repay anyone evil for evil." "Never avenge yourselves." Give your enemies food and drink if they need them. "Do not be overcome by evil, but overcome evil with good" (Rom. 12:13-21). This is what it means to be "living sacrifices" in a social and political context that is still governed by the powers of Sin and Death and in which the "reasonable public service" the messianic community renders is viewed as a threat rather than a blessing.

Ingredient in the political being of the messianic community is also a specific kind of relationship to "the governing authorities." Since God himself has set those authorities in order (θεοῦ τεταγμέναι εἰσίν — 13:1), the messianic community may not set itself against those authorities (13:2) but must rather order itself under them (Πᾶσα ψυχὴ ἐξουσίαις ὑπερεχούσαις ὑποτασσέσθω — 13:1). The authorities whom God has "set

---

30. A careful and compelling attempt to describe what this new messianic community in Rome might have looked like "at ground level" is given in Peter Oakes, *Reading Romans in Pompeii: Paul's Letter at Ground Level* (Minneapolis: Fortress, 2009).

in order" or "put in their place" are not finally free agents and masters of their own (and others') destinies, despite their often vaunted self-claims. Nor are they pioneers and agents of freedom, justice, peace, and salvation in history, since those come from God through Jesus Messiah. However they might construe their own image and agendas, the ruling authorities are, in fact, according to Paul, *conscripted* by God into service for what is finally a rather inglorious "ministry," namely, to be the agents in history of "wrath" toward those who do evil and "praise" toward those who do good. For that purpose alone (and not for many other purposes of their own defining) they also wield the "sword" as servants of God. One thing is certain: "wrath" cannot be a "ministry" taken up by those in the messianic political community, for not only have they themselves been "saved [by grace alone] from wrath through [the Messiah]" (5:9), they are also not (no doubt for that very reason) to be the executors of wrath, but to leave that to God (12:19). The messianic community and its members under the sovereignty of Messiah Jesus have a single calling in relation to the worldly political powers, as to everyone else: to do good (which may win praise from the authorities), to owe no one anything except love. In this manner they fulfill the law and share in the Messiah, who is himself the τέλος of the νόμος (10:4). In terms of messianic political responsibility, we must not read into Romans 13:1-7 anything other than the pattern of the Messiah Jesus, who did not resist the ungodly, the sinners, the enemies of God's purpose, but gave himself up to them (or, was handed over to them), and died for them.

It may be just as important to make clear what is *not said* in this text. There is no hint that those in the Messiah owe their political devotion, their praise, their allegiance (πίστις), their obedience (ὑπακοή), their bodies, their public service (λογικὴ λατρεία), or their sacrifice to the ruling authorities.[31] None of that is implied in ὑποτάσσω, a verb that we have to believe Paul chose very deliberately. Moreover, all of that is owed to God and his Messiah alone, for the sake of building up the political body of the messianic community and as a testimony to the ungodly and arrogant nations of their own truest destiny. What do "messianics" owe to those with whom they carry on their daily concourse in the wider society? "Love your

---

31. That all of these things have been and are even now thought to be owed by Christians to kings, or presidents, or governments, or nations, or grand ideals such as freedom and justice, or flags, rather than to the one God and his Messiah, is what William Cavanaugh has identified as "migrations of the holy." See Cavanaugh, *Migrations*.

neighbor as yourself." What that might mean concretely in any sphere of life is a matter of continual messianic discernment by those who have "put on the Sovereign Jesus Messiah" (13:14), who have "put on the armor of light," who know what time it is — that "the night is far gone, the day is near" (13:12).[32]

32. Among the many writers who might help with that discernment, by our Romans criteria we would seek out those that acknowledge the triune God over all political life, the Messiah Jesus as its center and pattern, the universal/local *ecclesia* in the Spirit as its base, and local, small-scale, short-range, nonviolent engagement with society as its mission. The writings of John Howard Yoder are essential. Among recent works, two books come especially to mind: Stanley Hauerwas and Romand Coles, *Christianity, Democracy, and the Radical Ordinary: Conversations between a Radical Democrat and a Christian* (Eugene, OR: Cascade, 2008); Luke Bretherton, *Christianity and Contemporary Politics* (Malden, MA: Wiley-Blackwell, 2010). Also, two essays: William Cavanaugh, "A Politics of Vulnerability," in *Migrations,* pp. 170-95; Paul J. Griffiths, "The Cross as the Fulcrum of Politics: Expropriating Agamben on Paul," in Harink, ed., *Paul,* pp. 179-97.

Creation, Gender, and Identity in (New) Cosmic Perspective: 1 Corinthians 11:2-16

Alexandra R. Brown

Among Beverly Gaventa's many exemplary contributions to the field of Pauline studies is her attention to the theme of creation (κτίσις) in Paul's apocalyptic rendering of the gospel. In *Our Mother Saint Paul* she approaches the theme by way of Paul's maternal imagery in 1 Thessalonians and Galatians and then, in an exposition of Romans 8, shows how Paul in that context shifts from images of birthing to the image of adoption in discourse that reaches its climax in the cry of *all* creation (human and nonhuman) for God's redemption.[1] Not surprisingly, for readers of Paul, the apostle's metaphors present new alignments and disrupt expected paradigms. The creation groans in labor pains but does not itself give birth. Nor is there some sort of self-restoring scheme at work in the creation narrative. Rather, the groaning creation awaits the adoption and redemption by God of the entire cosmos. In this act of deliverance, as Gaventa reads Paul, the whole creation will be reclaimed "out of the powers of Sin and Death."[2] Elsewhere, Gaventa has argued that in Romans the entity known as "Israel" is "not and never has been defined by birth," that is, by genetics, "but only by God's creation; it is not a biological but a theological category."[3] Her insights align with John Barclay's observation that for Paul the language of God's "mercy" in Romans 9:15 ("I will have mercy on whom I have mercy") and God's call in Romans 9:24-25 ("Those not my people I

---

1. Beverly Roberts Gaventa, *Our Mother Saint Paul* (Louisville: Westminster John Knox, 2007), pp. 51-62.

2. Gaventa, *Mother*, p. 60.

3. Beverly Roberts Gaventa, "On the Calling into Being of Israel: Romans 9:6-29," in *Between Gospel and Election: Explorations in the Interpretation of Romans 9–11*, ed. Florian Wilk and J. Ross Wagner, WUNT 257 (Tübingen: Mohr Siebeck, 2010), p. 259.

will call my people") is testimony to God's powerful redemption of *all*, Jew and Gentile, through the Christ-gift, or, as Barclay puts it, "the final merciful *recreation* of the world," a divine action that "encompasses 'the nations' as well as Israel."[4]

Paul's introduction of a theological distinction between natural birth and apocalyptic adoption and his collapsing of divine calling, creation, and deliverance terminology not only allow but demand our attention to questions surrounding ethnicity and gender in Paul's letters. Indeed, the circumstances that elicit his exposition of a new "grammar of creation" arise frequently from disputes in his churches about distinctions between Jew and Gentile, male and female, slave and free.[5] Paul's citation in Galatians 3:27-28 of the baptismal formula — "[f]or as many of you as were baptized into Christ have put on Christ. There is neither Jew nor Gentile, neither slave nor free, no male *and* female" — is no temporary rhetorical ploy but expresses Paul's fundamental and startling insight that in Christ a new creation is called into being, a new creation in which old orders of hierarchy and identity give way to what J. Louis Martyn calls "an eschatological *novum*," that is, "[a] new corporate person."[6] The corporate identity now newly created is determined not by the ethnic, gender, class, and religious factors that characterized the old creation (Gal. 5:6; 6:15). Rather, as Martyn concludes, for Paul, "[T]his people is determined solely by incorporation into the Christ in whom those factors have no real existence."[7] Gaventa similarly expresses the theological and anthropological consequence of the gospel encapsulated in Galatians 3:28: "Every difference is subordinated to the gospel; more than that, every source of human identity is taken up into the gospel."[8]

---

4. John M. G. Barclay, "'I Will Have Mercy on Whom I Have Mercy': The Golden Calf and Divine Mercy in Romans 9–11 and Second Temple Judaism," *Early Christianity* 1 (2010): 105, emphasis added. See also Gaventa, *Mother*, p. 155.

5. George Steiner, *Grammars of Creation* (New Haven: Yale University Press, 2001).

6. J. Louis Martyn, *Galatians: A New Translation with Introduction and Commentary*, AB 33A (New York: Doubleday, 1997), pp. 380, 382. The grammatical change from "neither/nor" in the first two pairs in Gal. 3:28 to "not/and" in the last may signal direct citation of LXX Gen. 1:27, where we read "male and female he created them."

7. Martyn, *Galatians*, p. 382.

8. Beverly Roberts Gaventa, "The Singularity of the Gospel Revisited: Exegetical Reflections on Galatians 1 and 2" (paper presented at the St. Andrews Conference on Scripture and Christian Theology: Paul's Letter to the Galatians and Christian Theology, St. Andrews, 11 July 2012).

ALEXANDRA R. BROWN

Creation and Cosmology in 1 Corinthians

When Paul addresses in 1 Corinthians 11:2-16 the worship practices of
women and men assembled as the body of Christ in Corinth, the apostle's
recourse to Genesis recalls the larger frame of his creation/new creation
formulations. Here we think not only of the baptismal formula (cited
without the male/female pair in 1 Cor. 12:13) but also, in this letter's opening chapter (1:26-31), of God's calling into being a new people out of nothing (τὰ μὴ ὄντα, 1:28), in chapter 8, of "one God . . . from whom all things
[ἐξ οὗ τὰ πάντα] come into being" and "one Lord Jesus through whom all
things [δι' οὗ τὰ πάντα] come into being" (8:6), and, in chapter 15, of the
Old and New Adam, "the first man from the earth, a man of dust," and the
second, the "man from heaven" whose "image we will bear" (15:45-49).
Seen within Paul's larger discourse on new creation in 1 Corinthians, his
peculiar focus on gender roles in worship in 1 Corinthians 11:2-16 comes
into new perspective. In this letter where worldly markers of identity are so
often the source of strife and division among the Corinthians, Paul finds
reason to reframe gender markers as real to the created order — the order
currently under the power of alien forces — but provisional in consequence of God's new creation.

Paul's sensitivity to this cosmological shift and his conviction that it is
under way in Corinth are apparent in the discourse on idols and food in
1 Corinthians 8:4-6. Here, in a text that combines the cosmological terminology of κόσμος, heaven (οὐρανός), and earth (γῆ) with the expression of the
creation by God the Father out of whom "all things" (τὰ πάντα) exist, Paul
juxtaposes God's πάντα — that is to say, the real-world creation announced
in the gospel — with the merely apparent idols, so-called "gods" and "lords"
in heaven and on earth (vv. 5-6). When the πάντα reappears in 15:28, in the
final act of divine deliverance of the creation "in order that God may be all in
all" ([τὰ] πάντα ἐν πᾶσιν), we see the fulfillment of a pattern of cosmological
transformation evidenced at several key moments across the letter, beginning with God's election of "things without being" at 1:28, and present at
points of controversy about identity markers (e.g., sexuality, eating practices,
gender in worship) in the community. In 1 Corinthians 15:35-58, the created
body (σῶμα) itself undergoes, at death and resurrection, the final cosmological transformation. Here, Paul seems to operate within what Sarah Coakley
has termed "an eschatological horizon which will give mortal flesh final significance." What is raised incorruptible in 1 Corinthians 15 is a body, but
surely a completed body that does not succumb to "'appropriate' or restric-

tive gender roles" or, we might add in the spirit of the corpus as a whole, any exclusionary identity marker.[9] In the meantime, in the time between the ages, Paul's grammar of creation is filled with the *aporiae* that mark both the rupture of the old creation and the promise of the new.

Sex, Gender, and the New Creation in Corinth

An interpretation of 1 Corinthians 11:2-16 nuanced by attention to the larger frame of creation/new creation in Paul's letters opens new possibilities for understanding his views on human identity, especially gender identity, in the time that is now or, as he says in 1 Corinthians 7:29, the time that is "drawn up, contracted," that is to say, the eschatologically charged "time that remains" between the death and resurrection of Christ Jesus and his Parousia.

Tensions will arise, of course, in the daily life of a newly created people when the accustomed patterns of identity are called fundamentally into question. Whereas in Galatians and Romans the primary tension resulting from Paul's gospel was located in the fate of the distinction between Jew and Gentile, in 1 Corinthians tensions around sexuality and gender are especially prominent. Indeed, four chapters of the letter (1 Corinthians 5, 6, 7, and 11) devote significant space to issues of sexuality, marriage, and gender distinctions in worship. Far from reiterating conventional standards when faced with questions of sexual practice, Paul here gives instructions that sound in context quite peculiar: a man who lives with his father's wife should be removed from the assembly, "delivered to Satan for the destruction of his flesh," but that action is to allow "his spirit to be saved on the day of the Lord Jesus" (5:1-5). Or again, πορνεία (sexual immorality), a clear threat to the integrity of the body of Christ, is characterized as a sin against one's own body, even as the new identity of that (individual) body as "the temple of the Holy Spirit," "bought with a price," is confirmed (6:12-20). A related image confounds the view of *porneia*'s contagion: in 7:15-16, the believer joined to an unbeliever may effect the opposite of contamination, cleansing the nonbeliever.[10] Least straightforward of all, but perhaps most

9. Sarah Coakley, "The Eschatological Body: Gender, Transformation, and God," *Modern Theology* 16 (2000): 70.

10. For extensive treatment of the body as portal for pollution in antiquity, see Dale B. Martin, *The Corinthian Body* (New Haven: Yale University Press, 1995).

provocative, is the instruction on marriage, divorce, and celibacy in 7:1-40, where the dislocation of conventional sexual customs and ideologies is evidenced in Paul's own preference for celibacy (although he approves marriage as a prophylactic against desire).[11] This dislocation is most pronounced in the strange advice to the married to live "as though not [ὡς μή] married," "for the form [τὸ σχῆμα] of this world is passing away" (7:29-31).

Throughout the letter, then, the division that marks humanity as male and female is strangely presented as both present and passing away. This difference, more insistently than ethnic or class distinctions, inheres in the creation itself; both Paul and the Corinthian congregants seem to struggle with this persistent anthropological and theological datum. How, indeed, is the distinction "male and female," so clearly embedded in the biblical account, to be understood in light of the radical new grammar of creation announced in the baptismal formula?

1 Corinthians 11:2-16 in Context

In 1 Corinthians 11:2-16, Paul seems to diverge from the earlier and surprisingly egalitarian discussion of celibacy, marriage, and sexual reciprocity within marriage in 1 Corinthians 7:1-40 by offering a set of directives about how women and men are to behave in communal worship. Specifically, he takes up the dress, or at least the hairstyles and head coverings, of women and men as they pray and prophesy in the congregation and, on the surface of the text at least, recommends a gender-distinctive dress or hair code justified — although not very straightforwardly — both by the creation accounts in Genesis (1 Cor. 11:7-12) and by an argument from "nature" (φύσις, v. 14): the women converts in Corinth, he says, are to "pray with their heads covered" (or is it to wear their hair coiled on top of their heads?) while men are advised to keep their heads *un*covered.[12] The con-

---

11. Martin, *Corinthian,* pp. 217-18.

12. Generally speaking, in the Greco-Roman world, women's head coverings are dictated by religion and status. In pagan culture, the situation is quite fluid. Paul's probable hometown, Tarsus in Cilicia, is praised by Dio Chrysostom (*1 Tars.* 33.49) for the modesty of its women in covering. Plutarch reports that "it is more usual for women to go out in public with their heads veiled, and for men to go out with their heads uncovered," although Plutarch is speaking of Roman women (*Mor.* 267A; see J. Hinton and L. L. V. Matthews, "Veiled or Unveiled? Plut. *Quaest. Rom.* 267B-C," *CQ* 58 [2008]: 336-42). Sculptures and mosaics in Syria, Lebanon, and Palestine do not, however, show veiled women. Ramsay MacMullen

troversial part of this "style" section of the letter is that style is apparently keyed to status. Does Paul here "baptize" for Christian worship conventional hierarchical arrangements of human beings? Does he now diverge from his otherwise moderately egalitarian position in 1 Corinthians 7, where the *reciprocity* of male and female partners stands out? At issue for contemporary commentators on this text is the claim of women to the same dignity of status in Christ that Paul preached for the Gentile and the slave, indeed the dignity of status implied by the baptismal formula that emerges in practical advice for women in 1 Corinthians 7.

What is at issue in Paul's own context is less clear. As David Horrell points out, the anti-emancipatory ideological potential of this text (not necessarily reflecting Paul's own preferences) may be reified by Paul's reflection on Genesis and God-given patterns of creation.[13] As we see in contemporary public debate, the creation narrative tends to be used to underwrite conservative social positions. But a careful reading of this very language of the creation account in the context of Paul's wider frame of creation/*new* creation reveals interruptions in the Genesis account itself. When "taken up into the gospel," these interruptions reveal a radically recast human identity in which every difference is subordinated to the "singular identity" of belonging to Christ.

Ancient Cosmology and Gender Identity

Recent studies have helpfully explored the ways in which Paul takes up, adapts, or subverts ancient Jewish and/or Greco-Roman ideas and practices about gender difference.[14] Most of these agree that Paul is acutely

---

posits class as the reason for this distinction, with humbler women wearing veils while those capable of commissioning sculpture mimicking the hairstyles of the imperial elite ("Women in Public in the Roman Empire," *Historia* 29 [1980]: 218). Roughly speaking, head coverings are seemingly related to both class distinctions and to mores about women's modesty in maintaining honor/shame societies. I will argue that Paul both knows and seeks to revise the cultural potencies of the veil. See "Covering of the Head," *The Oxford Dictionary of the Jewish Religion,* ed. Adele Berlin and Maxine Grossman, 2nd ed. (Oxford: Oxford University Press, 2011), p. 192. See also the very helpful article by Cynthia L. Thompson, "Hairstyles, Head-coverings, and St. Paul: Portraits from Roman Corinth," *BA* 51 (1988): 99-115.

13. David G. Horrell, *The Social Ethos of the Corinthian Correspondence: Interests and Ideology from 1 Corinthians to 1 Clement,* SNTW (Edinburgh: T. & T. Clark, 1996), p. 176.

14. For a model study of how Paul's message played in Christian antiquity, see the essay by Mary Rose D'Angelo, "Veils, Virgins and the Tongues of Men and Angels: Women's

aware of both Jewish and pagan (particularly Stoic) mores and that, with regard to matters of sexuality, his Jewish sensitivities are often in the lead. That he has both Jewish and pagan standards in mind in 1 Corinthians 11 is evident as he cites both the Genesis 1–2 accounts of creation (1:27: man is image of God; 2:18-24: woman created for man) and, as a second line of defense, arguments from "nature." Some critics suggest, as we have begun to do here, that Paul regularly in his letters *subverts* both Jewish and pagan constructions of gender by articulating a new theological principle of unity in Christ, a unity that *ultimately* (if not immediately) transcends status and gender difference. Others find Paul adhering more closely to the gender definitions of his time. Dale Martin, for example, finds Paul rather more resistant to claims of equality where male/female difference is concerned than in Paul's teachings on ethnic and class difference. The cause of this reticence, according to Martin, is the overpowering influence of ancient notions of physiology, both pagan *and* Jewish. The pervasive ancient belief in "the inferior nature of their female stuff" and its unique vulnerability to pollution is not only taken for granted by Paul, according to Martin, but explains Paul's anxiety to keep women veiled as a prophylactic against the pollution of the communal body, the church.[15]

Tension within the Corpus

How should the tension be understood, then, between Paul's citation in Galatians 3:27-28 of the baptismal formula negating *ethnic and gender* distinctions, a formula perhaps invoking a more equal creation formula — "in God's image he created male and female" — from Genesis 1:27, on one hand, and his apparent recourse in 1 Corinthians 11 to a gender hierarchy patterned on Adam's priority in Genesis 2, on the other? Paul's own awareness of the tension within his epistolary history may be evident when in 1 Corinthians 12:13, with explicit reference to baptism, he partly repeats the

---

Heads in Early Christianity," in *Off with Her Head: The Denial of Women's Identity in Myth, Religion and Culture,* ed. Wendy Doniger and Howard Eilberg-Schwartz (Berkeley and Los Angeles: University of California Press, 1995), pp. 131-64.

15. Martin, *Corinthian,* pp. 248-49. That female inferiority is not to be transcended even in resurrection (where the female will be subsumed into the superior stuff of the male) is thematic in *Gos. Thom.* 114, "For every woman who makes herself male will enter the Kingdom of God" (*The Gospel according to Thomas: Coptic Text with Translations into French, German and English,* ed. A. Guillaumont et al. [New York: Harper & Row, 1959], p. 57).

Galatians formula but now *without* the gendered pair, male and female. Something, it seems, prevents Paul from reiterating here the unity of male/ female accomplished by baptism in the Galatians formula. But what is it? Can it be, as Martin holds, a caution grounded in beliefs about physiology, lest the prophylactic function of veiling be abandoned, leaving the church vulnerable to cosmic pollution?[16] Or do we see an exegesis designed, as Judith Gundry-Volf proposes, to uphold *both* a patriarchal gender narrative (for the sake of honoring sexual difference in the world at large) *and* an egalitarian narrative (recognizing the breakdown of hierarchical structures within the new cosmos constituting the church)?[17] Why, after all, will women in Corinth have been unveiling if such was the deeply encultured understanding of purity and pollution? Perhaps, as Antoinette Wire has argued, the Corinthian women, encouraged by the baptismal erasure of male and female distinctions (as in the full formula in Galatians) and welcomed into the assembly as pray-ers and prophets, had shed their veils to announce and to celebrate their freedom.[18] Perhaps these women wished explicitly to signify through celibacy a departure from marriage, childbearing, and male authority, and in that context discarded the veil. If so, does the ascetical practice of *women* pose a threat to Paul or to the Corinthian congregation that his *own* choice of celibacy (see 7:6-7) does not? So once again we are in ambiguous territory, but territory that comes into better focus when seen as a landscape defining the gap between two cosmic ages — the old passing away, the new dawning.

16. Martin, *Corinthian*, pp. 241-45.

17. Gundry-Volf's elegant proposal takes account of the tensions in the uses of Genesis, finding three overlapping areas of points of reference in Paul's understanding: culture, eschatological life in Christ, and creation. For the sake of preserving key social values in culture, Paul reinforces conventional constructions of gender; the eschatological life in Christ, however, allows the pneumatic crossing of gender values already evident in Corinthian worship. Paul affirms this pneumatic equality of male and female "in the Lord" while "affirming the difference between them" (Judith M. Gundry-Volf, "Gender and Creation in 1 Corinthians 11:2-16: A Study in Paul's Theological Method," in *Evangelium, Schriftauslegung, Kirche: Festschrift für Peter Stuhlmacher zum 65. Geburtstag*, ed. Jostein Ådna et al. [Göttingen: Vandenhoeck & Ruprecht, 1997], pp. 151-71).

18. Antoinette Clark Wire, *The Corinthian Women Prophets: A Reconstruction through Paul's Rhetoric* (Minneapolis: Fortress, 1990). Perhaps, in moments of ecstatic prophesying, flowing female hair (fallen or never bound) bore too close a resemblance to pagan Dionysiac frenzy and misled potential converts. This is a reading of the "problem" at Corinth popularized by Elisabeth Schüssler Fiorenza, *In Memory of Her: A Feminist Theological Reconstruction of Christian Origins* (New York: Crossroad, 1983), pp. 227-30. There was quite probably an active Dionysus cult in Corinth, noted by Pausanias in the second century (*Descr.* 2.2.6-7).

A Conservative "Pauline" Trajectory

Later texts in the disputed Pauline Epistles settle into easier conventions of gender and reveal an anti-ascetic dimension as they promote both procreation and a hierarchical organization of male and female on the model of the Genesis 2 creation account: Colossians 3:18-25, Ephesians 5:22-33, and 1 Timothy 2:11-12 inscribe the traditional hierarchy (male over female, master over slave) and, in 1 Timothy 2:15, the necessity for Christian women to "be saved through childbearing." Alluding to Genesis 2:18-25, the author of 1 Timothy says:

> I do not permit a woman to be a teacher, nor must woman domineer over man; she should be quiet. For Adam was created first and Eve afterwards; and it was not Adam who was deceived; it was the woman, who, yielding to deception, fell into sin. Yet she will be saved through motherhood — if only women continue in faith, love and holiness, and with a sober mind. (1 Tim. 2:12-15)

Like 1 Corinthians 11, these later "Pauline" teachings on gender and communal order freely employ, implicitly and explicitly, the Genesis creation accounts, but now more straightforwardly. In these later teachings, the dialogical and finely nuanced exegesis of Genesis 1–2 in 1 Corinthians 11:8-12 ("on one hand this, but on the other that") disappears into unambiguous structures built to last in this world. Clearly, then, multiple and conflicting readings of Genesis support divergent views of gender across the Pauline corpus, into the church fathers, and to the present. In Paul's time, as in ours, ideologies of gender supported by philosophical and physiological argument determined both how Paul's gospel was pitched to his churches (during and after his own lifetime) and how these communities interpreted the gospel's radical claims for daily life and practice. For reasons not entirely clear, the egalitarian implications of the gospel with respect to gender and sexuality — or rather, in Gaventa's terms, the *singularity* of the gospel with respect to identity — are rendered more ambiguously by Paul and with greater diversity and controversy in the history of the church than implications for class and ethnic distinctions.

At the heart of the matter is Paul's theology of creation. Not only does he reflect to some degree his contemporaries' mores and theories about sex and marriage, pollution and purity, honor and shame; Paul also crafts his letters as a biblically informed Jew engaged with the creation texts of Genesis 1–2. Yet all of this reflection takes place for him in the extraordinary "now time" (Rom. 13:12-13) of the dawning *new* creation. The difference Paul's apocalyptic cosmology and eschatology make to the argument in 1 Corinthians 11 is the difference between a rule of restrictive binaries made normative by culture and a transformational gesture toward the singular identity of *all* in the gospel. The force of Paul's argument across the letter for the new creation *breaking in* to the old and not merely presenting another option for diversity pushes toward a somewhat more daring, if perhaps more precarious, reading of this strangely disjointed discourse on gender and worship.

Head, Image, and Glory: Key Terms in a (New) Creation Setting

I turn briefly now to three central elements in the text that bear significantly on how we read Paul's understanding of gender difference at the dawning of the new creation:

(1) the term κεφαλή (head) and its links to creation motifs in Genesis 1–2;
(2) the coincidence of the terms "image" (εἰκών) and "glory" (δόξα) in allusion to Genesis 1:26-27;[19] and
(3) the summation of the argument at verse 11 (πλὴν οὔτε . . .) geared toward the new creation formula — already thematic for the letter at 8:6 and recurring at 11:12b (cf. 15:28) — "all things are from God" (τὰ δὲ πάντα ἐκ τοῦ θεοῦ).

Here I want to stress the formulation "how we read," for what I will offer is a theological reading that draws Paul's argument in 1 Corinthians 11 into correspondence with the theology of creation that emerges from other parts of the letter. The argument is not that the *aporiae* in the text are resolved by a new-creation reading, but that the new-creation reading places these *aporiae* in a particular cosmological context consonant with Paul's conviction that "in the Lord" (v. 11) all are taken up into the singular iden-

19. While in 1 Corinthians Paul uses γυνή and ἀνήρ and not the pair ἄρσην and θῆλυς in LXX Gen. 1:27, the proximity of the terms to the Genesis narrative is clear. The terms selected for male and female in 1 Corinthians 11 may reflect Paul's intentional distancing of the baptismal formula pair ἄρσεν καὶ θῆλυ of Gal. 3:28 or may simply reflect his accommodation to the more common terms for the distinction in this environment.

tity of new creation, a new communal subject in whom the factors of gender, ethnicity, and class have "no real existence."[20]

1. Veiling and Revealing the Head (κεφαλή): Literal and Metaphorical Meanings

From antiquity, this entire text has been a puzzle to its learned interpreters, not least because of its lexical ambiguity. An initial difficulty is that Paul does not use the term κεφαλή outside of 1 Corinthians, except for the single unambiguous citation from Proverbs 25:21-22 in Romans 12:20. Most interestingly, he does not use it *in this very letter* when he describes the church as the body of Christ but resists assigning to that body Christ as its head (12:12-31).[21] But the term is central here, used nine times in fifteen verses. Verse 3 begins the discourse:

> But I want you to understand that the head (ἡ κεφαλή) of every man is Christ, the head (κεφαλή) of woman is the man, and the head (κεφαλή) of Christ is God.

Grasping the meaning here is made more difficult by the fact that the term κεφαλή occurs alternately throughout the passage with literal (what one wears on one's physical head) and metaphorical (e.g., the "head" of the man is Christ) connotations and in a context that thematizes both hierarchy and unity.[22] What is clear is that the metaphorical "head" is linked somehow to the literal practice of head covering; that women's heads

20. This is Martyn's expression regarding identity markers in Gal. 3:28 (*Galatians*, p. 382).

21. Paul does employ the noun κεφαλή in 1 Cor. 12:21. This text and 1 Cor. 11:2-16 famously contrast the later, post-Pauline conception in Colossians, where Christ is decidedly the head of the body, which is the church (Col. 1:18: αὐτός ἐστιν ἡ κεφαλὴ τοῦ σώματος τῆς ἐκκλησίας).

22. These options assume, of course, that all of the words in this text are Paul's own formulations. In addition to theories of wholesale interpolation, some understand the opening verses to be the words of Paul's opponents. Indeed, we might well imagine Paul engaging in wordplay here, perhaps quoting his audience — as he often does when he cites various Corinthian slogans in the letter — subverting their usage, or otherwise rendering subtle meanings no longer available to us. There would seem to be little doubt, especially as the argument progresses, that Paul is aware of multiple meanings of the term κεφαλή and employs the pun in rhetorical turns that would intentionally destabilize the linguistic context.

should be covered, or veiled, and men's uncovered is the apparent advice. But what the covered κεφαλή signifies is opaque.

Ancient usage of κεφαλή allows a semantic range that includes (1) opposition or hierarchy, "ruler" (ἀρχή) as distinct from ruled subject; (2) meanings that suggest synecdoche, e.g., head as in "standing for and representing the whole"; and (3) head as "source," as in "headwaters of a river" or first in a sequence where local or temporal beginning is in view. Anthropologies and christologies of various stripes might attach to the different lexical meanings. The patristic period, steeped in controversies about the identity of Christ, found the text affirming alternately both the Arian subordination of Christ to God and the unity of God and Christ, i.e., God is "head" of Christ while sharing the same substance and being (οὐσία) as Christ's. We find the latter strategy, for example, in Chrysostom (347-407 CE) and Augustine (354-430 CE), contemporaries and still early figures in the development of orthodox Trinitarian doctrine and theology, who argue from 1 Corinthians 11 against Arian Christology. Augustine cites 1 Corinthians 11:3 (*via* Phil. 2:5-11) in the following: "The Son, therefore, is equal with the Father and the working of the Father and the Son is indivisible . . . 'Who, being in the form of God'. . . . 'But the head of Christ is God'" (*Trin.* 1.6.12).

Similarly, Chrysostom makes a theological distinction between *nature* and *relationship.* God and Christ, then, are of the same nature, but of differing relations, Father and Son. Chrysostom then raises the question: Does κεφαλή mean the *same* thing each time it is used in the verse? That is, are God, Christ, and man "head" (κεφαλή) in the *same* sense? On one hand, Chrysostom concedes that as God and Christ are of one substance, so man and woman are one substance, and neither instance of headship, God's nor man's, includes rule or subjection:

> For had Paul meant to speak of rule and subjection . . . he would not have brought forward the instance of a wife, but rather of a slave and a master. . . . It is a wife as free, as equal in honor. And the Son also, though he did become obedient to the Father, it was *as the Son of God;* it was *as God.* (*Hom. 1 Cor.* 26.3)

But in practically the same breath, Chrysostom goes on to distinguish between woman as originally created and woman *after the fall.* While in creation there is no subjection, the post-fall situation is quite different. Now the headship of man in the sense of *dominance* reflects the divine will that the male shall rule and the woman be subject (Gen. 3:14-19). Specifically with respect to Paul's advice to cover a woman's head in worship and to uncover a man's, Chrysostom writes:

> If, then, such things [i.e., covered and bare heads] are distinctive marks, they both sin if they violate the proper order and command of God and transgress their proper boundaries, with the man descending to her inferior status and the woman, through her outward appearance, rising up over him. For it is not permitted for them to exchange garments and for her to wear a woolen cloak while he wears a mantle or a veil — "*A woman shall not wear anything that pertains to a man, nor a man put on a woman's garment*" (Deut. 22:5). . . . Thus, the one who transgresses in this matter confuses everything and betrays the gifts of God and casts to the ground the glory (v. 7) given from above. . . . For in fact it is the woman's greatest honor to maintain her own status, just as it is her greatest shame to rise in revolt. (*Hom. 1 Cor.* 26.4)

And so it goes. Chrysostom, like the majority of his ancient contemporaries, considers the subordination of woman to be a fact decreed by God after the fall; because of the fall, then, the metaphor finally works differently for God/Christ than for man/woman. Like other commentators of his time and ours, he takes Paul to be affirming this natural and divine post-fall order in his instructions on clothing in worship. In such a reading, the framing language of *new* creation in 1 Corinthians has left scarcely a trace.

Head as Source: Returning Woman's Authority (ἐξουσία) Interpreters closer to our times — there is a trend since the 1970s connected to the rise of feminist hermeneutics in biblical studies — tend to read the κεφαλή/ head language as connoting "source," not rule, in a way that frees Paul from the charge of making female ontologically inferior to male. Paul does not say that man is the *lord* of the woman, only that he is the *origin* of her being, now referring to the Genesis 2 account of creation. Here κεφαλή as "source" is taken to mean temporal priority but not preeminence: as God is *fons divinitatis* for Christ without subordinating Christ, so man is *fons humanitatis* for woman, without subordinating woman.[23] This reading, it is argued, makes a clearer break — one more attuned to Paul's *eschatologi-*

23. C. K. Barrett, *The First Epistle to the Corinthians* (New York: Harper & Row, 1968), p. 249.

cal vision — from connotations of domination and subordination. Now Paul can be read as arguing for a new authority bestowed on the "eschatological woman."[24] The distinction between male and female remains but without the relationship of dominance and subordination that characterized the old world.[25] Since the baptismal formula in Galatians has already established for Paul the "societal leveling quality" of Christian life, 1 Corinthians 11:3 carries "no hint of female subordination."[26] In fact, woman wears a veil to demonstrate that she has left the old order and now lives in the new. This is what is meant by the expression, "That is why a woman ought to have authority [ἐξουσία] on her head" (1 Cor. 11:10).[27] Morna Hooker summarizes the point: "Far from being a symbol of the woman's subjection to the man, therefore, her head-covering is what Paul calls it — authority: in prayer and prophecy she, like the man, is under the authority of God."[28]

24. Robin Scroggs, "Paul and the Eschatological Woman," *JAAR* 40 (1972): 283-303. A rejoinder by Elaine Pagels argues to the contrary that, had Paul meant to move away from subordinationist norms, he would not have constructed his argument around Genesis 2, a text rife with hierarchical implications, but would have focused instead on Gen. 1:26-27, where equality in creation makes a stronger appearance. See Elaine H. Pagels, "Paul and Women: A Response to Recent Discussion," *JAAR* 42 (1974): 538-49.

25. Scroggs finds company for this "source" reading in Cyril of Alexandria (d. 444): "Thus we say that the head of every man is Christ, because he was excellently made through him. And the head of woman is man, because she was taken from his flesh. Likewise the head of Christ is God, because he is from Him according to nature" (*De recta fide ad Arcadiam et Marinam* 5.6e; cited in Robin Scroggs, "Paul and the Eschatological Woman: Revisited," *JAAR* 42 [1974]: 535 n. 8).

26. Anthony C. Thiselton, *The First Epistle to the Corinthians*, NIGTC (Grand Rapids: Eerdmans, 2000), p. 814.

27. The full expression, "a woman ought to have ἐξουσία on her head because of the angels," leads to more speculation. Does Paul have in mind the lustful angels of Gen. 6:1-2 who gaze upon and desire the daughters of earth? Or should we envision, as commentators from Augustine to Aquinas have, holy angels who approve the propriety of women's covered heads and are hostile to the new-creation equality of men and women? More promising may be the association of angels "neither marrying nor giving in marriage" in Jesus' response to the query about marriage in heaven (Mark 12:25). This last possibility may in the minds of some (ancients and moderns) combine with the elimination of gender markers in the baptismal formula "not male and female, but one in Christ."

28. Morna Hooker, "Authority on Her Head: An Examination of 1 Cor 11:10," *NTS* 10 (1964): 416; cited in Scroggs, "Eschatological," p. 302.

2. Image and Glory in the New Creation

On the reading above, Paul's midrash on Genesis 2 is designed, then, not to invoke hierarchy, but to *correct* the theory of domination. Key terms complicating this reading are "image" (εἰκών) and "glory" (δόξα), terms used together six times in Paul's letters, four of them in the Corinthian correspondence (1 Cor. 11:7; 15:49; 2 Cor. 3:18; 4:4; cf. Rom. 1:23; 8:29). The repeated coincidence of the terms in the Corinthian correspondence is, I think, significant. In this instance, man is said to be "the image [εἰκών] and glory [δόξα] of God," but woman, "the glory [δόξα] of man" (1 Cor. 11:7). Scroggs reads the term δόξα in both instances as "manifestation" in the order of creation:

> For a man ought not to cover his head
> since he is the image and manifestation of God
> but the woman is the manifestation of man.[29]

The term εἰκών, in Jewish usage, Scroggs argues, means the "revelation of someone's being," so that when one sees God's εἰκών, one sees "the 'visible' manifestation of God's nature and power." This *image* manifestation would apply to both man *and* woman according to Genesis 1:26-27.[30] "Glory" (δόξα), he says, bears a different but closely associated nuance of "manifestation." Woman is not in man's *image* since she, like the male according to Genesis 1:26, is in the *image* of God. But precisely what nuance distinguishes the pair in *"glory,"* Scroggs does not explain.

Why then, we ask, the disequilibrium with respect to glory (δόξα)? This vexing text has provoked a number of compelling (and competing) theories about the veil, among them the idea that its purpose is to shield woman from the subjugating male gaze — she is his glory in the sense of erotic desire — and hence lift her into equality with the man in worship.[31] Another possibility — following on the "source" theory outlined above, and to some extent suggesting the use of head as a synecdoche in which part stands for whole — envisions something rather different and highlights Paul's use of "glory" imagery here and elsewhere in creation-related texts.

29. Scroggs, "Eschatological," p. 299.

30. Scroggs, "Eschatological," p. 299 n. 43.

31. Francis Watson, "The Authority of the Voice: A Theological Reading of 1 Cor 11:2-16," *NTS* 46 (2000): 520-36. Watson understands the veil to be an innovation by Paul designed (not reinstated against enthusiast unveiling) to signal the interdependence of woman and man in "shared practice."

Comparing the initial three headship pairs in verse 3 to the "glory" pairings in verse 7, we recall the logic that sees (1) God as the "source" of all (cf. 8:6: "God, out of whom all things have their being . . ."), (2) Christ as proceeding from that divine source and therefore becoming the new-creation "source" of humanity (cf. 8:6: "through whom all things have their being"), and (3) woman proceeding out of man who is the "source" of humanity. In the diagram below this order of procession is given in column B:

A. Order in the Text	B. Order in Procession from God to Human Beings
Head of man = Christ	Head of Christ = God
Head of woman = man	Head of man = Christ
Head of Christ = God	Head of woman = man

Augustine and Chrysostom, as we noted above, saw the formula as denoting unity between God and Christ, on one hand, and between man and woman, on the other, at least in their prelapsarian condition. With the pairing in verse 7 around the theme of glory comes a development on the original formula, further specifying conditions for worship:

Man is image and glory of God.
Woman is glory of man.

Glory: Divine Light Reflected in Relationship, Divine and Human If by "glory" Paul means, as commentators generally agree, something related to the Hebrew notion of כָּבוֹד *(kābôd)*, the "inner, essential, objective strength which [one] has and which expresses itself in the force of [one's] appearance and activity, in the impression that [one] makes on others," and if we understand his glory language here and elsewhere to denote the way in which divine being shows forth in the creation, a nuance of glory as God's illuminating *relationship*, first, divine to human (man = glory of God), and then, human to human (woman = glory of man), becomes plausible.[32] In the context of the "source"/headship pairs in verse 3, then, we read here a

---

32. The quotation is taken from Karl Barth, *Church Dogmatics* II/1, trans. Geoffrey Bromiley et al. (Edinburgh: T. & T. Clark, 1957), §31, p. 642. Thiselton renders "glory" from the Hebrew context with A. Feuillet ("La dignité et le rôle de la femme d'après quelques textes pauliniens: Comparaison avec l'Ancien Testament," *NTS* 21 [1975]: 157-91) as "the manifestation of God's attributes," which Thiselton takes to include not only divine power but also mercy, love, and self-giving. See Thiselton, *First Corinthians*, p. 835.

sequence that connotes in two steps the relationship of God to God's Other, the human being, and the shared reflection of that glory in the relationship between the human creature, Adam, whose loneliness is answered by another, Eve. The male-female sequencing of the creation story in Genesis 2 does not bear on status if we (1) understand the image (εἰκών) of God to describe both man and woman, as in Genesis 1:26-27, and (2) take the essence of the "glory" pairings to be the manifestation of divine *relationship*, first, divine to human, and second, human to human. In the second instance, a type of synecdoche is in view: reflection of glory in human beings is represented by the headship of the first human being. In such an understanding, the veil may indeed symbolize the woman's authority (v. 10) to bear the dignity of relationship, symbolizing that without her the male would be unable to realize the human means of reflecting divine glory. The unity of the man and woman as relational — *hence differentiated* — reflections of divine glory is the focus in this rendering of the language. The following statements in verses 11-12 then draw the differentiated, glory-reflecting human beings now into the fully reciprocal terminology of shared and interdependent identity in new creation. While differentiation in 1 Corinthians 11 focuses on gender, elsewhere in Paul's new-creation account other particular loci of differentiation are shown to be indifferent, except as the Spirit, passing through them, as it were, enables them to reflect through mutual service the singular glory of God.[33]

3. Relationship and Reciprocity in the New Creation

The whole matter comes to a point at verses 11-12:

> The key thing is [πλὴν οὖτε], in the Lord, the woman is not independent of the man nor the man of the woman, for as woman was made

---

33. The figure of "indifference that tolerates difference" comes from Alain Badiou: "What matters, man or woman, Jew or Greek, slave or free man, is that differences *carry the universal that happens to them like a grace*" (*Saint Paul: The Foundation of Universalism*, trans. Ray Brassier [Stanford: Stanford University Press, 2003], p. 106; emphasis original). Badiou ends his chapter "Universality and the Traversal of Differences" with a citation from 1 Cor. 14:7: "'If even lifeless instruments, such as the flute or the harp, do not give distinct notes, how will anyone know what is being played on the flute or the harp?' (Cor. I.14.7). Differences, like instrumental tones, provide us with the recognizable univocity that makes up the melody of the True" (p. 106).

from man [ἐκ τοῦ ἀνδρός], so is the man (made) through the woman [διὰ τῆς γυναικός]. And everything is of God [τὰ δὲ πάντα ἐκ τοῦ θεοῦ].

By beginning with the phrase "the key thing is," Paul signals that he means to complete the meaning of the preceding verses by way of the obviously reciprocal figure in verse 11: neither the man nor the woman is independent with respect to source.[34] The equalizing creation formula of Genesis 1:26-27 — "In the image of God created he them, male and female . . ." — is closer to hand, to be sure, but the more telling figure for our reading is the new-creation formula at verse 12b: "all things come from God." This expression echoes statements in 1 Corinthians 8:5-6 that will have been heard only moments before in the public reading:

> For although there may be many so-called gods in heaven or on earth . . . yet for us there is one God the Father, from whom all things are [ἐξ οὗ τὰ πάντα] and for whom we exist, and one Lord, Jesus Christ, through whom are all things [δι' οὗ τὰ πάντα] and through whom we exist. (1 Cor. 8:5-6)

The sequence of prepositional phrases in 8:6 — *out of whom (ἐξ οὗ) the Father//through whom (δι' οὗ) Christ* — are echoed in 11:12 — ἐκ τοῦ ἀνδρός// διὰ τῆς γυναικός — with striking implications for worshiping God as new creatures. As in the gospel, "Out of God we all exist; through Christ we all exist," so in the New-Age vocation to glorify God, "Out of the man we came and through the woman we came," for "all things are from God through Christ." Prayer and prophecy, equal opportunities for women and men, reflect the glory of Creator God who said, "Let light come out of darkness," for it is that One through the gospel "who has shone in our hearts to give the light of the knowledge of the glory of God in the face of Christ" (2 Cor. 4:6). At the end of 1 Corinthians, questions of the equality of male and female are left in the dust, so to speak, as the glorious body of resurrection (1 Cor. 15:42) is fully transformed from the "image [εἰκών] of the human being [ἄνθρωπος] of dust" into the "image [εἰκών] of the human being [ἄνθρωπος] of heaven" (1 Cor. 15:42-49).

Paul appears, then, to weave the Genesis texts together as a way of ex-

---

34. Scroggs renders the phrase πλὴν οὔτε as "the key thing" to reflect the grammatical judgment in Blass-Debrunner that Paul uses the term "to conclude a discussion and emphasize what is essential" (see BDF §449, p. 234, cited in Scroggs, "Eschatological," p. 300 n. 47).

pressing the conviction that divine in-breaking takes place precisely within the earthly order and within Scripture itself, all the more vividly within the worshiping *ecclesia,* transforming but not eliminating (originally) created distinctions that themselves show forth in Spirit-transformed relationship the unifying and singular glory of God. How, we rightly wonder, would such a gesture toward transformation have been received? Would the nuance "distinction-without-hierarchy" have been too subtle for the Corinthian ear? How *would* it be heard as other than merely sanctioning old cosmic patterns of domination?

The Image of the Androgyne:
An Alternate New Creation Account

Some in Corinth, Wayne Meeks famously proposed, may have read the Genesis citations elsewhere in Christian preaching and baptism as signaling a restoration in Christ of the original, sexually undifferentiated androgyne. In his landmark essay, Meeks argued that in reaction to pressures on traditional roles for men and women that followed the consolidation of Rome's imperial power, the differentiation of male and female became a "powerful symbol for the fundamental order of the world," such that any modification of the traditional order could become a "potent symbol of social criticism or even of total rejection of the existing order."[35] The early Christian adaptation of a particular reading of Genesis 1 as the narration of humanity as an original androgyne, and the linking of that myth to Christian baptism, led some Christian groups to see themselves, through unity with Christ the second Adam, as the restored, pre-fall humanity.[36] Through form-critical and philological analysis of the instances of the unification formula in the Pauline corpus (Gal. 3:28; 1 Cor. 12:13; Col. 3:11), Meeks concluded that the reunification formula was the baptismal formula used in congregations associated with Paul:[37]

35. Wayne A. Meeks, "Image of the Androgyne: Some Uses of a Symbol in Earliest Christianity," *HR* 13 (1974): 207.

36. In the Colossian church, at least, the act of baptism is said explicitly to reconnect the baptized person to the image of the creator: "Do not lie to one another, seeing that you have put off the old nature with its practices and put on the new nature which is being renewed in knowledge after the image of the creator" (Col. 3:9-10).

37. Elisabeth Schüssler Fiorenza sees the practice of egalitarian self-identity as stemming from the Jesus movement itself and defining the earliest layers of Christian practice.

[A] resident of one of the cities of the province Asia who ventured to become a member of one of the tiny Christian cells in their early years would have heard the utopian declaration of mankind's reunification as a solemn ritual announcement. Reinforced by dramatic gestures (disrobing, immersion, robing), such a declaration would carry — within the community for which the language was meaningful — the power to assist in shaping the symbolic universe by which that group distinguished itself from the ordinary "world" of the larger society. A modern philosopher might call it a "performative utterance."[38]

In Corinth, Meeks surmises, the reunification myth became a locus of identity. Paul himself seems to have held a partial and positive reading of the myth in 1 Corinthians 7, where he allows a reciprocity and mutuality between men and women in domestic affairs that is "virtually unparalleled in Jewish or pagan society of the time."[39] Even in 1 Corinthians 11 there is, says Meeks, no question of functionally inferior roles for women, only symbolic differentiation through clothing. Women are, indeed, clearly invited to participate in charismatic leadership of worship. The symbolic differentiation through clothing recommended by Paul comes as his response to the spiritual enthusiasm in Corinth that threatened to so elevate the spirit over the body as to deny the goodness of the creation altogether.[40] Against this "cosmic audacity" to disregard the conventions of what it means to be human, and preserving his native trust in the goodness of creation, then, Paul himself holds to the distinction male and female as a relational, bodily reflection of divine glory through mutuality and equality "in the Lord."[41]

She resists the notion that egalitarian forms of worship are a result of enthusiasm based in realized eschatology. See *Memory*, pp. 97-241.

38. Meeks, "Androgyne," p. 182.

39. Meeks, "Androgyne," p. 200. There is widespread agreement on the unusual degree of reciprocity and mutuality Paul allows in 1 Corinthians 7. That the androgyne myth is Paul's inspiration is less certain; that conclusion is not necessary to the reading presented here, where gender difference in Genesis is retained but transformed.

40. Meeks looks forward in Christian development to the emergence of gnostic and encratite circles, where denial of the body through gnostic theory or extreme asceticism became popular Christian expressions.

41. The phrase "cosmic audacity" comes from Meeks, "Androgyne," p. 207, citing Jonathan Z. Smith, "Birth Upside Down or Right Side Up?" *HR* 9 (1970): 281-303.

Conclusion

In our text and throughout his letters, Paul occupies, one could say, an *unstable middle position* with respect to the human body and its particularities.[42] In this time that is being "drawn up" (συνεσταλμένος), in which the "form [τὸ σχῆμα] of this world is passing away" (1 Cor. 7:29, 31), Paul sees the good creation of God *recreated* in the baptismal act for mutuality, service, and praise "in the Lord." As such, the body is now, post-baptism, the material and spiritual entity (both individual and corporate) that reflects the glory of God revealed singularly in Christ crucified and resurrected, the first fruit of the final, full, and free participation of the whole creation (Rom. 8:21) in divine glory.[43] The body is at once the instrument for mutual sharing of the glory revealed in the gospel, and the "earthly frame in which we are enclosed" (2 Cor. 5:1); it is the body in which "we groan, yearning to be covered by our heavenly habitation put on *over this one so that our mortality may be absorbed into life immortal*" (2 Cor. 5:4).[44] Above all, it is the body groaning to be liberated from its "slavery to decay" for the "freedom of glory of the children of God" (Rom. 8:21) and, at the same time, the body "being changed from glory into glory" (2 Cor. 3:18).

From this utterly realistic and utterly hope-filled middle position, Paul advises congregation after congregation according to the specific circumstances in which they strive to realize the transformation already begun (1 Cor. 9:19-23). In Corinth, he is compelled by local circumstances to em-

42. The late British philosopher Gillian Rose articulates the "broken middle" as a dynamic space for justice-seeking between the worlds of legal coercion and postmodern antinomianism; see *The Broken Middle: Out of Our Ancient Society* (Hoboken: Wiley-Blackwell, 1992).

43. Karl Barth, in his extended discussion of divine glory in *CD* II/1 §31, traces the image from the Hebrew Bible into the New Testament, stressing that in both testaments "the glory of God belongs to the context of the doctrine of the love of God" (ET: p. 643). Here, for Barth, God's "condescension and friendliness," i.e., his relating in love to the human creature, is especially in view. "God's glory is the indwelling joy of His divine being which as such shines out from Him, which overflows in its richness, which in its super-abundance is not satisfied with itself but communicates itself" (ET: p. 647).

44. Much rests here on Paul's understanding of σῶμα (body). Generally he treats the σῶμα positively and the flesh (σάρξ) as a negative, worldly power inimical to the proper relationship of the human being to God. Note, too, his insistence on the middle position in 1 Corinthians 15, where it is the *spiritual* σῶμα that will be raised in the resurrection of the dead (15:44). For Paul, the apocalypse of Jesus Christ has caused a radical transformation of the human being, a transformation to be realized fully in the resurrection of this pneumatic σῶμα.

phasize the gendered body now freed "in the Lord" from hierarchical or re-strictive identities to reflect in the practices of worship the singular glory now revealed in the face of Christ. Neither letting go of the profound mysteries of gender embedded in Genesis, nor leaving them untouched by new creation, Paul argues for a transformative way through the accustomed binary patterns of gender within a new language and practice of divine glory.[45] Far from eschewing the narrative of gender he reads in Genesis, Paul's exegesis of Genesis has the effect, ultimately, of embracing the gendered body as a changing and ever-reflective organ of God's own creative and re-creative glory. But gendered identities *as culturally or naturally defined* are never by Paul reified, and this refusal allows him to show *all* identities being drawn up into the unifying, singular gospel of Christ "through whom all — even things that had no being — exist" by God's gracious act of new creation (1 Cor. 1:28; 8:6).[46]

45. For the expression "transformative way through [gender binaries]," I am indebted to Coakley, "Eschatological," p. 67. Taking up 1 Cor. 11:2-16, Badiou writes: "Ultimately, Paul's undertaking . . . consists in making universalizing egalitarianism pass through the reversibility of an inegalitarian rule. This allows him . . . to arrange the global situation so that universality is able to affect particularizing differences in return: in this instance, the difference between the sexes" (*Paul,* pp. 104-5).

46. Paul's refusal to reify cultural or natural definitions of gendered identities seems to be the point of Paul's brief final appeal to "nature herself" in 1 Cor. 11:14. Nature's dictates, however compelling, are of provisional not final significance to the Apostle of the New Creation. On the view that "nature functions in this text as a competing moral authority alongside that of God as Creator and God's New Creation in Christ," see Jennifer Thweatt-Bates, "On Creation, New Creation and the Natural Order: A Theological Reading of 1 Corinthians 11.2-16," *Leaven* 16 (2008): 86-90; available at: http://digitalcommons.pepperdine.edu/leaven/vol16/iss2/9.

Ashes on the Frontal Lobe: Cognitive Dissonance and Cruciform Cognition in 2 Corinthians

Susan Grove Eastman

Ashes on the Frontal Lobe

Many churches, including my own tradition, begin the liturgical season of Lent with an Ash Wednesday service. During the liturgy, participants are marked individually on the forehead with a cross made from the burned palm fronds of the previous year's celebration of Palm Sunday. As the black, messy ashen cross is inscribed on each person's face, the celebrant intones, "Remember that you are dust, and to dust you shall return."

It is a solemn service, with an element of cognitive dissonance provoked by the lectionary readings for the day, which always include Jesus' exhortation in the Sermon on the Mount: "Beware of practicing your piety before other people in order to be seen by them" (Matt. 6:1).[1] The very public facial disfiguration surely seems like practicing one's piety before others, especially if the devotee has attended an early-morning service and goes through the rest of the day with a black smudge on her forehead announcing to all and sundry, "I went to church today!" What's a person to do? Wash off the cross afterward, remembering that Jesus also said, "When you fast, anoint your head and wash your face" (Matt. 6:17)? Go to evening service instead? Or wear the ashes boldly, perhaps

1. All biblical translations in this essay are my own.

It is a joy and privilege to dedicate this essay to Beverly Gaventa, in deep thankfulness for her friendship and collegiality over the years. Like many, I am the happy recipient of her sharp wit, seasoned wisdom, and passionate commitment to communicating the grace of God in Jesus Christ.

viewing them sacramentally as an "outward and visible [sign] of inward and spiritual grace"?[2]

The conundrum arises from thinking of the ashen cross primarily as an outward sign that others see. But what if we understand it as a way of changing our own perception through imprinting the cross on our modes of perception, our intentions, and our actions? Hence the title of this essay: "Ashes on the Frontal Lobe." I use the precise term "frontal lobe" to denote our embodied brains rather than a disembodied mind. Recent discoveries in neuroscience have led to an explosion of insights about the human brain, which are overturning Cartesian assumptions of mind/body dualism and free-floating individualism.[3] It turns out that the frontal lobe, which is the executive part of the brain where memory, intention, and action planning are located, receives and processes input from perceptive, sensory, and motor regions of the brain.[4] Once thought to inhabit rigidly distinct areas of the brain, these functions now are understood as strongly interrelated in their activity. The result is that the activity of the motor system that generates bodily movement is integral to perception and the processing of sensory input. In other words, action shapes perception, and perception shapes action, such that cognition happens in the interplay between the brain, the body, and the environment.[5] In the words of philoso-

---

2. *The Book of Common Prayer* (New York: Church Publishing, 1979), p. 857.

3. The literature on this subject is vast; for helpful introductions, see Stein Bråten, ed., *On Being Moved: From Mirror Neurons to Empathy*, Advances in Consciousness Research 68 (Amsterdam/Philadelphia: John Benjamins, 2007); Susan Hurley and Nick Chater, eds., *Perspectives on Imitation: From Neuroscience to Social Science*, vol. 2: *Imitation, Human Development, and Culture* (Cambridge, MA: MIT Press, 2005). On the relationship between the body and the mind, see Shaun Gallagher, *How the Body Shapes the Mind* (Oxford: Oxford University Press, 2005). On the idea of embodied cognition, see Andy Clark, *Supersizing the Mind: Embodiment, Action, and Cognitive Extension* (Oxford: Oxford University Press, 2008).

4. For a brief overview of the brain, see Giacomo Rizzolatti and Corrado Sinigaglia, *Mirrors in the Brain: How Our Minds Share Actions and Emotions*, trans. Frances Anderson (Oxford: Oxford University Press, 2008), pp. 1-20. The anterior part of the frontal lobe performs executive functions, linking sensory input with motor mechanisms. It receives input from the prefrontal lobe, associated with memory, planning, and intention, and from the cingulate cortex, "involved in the processing of motivational and emotional information which are the basis of our intentions and influence the course of our actions" (p. 13). The posterior region of the frontal lobe receives input from the posterior parietal lobe, which controls action and movement (see pp. 13-17).

5. For a helpful overview of theories about the degree and mode of this interplay, see Lawrence Shapiro, *Embodied Cognition* (New York: Routledge, 2010). The link between per-

pher of mind John Haugeland: "If we are to understand mind as the locus of intelligence, we cannot follow Descartes in regarding it as separable in principle from the body and the world. . . . Mind, therefore, is not incidentally but *intimately* embodied and *intimately* embedded in its world."[6]

What does all of this have to do with the Ash Wednesday liturgy? Simply this: if we think of the mark of the cross as an inscription on our frontal lobe and not merely as a visible sign on our foreheads, then we associate it with our own perceptions and actions rather than our appearance. It is not about how we look *to* others, but how we look *at* others, and, furthermore, how that perception then interacts with our cognitive processes and our bodily movements. The knowledge we receive from bodily experience and perceptions, which in turn shapes our intentions and actions, is processed through the death of Christ. Even our memories become accessed through the cross. We look both outward and inward through this sign — this lens — of Christ's death planted in the dust of our own mortality. The only marker visible to others — if we don't wash it off! — is the sign of our own transitory mortality, yet paradoxically in the shape of the cross that carries us from death to life.

In the following essay, I shall suggest that the neuroscientists who talk of an embedded and embodied brain are closer to Paul than they are to Descartes. Paul certainly knew that there is a very close link between perception and action, and in this he was not alone; as many scholars have noted, the idea of transformation through vision was widespread in the ancient world. My focus is 2 Corinthians 2:14–7:4, a complex and convoluted text in which verbs of perception and cognition figure prominently.[7]

---

ception and action has received intense attention through the discovery of "mirror neurons," motor neurons that are activated simply by observing an action. For example, the sight of a coffee cup activates the neurons that control the actual movement of picking it up. As Rizzolatti and Sinigaglia put it, this neural response to vision is "a preliminary form of action, a call to arms so to speak" (*Mirrors*, p. 49, see also pp. 79-138).

6. John Haugeland, *Having Thought: Essays in the Metaphysics of Mind* (Cambridge, MA: Harvard University Press, 1998), pp. 236-37, emphasis original.

7. Regardless of their views on the unity of 2 Corinthians, most scholars treat 2:14–7:4 as an intact unit. So Dieter Georgi, *The Opponents of Paul in Second Corinthians* (Philadelphia: Fortress, 1986); F. F. Bruce, *1 and 2 Corinthians*, NCB (London: Oliphants, 1971), who puts 2:14–7:1 under the heading "The Apostolic Ministry"; Scott J. Hafemann, *Suffering and Ministry in the Spirit: Paul's Defense of His Ministry in II Corinthians 2:14–3:3* (Grand Rapids: Eerdmans, 1990), p. 8; Sze-kar Wan, *Power in Weakness: Conflict and Rhetoric in Paul's Second Letter to the Corinthians*, The New Testament in Context (Harrisburg, PA: Trinity Press International, 2000), p. 57.

In his appeal to the Corinthians Paul is metaphorically imposing ashes on the frontal lobes of his converts; he wants their vision and understanding, motivation and action, to be filtered through the lens of the cross, so that they see the action of God subversively at work in their own lives.

To trace the movement and effectiveness of Paul's appeal, the following section will investigate two thematic strands that seem to contradict one another in the letter, setting up a certain tension in the letter. The first line of thought contrasts the boldness and visibility of Paul's abiding ministry with the veil over Moses' ministry, a ministry that is being annulled. The second contrasts the perpetuity of what is unseen with the transience of what is seen.

Cognitive Dissonance

The result of these thematic crosscurrents is a cognitive dissonance that threads through 2 Corinthians 2:14–7:4, precisely concerning perception, knowledge, and the transformation of information into motivation and action. The dissonance emerges in a nutshell when we consider two passages in tandem:

> Having such a hope, we exercise great boldness [παρρησίᾳ], not like Moses, who put a veil over his face [πρόσωπον] so that the sons of Israel could not gaze intently at the end of what was being annulled. (3:12-13)

> Therefore, knowing the fear of the Lord, we persuade human beings, but we are known [or "manifest," πεφανερώμεθα] to God, and I hope we also are manifest to your consciences. We are not commending ourselves to you, but we are giving you a basis [ἀφορμήν] for boasting about us, so that you may have an answer to those who boast in the face [ἐν προσώπῳ] and not in the heart. (5:11-12)

The first passage is the linchpin of Paul's comparison between his ministry and that of Moses in 3:1–4:6. Bringing together references to both vision and speech, it contrasts Paul's liberty of expression with Moses' veiled face.[8] In stark contrast, in 2 Corinthians 5:11-12 Paul bases his appeal to the

---

8. "Paul has set up the veiled figure of Moses as a foil against which to commend the candor and boldness of his own ministry" (Richard B. Hays, *Echoes of Scripture in the Letters of Paul* [New Haven: Yale University Press, 1989], p. 147).

Corinthians on the superiority of the unseen heart to the visible face in 4:7–7:4. That is, he draws out the relational implications of his argument for the superiority of what is unseen to what is seen, and what is inward to what is outward. What is outward and visible is transient; what is inward and invisible is eternal — indeed it is being made new daily (4:16-18).

Thus each of these subsections of the letter employs the language of perception and cognition, but in apparently contradictory ways. The result is a brilliant cognitive bait and switch. To begin to grasp this paradoxical movement in Paul's argument, it will be helpful to look in greater depth at each subsection.

2 Corinthians 3:1–4:6: From the Lesser to the Greater Glory

In 3:1–4:6, Paul employs the rabbinic exegetical technique of arguing "from the lesser to the greater" to establish a contrast between his ministry and that of Moses. The contrast is between the lesser glory of Moses' ministry, when his face shone after his encounter with God on the mountain, and the greater glory of the ministry of righteousness and the Spirit. Hence, "If the ministry of death, carved in letters on stone, came with such glory that the Israelites could not gaze intently at Moses' face because of its glory, even though it was being annulled, how much more will the ministry of the Spirit be in glory?" (3:7-8). Again, "If the ministry of condemnation [came] in glory, how much more does the ministry of righteousness surpass it in glory?" (3:9). Paul summarizes the point in 3:10-11: "What once had glory no longer has glory because of the glory that surpasses it. For if what is being annulled came through glory, how much more does what abides [τὸ μένον] come in glory?"

Building on this argument from the lesser to the greater, Paul then amplifies the story of Moses' shining face through a focus on Moses' veil.[9] Of particular interest is the way motifs of perception and communication are interwoven, first in the Exodus narrative itself, and then in Paul's use of

---

9. The literature on Moses' veil is voluminous. For an in-depth analysis and proposal, see Scott J. Hafemann, *Paul, Moses, and the History of Israel: The Letter/Spirit Contrast and the Argument from Scripture in 2 Corinthians 3*, WUNT 81 (Tübingen: J. C. B. Mohr [Paul Siebeck], 1995), pp. 335-436; Linda L. Belleville, *Reflections of Glory: Paul's Polemical Use of the Moses-Doxa Tradition in 2 Corinthians 3.1-18*, JSNTSup 52 (Sheffield: Sheffield Academic Press, 1991); Carol Kern Stockhausen, *Moses' Veil and the Glory of the New Covenant: The Exegetical Substructure of II Cor. 3,1–4,6*, AnBib 116 (Rome: Pontificio Instituto Biblica, 1989).

that narrative. In Exodus 34:29-35, Moses puts on the veil when he is silent and separated, not talking with either the people or God. As Brian Britt observes, "[The veil] divides times when Moses performs as a prophet from other times. The veil is thus a temporal rather than a spatial barrier between the sacred and the ordinary. When he wears the veil, there is no prophecy, no divine revelation. The covered prophet is a silent prophet."[10] Britt backs up this claim by noting the emphasis on communication and patterns of repetition within the narrative. The Lord tells Moses to write the words, and he does. When Moses descends the mountain, his face shines because he has been speaking with the Lord. The people are afraid when they see the shining of Moses' face, but nonetheless he speaks to them; it is only when he has finished talking that he puts the veil on his face (Exod. 34:33). He takes off the veil whenever he speaks with the Lord (Exod. 34:34-35).[11]

"The covered prophet is a silent prophet." The veil marks the times when Moses is incommunicado. As such it also obstructs the senses and thereby creates a cognitive barrier: what is not seen is also not heard.[12] Hence the veil functions as a means or marker of both separation and incomprehension. It quite literally comes between Moses and the people. When Paul reframes the story, he capitalizes on this theme: "When they [the Israelites] read the old covenant, that same [τὸ αὐτό] veil remains unlifted. . . . Yes, to this day, whenever Moses is read a veil lies over their minds" (2 Cor. 3:14-15). "That same veil" is the cognitive barrier that signifies the prophet's silence and separation.[13]

Paul exploits this motif in two ways. First, he attributes a motive to Moses' self-covering: "Moses, who put a veil on his face so that the sons of Israel could not gaze intently at the end [τέλος] of what was being annulled" (2 Cor. 3:13). The cultural resonance of veils in Greco-Roman cul-

---

10. Brian Britt, "Concealment, Revelation, and Gender: The Veil of Moses in the Bible and in Christian Art," *RelArts* 7 (2003): 230.

11. Britt, "Concealment," pp. 230-31.

12. Contrast 1 Kings 19:13, where Elijah covers his face with a veil while the Lord passes by the cave and speaks to him.

13. Arguing that the veil is a metonym for the hardening of the Israelites' minds in 2 Cor. 3:14, Hafemann states: "The problem signified by the veil is thus not a *cognitive* inability due to the lack of a special spiritual endowment, but an inescapable *volitional* inability as a result of a hardened heart untouched by the Spirit's transforming power" (*Paul,* p. 374, emphasis original). But this is to downplay the preponderance of verbs of perception in 2 Corinthians 3 and to impose a misleading dichotomy between cognition and volition.

ture strongly suggests that Paul's auditors would hear in this passage a motivation of shame, of hiding a loss of status or of a change of identity.[14] Women were expected to be veiled as an expression of modesty and a mode of seclusion, but it was suspect for a man to be veiled. A man might cover his face to hide unmanly emotions, as did David when he wept over Absalom's treachery (2 Sam. 15:30). The veil signified separation, feminine seclusion, or the covering of shame.[15] Even if a man did not feel shame, the existence of a veil could communicate such dishonor or weakness. Evident in ancient Greek culture, this connotation for the veil persisted into Roman times. For example, in Plutarch's retelling of the suicide of Demosthenes, the hero entrapped by his enemies veils his head, turns away from them, and sucks the poison out of his pen. While he is veiled, his captors accuse him of effeminacy (μαλακόν), but when the poison begins to work, he throws back the veil and looks them in the eye before he dies (*Life of Dem.* 28-29).[16] The veil hides the hero's action, it hides the transition from life to death, and it carries cultural connotations of feminine weakness and therefore a loss of status.

Perhaps for this reason, neither Philo nor Josephus talks about Moses' veil. Indeed, Philo contrasts being confident before God with boldness (θαρρέω) and hiding or veiling one's face (*Spec.* 1.270).[17] For Philo, God's Spirit dwells only in those who have "disrobed themselves of all created

---

14. See, e.g., W. C. van Unnik, "'With Unveiled Face': An Exegesis of 2 Corinthians iii 12-18," *NovT* 6 (1963): 153-69. Van Unnik notes an equivalence between the Aramaic for "unveiled" and the meaning of παρρησία. It is not necessary to argue, as does van Unnik, that Paul thought in Aramaic. The linguistic parallels simply serve as further evidence for an association between confident, bold speech and unveiled rather than veiled faces. In my view, this widespread connotation for the veil argues against interpretations of τέλος as the glory of God in the face of Christ (so, e.g., Hays, *Echoes*, p. 146).

15. In this regard, it is notable that there are very few depictions of Moses' veil in either Jewish or Christian art, and that in Christian art the trope becomes transmuted into the image of the synagogue as a veiled female figure. The most famous of these depictions are the statues of church and synagogue in the south transept of Strasbourg cathedral. See the discussion in Britt, "Concealment," pp. 243-50. For an analysis of the veil in ancient Greece, with an argument that its cultural resonances carried over to the Roman era, see Douglas L. Cairns, "The Meaning of the Veil in Ancient Greek Culture," in *Women's Dress in the Ancient Greek World*, ed. Lloyd Llewellyn-Jones (London: Duckworth; Swansea: Classical Press of Wales; Oakville, CT: Distributor in the United States of America, David Brown Book Co., 2002), pp. 73-93. I am grateful to my research assistant Jared Wortman for bringing the articles by Britt and Cairns to my attention.

16. Cairns, "Veil," pp. 79-80.

17. Belleville, *Reflections*, pp. 33-34.

things and of the innermost veil and wrapping of mere opinion" (*Gig.* 53, LCL). The veil is a cover for wrongdoing (*Spec.* 2.11; 4.7; *Conf. Ling.* 116). Similarly, in Jeremiah 14:3-4, the servants and the farmers cover their faces to hide their shame when God sends a drought as judgment for Israel's apostasy (cf. Jer. 3:25).

Does Paul intend to say that Moses was ashamed when his face ceased to shine? Or that he was undergoing a change in status and identity? It is difficult to determine. What we can assume is that his auditors would be aware of the cultural associations between veiling and shame or change in status, and that such awareness would be strengthened by the implicit contrast between Moses' veil and Paul's subsequent claim in 2 Corinthians 4:2: "We have renounced the secret things of shame [τὰ κρυπτὰ τῆς αἰσχύνης]." Rather, says Paul, "by the open manifestation [φανερώσει] of the truth we commend ourselves to every person's conscience in the sight of God" (4:2). Here secrecy and shame contrast with public manifestation.

This contrast between what is veiled and public proclamation brackets and permeates 2 Corinthians 3:1–4:6, alerting us to the second way in which Paul exploits the motif of Moses' veil as he proclaims, "We exercise great boldness, not like Moses, who put a veil over his face" (3:12). In contrast with the veil that impedes understanding when Moses is read (3:14-15), Paul writes "nothing but what you can read [ἀναγινώσκετε] and understand [ἐπιγινώσκετε]" (1:13). Unlike those who peddle God's word, Paul and his associates are sincere, commissioned by God, and speak in Christ in the sight of God (2:17). The Corinthians themselves are their letter of recommendation, "to be known [γινωσκομένη] and read [ἀναγινωσκομένη] by all people" (3:2). Just as Moses removed his veil when he entered the presence of the Lord, so now, "whenever a person turns [ἐπιστρέψῃ] to the Lord, the veil is removed" (3:16). The effect of this unveiling is freedom (3:17), which in contrast to veiled silence implies the liberty to speak boldly, without fear or shame. Hence, when shortly Paul contrasts his public manifestation of the truth with shameful secrets (4:2), he is expressing precisely the freedom that the Spirit of God gives. He can do this because God the creator, who spoke light into existence, now "has shone in our hearts to give the light of the knowledge of the glory of God in the face of Christ" (4:6). Paul's faith impels him to speak (4:13). His free speech certainly describes his public proclamation of the gospel. But it also conveys his openness of heart towards the Corinthians themselves: "Our mouth is open to you, Corinthians; our heart is wide" (6:11).

All of this is a movement from the lesser glory of Moses under the veil, to the greater glory that surpasses it. Associated with boldness and openness of speech, this glory is also visible and transforms those who behold it. So Paul proclaims the stunning promise: "We all, with unveiled face, beholding as in a mirror [κατοπτριζόμενοι] the glory of the Lord, are being changed into the same likeness from glory to glory, from the Lord, the Spirit" (3:18). This greater glory is found in the face of Christ, the image of God who mirrors God's glory so that through him we are given "the light of the knowledge [γνώσεως] of the glory of God" (4:4, 6).[18] In sum, the movement from the lesser to the greater is from shamefaced secrecy to public proclamation, from lower to higher status, from silence to speech, from transitory to lasting hope, from veiled cognition to the knowledge of God. Paul amplifies the contrast through his repeated use of ἔχω to denote the treasures that come through Christ.[19] Through Christ, Paul and his fellow believers have confidence toward God (3:4). Because they have a hope that abides, they are very bold (3:12). They have the ministry of transformation by the mercy of God (4:1). They have the psalmist's spirit of faith and so publicly proclaim their faith (4:13). They have an eternal dwelling from God (5:1).

This is a very triumphant picture of Paul's ministry, suffused with glory and highly visible. It is not surprising that subsequent interpreters have read Paul's argument in triumphal ways. It is tempting to contrast the lesser glory of Moses, for example, with the greater glory of Christian preachers with shining faces.[20] One anticipates a highly visible — and victorious — profile for Paul's own ministry. The ministry of the Spirit and of righteousness (3:8-9) surely is also a ministry of glory, is it not?

The discerning reader will expect a negative answer at this point, and

18. See the extensive discussion in Victor Paul Furnish, *II Corinthians*, AB 32A (Garden City, NY: Doubleday, 1984), pp. 238-42.

19. Noted by Hafemann, *Paul*, p. 340.

20. As argued by Belleville, *Reflections*, p. 281. See also N. T. Wright, "Reflected Glory: 2 Corinthians 3:18," in *The Glory of Christ in the New Testament: Studies in Christology in Memory of George Bradford Caird*, ed. L. D. Hurst and N. T. Wright (Oxford: Clarendon, 1987), pp. 139-50; Jacques Dupont, "Le Chrétien, miroir de la gloire divine d'après II Cor., III, 18," *RB* 56 (1949): 392-411. Belleville, Wright, and Dupont all interpret κατοπτριζόμενοι in 2 Cor. 3:18 as a reference to the glorified countenances of Christians who reflect God's glory rather than beholding it as in a mirror. The difficulty with this interpretation is that it focuses on glorified human faces — precisely what Paul argues against in 5:12 — rather than on the face of Christ (4:6). Paul himself is lowly in face and weak in body (1 Cor. 10:1, 10). See J. Louis Martyn, *Theological Issues in the Letters of Paul* (Nashville: Abingdon, 1997), pp. 103-4 (esp. n. 47), 108.

she will be right. For as already indicated, there is a counter-narrative, a cognitive crosscurrent, that undercuts such a reading. So we turn to the second subsection, 2 Corinthians 4:7–7:4.

2 Corinthians 4:7–7:4: From the Greater Glory to Cruciform Cognition

Indeed, in addition to confidence, abiding hope, ministry, and the spirit of faith, Paul and his fellow preachers have (ἔχομεν), according to 2 Corinthians 4:7, the treasure of the knowledge of the glory of God in the face of Christ (taking this treasure to refer to the immediately preceding referent, in 4:6). But they have this knowledge in clay vessels (ὀστρακίνοις σκεύεσιν) so that the surpassing power is from God and not from them. Paul immediately describes what these "clay pots" experience: affliction, perplexity, persecution, being struck down — in short, extreme hardships (4:8-9). Nonetheless, these hardships do not destroy them. Rather, Paul sees and narrates their suffering through the death of Christ: "always carrying in the body the death of Jesus, so the life of Jesus may be manifested [φανερωθῇ] in our bodies" (4:10). Experientially this means "being given up to death for Jesus' sake, so that the life of Jesus may be manifested in our mortal flesh" (4:11). The knowledge of divine glory mediated through the face of Christ suddenly becomes hidden, known through being given over to death. The faces of Christ's followers do not shine; they are marked with ashes. This is cruciform cognition in a double sense: Paul interprets his bodily experience through the death of Jesus, as in fact embedded in the crucified body of Christ. And the public display of this christological union is a paradoxical combination of suffering and indestructible life. Embodied in his life, and embedded in Christ, Paul sees and is seen through union with the Christ who acts in and among believers through the Spirit.

Paul, who rejoiced in boldness and open communication, now begins to distinguish between the outer and the inner person (4:16), and between what is seen and what is unseen (4:18). Irony of ironies, having depicted Moses' veil as hiding the transience of the lesser glory, now Paul states that what is outward and visible is transient, and what is inward and unseen is eternal (4:16-18). The transformation of those who behold God's glory with unveiled faces is now described as an inner re-creation (4:16), accomplished through affliction, and awaiting a future, surpassing weight of glory (4:17) that is not visible in the present time. Having proclaimed that we all are being transformed into the image of Christ, as with unveiled faces we see the reflected glory of the Lord, now Paul proclaims, "We walk by faith, not by sight" (5:7).

At work here is an interplay between how Paul sees and knows others, and how he wants to be seen and known. He interprets his own afflictions as representing and making known the death of Jesus. His physical experiences, shared with his fellow missionaries, are a mode of knowledge — for himself, as knowledge of Jesus, and for others, as a visible sign of Jesus. We recall his appeal to the Corinthians: "What we are is manifest to God, and I hope we also are manifest to your consciences. We are not commending ourselves to you, but we are giving you a basis [ἀφορμήν] for boasting about us, so that you may have an answer to those who boast in the face [ἐν προσώπῳ] and not in the heart" (5:11-12). Paul wants the Corinthians to see him as he sees himself, through the cognitive lens of the cross. His own experiences — his bodily sensory input to the frontal lobe, we might say — in turn shape Paul's intentions and actions from within: "For the love of Christ controls [συνέχει] us, because we are convinced that one has died for all; therefore all have died. And he died for all, that those who live might live no longer for themselves but for him who for their sake died and was raised" (5:14-15). For this reason and in this way, Paul no longer sees others on the basis of outward appearances (κατὰ σάρκα) but also, as J. Louis Martyn has argued, through the prism of the death of Jesus (5:16).[21]

I have labeled this way of knowing and being known as a kind of cognitive dissonance. One effect of such dissonance is to undercut any confidence in knowledge based on appearances. When, in 5:16, Paul says that we regard no one according to the flesh (οὐδένα οἴδαμεν κατὰ σάρκα), his auditors would have heard, and agreed with, a rejection of knowledge gained only through sensory experience and an embrace of knowledge gained through the indwelling Spirit.[22] Furthermore, taking into account Paul's distinction between the "inner" and "outer" person in 4:16, it is tempting to conclude that Paul rejects sensory knowledge in favor of a disembodied knowledge held by the individual soul in whom the Spirit dwells. To do so, however, would be to ignore the detailed lists of physical as well as emotional experience that precede and follow 5:16-21 (namely, 4:7-12; 6:4-10).[23]

21. Martyn, *Issues,* pp. 89-110.
22. Martyn, *Issues,* pp. 95-97.
23. "Thus, the new way of knowing is not in some ethereal sense a spiritual way of knowing. It is not effected in a mystic trance, as the pseudo-apostles claimed, but rather right in the midst of rough-and-tumble life" (Martyn, *Issues,* p. 109).

Paul does not reject knowledge gained through the body; rather, he rejects reliance on immediate knowledge unmediated by the death of Jesus. His embodied cognition is mediated and transmuted through the cruciform body of Christ, known through the community in which Paul and his believers are embedded.

This cruciform, embodied, and embedded cognition is, for Paul, the only way the saints can truly see and be seen. It allows him, or rather compels him, to commend his ministry paradoxically "through glory and dishonor, through poor repute and good repute" (6:8). He acknowledges and even seems to rejoice in the disconnect between what others see and know of him, and his own experience of God's provision: "as imposters, and yet true; as unknown, and yet well known; as dying, and behold [ἰδού], we live; as punished, yet not killed; as sorrowful, yet always rejoicing; as poor, yet enriching others; as having nothing, and possessing everything [ὡς μηδὲν ἔχοντες καὶ πάντα κατέχοντες]" (6:8b-10). The only sign that Paul will show to the Corinthians and to the world is an ashen smudge shaped in a cross, imposed on his vision and directing his speech and action.

From Cruciform Cognition to Christ's Act of Reconciliation

Paul's appeal to his beloved Corinthians is, in effect, an exercise in recognition, through which he directs his auditors' attention to God's subversive way of acting to reconcile us to God and to each other, and to God's hidden but powerful presence in the midst of daily hardships. The ascending movement from lesser to greater glory in 3:1–4:6, and the abrupt plunge to the depths in 4:7–6:10, is the movement of Christ himself, who plunged "to the depths" on our behalf (5:16-21). It is Christ's plunge into humanity's sin that reconciles and makes new, not least through transforming our vision (5:21).

Sometimes we gain a new recognition of this reconciliation and paradoxical transformation through new media. So I close with a poem by Gerard Manley Hopkins as a particularly eloquent and poignant exposition of the movement from glory to glory through cruciform re-cognition:[24]

---

24. Cited from Gerard Manley Hopkins, *Poems and Prose* (London: Penguin, 1953), p. 30.

"The Windhover"
To Christ Our Lord

I caught this morning morning's minion, king-
> dom of daylight's dauphin, dapple-dawn-drawn Falcon, in his
>> riding
> Of the rolling level underneath him steady air, and striding

High there, how he rung upon the rein of a wimpling wing
In his ecstasy! then off, off forth on swing,
> As a skate's heel sweeps smooth on a bow-bend: the hurl and
>> gliding
> Rebuffed the big wind. My heart in hiding

Stirred for a bird, — the achieve of, the mastery of the thing!

Brute beauty and valour and act, oh, air, pride, plume, here
> Buckle! AND the fire that breaks from thee then, a billion
Times told lovelier, more dangerous, O my chevalier!

No wonder of it: sheer plod makes plough down sillion
Shine, and blue-bleak embers, ah my dear,
> Fall, gall themselves, and gash gold-vermillion.

There are two themes here: the heart in hiding and the revelation of glory at the point of falling. The poet's heart is "in hiding," and from his hiding place he sees a falcon silhouetted against the dawn sky. It is the prince of the "kingdom of daylight," soaring effortlessly with the wind. It is masterful, glorious. The "heart in hiding" is stirred, lifted up by this glorious vision.

But then this glory is surpassed by an even greater glory, revealed, not by the falcon's higher ascent into the heavens, but at the moment when rays of the rising sun reflect off the bird's wings as it dives. The turning point of the poem, its literal cincture, is the word "buckle," when the falcon's body contracts and it plummets to earth. "Buckle" cinches together the bird's attributes of power and majesty and paradoxically also evokes crumpling and falling, like knees buckling, like falling to one's knees in prayer or anguish.

Insofar as the falcon enacts Christ's own descent to earth, the second theme is christological, and it speaks to the condition of the first in a way that the falcon's airborne glory cannot. The falcon in flight does move the secret places of the heart, but it does not transform them. That transformation comes into view in the final stanza. "No wonder of it," says the poet, but it *is* wonder, only the wonder is hidden. The shine in the muddy furrow when the farmer tramps through it, and the vermillion gash in the blue-bleak embers, are revelations of the reflected glory that comes with the buckling. This is a movement from the lesser to the greater in a counterintuitive way, from the lesser glory of the bird in flight, to the greater glory of the fire glancing off the bird as it dives, to the gleam of a muddy furrow in the rain.

The ashen embers spill over the grate and break open to reveal the fire inside.

Glory.

Cross and Cosmos in Galatians

Martinus C. de Boer

Paul uses the term κόσμος in two passages of Galatians, and these shall be the focus of this essay:

(1) In 4:3, while looking back to the common past of believers in Christ, Paul writes that "when we were children, we were enslaved under the στοιχεῖα of the κόσμος."

(2) In 6:14, where the term occurs twice, Paul writes about "the cross of our Lord Jesus Christ, through which to me the κόσμος has been crucified and I to the κόσμος."[1]

At issue here is the precise reference of the term κόσμος in these two passages. Does the term refer to the same reality in 4:3 and 6:14? A second question naturally follows when we take into account that in both passages the κόσμος being referred to belongs to the past of believers: To

---

1. Translations of passages from Galatians follow those defended in my commentary (Martinus C. de Boer, *Galatians: A Commentary*, NTL [Louisville: Westminster John Knox, 2011]).

I shared a podium with Beverly Roberts Gaventa when we both presented papers on the theme of the cosmos in Paul for the Pauline Soteriology Group of the Society of Biblical Literature at its Annual Meeting in Atlanta in November 2010. It therefore seems appropriate to allow the substantially revised version of my paper to be included in this Festschrift in her honor. She has convincingly reminded us that "the governing theological antithesis in Galatians" is actually not "between Christ and the law and between the cross and circumcision" but "between Christ/new creation and cosmos" (Beverly Roberts Gaventa, *Our Mother Saint Paul* [Louisville: Westminster John Knox, 2007], pp. 103, 108). "The theology reflected in Galatians," she points out, "is first of all about Jesus Christ and the new creation God has begun in him (1:1-4; 6:14-15), and only in the light of that christocentrism can Paul's remarks concerning the law be understood" (p. 102).

what extent are the two passages related to one another at the level of soteriology?

I shall argue that in 4:3 the κόσμος in view is evidently the physical universe that is comprised of certain elements; in 6:14, however, the κόσμος in view pertains to the religion of the law, represented in the immediate context by the practice of circumcision (6:12-13, 15). On this point I differ from a number of exegetes who argue that the term has the same referent in the two passages.[2] I shall also argue, however, that despite the different *referential* meanings of the term κόσμος in the two passages, they do bear a close relationship to one another at the level of soteriology.

Before I turn to an exegetical analysis of Galatians 4:3 and 6:14, a very brief word about the rhetorical situation of the letter is in order. Paul addresses his Galatian readers in 4:21 as "you who want to be under the law." This characterization of the Galatians reflects the fact that after Paul founded the churches in Galatia (cf. 1:2, 8-9, 11; 3:1; 4:13) new preachers (Christian Jews who have a close relationship with the mother church in Jerusalem) have come into the Galatian churches and have been putting pressure on the new believers in Galatia to adopt the practice of circumcision (1:6-9; 3:1; 4:17; 5:2-4, 7-12; 6:12-13).[3] The practice of circumcision is a communal and a family matter, pertaining not simply to individuals or men. By adopting the practice of circumcision, the churches in Galatia, consisting of both women and men, will be incorporated into God's people, also known as the offspring of Abraham (3:29), and as a result will be under obligation to observe the remainder of the covenantal law. Among that remainder is, for example, the obligation to observe feast days such as the Sabbath and Passover. Paul writes in 4:10 about the Galatians "observing days and months and seasons and years." His consternation about this turn of events is palpable. The letter to the Galatians represents Paul's passionate attempt to prevent this turn to the law in Galatia from going any further, indeed to reverse it, and to announce to the believers in Galatia

---

2. Cf. esp., on different grounds, Edward Adams, *Constructing the World: A Study in Paul's Cosmological Language*, Studies of the New Testament and Its World (Edinburgh: T. & T. Clark, 1999), p. 229; J. Louis Martyn, *Galatians: A New Translation with Introduction and Commentary*, AB 33A (New York: Doubleday, 1997), pp. 405-6.

3. For more detail and support, see Excursus 4 in my commentary on Galatians (*Galatians*, pp. 50-61). An earlier version of this excursus is in Martinus C. de Boer, "The New Preachers in Galatia: Their Identity, Message, Aims, and Impact," in *Jesus, Paul, and Early Christianity: Studies in Honour of Henk Jan de Jonge*, ed. Rieuwerd Buitenwerf, Harm W. Hollander, and Johannes Tromp, NovTSup 130 (Leiden: Brill, 2008), pp. 39-60.

that as the recipients of what was promised to Abraham, namely, the Spirit of God's Son (3:14, 18, 22, 29; 4:6-7), they *are* the offspring of Abraham apart from any observance of the law (2:15-16; 3:1-5, 29).

Finally, I should note that in this essay I shall refer to what I call Paul's "negative soteriology" and his "positive soteriology." What I mean by these terms can perhaps best be illustrated by what Paul says in 2:19-20: "I . . . died to the law" (negative soteriology) "so that I might live to God" (positive soteriology). "It is no longer I who live" (negative soteriology) "but Christ who lives in me" (positive soteriology). They are two sides of the same coin for Paul, the positive presupposing the negative.

Galatians 6:14

Because the occasion of the epistle finds its clearest expression in the letter closing in 6:11-18, I begin with 6:14, which is part of that closing. In this passage, Paul's focus is on those who would seek to impose the law on the Galatians, beginning with the rite of circumcision, whereas in 4:3 his focus is on the believers in Galatia, former Gentiles who now want to be under the law.

Apart from the final benediction in verse 18, the closing constitutes a recapitulation of the letter's argument, which Paul writes in his own hand (v. 11). In verses 12-13, Paul offers a final rebuke of the new preachers in Galatia, focusing on their central demand for circumcision. Verses 14-15 then emphasize the significance of the cross of Christ and provide a final contextualized summary of the gospel as preached by Paul. The closing thus places over against one another two central topics of the epistle: circumcision and the cross.[4] The former (circumcision) encompasses the primary aim of the new preachers in Galatia, to get the Galatians to adopt the practice of circumcision and then, as the necessary result of that first step, to observe the remainder of the law; the latter (the cross) encapsulates Paul's theology with respect to circumcision and the law and does so in a particular way.

In Galatians 6:12-13, Paul provides a catalogue of accusations against the new preachers active in Galatia. These accusations are a mix of historically plausible facts about the new preachers (vv. 12b, 13b) and unprovable

---

4. See Jeffrey A. D. Weima, "Gal 6:11-18: A Hermeneutical Key to the Galatian Letter," *CTJ* 28 (1993): 90-107.

assumptions about their supposed motivations and aims (vv. 12a, 12c, 13a, 13c). Historically plausible is certainly the charge that the new preachers are "putting pressure" on the Galatians "to practice circumcision" in verse 12, a charge repeated in verse 13 in slightly different words: "they are wanting you to practice circumcision." Although the nature of the pressure being exerted is not elaborated, neither the new preachers nor the Galatians will disagree with what Paul says here. With respect to the new preachers' supposed motivation for and aims in insisting on the practice of circumcision in the Galatian churches, Paul makes two related but unprovable accusations: the new preachers, he writes, "want to make a good showing in the flesh" (v. 12) and they "want to boast" in "the flesh" of the Galatians (v. 13). The term "flesh" is here surely an allusion to their demand for circumcision (cf. LXX Gen. 17:9-14: circumcision involves removing "the flesh of your foreskin"). Paul virtually accuses the new preachers of counting the number of foreskins severed with the circumcision knife. These preachers are, he suggests, after trophies, presumably (so Paul intimates) in order to impress their fellow Jews, perhaps especially law-observant Christian Jews such as James and the circumcision party in Jerusalem (cf. 2:12).

A deeper meaning may be that Paul accuses the new preachers of wanting to make a good showing "in the realm of the Flesh," with a capital F, rather than in that of the Spirit (5:13–6:10; cf. 3:3). In 5:13–6:10, Paul presents the fleshly circumcision being recommended by the new preachers as an indication of a greater problem, that of "the Flesh."[5] In that earlier passage, Paul widens the scope, as it were, moving from the particular instance of the fleshly circumcision being demanded by the new preachers to a consideration of "the Flesh" as a cosmic power equivalent to and interchangeable with "Sin" (2:17; 3:22). Only the Spirit of Christ is sufficient to counter its attacks on human life, i.e., its destructive impact on relations between human beings. The coming of the Spirit has unmasked this power in all its malignancy and at the same time inaugurated a victorious apocalyptic struggle against it. Those "wanting to make a good showing in the Flesh" (capital F) do not know that there has been a change of regimes (3:25); they still orient their lives to the Flesh instead of to the Spirit of God's Son (cf. 4:6; 6:8), with all the dangers for communal life that involves, as given expression in 5:13-24 ("works of the Flesh"). The Flesh threatens to undo what Paul's initial preaching of the gospel in Galatia had brought about (3:1; 4:13-14). So the accusation that the new preachers "want to make a

---

5. Cf. de Boer, *Galatians*, pp. 329-32, 335-39, 403.

good showing in the flesh" in the letter closing could be a reference to "the Flesh" with a capital F. However, it must also be said that Paul himself does not connect the dots explicitly; he leaves it up to his readers/hearers in Galatia to do that. But that may well be his intent, and, if so, there are consequences for how he wants the Galatians to understand the κόσμος to which he refers in 6:14.

Paul also charges that the new preachers insist on circumcision "only in order that they not be persecuted for the cross of Christ" (v. 12). This charge recalls 5:11, where Paul has also linked what he there calls "preaching circumcision" to the avoidance of persecution for the sake of the cross: "if I am still preaching circumcision, why am I still being persecuted? Then the offense (σκάνδαλον) of the cross has been destroyed (κατήργηται)," i.e., devoid of all significance (cf. 3:17; 2:21). In both 5:11 and 6:12, "circumcision" and "the cross (of Christ)" stand in stark opposition to one another; to reject the former (preaching circumcision) is to incur persecution for the sake of the latter (preaching the cross). In Paul's view, then, the new preachers are advocating circumcision for the believers in Galatia not from altruistic motives (i.e., the presumed salvation of the Galatians through their incorporation into Israel as a first and necessary step) but from selfish concerns: they want to avoid persecution for the cross of Christ. It is impossible to know whether Paul is right in this charge against the new preachers (the word "only" in any event points to a polemical exaggeration of this charge) or whether he is here merely extrapolating from his own experience, both as a former persecutor of the church and as the persecuted apostle of Christ (cf. 6:17). However that may be, in 6:12, as in 5:11, Paul effectively accuses the new preachers of being unwilling to discern and to accept the radical implications of the cross of Christ for the observance of the law (2:16, 21), beginning with the rite of circumcision (2:3; 5:2-4), implications that he himself has painfully experienced in his own body (cf. 6:17, referring to "the στίγματα [scars] of Jesus" that Paul carries on his own body). It remains for them "an offense." In 1 Corinthians 1:23, Paul writes that "we preach Christ crucified, an offense to Jews." In Galatians, the proclamation of the crucified Christ, the cross (cf. 1 Cor. 1:18), is evidently an offense to Christian Jews such as the new preachers active in Galatia because, so Paul claims, it has brought about the end of the law as the reliable basis for righteousness and life (cf. Gal. 1:13-16; 2:16, 21; 3:1, 13-14, 21, 23-25; 4:4-5).

Paul's charge in 6:13 that the new preachers have as their goal to "boast in the [circumcised] flesh" of the Galatians provides a rhetorical foil for his articulation, in 6:14, of what in his view legitimate boasting entails: "But let it not be for me to boast except in the cross of our Lord Jesus Christ. . . ." Paul becomes personal here ("me"), as he had been in chapters 1–2, a strategy that suggests Paul is here contrasting two forms of evangelism, one carried out by the new preachers (vv. 12-13), the other carried out by Paul (vv. 14-17; cf. 5:11). Whereas they (according to Paul's perception) aim to boast in the number of converts they have made (cf. 6:4) and then on the basis of a theology that in Paul's view "turns the gospel of Christ into its opposite" (so 1:7), Paul aims, in his preaching of the gospel (2:2; 3:1), "to boast . . . [only] in the cross of our Lord Jesus Christ." The reference to "our Lord Jesus Christ" is notably confessional and solemnly calls attention to the one who is the Lord not only of Paul but also of the Galatians and the new preachers among them. By using the word "our," Paul calls the Galatians and the new preachers to his side. Their common Lord has a cross, and this fact cannot be ignored or evaded.

As I have already intimated, "the cross" (5:11), which is "the cross of Christ" (6:12) or "the cross of our Lord Jesus Christ" (6:14), is Pauline shorthand for "the crucifixion of Christ" and, in the context of the letter to the Galatians, everything that this event entails with respect to circumcision and the law.[6] In that sense, the cross — the crucifixion — is also a matter of soteriology. The soteriology of "the cross" represents, however, what I have called "the negative side" of Paul's soteriology, as is seen on the basis of what Paul writes in the remainder of 6:14. The cross "of our Lord Jesus Christ" has effected a double crucifixion, that of the κόσμος and that of Paul himself, each in relation to the other: ". . . through which [the cross] to me the κόσμος has been crucified and I [have been crucified] to the κόσμος" (v. 14b). Paul's language of crucifixion is here metaphorical and hyperbolic, yet also realistic and serious. It is not just a figure of speech, but a vivid interpretation of a truly painful and real experience. Paul here articulates the "negative" soteriological consequences of Christ's faithful death on the cross (cf. 2:16, 19-21; 3:1). In other places and contexts Paul can use the expression "to die to [something]" to articulate these negative soteriological consequences, as in 2:19 where as we have seen he writes, "I . . . died to the law" (cf., e.g., Rom. 6:2). To be crucified "to"

---

6. Paul here uses the figure of metalepsis, or double metonymy (cf. E. W. Bullinger, *Figures of Speech Used in the Bible: Explained and Illustrated* [London: Eyre & Spottiswoode, 1898; repr., Grand Rapids: Baker, 1968], pp. 608-11). The "cross" stands for the very real, literal crucifixion of Christ but also for the soteriological effects of this event.

someone or something, i.e., with respect to someone or something, is an intensification of this "dying to" language. It suggests a violent and painful death with respect to someone or something. Paul uses the language of crucifixion in this context to underscore the destructive soteriological effects of Christ's death by crucifixion.[7]

Paul announces, first, that with respect to himself ("to me," ἐμοί, emphatic by position) the κόσμος has been crucified, violently put to death. What is this κόσμος? The word carries the strong nuance of "order" (cf. LSJ 985). A (or the) κόσμος is assumed to be an orderly, coherent whole. Consistent with contemporary usage (BDAG, 561-63), furthermore, Paul uses the term elsewhere to refer to "the (whole) human world" (e.g., Rom. 5:12), "planet earth" (e.g., Rom. 1:8), or "the physical universe in its entirety" (e.g., Rom. 1:20).[8] None of these meanings easily applies here. Given the immediate context, the κόσμος to which Paul here refers is most probably the religion of the law, what he has earlier in this letter characterized as Ἰουδαϊσμός (1:13-14) and as ἔργα νόμου (2:16; 3:2, 5, 10), which includes circumcision (2:3; 5:2-12; 6:12-13).[9] That particular κόσμος, the κόσμος structured by the practice of circumcision and the observance of the law, has been utterly destroyed, in any case, for Paul himself as a believer in Christ (cf. Rom. 6:6).[10] He is probably not here simply giving his personal, subjective opinion ("As far as I am concerned . . .") but describing what he takes to be an objective situation, the effect of Christ's death on an objective cross and (the effect of) his own experienced participation in that objective death. That world of the law no longer exists "for him." For that reason, Paul can go on to say that, with respect to the world of the law, he himself has also been crucified ("and I to the κόσμος"), a claim that echoes 2:19, where he writes: "I died to the law . . . I have been crucified with Christ," i.e., to the law. Faith *in* Christ is participation in "the faith *of* Christ" (2:16), that is to say, in Christ's faithful death (2:20-21).[11] For this very reason, Paul can speak of this participation as crucifixion *with* Christ — in this case, to the law. In both 2:19 and 6:14, then, Paul has in view his

7. See de Boer, *Galatians*, p. 172, on 3:1.

8. It is not always possible to distinguish clearly between these three meanings in all instances. Especially the first two can overlap.

9. For this reason the omission here of the article with the word κόσμος may be significant, although it may also be purely stylistic (cf. 1 Cor. 3:22; 2 Cor. 5:19); see BDF §253:4.

10. Ernest DeWitt Burton, *A Critical and Exegetical Commentary on the Epistle to the Galatians*, ICC (Edinburgh: T. & T. Clark, 1921), p. 354.

11. Cf. de Boer, *Galatians*, pp. 148-50.

nomistic "I," the "I" whose existence and identity were given shape and direction by the practice of circumcision and the observance of the law. Paul's "previous, cherished and acknowledged identity" was put to death and separated from the ordered nomistic κόσμος into which he was born, in which he was nurtured, and in which he grew up.[12] That κόσμος still exists, of course, but not for Paul as a participant in the crucifixion of Christ.

In 6:14, as in 2:19, Paul employs a verb in the perfect tense (ἐσταύρωται), indicating a past action with continuing effect on the present (cf. 3:1). In both passages, Paul refers to himself ("I") not in an exclusive sense but as a paradigm for all believers who take their bearings from "the cross of *our* Lord Jesus Christ." Both Paul's nomistic self and the nomistic world he once inhabited have been put to death by his participation in the crucifixion of Christ. The two crucifixions are two sides of the same coin, as it were; his crucifixion with Christ also involves the crucifixion of the world in which he had found his identity and his bearings. This is Paul's way of emphasizing the complete break with his past as a devotee of the law and the pain this break caused him. For him, a world has been destroyed and he has suffered the loss of that world.

Does the crucified κόσμος include the Flesh, with a capital F? We have seen that Paul's accusation that the new preachers want to make a good showing "in the flesh" (6:12) may refer to the realm of "the Flesh" as a malevolent, cosmic power against which the law is ineffectual (3:21; 5:23). In 5:24, again using the language of crucifixion, Paul has written that "those who belong to Christ [i.e., all believers who have received the Spirit] have crucified the Flesh with its desire." Given the implicit link Paul establishes between fleshly circumcision and the realm of the Flesh, the κόσμος crucified in 6:14 seems also to encompass "the Flesh with its passions and desires" (5:24). The word κόσμος in 6:14 then has a much broader reference than the religion of the law, and comes (more emphatically) to signify a realm that is hostile to God and inimical to human life before God (cf. ὁ κόσμος οὗτος in 1 Cor. 3:19; 5:10a; 7:31b). Again, Paul himself does not connect the dots explicitly; he leaves it up to his readers to do that.

Whatever the case may be, the extreme language of crucifixion with Christ in 2:19 or crucifixion to the world in 6:14 gives expression to a key element of participation in Christ's faithful death, the end or the permanent loss of a previous manner of life (cf. 5:24; Rom. 6:6), in this case an existence determined by fleshly circumcision and the law. Crucifixion with

---

12. Martyn, *Galatians*, p. 564.

Christ represents for the individual believer the destruction of his or her participation in the old age where the law functions as a cursing, imprisoning, and enslaving power on a cosmic scale (3:10, 13, 19-23; 4:4-5).[13] A crucifixion with Christ is thus also a crucifixion to this world of law observance. This is Paul's soteriology of the cross in Galatians, and it is a negative soteriology.

It must also be said, however, that when Paul says he has been "crucified with Christ" or "to the world," he also means he has been rescued from the present evil age (1:4) or redeemed from the curse of the law (3:13; cf. 4:4-5; 5:1). On the other side of the crucified religion of the law lies a new creation: "For neither circumcision is anything nor uncircumcision but [only] a new creation."[14] Where there is circumcision, there is also uncircumcision.[15] The law also implies, and in a sense encompasses, the not-law.[16] So, when circumcision (the rite and the condition) becomes irrelevant, so of necessity does uncircumcision (the absence of the circumcision rite and the presence of the foreskin). The religious, ethnic, and social distinctions caused by a world divided into circumcision and uncircumcision have in Paul's view been violently replaced by "a new creation" (καινὴ κτίσις), a new reality brought into being by the action of God in Christ. That "world" of religious, ethnic, and social differentiation came to an end in the cross, the crucifixion of Christ, at least for those who are "in Christ." What matters now is the new creation that has replaced a world divided by circumcision and uncircumcision.[17] The new creation represents the positive side of Paul's soteriology. This positive soteriology has a negative soteriology as its foundation.

---

13. For the law as a cosmic power before and apart from Christ, see de Boer, *Galatians*, pp. 35, 201, 209-10, 264. For those "in Christ," that is no longer the case.

14. Adams rightly remarks: "With the terms κόσμος and καινὴ κτίσις, Paul is invoking the apocalyptic spatio-temporal dualism of 'this world' and 'the world to come' / 'the new creation'" (*Constructing*, p. 227).

15. "Circumcision" can here refer both to the practice of circumcision (cf. Rom. 4:11) and to the condition of being circumcised. "Uncircumcision" (ἀκροβυστία, lit. "foreskin") can in turn refer both to the absence of the practice of circumcision and to the condition of being uncircumcised (cf. 1 Cor. 7:19). In Gal. 2:7-9, Paul uses the two terms metonymically for groups of people practicing ("Jews") or not practicing ("Gentiles") circumcision.

16. Martyn, *Galatians*, p. 571.

17. Cf. Adams, *Constructing*, pp. 227-28.

Galatians 4:3[18]

The meaning of the phrase τὰ στοιχεῖα τοῦ κόσμου has been debated since antiquity. Commentators on the passage routinely discuss the four meanings proposed in the English versions of the standard Greek lexicon of Walter Bauer, i.e., BAG (1957) and BAGD (1979):

1. Elements (of learning), fundamental principles.
2. Elemental substances, the basic elements from which everything in the natural world is made, and of which it is composed, namely, earth, air, fire, and water.
3. Elemental spirits, which the syncretistic religious tendencies of later antiquity associated with the physical elements (cf. RSV; NRSV).
4. Heavenly bodies (as in "the twelve στοιχεῖα of heaven," the twelve signs of the zodiac).

In the most recent English edition of Bauer, that of Danker (BDAG 2000), the first of these meanings is given preference. The lexicon approvingly cites the translation "elementary ideas belonging to this world," taken from a footnote of the NEB. This interpretation of the phrase follows in the footsteps of the commentators Lightfoot and Burton, both of whom translate: "elementary teaching" (cf. Heb. 5:12).[19] Longenecker continues this tradition of interpretation in his commentary ("the principles of the world").[20] In this line of interpretation, κόσμος evidently means "the human world."

The research carried out by three scholars — Blinzler, Schweizer, and Rusam[21] — has shown conclusively, however, that the full Greek phrase τὰ στοιχεῖα τοῦ κόσμου was a common, technical expression, derived primar-

---

18. For the next several pages, see de Boer, *Galatians*, pp. 251-58, which incorporates a previous article ("The Meaning of the Phrase τὰ στοιχεῖα τοῦ κόσμου in Galatians," *NTS* 53 [2007]: 204-24).

19. J. B. Lightfoot, *Saint Paul's Epistle to the Galatians: A Revised Text with Introduction, Notes and Dissertations* (London and New York: Macmillan, 1887), p. 167; Burton, *Galatians*, p. 517.

20. Richard N. Longenecker, *Galatians*, WBC 41 (Dallas: Word, 1990), p. 165.

21. Josef Blinzler, "Lexikalisches zu dem Terminus *Ta stoicheia tou kosmou* bei Paulus," in vol. 2 of *Studiorum Paulinorum Congressus Internationalis Catholicus 1961* (Rome: Pontifical Biblical Institute, 1963), pp. 429-43; Eduard Schweizer, "Slaves of the Elements and Worshipers of Angels: Gal 4:3, 9 and Col 2:8, 18, 20," *JBL* 107 (1988): 455-68; Dietrich Rusam, "Neue Belege zu dem *Stoicheia tou kosmou* (Gal 4,3.9; Kol 2,8.20)," *ZNW* 83 (1992): 119-25.

ily from Stoic thought, designating the four elements from which the ancients thought the physical universe was composed: earth, water, air, and fire.[22] These three scholars show that this is by far the most common referential meaning of the term στοιχεῖα and the *only* referential meaning attested for the full expression τὰ στοιχεῖα τοῦ κόσμου in Paul's time. The word κόσμος in this full expression refers to the physical universe. Now, Paul's concern in 4:3 is certainly not to expatiate on the nature of the physical universe when he writes that "we were [all once] enslaved under τὰ στοιχεῖα τοῦ κόσμου." Something more is surely involved in Paul's use of the term. The question is: What?

In 4:8-10, Paul mentions the στοιχεῖα a second time, and in this passage it becomes clear that the στοιχεῖα, the "elements," lay at the basis of the religion of the Galatians before they became believers in Christ:

> Then, when you did not know God, you served[23] beings not gods by nature. But now having come to know God, or rather having become known by God, how can you be turning again to the weak and impotent στοιχεῖα which you are wanting to serve[24] once more? You are observing days and months and seasons and years!

Paul here works from two assumptions. First, the στοιχεῖα have something to do with the gods the Galatians once venerated.[25] Paul is telling the

---

22. Cf., e.g., Philo, *Aet.* 107, 109-10: "there are four elements (στοιχεῖα), earth, water, air and fire, of which the world (κόσμος) is composed . . . all these have transcendent powers. . . . For just as the annual seasons circle round and round, each making room for its successor as the years ceaselessly revolve, so, too, the elements of the world (τὰ στοιχεῖα τοῦ κόσμου) in their mutual interchanges seem to die, yet, strangest of contradictions, are made immortal as they ever run their race backwards and forwards and continually pass along the same road up and down . . ." (trans. F. H. Colson, LCL [Cambridge, MA: Harvard University Press, 1941]).

23. The verb here is δουλεύω, which means "to serve (as a slave)" or "to be a slave." Paul's choice of this word to signify veneration or worship is probably rhetorically motivated. See de Boer, *Galatians*, p. 272.

24. See previous note.

25. Cf. Philo, *Contempl.* 3-4: "Can we compare those who revere the elements (τὰ στοιχεῖα), earth, water, air, fire, which have received different names from different peoples who call fire Hephaestus . . . , air Hera . . . , water Poseidon . . . , and earth Demeter . . . ? Sophists have invented these names for the elements (τὰ στοιχεῖα) but the elements themselves are lifeless matter incapable of movement of itself and laid by the Artificer as a substratum for every kind of shape and quality" (trans. F. H. Colson, LCL [Cambridge, MA: Harvard University Press, 1941]).

Galatians something about the στοιχεῖα that they already know. Second, the veneration of the στοιχεῖα by the Galatians involved, according to Paul, calendrical observances.[26] Here, too, Paul is telling the Galatians something they already know. Paul also tells them something that they do not already know: to turn to the law and its calendrical observances is to return to the στοιχεῖα and the calendrical observances associated with them. I will come back to this startling equation below.

If we bring what Paul writes in 4:8-10 to bear on the full phrase τὰ στοιχεῖα τοῦ κόσμου in 4:3 — which, as I have indicated, was a common, technical expression referring specifically to the four constituent elements of the physical universe — then we may conclude that the full phrase is being used by Paul as *a summary designation* for a complex of religious beliefs and practices at the center of which were the four elements of the physical cosmos to which the phrase concretely refers. In Paul's usage, the full phrase is an instance of *metonymy,* whereby an aspect or attribute stands for a larger whole of which it is a part. In this case, τὰ στοιχεῖα τοῦ κόσμου — the four elements of physical reality — stand for the religious beliefs and practices of the Galatians associated with the στοιχεῖα prior to their becoming believers in Christ. Calendrical observances and the physical phenomena associated with such observances — the movements of sun, moon, stars, and planets — were an integral part of these religious beliefs and practices. The gods whom the Galatians worshiped were so closely linked to the four στοιχεῖα that the worship of these gods could be regarded, at least by Paul, as tantamount to the worship of the στοιχεῖα themselves.[27] The sense of Galatians 4:3 can be captured with the following paraphrase: "we were [all once] enslaved under the religious beliefs and practices associated with the four elements of the universe (earth, water, air, and fire)."

---

26. Cf. Wis. 7:17-19: "For it is he [God] who gave me unerring knowledge of what exists, to know the structure of the world (κόσμος) and the activity of the elements (στοιχεῖα): the beginning and end and middle of times, the alternations of the solstices and the changes of the seasons (καιροί), the cycles of the year (ενιαυτός) and the constellations of the stars . . ." (NRSV). See also Wis. 19:18-20.

27. It is for this reason that the phrase is frequently taken to mean "elemental spirits" or the like. But that is not the *referential* meaning of the phrase. On the relationship between worship of gods and worship of the four elements, see Wis. 13:1-3: "For all people who were ignorant of God . . . supposed that either fire or wind or swift air, or the circle of the stars, or turbulent water, or the luminaries of heaven were the gods (θεοί) that rule the world. If through delight in the beauty of these things people assumed them to be gods (θεοί), let them know how much better than these is their Lord, for the author of beauty created them" (NRSV).

One of the difficulties presented by 4:3 is Paul's use of the first person pronoun "we" (ἡμεῖς, emphatic in the Greek). This "we" must include Jewish believers such as Paul himself. Yet that seems strange, since Jews, for whom God was "one" (Deut. 6:4; cf. Gal. 3:20), certainly did not as a rule venerate the στοιχεῖα as gods, as did the Galatians before they came to believe in Christ (cf. Wis. 13:1-3). How, then, can Paul claim that Jewish believers and not only Gentile believers were once enslaved under the στοιχεῖα when these στοιχεῖα evidently concern pagan religious beliefs and practices?

The answer to this question probably lies in the fact that Paul has in view the calendrical observances related to these four elements of the κόσμος, particularly, even exclusively, as indicated by 4:8-10, where, as we have seen, Paul reproaches the Galatians for "returning again to the . . . στοιχεῖα, which you want to serve once more: You observe days and months and seasons and years!" Calendrical observances, therefore, were for the Galatians an integral part of the religious beliefs and practices associated with the στοιχεῖα prior to their becoming believers in Christ. Calendrical observances (e.g., Sabbath, Passover) linked to the primal elements and associated phenomena (the movements of sun, moon, planets, stars) were also an integral part of Jewish belief and practice (cf. *Jub.* 2:8-9; *1 En.* 82:7-9; Wis. 7:17-19). In this particular, limited sense both Gentile and Jewish believers in Christ were once "enslaved [together] under τὰ στοιχεῖα τοῦ κόσμου," i.e., under the religious beliefs and practices connected to the four elements that make up the physical universe and determine its specific character.

This also explains how Paul can in the verses preceding and following 4:3 refer to all believers in Christ as once having been "under the law" (ὑπὸ νόμον; 3:23-25; 4:4-5; cf. 3:10-14). To be under the law is evidently to be under τὰ στοιχεῖα τοῦ κόσμου as well. For this reason, to place oneself under the law (as the Galatians are wanting to do) is to place oneself once again under τὰ στοιχεῖα τοῦ κόσμου. Paul has introduced a reference to τὰ στοιχεῖα τοῦ κόσμου into his argument at this point precisely because he wants the Galatians to realize that there is a conceptual and functional overlap between being under the law and being under τὰ στοιχεῖα τοῦ κόσμου, i.e., between the religion of the law and the religion of τὰ στοιχεῖα τοῦ κόσμου. That conceptual and functional overlap may be found in calendrical observances related to the four elements of the universe found in both forms of religion.[28] It hardly needs to be said that this equation be-

---

28. In 4:1-7, Paul says that the religion of the στοιχεῖα, which the Galatians left behind,

tween the two situations supports Paul's rhetorical agenda, which is to prevent the believers in Galatia from becoming observers of the law, beginning with the rite of circumcision. He wants to make plain to the Galatian believers, who are tempted to observe the law as the new preachers in Galatia are insistently recommending, that their liberation from the στοιχεῖα (and the calendrical observance associated with these στοιχεῖα) was also, at the same time, their liberation from the law (and the similar calendrical observances associated with that law).

Paul's reference to τὰ στοιχεῖα τοῦ κόσμου in Galatians 4:3 occurs, then, in connection with the religious beliefs and practices once adhered to by the Galatians. The term κόσμος in the phrase refers to the physical universe. There is no indication that the κόσμος so understood has come to an end. It continues to exist. The physical κόσμος does not disappear; nor then do the στοιχεῖα that comprise this physical κόσμος. What has come to an end is the religion of the στοιχεῖα that make up the κόσμος. Put otherwise: What has changed is the *relationship* of the Galatians to this κόσμος. As is seen in 4:8-10, Paul calls the gods the Galatians had once worshiped "beings not gods by nature." These "gods" (θεοί) are not here specified; they are simply distinguished from the singular one "God" (θεός) who by implication *is* God "by nature." The phrase "by nature" (φύσει) here means simply "in reality" or "in fact": the Galatians had worshiped beings that were not in fact gods at all. Upon becoming believers in Christ, the Galatians had come to see, following Paul, that the gods they had been worshiping were not really gods. He reminds them of this fact, that the gospel has removed the aura of divinity from the beings they had once worshiped, reducing the στοιχεῖα to the merely natural phenomena they in fact always were.

The στοιχεῖα became gods in Paul's view, and can become gods once again, only if and whenever human beings venerate them as such. It is evidently Paul's position that once human beings begin venerating the στοιχεῖα they in effect become enslaved to the gods they have created for themselves (4:3). The gospel liberates human beings from such enslaving delusions. For such reasons, Paul characterizes the στοιχεῖα as "weak and impotent" (ἀσθενῆ καὶ πτωχά, cf. 4:9), which is what they actually are apart from the power that human beings grant them. This characterization

---

is equivalent to the religion of the law, from which Christ delivered human beings; in 4:8-10, however, he says the reverse: the religion of the law the Galatians are in the process of adopting is equivalent to the religion of the στοιχεῖα they had left behind.

of the στοιχεῖα is part of Paul's rhetorical strategy of dissuading the Galatians from becoming observers of the law: the στοιχεῖα are just as ineffectual for salvation as the law, which is unable to give life (3:21).[29]

Is Paul's "demythologization" of the gods behind the στοιχεῖα a consequence of his theology of the cross as it comes to expression elsewhere in Galatians? One sign that this is the case is found in 3:1, where Paul claims that when he came to Galatia he portrayed Christ as "having been crucified" before their very eyes. As Paul's reference to his crucifixion with Christ in 2:19 indicates, the appeal to Christ's crucifixion here instead of merely to his death (as in 2:20c-21) calls attention to the manner of Jesus' death as an apocalyptic event, i.e., as an event that announces and effects the end of the world (cf. 1 Cor. 1:18-19), in this case the world of law observance (cf. Gal. 2:16, 19; 3:25; 4:4-5; 6:14-15), which is the point at issue in 3:1-5 and, in fact, throughout Galatians. In Christ's crucifixion a world has been destroyed, and that is what Paul wishes to emphasize in this context by characterizing Jesus Christ as "having been crucified" (cf. 1:4; 2:19-20; 5:11; 5:24; 6:14). For the Galatians to take up law observance as part of their new Christian identity would thus be tantamount to returning to that world from which Christ has delivered them (4:8-11). Paul here already assumes (perhaps only subconsciously) an equation between the religion of the law and the religion of the στοιχεῖα. For when he came to the Galatians with the gospel, he did not preach Christ crucified in connection with the religion of the law but in connection with their religion of the στοιχεῖα τοῦ κόσμου. For those who "came to believe in Christ" (2:16b), the cross has put an end both to the religion of the law and to that of the στοιχεῖα. In fact, Paul makes it appear as if there is in essence and in practice no difference between these two religions whatsoever. So when Paul says in 6:14 that "the κόσμος has been crucified to me and I to the κόσμος," he could in principle be including the religion of the στοιχεῖα τοῦ κόσμου.[30]

That is Paul's negative soteriology with respect to the στοιχεῖα. For the positive side, we return briefly to 4:3 in its context. Paul's claim that "we were enslaved under the στοιχεῖα τοῦ κόσμου" is followed in verse 4 by what may well be the central theological announcement of the letter: "When the fullness of time came, *God.* . . ." God did something. In Christ a new time has begun — the time of faith, the time of the Spirit, succeeding

29. Cf. Martyn, *Galatians,* p. 412.

30. Exegetical honesty requires us to note, however, that Paul does not himself explicitly say this.

the time of the law (cf. "no longer" in 3:25 and 4:7). The contrast prominent in 4:1-2 (between the childhood and adulthood, or between immaturity and maturity) gives way in verses 4-5 to a contrast between a situation of enslavement "under the law" before Christ and a situation of adopted sonship for believers after "the fullness of time" has come. Adopted sonship has as its presupposition liberation from (the religion of) the law and from (the religion of) the στοιχεῖα τοῦ κόσμου. The "fullness of time" thus signifies a clean break with the past and may be regarded as an apocalyptic assertion on Paul's part: the fullness of time signals the end of "the present evil age" (1:4) and the beginning of the "new creation" (6:15). In Christ, God has destroyed a world, the world of the religion of the law and that of στοιχεῖα τοῦ κόσμου, which amounts to the same thing, and God has given human beings another world to live in, the new creation, in this context called the Spirit of God's Son, whereby a believer knows himself or herself to be "no longer a slave, but a son, and if a son, also an heir" (4:7) of the promise God made to Abraham. Paul's positive soteriology here presupposes a negative soteriology, the end or destruction of a previous, familiar "world," in this case one determined by τὰ στοιχεῖα τοῦ κόσμου.

Three Concluding Observations

Paul uses the term κόσμος in two different referential meanings in the two passages analyzed. In 4:3, the word κόσμος refers to the physical universe composed of certain elements (earth, water, air, and fire). In 6:14, it refers first and foremost to (the religion of) the law, which effects a dichotomy between circumcision and uncircumcision, thus also a division between those who practice circumcision and those who do not (cf. 2:7-9). At the level of soteriology there is a connection between the two uses of the term, although Paul does not make this connection explicit. In 4:1-5 and 4:8-11, he establishes a functional and a conceptual similarity between (the religion of) the law and (the religion of) the στοιχεῖα τοῦ κόσμου. For this reason, we can say that the end (the crucifixion) of the κόσμος of the religion of the law in 6:14 is also the end (the crucifixion) of the religion of the στοιχεῖα τοῦ κόσμου. In that sense, Martyn is right when he insists that the new creation replaces "not Judaism as such, but rather the world of *all* religious differentiation."[31] We can extend that claim, as Martyn does, to the

---

31. Martyn, *Galatians*, p. 565, emphasis original.

pairs of opposites in Galatians 3:28: the dichotomies of the present world (Jew/Greek, slave/free, male/female, circumcision/uncircumcision) have been abolished, or at least relativized, for those who have come to believe in Christ.[32]

Second, in the hortatory section of the letter (5:13–6:10), Paul casts the human conflict over fleshly circumcision, the explicit topic of both the preceding and following passages (5:2-12; 6:12-13), as an instance of a cosmological conflict between the Spirit and the Flesh. He informs the Galatians at one point that they "have crucified the Flesh with its passions and desires" (5:24). The κόσμος crucified in 6:14 can then also be understood to encompass the realm of the Flesh. Paul does not, however, make this (seemingly probable) link between the κόσμος of 6:14 and the realm of the Flesh explicit in the closing. Paul has not thought through, or at least not fully or systematically articulated, all the possible ramifications of his assertions.[33]

Finally, it may be significant that Paul does not use the word κόσμος for the new creation. For him the new world, the new κόσμος, for which he does not use this particular term, carries such descriptive labels as "the kingdom of God" (5:21), "eternal life" (6:8), and, of course, "new creation" (6:15). Perhaps the main indicator of its character is to be found in 5:6, where Paul uses a formulation that is quite similar to that found in 6:15:

5:6a   for in Christ Jesus neither circumcision avails anything nor uncircumcision,

5:6b   but faith becoming effective through love

6:15a   for (in Christ Jesus)[34] neither circumcision is anything nor uncircumcision,

6:15b   but a new creation.

Galatians 5:6a and 6:15a describe the crucified κόσμος in similar terms. This parallel between the two verses suggests that "new creation" in 6:15b is to be equated with "faith becoming effective through love" in 5:6b (cf.

---

32. Cf. Gaventa, *Mother*, p. 72.

33. Paul has thereby de facto left room for believers in general and systematic theologians in particular to make their own contributions to the discussion.

34. This phrase is missing from important manuscripts and may have been included under the influence of 5:6. See the discussion in de Boer, *Galatians*, pp. 394, 403 n. 498.

2:20; 5:13-14, 22).[35] The new creation is both God's newly creative act in Christ[36] and the result of this newly creative act, a community of mutual love and service in the Spirit of Christ (cf. 4:6-7; 5:13-24).[37]

---

35. For the interpretation of this compact phrase, see de Boer, *Galatians,* pp. 317-19, 403, where I argue that it has both a christological dimension and an anthropological one.

36. As Gaventa has written in a comment based on Gal. 6:15: "The good news Paul proclaimed to the Galatians is that the release that could not be secured by human effort of any sort has come about through the action of God in Jesus Christ" (*Mother,* p. 74).

37. See Adams (*Constructing,* pp. 226-28) for a nuanced discussion of the possible cosmological, anthropological, and ecclesiological dimensions of the "new creation" for Paul. The various dimensions are not necessarily mutually exclusive. On the use of the term κτίσις in Romans 8, see the helpful discussion of Gaventa, *Mother,* pp. 53-55. She rightly questions the tendency to limit the reference of the term to the nonhuman parts of the (old) creation, and convincingly argues that the term includes a reference to all humanity as well.

Unity in the Community:
Rereading Galatians 2:15-21

William Sanger Campbell

As a professor and adviser, Beverly Gaventa has passed her love of Paul's theology on to numerous graduate students, including me. For this essay, I shall focus on Paul's eschatology in Galatians, notably his understanding that God's plan involves the inauguration of the end-time with the crucifixion of Christ and what that means for Christ-believers.[1]

It is clear from even a casual reading of the undisputed letters of Paul that one of the principal issues he addressed was unity within his communities. Paul believed that they were living in the end-time between the Christ event and the Parousia, and that his eschatological communities should model the kingdom fulfilled in all ways, especially in unity. An interesting passage in this regard is Galatians 2:15-21. Often this pericope is interpreted as referring to Paul's theology of justification. This has been the case, partially, because the text has been read in the context of Galatians 3–4. Before Hans Dieter Betz's groundbreaking analysis, however, commentators tended to emphasize the role of 2:15-21 as summary of and conclusion to the letter's first two chapters, and in particular to the passage immediately preceding it regarding the Antiochene incident (2:11-14).[2] Indeed, a perennial question is whether all or part of 2:15-21 should be

---

1. Beverly Roberts Gaventa, "The Singularity of the Gospel: A Reading of Galatians," in *Pauline Theology*, vol. 1: *Thessalonians, Philippians, Galatians, Philemon*, ed. Jouette M. Bassler (Minneapolis: Fortress, 1991), pp. 147-59.

2. Ernest DeWitt Burton calls this passage a "[c]ontinuation and expansion of Paul's address at Antioch" (*A Critical and Exegetical Commentary on the Epistle to the Galatians*, ICC [Edinburgh: T. & T. Clark, 1921], p. 117). J. B. Lightfoot suggests that Paul might be "adding a comment while narrating the incident afterwards to the Galatians" (*The Epistle of St. Paul to the Galatians*, 10th ed. [London: Macmillan, 1890; repr., 1900], p. 113).

considered a continuation of Paul's rebuke of Peter. Long ago, J. B. Lightfoot concluded it was impossible to determine a definitive answer to this question.[3]

Betz shifted the perspectives of many when he proposed that Galatians be classified as an "apologetic letter" organized in accordance with categories employed in Greco-Roman rhetoric and epistolography.[4] He argued that 2:15-21 "conforms to the form, function, and requirements of the *propositio*. Placed at the end of the last episode of the *narratio* (ii. 11-14), it sums up the *narratio*'s material content. But it is not part of the *narratio*, and it sets up the arguments to be discussed later in the *probatio* (chapters iii and iv)."[5] Although some interpreters have argued against Betz's classification of Galatians as apologetic, the influence of his proposal has been widespread, leading many interpreters to stress the function of 2:15-21 in the context of the following two chapters, thereby neglecting its relation to the first two chapters.[6] For instance, in Richard N. Longenecker's estimation, "Betz's thesis also gives guidance as to how the compressed language of Paul's *propositio* [2:15-21] should be treated. For if the *probatio* [chapters 3 and 4] contains the proofs or arguments introduced by the *propositio*, then we must look to Paul's *probatio* . . . for an understanding of how to unpack the terms of the *propositio*."[7]

Disconnecting this passage from the rest of chapters 1 and 2 has been unfortunate. First, the fact that 2:15-21 is so interwoven with 2:11-14 that it is impossible to ascertain with any confidence "[w]hen [Paul] leaves the Antioch situation behind, or whether he really does so at all," suggests that 2:15-21 must be read primarily in light of what has come before, whatever its

---

3. Lightfoot, *Galatians*, pp. 113-14. See also Burton, *Galatians*, p. 117; F. F. Bruce, *The Epistle to the Galatians: A Commentary on the Greek Text*, NIGTC (Grand Rapids: Eerdmans, 1982), p. 136. Nevertheless, the lack of a connecting particle between verses 14 and 15 supports — however tenuously — the conclusion that there is a break at that point. For example, after surveying the instances of asyndeton in Galatians, Michael Winger judges that although "[n]o firm conclusion can be drawn from the absence of any such connective . . . it does cast doubt on the theory that 2:14-15 is a continuous address to Peter" (*By What Law? The Meaning of Νόμος in the Letters of Paul*, SBLDS 128 [Atlanta: Scholars Press, 1992], p. 127 n. 15).

4. Hans Dieter Betz, "The Literary Composition and Function of Paul's Letter to the Galatians," *NTS* 21 (1975): 354; see also Betz, *Galatians: A Commentary on Paul's Letter to the Galatians*, Hermeneia (Philadelphia: Fortress, 1979), pp. 14-25.

5. Betz, "Literary Composition," p. 368; see also Betz, *Galatians*, p. 114.

6. One who has argued against classifying Galatians as an apologetic letter is J. Louis Martyn, "Apocalyptic Antinomies in Paul's Letter to the Galatians," *NTS* 31 (1985): 420.

7. Richard N. Longenecker, *Galatians*, WBC 41 (Dallas: Word, 1990), p. 81.

relationship to the subsequent chapters.[8] Thus, J. Louis Martyn maintains that "Paul's failure formally to close the quotation begun in v. 14 is no accident. It reflects his determination to connect his account of the Antioch incident to the situation in Galatia."[9] Second, as George A. Kennedy has argued, Betz's position slights the rhetorical principle of linearity:

> Rhetoric originates in speech and its primary product is as a speech act, not a text. . . . A speech is linear and cumulative, and any context in it can only be perceived in contrast to what has gone before, especially what has immediately gone before. . . . To a greater extent than any modern text, the Bible retained an oral and linear quality for its audience.[10]

With this in mind, I contend that the meaning of 2:15-21 must be derived primarily from what has been said previously to it, especially in 2:11-14. This is not to suggest that 2:15-21 be dissociated from the remainder of the letter, but that subsequent chapters should be interpreted in light of what precedes them, including the present passage, and not vice versa. When viewed this way, the problem that Paul is addressing to the Galatian churches in 2:15-21 is not limited to adherence to and justification by the law, but concerns equally the communal disunity that can be caused by observance of the law.

Unity in Paul's Letters

Unity is for Paul an important characteristic of his communities.[11] More than once he decries disunity within his churches (e.g., Gal. 2:11-14; 1 Cor. 1:10-17; 11:19-22). Paul believes that the Parousia will bring about the eschatological unity of humanity, and he urges his communities to model this unity — "unity in Christ and, therefore, unity with and for one another" — during the end-time period that was inaugurated with the Christ event

8. Burton, *Galatians*, p. 117.

9. Martyn, *Galatians: A New Translation with Introduction and Commentary*, AB 33A (New York: Doubleday, 1997), pp. 229-30. See also T. David Gordon's assertion that 2:15-21 is "a continuation of the discussion generated by Peter's behavior at Antioch" ("The Problem at Galatia," *Int* 41 [1987]: 34).

10. George A. Kennedy, *New Testament Interpretation through Rhetorical Criticism* (Chapel Hill: University of North Carolina Press, 1984), p. 5; see also pp. 144-52.

11. For a discussion of unity in the Pauline Epistles, see William Sanger Campbell, "Unity," *NIDB* 5:703.

(e.g., Gal. 5:25-26; Rom. 12:15-16; 15:5-6; 1 Cor. 3:21-23; 6:1-11; Phil. 1:27–2:11; 4:2-3).[12] He often uses the human body with its unified whole made up of many parts to image the unity that he is advocating (Rom. 12:3-8; 1 Cor. 10:16-17; 12:12-26). His point is that, in baptism, all differences that might otherwise divide community members must be eliminated (Gal. 3:27-38; see also Rom. 10:12; 1 Cor. 12:13). Unity, then, is often on Paul's mind and with it the concomitant responsibility for local community members (for example, Gal. 5:13-14; 6:1-9; Rom. 12:9-21; 13:8-11; 14:1-4, 13-21; 15:1-6; 1 Cor. 13:1-13) and the wider church (Gal. 2:10; Rom. 15:25-27; 1 Cor. 16:1-4; 2 Cor. 8–9) to demonstrate unity in action. As the examples indicate, this is no less the case in Galatians than in Paul's other letters.[13]

Indeed, Galatians opens with allusions to the unity of the gospel itself (1:6-9) as well as the unity of the Gentile mission under Paul's apostleship (1:10-24) and the unity of the church leaders in accepting Paul's authority with respect to the Gentile mission (2:1-10). Those who would upset the oneness of the gospel, Paul's leadership in preaching it, or the gospel's implications for the unity of Christ-believers are to be cursed (1:7-9) and opposed (2:4-5).

One of those whom Paul opposes is Peter (Κηφᾶς) in 2:11-14. E. P. Sanders and James D. G. Dunn have argued that the charges made in 2:14b have been overstated.[14] Peter likely did not abandon all Jewish practices (ἐθνικῶς καὶ οὐχὶ Ἰουδαϊκῶς ζῆς) at Antioch, nor did he compel the Gentiles there to observe all Jewish customs (τὰ ἔθνη ἀναγκάζεις ἰουδαΐζειν). Dunn, for example, suggests that ἰουδαΐζειν is a relative term denoting a "range of possible degrees of assimilation to Jewish customs."[15] Sanders summarizes, "Paul's statement that Peter had been 'living like a Gentile' (Gal 2:14) was exaggerated. He probably had not been doing any-

---

12. Campbell, "Unity," 5:703; see also Gaventa, "Singularity of the Gospel," p. 149.

13. Martyn also notes Paul's interest in unity within and among Christ-believing communities (*Galatians*, p. 274).

14. E. P. Sanders, "Jewish Association with Gentiles and Galatians 2:11-14," in *The Conversation Continues: Studies in Paul and John in Honor of J. Louis Martyn*, ed. Robert T. Fortna and Beverly R. Gaventa (Nashville: Abingdon, 1990), p. 186; James D. G. Dunn, "The Incident at Antioch (Gal 2:11-18)," *JSNT* 18 (1983): 25-26.

15. Dunn, "The Incident at Antioch," p. 26. But see Mark D. Nanos, who argues that the Gentiles at Antioch needed to become Jewish proselytes ("What Was at Stake in Peter's 'Eating with Gentiles' at Antioch?" in *The Galatians Debate: Contemporary Issues in Rhetorical and Historical Interpretation*, ed. Mark D. Nanos [Peabody, MA: Hendrickson, 2002], pp. 310-16), and Martinus C. de Boer, who maintains that they had to observe the entire law, including circumcision (*Galatians*, NTL [Louisville: Westminster John Knox, 2011], p. 138).

thing as drastic as eating pork, shellfish, or hare. Exaggeration on this point fits perfectly since the charge that Peter was 'forcing Gentiles to live like Jews' in the same verse goes beyond the story as he tells it."[16] The use of the postpositive γάρ in 2:12 signals that the reason for Peter's condemnation follows, namely, that because of the arrival of emissaries from James, he had withdrawn and separated himself from the Gentile Christ-believers out of fear of those ἐκ περιτομῆς (lit. "those from circumcision"; 2:12), and his actions had caused other Jewish Christ-believers to do likewise (2:13).[17] Paul's frustration with Peter, therefore, was not over customs or practices or even doctrine, but because Peter had disengaged from table fellowship with the Gentile members of the Jesus-community in Antioch and in so doing had influenced Jewish members of the movement — including Paul's colleague Barnabas — to do the same, notwithstanding the fact that it was neither prohibited nor unusual at the time for Jews to associate with Gentiles (e.g., 1 Cor. 5:9-13; 8:10; 10:27).[18] In other words, Paul's dispute with Peter was over Peter's introduction of a rift within the Christ-believing community at Antioch. Although the reason for Peter's withdrawal is still debated (whether it had to do with the food served or with the Gentiles themselves), it might be, as Mark D. Nanos proposes, that

> [that] to which the ones advocating circumcision objected had nothing to do with the food being eaten or with the fact that it was being eaten with Gentiles, and it was not the threat of impurity or idolatry either. Rather, it was the way that these Gentiles were being *identified* at these meals. These Jews were not "eating with" these Gentiles according to

16. Sanders, "Jewish Association with Gentiles," pp. 186-87. Others agree with this assessment. Martyn, for instance, speaks of Paul's "intemperate and quasi-gnostic comments about the Law in Galatians" and how "interpreters feel somewhat embarrassed that Paul should have written the letter in a state of unrepentance for the inflexible and even hostile words he spoke to Peter" ("Apocalyptic Antinomies," p. 410). J. Christiaan Beker claims that the polemical nature of the letter causes a distortion of any theological claims in it (*Paul the Apostle: The Triumph of God in Life and Thought* [Philadelphia: Fortress, 1980], p. 57).

17. It is not clear whether "those who came from James" and "those from the circumcision" in 2:12 are one group or separate groups and, if separate, whether "those from the circumcision" are Christ-believing Jews or not. According to de Boer, the emissaries from James are "Christian Jews . . . [who] represented the interests and the viewpoints of the circumcision party in Jerusalem" (*Galatians*, p. 133). For a discussion of these groups, see Nanos, "What Was at Stake," pp. 285-92.

18. Sanders makes this point as well in "Jewish Association with Gentiles," p. 179. See also Nanos, "What Was at Stake," pp. 296, 299.

prevailing norms for eating with Gentiles: on the one hand, as pagan guests or, on the other hand, as proselyte candidates. The food was Jewish, and the Gentiles were eating it Jewishly, that is, as deemed appropriate for non-Jews to eat with Jewish people. But they were eating together as though these Gentiles and Jews were all equals, although these Gentiles were not Jews; in fact, they were — on principle — not even on their way to becoming Jews, meaning proselytes. The ones advocating the proselyte conversion of these Gentiles objected to circumventing the place of this rite to reidentify these Gentiles as *full and equal members* of this Jewish subgroup [that is, the Antiochene Christ-believing community].[19]

That is to say, Nanos's argument is that these Gentiles were "marginalized for . . . having believed that in Christ they have become already full members of the Jewish community."[20] But as far as Paul was concerned, the Christ-believing Gentiles at Antioch were part of the covenant community and thereby just like other groups within Judaism that had different beliefs and practices (for example, Pharisees and Sadducees).

Galatians 2:15-21

In 2:15-21, Paul provides a theological defense of his assertion that there should be no disunity between Jewish and Gentile members of the Christ-believing community.[21] The passage breaks down into three sections: 2:15-17; 2:18; and 2:19-21. The first and third sections are identifiable from the repetition of the prevalent terminology in each, namely, δικαιόω, ἐξ ἔργων νόμου, and πίστις/πιστεύω ᾽Ιησοῦ Χριστοῦ in the first section and ἀποθνήσκω and ζάω in the third section. In addition, they each end with a conditional sentence in which the apodosis, introduced by the particle ἄρα, contains a christological absurdity.[22]

19. Nanos, "What Was at Stake," pp. 300-301, emphases original.
20. Nanos, "What Was at Stake," p. 317.
21. Here Paul has the Galatian community in mind, but he would certainly have felt likewise about the other churches that he established.
22. NA[27] has the interrogative particle (ἆρα) in 2:17, but this is not attested in any of the constant witnesses. The interrogative particle is not needed to indicate that a question is meant because this is made clear by the subsequent exclamation (μὴ γένοιτο). Bruce points out that "every other Pauline instance of μὴ γένοιτο, used thus as an independent sentence, follows a question . . . there is thus a presumption that it does so here" (*Galatians,*

Galatians 2:15-17

In the first section, Paul takes up the proposition that Jewish and Gentile Christ-believers receive "status before God" in identical fashion.[23] He opens with a declaration of the ethnic identity that he and the rival preachers in Galatia share with Peter, Barnabas, and the other Christ-believers who separated themselves from the Antioch community, namely, they are all Jews by birth (2:15a).[24] Paul draws attention to this fact in order to contrast Jewish Christ-believers, not with Gentiles, but with other ethnic Jews. In Paul's view, Jewish Christ-believers represent Jews who discovered through their experience of Christ Jesus that the requisites of the law were inadequate for being made righteous before God (2:16). It is important to notice that Paul does not condemn Jewish practices, he qualifies them; that is, they are not antithetical, but subsidiary (ἐὰν μή) to faith.[25] Twice in the letter Paul states

---

p. 141). Given the lack of textual support or need for the interrogative, I have read it as an inferential particle (ἄρα), which is supported by a number of witnesses (note, however, that several of the most important manuscripts contain the particle unaccented [αρα; e.g., P[46], ℵ, B*]). See also Longenecker, *Galatians*, p. 90; Burton, *Galatians*, pp. 125-26; BDF §440 (2); C. F. D. Moule, *An Idiom Book of New Testament Greek* (Cambridge: Cambridge University Press, 1959), p. 164; Marion L. Soards, "Seeking (Zētein) and Sinning (Hamartōlos & Hamartia) according to Galatians 2.17," in *Apocalyptic and the New Testament: Essays in Honor of J. Louis Martyn*, ed. Joel Marcus and Marion L. Soards, JSNTSup 24 (Sheffield: Sheffield Academic Press, 1989), p. 239.

23. Betz, *Galatians*, p. 115.

24. See A. Andrew Das, *Paul and the Jews*, Library of Pauline Studies (Peabody, MA: Hendrickson, 2003), p. 24.

25. See also James D. G. Dunn, "The Theology of Galatians: The Issue of Covenantal Nomism," in *Pauline Theology*, vol. 1, pp. 140-41; C. K. Barrett, *Freedom & Obligation: A Study of the Epistle to the Galatians* (Philadelphia: Westminster, 1985), p. 20.

In addition, ἐὰν μή in 2:16 is usually rendered as adversative in translations and commentaries ("knowing that a person is not justified from works of the law, but [ἐὰν μή] through faith in Jesus Christ"). There is little grammatical justification for such a translation, however, and many commentators do not offer any; e.g., Bruce simply states that "[h]ere ἐὰν μή means 'but,' the previous option, ἐξ ἔργων νόμου, being excluded" (*Galatians*, p. 138). De Boer argues that it is adversative here while admitting that everywhere else in Paul it is exceptive (*Galatians*, p. 144). Others, like Heikki Räisänen, claim that it follows on the adversative use of εἰ μή in Gal. 1:7 and elsewhere in the NT, e.g., Matt. 12:4 and Luke 4:26-27 ("Galatians 2.16 and Paul's Break with Judaism," *NTS* 31 [1985]: 547). But, as A. Andrew Das argues, εἰ μή is not a good comparison because it "is used adversatively [in the NT] proportionately more frequently than ἐὰν μή. . . . In the Pauline context the occasional adversative use of εἰ μή is of even less value because of the apostle's complete avoidance of the adversative ἐὰν μή. Paul may choose to use εἰ μή adversatively but never ἐὰν μή" ("Another Look at ἐὰν μή

explicitly that the overriding issue is not whether or not the Galatian Christ-believers are circumcised (ἐν γὰρ Χριστῷ Ἰησοῦ οὔτε περιτομή τι ἰσχύει οὔτε ἀκροβυστία; 5:6; 6:15; see also 1 Cor. 7:19). Taking Paul at his word, I understand him to mean by this that *either* is acceptable, but that *neither* is sufficient.[26] Those who interpret Galatians as demanding that the law *must* not be observed by the Gentile Christ-believers appear to be denying the indifference toward the matter that Paul claims repeatedly.

Dunn argues that the phrase "works of the law," while referring to religious practices, encompasses particular social implications as well. According to him, ἔργα νόμου are "religious practices which demonstrate the individual's 'belongingness' to the people of the law. . . . Paul's way of describing in particular the identity and boundary markers."[27] Paul's critique

in Galatians 2:16," *JBL* 119 [2000]: 531-32; *Paul and the Jews*, pp. 31-32). Still others retain the exceptive quality of ἐὰν μή and solve the dilemma by applying it to the preceding clause taken without "works of the law" (e.g., Burton, *Galatians,* p. 121; Lightfoot, *Galatians,* p. 115; Longenecker, *Galatians,* p. 84; thus "a person is not justified except through faith in Jesus Christ"). Years ago, the grammarian A. T. Robertson applied to ἐὰν μή what he wrote about εἰ μή, that while the construction is exceptive, the effect "is to make [ἐὰν μή] *seem* adversative instead of exceptive" (*A Grammar of the Greek New Testament in the Light of Historical Research* [New York: George H. Doran, 1914], p. 1025, emphasis added). Das appears to build on Robertson's argument by maintaining that ἐὰν μή is (purposely?) ambiguous, and that Paul's opponents in Galatia would have read it as exceptive while the Gentile Christ-believers there would have read it adversatively ("Another Look," pp. 537-39). James D. G. Dunn, on the other hand, accepts the construction in its "most obvious grammatical sense" as introducing a clause in which "faith in Jesus is described as a *qualification* to justification by works of the law, not (yet) as an antithetical alternative," although he adds that the remainder of the verse "pushes what began as a qualification . . . into an outright antithesis" ("The New Perspective on Paul," *BJRL* 65 [1983]: 112-13; emphasis original). I would also appeal to Dunn's discussion of 3:11-12, viz., "In setting faith and law in such contrast here Paul would not want them to be understood as mutually exclusive; nor would he want to disparage the idea of 'doing the law' as such. . . . Once again it is a question of priorities" ("Works of the Law and the Curse of the Law [Galatians 3.10-14]," *NTS* 31 [1985]: 535).

26. James D. G. Dunn argues that circumcision and uncircumcision in these passages refer to ethnic identity similar to 3:28, i.e., circumcision/Jew, uncircumcision/Gentile ("'Neither Circumcision nor Uncircumcision, but . . .': Gal. 5.2-12; 6.12-16; cf. 1 Cor. 7.7-20," in *The New Perspective on Paul,* rev. ed. [Grand Rapids: Eerdmans, 2008], p. 330), but see 1 Cor. 7:18-20, which is clearly about the practice of circumcision. See also David A. Carson, who argues that Paul is inconsistent in his treatment of the law ("Pauline Inconsistency: Reflections on 1 Corinthians 9.19-23 and Galatians 2.11-14," *Chm* 100 [1986]: 19, 36).

27. Dunn, "Works of the Law," p. 528. Dunn confines "works of the law" in Galatians to circumcision and dietary restrictions, but others broaden the term to mean all Torah regulations (e.g., de Boer, *Galatians,* pp. 145-48).

of such practices has to do with this "social function as distinguishing Jew from Gentile."[28] The Jewish Christ-believers in Galatia are insisting on certain social consequences if Gentiles do not follow the law, likely separation from them as happened at Antioch. In Paul's experience, however, ethnic Jews did not dissociate from other Jews whose practices were different from their own. Regardless of their dissimilarity with respect to orthodoxy or orthopraxy, Jews accepted other Jews as Jews. For Paul, therefore, Christ-believing Gentiles were part of the covenant community, that is, Jews (in the Jesus-movement party), and there should be no separation of party members whether they be ethnically Jewish or Gentile.[29] Paul's view must have been that of Peter and the other Jewish Christ-believers in Antioch initially; otherwise, why were they eating with the Gentile members in the first place?

Paul goes on to argue that even for ethnic Jews who became Christ-believers justification was to be found "in Christ" (ἐν Χριστῷ; 2:17a). Longenecker explains that this phrase "appears frequently in Paul's letters to signal the sphere within which the believer lives and the intimacy of personal fellowship that exists between the believer and Christ."[30] The phrase most often refers as well to being a baptized member of the Jesus movement. There are, then, corporate overtones in Paul's use of ἐν Χριστῷ (for example, Gal. 3:28; Rom. 12:5).[31] Living in Christ means living in relationship with other Christ-believers, including Gentiles. The second part of the protasis in verse 17 confirms this corporate dimension while it sets out the potential consequences of such a relationship, namely, there is a risk that the Jewish Christ-believers will be perceived as "sinners" (ἁμαρτωλοί) just as the Gentiles have been (2:17b; see 2:15).[32] As far as Paul is concerned, this is not a threat at all because, for him, it is a false categori-

---

28. Dunn, "Works of the Law," p. 531.

29. Contra Francis Watson, *Paul, Judaism, and the Gentiles: Beyond the New Perspective*, rev. ed. (Grand Rapids: Eerdmans, 2007), pp. 100-135.

30. Longenecker, *Galatians*, p. 89; similarly Burton, *Galatians*, p. 124.

31. Martyn refers to this as "anthropological unity in Christ" ("Apocalyptic Antinomies," p. 415). See also Barrett, *Freedom & Obligation*, p. 36.

32. "Sinners" here seems to be, as Longenecker has suggested, "a colloquialism used by Jews with reference to Gentiles (cf. *Jub.* 23.23-24; on 'sinners' as a synonym for Gentiles, see Isa 14:5; 1 Macc 2:44; *Pss. Sol.* 1.1; 2.1; Matt 26:45; Luke 6:32-33)" (*Galatians*, p. 83; see also Bruce, *Galatians*, p. 137). In addition, there is a sense of irony about its use with ἔθνη (if indeed they are synonymous terms) and ἁμαρτία (Lightfoot, *Galatians*, p. 115; Robert G. Hamerton-Kelly, "Sacred Violence and 'Works of the Law': 'Is Christ Then an Agent of Sin?' [Galatians 2:17]," *CBQ* 52 [1990]: 61 n. 19).

zation for Gentile as well as Jewish Christ-believers.[33] He drives home his contempt for such characterizations with the absurd rhetorical question in the apodosis: "Is Christ then a servant of sin [διάκονος ἁμαρτίας]? Ridiculous [μὴ γένοιτα]!"

In the first section of the passage, therefore, Paul is arguing theologically for a sociological conviction. Just as they accepted as part of the covenant community other ethnic Jews whose orthopraxy might have differed from their own, so also Jewish Christ-believers must accept Gentile Christ-believers. Jewish practices, which are otherwise permissible and perhaps even helpful, must not be allowed to interfere with communal fellowship. As Dunn concludes, "it is the law in its social function which draws a large part of Paul's critique."[34]

Galatians 2:18

The significance of the second section to the passage's argument is highlighted by its brevity and its insertion between the two similarly constructed sections. Although Paul shifts from first person plural to first person singular, he likely still has in mind in a general way those Jewish Christ-believers to whom he has referred previously. But the shift in person is especially designed to contrast Paul with Peter. As Gaventa has argued, Paul intends to establish himself as a paradigm for the Galatians.[35] In the present verse, he distinguishes himself from Peter, an alternative — though unsatisfactory — model to follow. Here it is that he sets forth in clearest fashion his objection to the potential ramifications of the misapplication of ἔργα νόμου. On one level, 2:18 applies to the rebuilding (οἰκοδομέω) of the ἔργα νόμου with which Paul has previously dispensed.

---

33. The meaning of "sinner" is ambiguous, the choices being those outside the law and those who transgress God's will. In my view, the ambiguity should not be resolved, since, as Betz captures well, "the expression . . . presupposes the Jewish concept of human sinfulness, according to which sinners within Judaism must be distinguished from sinners who come from the non-Jewish population. . . . Jews commit sins when they transgress the Torah, and they can obtain forgiveness by various cultic means . . . that is, by the Torah. Gentiles, however, are 'sinners' as Gentiles, and outside of the Torah covenant there is no salvation" (*Galatians*, p. 115). For a discussion of the various interpretations of 2:17, see Soards, "Seeking and Sinning," pp. 237-54.

34. Dunn, "Works of the Law," p. 531.

35. Beverly Roberts Gaventa, "Galatians 1 and 2: Autobiography as Paradigm," *NovT* 28 (1986): 309-26.

On another level, however, it is acknowledging that Paul would be a transgressor if he reestablished social barriers between Jewish and Gentile Christ-believers that he has torn down (καταλύω) in his communities, as Peter did at Antioch and for which Peter rightly stood condemned (καταγινώσκω [2:11]).[36] Indeed, according to Jan Lambrecht,

> [t]he adverb πάλιν and the verb οἰκοδομῶ point the reader to the hypothetical step of Paul (and the actual step of Peter) "to live again like a Jew" (cf. 2,14). With ἅ and ταῦτα we must think in *the first place* of eating with Gentiles and, further, of calendar prescriptions (4,10), and circumcision (5,2-3).[37]

In other words, in the context of 2:11-14, Paul will not erect again the wall separating Jews from Gentiles in the Galatian churches the way that Peter did at Antioch. Lambrecht argues that to Paul's opponents in Galatia the transgression (παραβάτης) involved firstly eating with Gentiles.[38] For Paul, therefore, the transgression would include destruction of the social equality — unity — between Jewish and Gentile Christ-believers at Galatia. The use of παραβάτης conveys Paul's seriousness. He intends no irony as he did with ἁμαρτωλοί in verse 17. He is determined to dissuade the Galatians from following in the footsteps of Peter, Barnabas, and the other Jewish Christ-believers in Antioch.[39]

Galatians 2:19-21

In the final section, Paul unpacks his reasons for insisting that he and those who would imitate him must not revert to the previous social boundaries as

---

36. Elsewhere Paul uses the term οἰκοδομέω to refer to the upbuilding of the community (Rom. 15:20; 1 Cor. 8:1; 1 Thess. 5:11). The repetition of κατά (κατὰ πρόσωπον and καταγινώσκω in 2:11, and καταλύω in 2:18) emphasizes Paul's opposition to the disruption of the community caused by Peter at Antioch and advocated by the rival preachers at Galatia.

37. Jan Lambrecht, "Transgressor by Nullifying God's Grace: A Study of Gal 2,18-21," *Bib* 72 (1991): 223, emphasis added. Martyn acknowledges the dual-level meaning: "[Paul] assumes that the Galatians will know from the context . . . that the edifice is the Law, seen as the wall that separates Jews from Gentiles" (*Galatians*, p. 256). See also Hamerton-Kelly, "Sacred Violence," pp. 61, 65-66; C. K. Barrett, *Freedom & Obligation*, p. 20.

38. Lambrecht, "Transgressor," pp. 231-32; de Boer, *Galatians*, p. 158.

39. Bruce also sees this as a possible interpretation (*Galatians*, p. 142). Lambrecht comments as well that in 2:18 "Paul comes back to the concrete Antiochean incident which manifested Peter's behaviour of restoring what was pulled down" ("Transgressor," p. 219).

Peter did.[40] Paul himself interprets the obscure saying in 2:19, "I died to the law through the law in order that I might live to God." It means "I have been crucified with Christ" (2:19c).[41] The perfect-tense verb συνεστούρωμαι gives a durative quality to the statement; that is, Paul's crucifixion with Christ occurred in the past and its effects continue into the present. The point at which this death experience befell Paul has been disclosed in 1:13-16, a passage helpful for understanding 2:19a. Previously Paul had progressed beyond his peers in Judaism and was even more zealous in observing Jewish customs (1:14). He was, therefore, a strict Jew who would have been sensitive about his contact with Gentiles, although as I have previously noted, that is not to say that he would have had no contact with them.[42] In addition, he persecuted and tried to destroy the church of God (1:13). Paul was no friend to Christ-believers, Jew or Gentile. But then God revealed God's Son to him, that Paul might preach Christ to the Gentiles (1:15-16). It is at this point that he was crucified with Christ and that his views of the church and Gentiles were reversed.[43]

Paul specifies the continuing effects of this experience in 2:20. Christ has so completely taken over his being that he cannot even name his present existence.[44] Whatever state he is in, however, it is "in faith in the Son of

40. There is an ongoing debate as to whether Paul is speaking here of his own experience or that of Christ-believers in general. The emphatic pronoun (ἐγώ) and the context of the passage suggest that he is referring to himself (e.g., Bruce, *Galatians,* p. 143). Gaventa, on the other hand, perceives a connection between Paul's personal experience and that of the broader Christ-believing community: "Paul does not intend the first person singular here or earlier simply to refer to 'one.' Nor does he speak of his own experience in order merely to defend his apostolate or to boast of his relationship to Christ. Instead, he sees in his experience a paradigm of the singularity of the gospel, and he uses his experience to call the Galatians into that singularity in their own faith-lives" ("Galatians 1 and 2," p. 318).

41. Betz thus claims that "[t]he difficulty of interpreting this *crux interpretum* comes from its nature of 'abbreviation,' which must be 'decoded.' . . . The aorist ἀπέθανον . . . in a metaphorical way points to some kind of death experience, which is clarified by the following thesis: 'I have been crucified together with Christ'" (*Galatians,* p. 122).

42. See Sanders, "Jewish Association with Gentiles," pp. 170-88; Dunn, "Incident at Antioch," pp. 3-74.

43. Gaventa also notes the connection between chapter 1 and 2:19-20 ("Galatians 1 and 2," p. 318).

44. The neuter relative (ὅ) in 2:20 is sometimes considered to express a cognate accusative of inner content, "which simply puts into substantive form the content of the verb ζῶ" ("the life that I now live"; Burton, *Galatians,* p. 138; see also BDF §154; Robertson, *Grammar,* pp. 478-79; BDAG, s.v. ὅς 1.g.γ.). This appears to be the preferred construal of most translations and commentaries (see NRSV, RSV, NIV, NEB; Longenecker, *Galatians,* p. 93; Bruce,

God who loved me and gave himself up for me" (2:20d; cf. 1:4).[45] The Christ-believers in Galatia are to imitate Christ and Paul by living lives of love and self-sacrifice on behalf of others within the Jesus movement. This is, of course, impossible if they allow themselves to become separated from one another.

That 2:19-20 is as much related to the ethical exhortations in chapters 5 and 6 as it is to chapters 3 and 4 has been well argued by, among others, Bernard Lategan and Richard B. Hays.[46] Lategan maintains that "[t]he attributes used here to describe Christ . . . anticipate the theological and ethical sections which follow in 3–4 and 5–6: τοῦ ἀγαπήσαντός με is an abbreviated description of the ethical content of the gospel, as personified by Christ and his 'Verhalten,' and which forms the content of chapters 5 and 6."[47] Hays adds that participationist christology is an important unifying theme in the letter.[48] An essential aspect of such a christology is that it supplies "the pattern for Christian conduct. Paul's ethical directives to the Galatians presuppose a particular understanding of Jesus Christ as a *paradigm* for the life of the Christian believer and — to do justice to the full scope of Paul's vision — for the life of the *community* in Christ."[49] Paul believes that his own life and ministry correspond to Christ's and, therefore, are worthy of imitation by his communities.[50] Hays notes that "the most important text here, of course, is Gal 2:19b-20."[51]

The details about what conduct is needed to imitate Christ and Paul

---

Galatians, p. 144). Others take it as an adverbial accusative of inner content (accusative of general reference), which "limits and qualifies" that life ("to the extent that I have life"; Lightfoot, *Galatians*, p. 119; Betz, *Galatians*, pp. 124-25; NAB; see also Moule, *Idiom*, p. 131). Instead of these two possibilities, I understand the pronoun as an indefinite relative, used to convey the uncertainty of what being alive means in light of the preceding declarations in 2:19c-20b ("whatever I am living"; see Robertson, *Grammar*, pp. 719-20).

45. Given the context in 2:20, I consider πίστις Χριστοῦ to be an objective genitive; to paraphrase, whatever Paul is living now, he is living it believing in the Son of God who loved him and gave himself up for him.

46. Bernard Lategan, "Is Paul Defending His Apostleship in Galatians? The Function of Galatians 1.11-12 and 2.19-20 in the Development of Paul's Argument," *NTS* 34 (1988): 426-30; Richard B. Hays, "Christology and Ethics in Galatians: The Law of Christ," *CBQ* 49 (1987): 268-90.

47. Lategan, "Is Paul Defending His Apostleship?" pp. 429-30.

48. Hays, "Christology and Ethics," pp. 272, 282. See also the discussion of ἐν Χριστῷ, above.

49. Hays, "Christology and Ethics," p. 273, emphasis original.

50. Hays, "Christology and Ethics," pp. 280-81; see also p. 277.

51. Hays, "Christology and Ethics," p. 280.

are taken up in chapters 5 and 6. These exhortations have to do fundamentally with community among the Galatian Christ-believers, as Gordon Fee has observed:

> [T]he concern from beginning to end is with *Christian life in community, not with the interior life of the individual Christian.* Apart from 5:17c . . . there is not a hint that Paul is here dealing with a "tension" between flesh and Spirit that rages within the human breast — in which flesh most often appears as the stronger opponent. To the contrary, the issue from the beginning . . . has to do with the Spirit life within the believing community.[52]

The lists of vices and virtues in Galatians 5:19-23 support Fee's claim. Hays points out that the vice list defines "works of the flesh" primarily in terms of "the impulses which produce rivalry, disunity, and conflict among brothers and sisters in the community of faith."[53] Dunn calls attention to the fact that the virtue list also pertains to community life, that "joy and peace . . . [strengthen] bonds of community . . . includ[ing] all that makes for social well-being and harmonious relationships."[54] Indeed, Paul uses the strongest possible language to get across that unity among the Galatian Christ-believers is critical, commanding that in love they become slaves to one another (5:13).[55] Galatians 6:1-5 contains additional evidence of Paul's emphasis on unity among the Christ-believers in Galatia. His exhortations there are directed to the law-abiding (no pun intended) citizens, stressing that it is *their* responsibility to maintain solidarity with those whose misconduct might otherwise divide the community.

The concluding verse of the final section (2:21) deals with Paul's refusal to nullify God's grace (χάρις). It was by God's grace that Paul's mission to and, therefore, fellowship with Gentiles was initiated (1:15). Moreover, once the Jerusalem apostles recognized that Paul's mission to the

---

52. Gordon Fee, "Freedom and the Life of Obedience (Galatians 5:1–6:18)," *RevExp* 91 (1994): 205, emphasis original. See also Gaventa, "Singularity of the Gospel," p. 155.

53. Hays, "Christology and Ethics," p. 286.

54. James D. G. Dunn, *The Theology of Paul's Letter to the Galatians* (Cambridge: Cambridge University Press, 1993), p. 112.

55. Hays concludes that "[w]ith that exhortation, Paul urges the Galatians to participate in a paradoxical self-giving which mirrors the action of Christ who gave himself up. . . . This self-giving is paradoxical because it consists in the community's exercise of freedom (5:13a) in the interests of others in such a way that 'slavery' is the result" ("Christology and Ethics," p. 283).

Gentiles was by God's grace, they gave their approval to his work. His agreement to undertake a collection for the Jerusalem church (2:10), to which he devoted a considerable portion of his ministry thereafter if his letters are to be believed (Rom. 15:25-28; 1 Cor. 16:1-4; 2 Corinthians 8–9), punctuates his commitment to unity between Jewish and Gentile Christ-believers. God's grace, Paul realizes, is integrally related to this unity.

This section concludes with another christological absurdity (2:21c), which should be read with the other absurdity of 2:17 in view.[56] In light of what Paul has just articulated in emphatic fashion (ζάω is repeated four times in 2:20), no reader or hearer of the letter could take seriously the notion that Christ died in vain. This leads to an understanding of the protasis (2:21b) somewhat parallel to that in 2:17a, that is, there is a risk that some will cling to an understanding of the law that calls for a certain degree of separation of Jewish Christ-believers from Gentile Christ-believers. For Paul, this is as nonsensical as being characterized as "sinners" and is also a rejection of God's grace.

Conclusion

Galatians 2:15-21, then, is not wholly about the law and whether the Jewish orthopraxic customs (ἔργα νόμου), especially circumcision, must be rejected (or accepted, according to the rival preachers) by Gentile Christ-believers in Galatia. Indeed, Paul's view of the law in Galatians is much more nuanced than an "either/or" answer allows, as is suggested by my proposed translation of ἐὰν μή in 2:16 and serious consideration of 5:6 and 6:15 ("neither circumcision nor uncircumcision means anything"). Unity among Christ-believers, regardless of their ethnicity, is another primary issue in this passage. Jewish and Gentile Christ-believers alike have been called to live "in Christ," and to the extent that any works of the law disrupt that unity, they are to be reinterpreted or set aside.[57] As Sanders and Dunn have argued, there is a great distance from this demand to rejection of the law and all practices in conformity to it.

Throughout Galatians 2:15-21, Paul employs a number of contrasts:

---

56. Rudolf Bultmann also argued for the association of these verses ("Zur Auslegung von Galater 2,15-18," in *Exegetica: Aufsätze zur Erforschung des Neuen Testaments,* ed. Erich Dinkler [Tübingen: Mohr Siebeck, 1967], pp. 394-96).

57. Räisänen, "Gal 2.16 and Paul's Break," p. 549.

Jews and Gentiles, know and believe, seek and find, build up and tear down, live and die.[58] How can the use of such contrasting terminology be reconciled with a reading of the passage that focuses on unity? The rapprochement between these concepts may be less problematic than might first be supposed. Indeed, the implication seems clear, namely, that as far as Paul is concerned, just as in God's kingdom inaugurated at Christ's crucifixion and resurrection and (to be) fulfilled at the Parousia, *difference must not mean division.*

Finally, as I have noted, for Paul God acted in history to inaugurate God's kingdom through the death and resurrection of Jesus Christ. As Paul believed that God had selected him before birth to preach Christ to Gentiles (Gal. 1:15-16), he also understood that God was taking the initiative to unite Gentile and Jew under the banner of Christ. Paul believed this unity would begin with the end-time communities that he established but would — at the Parousia — end with the cosmos unified under Christ, who would then hand it as a unified whole over to God (1 Cor. 15:24-28). As Gaventa has shown, "ethnic tensions between Jew and Gentile," when divorced from the larger narrative of God's ultimate triumph over all things, present themselves as "mere social relations, while for Paul they are a matter of the unity of humankind in doxological response to God's action for all humankind."[59] For those in the church who work toward unity, either through ecumenical or interfaith action, this human endeavor must ultimately be rooted in an acknowledgment of God's gracious actions on behalf of the entire cosmos.

---

58. Martyn, "Apocalyptic Antinomies," pp. 410-24.

59. Beverly Roberts Gaventa, *Our Mother Saint Paul* (Louisville: Westminster John Knox, 2007), p. 135.

The God Who Gives Life That Is Truly Life: Meritorious Almsgiving and the Divine Economy in 1 Timothy 6

David J. Downs

Among the interpretative challenges offered by the final chapter of 1 Timothy, one literary and one theological question are especially resistant to easy answers. First, how does the personal charge to Timothy in 6:11-16 relate to its present literary context, particularly since the directives given to Timothy in verses 11-14, which are punctuated by a brief doxology in verses 15-16, appear at first glance to interrupt the focused teachings on wealth found in verses 6-10 and verses 17-19? Second, does the instruction to the rich in verses 17-19, with its suggestion that the wealthy are able through generous deeds to store up a treasury of credit from which funds can be used to purchase reward in the next life, contradict or stand in tension with the Pauline doctrine of justification by faith and not works?

This essay will suggest that the answers to these two questions are not only related but also indiscernible without careful attention to the character and activity of God in the "theologizing" of 1 Timothy.[1] I shall argue that all of 1 Timothy 6:6-19, including verses 11-16, represents discourse about wealth, but this unified passage is also, at the same time, discourse about the God who richly provides all things. In short, 1 Timothy 6 does promote meritorious almsgiving: the rich in the present age are able to secure heavenly treasure through the "enjoyment" of their wealth, enjoyment that takes the form of generous sharing of material resources (vv. 17-19). This exchange of possessions for heavenly reward, however, cannot be

---

1. The term "theologizing" is taken from Paul W. Meyer, "Pauline Theology: A Proposal for a Pause in Its Pursuit," in *Pauline Theology*, vol. 4: *Looking Back, Pressing On*, ed. E. Elizabeth Johnson and David M. Hay (Atlanta: Scholars Press, 1997), pp. 140-60, esp. p. 150. With Meyer, I use the term to suggest that the theology of a letter like 1 Timothy is not found behind the text but in the outcome of its composition.

separated from the author's emphatic insistence, in this chapter and elsewhere in the letter, that all things come from God (1 Tim. 6:13-17). Those who secure the treasure of a good foundation in order to take hold of life that truly is life do so with funds they have already received from God. Thus, even the human action of meritorious almsgiving is located in a larger divine economy in which God is proclaimed to be the source and provider of all things.[2]

The Literary Unity of 6:6-19

The literary structure of 1 Timothy 6 has frequently puzzled interpreters. The instructions to slaves in 6:1-2a conclude and naturally belong together with the household code from the previous chapter, material that has addressed the treatment of older and younger men and women (5:1-2), support of widows (5:3-16), and the payment, discipline, and appointment of elders (5:17-25).[3] It is more difficult to discern the organization and thematic relationship of the material that follows, not least because two sections that deal directly with the topic of wealth, 6:6-10 and 6:17-19, are ostensibly separated by a personal charge to Timothy in 6:11-16.[4] The material in verses 11-16 has been characterized as an "intrusion,"[5] an inter-

2. A brief note on methodology is in order. In this essay, I do not wish to engage the issue of the authorship of 1 Timothy, for I am interested in the theological witness of the letter in its present form as part of the Pauline canon. I shall speak of Paul as the author of 1 Timothy, for he is represented as the author of the epistle, regardless of whether he is the real author. For a fuller statement on this approach and the reasons for it, see David J. Downs, "Faith(fulness) in Christ Jesus in 2 Timothy 3:15," *JBL* 131 (2012): 143-60.

3. See David G. Horrell, "Disciplining Performance and 'Placing' the Church: Widows, Elders, and Slaves in the Household of God (1 Tim 5,1–6,2)," in *1 Timothy Reconsidered,* ed. Karl P. Donfried, Colloquium Oecumenicum Paulinum 18 (Leuven: Peeters, 2008), pp. 109-34. The directive that Timothy stop drinking only water in 5:23 does appear to be something of a digression, although it is probably linked to the preceding and following material through the concept of purity (so Jürgen Roloff, *Der Erste Brief an Timotheus,* EKKNT 15 [Zürich and Neukirchen-Vluyn: Benziger and Neukirchener, 1988], p. 315).

4. The discussion of wealth in 6:6-10 is linked to the previous material on false teaching in 6:3-5 by the repetition and alteration in verse 6 (Ἔστιν δὲ πορισμὸς μέγας ἡ εὐσέβεια μετὰ αὐταρκείας) of the phrase πορισμὸν εἶναι τὴν εὐσέβειαν in verse 5 that is used to describe the mistaken belief of false teachers that godliness is a means of profit; see Peter Dschulnigg, "Warnung vor Reichtum und Ermahnung der Reichen: 1 Tim 6,6-10.17-19 im Rahmen des Schlußteils 6,3-21," *BZ* 37 (1993): 60-77.

5. Martin Dibelius and Hans Conzelmann, *The Pastoral Epistles: A Commentary on the*

polation,[6] awkwardly placed baptismal or ordination tradition,[7] or an example of the author's tendency to combine material in a rough and disjointed manner.[8]

Nathan Eubank has recently offered a creative, and to my mind convincing, solution to the problem of the literary unity of 1 Timothy 6:6-19, a proposal that also solves the equally vexing question of the nature of the unspecified "commandment" that Timothy is exhorted to keep in verse 14.[9] In verses 13-14, Paul issues a solemn charge for Timothy to keep "the commandment" (τηρῆσαί σε τὴν ἐντολήν), yet there is no immediate indication of what specific action(s) keeping this commandment is intended to entail:

> I charge you in the presence of God, who gives life to all things, and of Christ Jesus, who witnessed in the time of Pontius Pilate the good confession, *to keep the commandment unblemished and above reproach until the manifestation of our Lord Jesus Christ,* which he will make known at the proper time — he who is the blessed and only Sovereign, the King of kings and the Lord of lords, who alone has immortality, who dwells in unapproachable light, whom no human has seen or is able to see; to him be honor and might forever. Amen. (1 Tim. 6:13-16)[10]

Eubank contends that "the commandment" in verse 14 refers to the practice of almsgiving, with the implication that 1 Timothy 6:11-16 is "not a vio-

---

Pastoral Epistles, trans. Philip Buttolph and Adela Yarbro, Hermeneia (Philadelphia: Fortress, 1972), p. 87.

6. James David Miller, *The Pastoral Letters as Composite Documents,* SNTSMS 93 (Cambridge: Cambridge University Press, 1997), pp. 88-95.

7. Roloff, *Timotheus,* pp. 340-45; Ernst Käsemann, "Das Formular einer neutestamentlichen Ordinationsparänese," in *Neutestamentliche Studien für Rudolf Bultmann: Zu seinem siebzigsten Geburtstag,* ed. Walther Eltester, BZNW 21 (Berlin: De Gruyter, 1954), pp. 261-68.

8. Samuel Bénétreau, "La richesse selon 1 Timothée 6,6-10 et 6,17-19," *ETR* 83 (2008): 49-60.

9. Nathan Eubank, "Almsgiving Is 'the Commandment': A Note on 1 Timothy 6.6-19," *NTS* 58 (2012): 144-50. Other proposals for the meaning of "the commandment" include: (1) the specific instruction in verses 11-12, (2) Timothy's baptismal or ordination commission, (3) the entire epistle, (4) the life of faith as it is summarized in verses 11-12, (5) Timothy's ministry or commitment to Christ, (6) the "deposit of faith" in 1 Tim. 6:20, (7) the gospel as a "rule of life," or (8) a reference to Jesus tradition; see the listing and discussion in I. Howard Marshall, *A Critical and Exegetical Commentary on the Pastoral Epistles,* ICC (London: T. & T. Clark, 1999), pp. 663-65.

10. Unless otherwise noted, all translations in this essay are my own.

lent intrusion into a discussion of the proper use of wealth, but an integral part of the author's argument — an argument that concludes in vv. 18-19 with a call for the rich to give alms."[11]

In order to support this claim, Eubank draws attention to Saul Lieberman's observation that in numerous rabbinic texts the term מצוה ("commandment") refers to the activity of providing material assistance to the needy (i.e., "almsgiving"), with the Aramaic phrase בר מצוותא denoting a "man of almsgiving."[12] For instance, the fifth-century *Leviticus Rabbah* 3.1 states, "Better is he who goes and works and gives charity of that which is his own, than he who goes and robs or takes by violence and gives charity of that belonging to others. . . . It is his ambition to be called a man of almsgiving [בר מצוותא]."[13] Although this usage of the term מצוה to mean "almsgiving" probably only became common in the fourth century of the Common Era,[14] Eubank points to an earlier parallel, outside of rabbinic literature, from the *Testament of Asher* 2:8, a text that has been dated to around 200 CE, although it also likely incorporates earlier traditions.[15] Similarly, Gary Anderson has suggested that the understanding of almsgiving as "*the* commandment" goes back to the Second Temple period, a contention Anderson maintains with reference to the prominence given to almsgiving in the narrative of Tobit (e.g., 4:5-11; 12:8-10; 14:8-11).[16]

11. Eubank, "Almsgiving," p. 145.

12. Saul Lieberman, "Two Lexicographical Notes," *JBL* 65 (1946): 67-72. More recently, Gary A. Anderson glosses בר מצוותא as "'a generous person,' that is, one who is in the habit of giving alms" (*Sin: A History* [New Haven: Yale University Press, 2009], p. 174).

13. The translation is Eubank's, slightly amended from Harry Freedman and Maurice Simon, eds., *The Midrash Rabbah, Leviticus* 4, trans. J. Isaelstram (London: Soncino, 1961), pp. 34-35.

14. So Michael L. Satlow, "'Fruit and the Fruit of Fruit': Charity and Piety among Jews in Late Antique Palestine," *JQR* 100 (2010): 244-77. Lieberman himself suggests that the development occurred "beginning not later than the third century" ("Two Lexicographical Notes," p. 69). To the evidence from third- through seventh-century Jewish and Christian sources that Lieberman cites for an identification between obedience to the commandments and almsgiving, we should probably add a third- or fourth-century (?) Jewish inscription from the catacombs in Rome that describes its honoree, Priscus, as φιλόλαος φιλ[έντολ-]ος φιλοπένης, "one who loved the people, the commandments, and the poor." See David Noy, *Jewish Inscriptions of Western Europe*, vol. 2: *The City of Rome* (Cambridge: Cambridge University Press, 1995), pp. 211-13 [#240].

15. See Joel Marcus, "The *Testaments of the Twelve Patriarchs and the Didascalia Apostolorum*: A Common Jewish Christian Milieu?" *JTS* 61 (2010): 596-626.

16. Anderson, *Sin*, p. 174. Eubank also identifies Sir. 29:1 ("The merciful lend to their neighbors; by holding out a helping hand they keep the commandments," NRSV); Sir. 29:8-

With regard to the structure and argument of 1 Timothy 6, Eubank shows that viewing "the commandment" in verse 14 as a reference to almsgiving both continues the discussion of wealth in verses 6-10 and anticipates the advice for the rich to share their wealth in verses 17-19. Indeed, Eubank points out that verses 17-19 neatly recapitulate the basic elements of the personal charge to Timothy in verses 11-16:

Charge[17] to Timothy (vv. 11-16)	Instructions to the rich (vv. 17-19)
Flee these things (i.e., the love of money in v. 10)	Do not be haughty, nor hope in the uncertainty of wealth (v. 17)
Instead of the love of money, pursue righteousness, godliness, faith, love, endurance, gentleness (v. 12)	Instead of hoping in wealth, hope in God (v. 17)
Take hold (ἐπιλαβοῦ) of the eternal life and keep the commandment, i.e., to give alms (vv. 12-14)	Generously share resources, thus storing up a good foundation for the future, so that they may take hold [ἵνα ἐπιλάβωνται] of that which is truly life (vv. 18-19)

As Eubank summarizes his argument, "If 'the commandment' [in 1 Tim. 6:14] refers to almsgiving then the author would simply be telling Timothy

---

13; Matt. 19:16-22 (and pars.); *Did.* 1.5 as texts that might suggest a link between almsgiving and obedience to the commandments. I would propose that *2 Clem.* 16-17 be added to this list of textual witnesses. With a clear allusion to Tob. 12:8-9 and a quotation of 1 Pet. 4:8, *2 Clem.* 16.4 states, "Therefore, almsgiving is good as repentance for sin. Fasting is better than prayer, but almsgiving is better than both, and 'love covers a multitude of sins.' Prayer from a good conscience delivers from death. Blessed is everyone who is found full of these things, for almsgiving lightens the burden of sin." The author of *2 Clement* then immediately follows this call to repentance in the act of almsgiving in 16.4 with another exhortation to repent and a reminder that repentance involves the practice of "the commandments" in 17.1: "For if we have commandments [εἰ γὰρ ἐντολὰς ἔχομεν] that we should practice this [i.e., repentance, which is demonstrated through almsgiving, according to *2 Clem.* 16.4], to draw people away from idols and to instruct them, how much more wrong is it that a person who already knows God should perish?" On the relationship between almsgiving and repentance in *2 Clement*, see David J. Downs, "Redemptive Almsgiving and Economic Stratification in *2 Clement*," *JECS* 19 (2011): 493-517.

17. Paul employs the verb παραγγέλλω in verse 13 to issue the formal charge to Timothy, and then in verse 17 Timothy is instructed to "charge" (παράγγελλε) the rich in the present age "not to be haughty, nor to hope in the uncertainty of wealth, but to hope in God, who richly grants to us all things for enjoyment" (cf. the use of παραγγέλλω in 1 Tim. 1:3; 4:11; 5:7).

the same thing that Timothy is to tell the rich: instead of pursuing money, pursue eternal life and give alms."[18] The entirety of 1 Timothy 6:6-19, then, encourages an appropriate theological perspective on and the proper employment of wealth.

Eubank's proposal can perhaps be sharpened by noting that the two adjectives used to describe *how* "the commandment" in verse 14 is to be kept — ἄσπιλος and ἀνεπίλημπτος — make sense especially in the context of Timothy's oversight of material distributions to the needy.[19] If the intended recipients of the directives in 1 Timothy 5:7 ("Give these instructions, so that *they* may be above reproach") are family members who provide for widows (as opposed to the widows themselves),[20] then the adjective ἀνεπίλημπτος has already been used in the letter to describe the "irreproachable" character of those charged with the responsibility of caring for the needy. To be sure, this summons to impeccable moral conduct in 1 Timothy 5:7 should not be limited to matters of financial integrity, for in the act of providing responsible care for godly widows family members demonstrate their general character and reputation (cf. 1 Tim. 3:1-13).

In the context of directives about how to care for the socially and economically marginalized, however, the issue of integrity when managing and distributing material resources is almost certainly at the forefront in the purpose-clause ἵνα ἀνεπίλημπτοι ὦσιν in 1 Timothy 5:7. Moreover, one need only examine the contentious history of Paul's efforts to organize a relief fund for impoverished believers in Jerusalem — an endeavor that led to charges of fiscal mismanagement and impropriety against the apostle in Corinth (cf. 2 Cor. 11:7-9; 12:14-21) — in order to appreciate the importance of caring for the poor in a manner that is "unblemished and above reproach" (1 Tim. 6:14). Although not offering an exact linguistic correspon-

18. Eubank, "Almsgiving," p. 149.

19. If this reading is accepted, a related question concerns the particular role that Timothy himself is intended to play in the distribution of alms in Ephesus. This question broaches larger issues concerning the structure and development of church leadership in 1 Timothy, the Pastoral Epistles, and second-century Christianity. My own view is that in keeping "the commandment" of almsgiving Timothy is intended to manage and oversee material contributions to the poor in a way similar to Paul's organization of the Jerusalem collection, even if Timothy's leadership is mediated by local ἐπίσκοποι (3:1-7) and διάκονοι (3:8-13). On the importance of care for the indigenous poor in Pauline communities, see Bruce W. Longenecker, *Remember the Poor: Paul, Poverty, and the Greco-Roman World* (Grand Rapids: Eerdmans, 2010).

20. So William D. Mounce, *Pastoral Epistles,* WBC 46 (Nashville: Thomas Nelson, 2000), p. 283.

dence, Paul's statements in 2 Corinthians 8:16-24 about his plans to collect offerings in Corinth for the saints in Jerusalem with at least two appointed delegates from the Macedonian churches represent a thematic parallel to the instruction given to Timothy in 6:14: "We are taking this preparation lest anyone blame us concerning this lavish gift that is being administered by us. For we pay attention to what is honorable, not only 'in the sight of the Lord' but also 'in the sight of human beings'" (2 Cor. 8:20-21).[21] In the same way, Paul charges Timothy to keep the commandment of providing for the needy in a manner that is unblemished and above reproach, lest Timothy encounter in Ephesus similar opposition to that experienced by Paul in Corinth during the apostle's efforts to arrange a contribution for needy believers in Jerusalem.

Meritorious Almsgiving in 1 Timothy 6:17-19

The solution to the literary unity of 1 Timothy 6:6-19 discussed above sheds important light on the interpretation of 6:17-19, a text that has often beguiled interpreters because of the implication of verse 19 that wealthy believers can accrue for themselves future treasure in exchange for generously sharing their resources. The text reads:

> [17]To the rich in the present age, charge them not to be haughty, nor to hope in the uncertainty of wealth, but to hope in God, who richly grants to us all things for enjoyment — [18]that is, to do good, to be rich in good works, to be generous, sharing, [19]storing up for themselves a good foundation for the future, so that they may take hold of the life that is truly life.

Helmut Merkel asserts that 1 Timothy 6:18-19 reflects the notion, which he maintains is commonly found in the Pastoral Epistles, that good works provide a foundation for the future, and Merkel calls this idea "completely un-Pauline."[22] Among those not inclined to posit so sharp a dis-

---

21. For a more detailed description of the troubles faced by Paul in his efforts to raise funds for Jerusalem, see David J. Downs, *The Offering of the Gentiles: Paul's Collection for Jerusalem in Its Chronological, Cultural, and Cultic Contexts*, WUNT 2:248 (Tübingen: Mohr Siebeck, 2008), pp. 40-60, 138-39.

22. Helmut Merkel, *Die Pastoralbriefe*, NTD 9/1 (Göttingen: Vandenhoeck & Ruprecht, 1991), p. 52 (my translation).

continuity between the soteriology of 1 Timothy (or the so-called Pastoral Epistles in general), on one hand, and the undisputed Pauline Epistles, on the other, a common strategy for explaining the relationship between charity and reward in 1 Timothy 6:19 is to draw a distinction between *demonstrating* one's godliness and *earning* one's salvation. For example, Philip Towner says of the ἵνα-clause at the end of verse 19, "[I]t requires not an earning of salvation or eternal life, but rather a demonstration of genuine godliness in the present age."[23] Similarly, William Mounce comments, "There is no suggestion that the rich can earn their way to heaven by doing these things; Paul is spelling out the results of certain actions. Salvation in [the Pastoral Epistles] is by God's grace and mercy alone (cf. 1 Tim 1:12-17)."[24] I. Howard Marshall's interpretation is slightly more nuanced in that he perceives verse 19 to be focused on "reward" instead of salvation, but Marshall nevertheless emphasizes the same distinction between earning and demonstration: "The purpose clause might almost be thought to suggest that people can lay up a treasury of credit for their generous deeds which will win reward in the next life (for the motif see Tobit 4.9); but 2 Tim 1.9 forbids this idea. Rather, we have the normal NT teaching that lack of the expression of faith in good works is an indication of the lack of faith itself, and conversely."[25]

This-Worldly or Eschatological Reward?

Before considering an alternative perspective on the relationship between generosity and reward, it is worth asking if 1 Timothy 6:17-19 refers to eschatological realities and divine recompense at all. In the economic world of Greco-Roman antiquity, a context in which episodic or conjunctural poverty was an ever-present threat for all but a very small number of the economic elite, might 1 Timothy 6:17-19 simply advocate the wisdom of generously sharing one's resources with others in the hope that the recipients of such munificence would reciprocate, should the original donor run into financial hardship at some point in the future? Even those in verse 17 characterized as οἱ πλούσιοι ἐν τῷ νῦν αἰῶνι ("the rich in the present age")

---

23. Philip H. Towner, *The Letters to Timothy and Titus,* NICNT (Grand Rapids: Eerdmans, 2006), p. 428.

24. Mounce, *Pastoral,* p. 368.

25. Marshall, *Pastoral,* pp. 673-74.

need not be exempt from economic trouble, especially if this term denotes those members of the early Christian movement who possess moderate to significant surplus resources but are not representatives of the imperial or regional elite. Thus, even though I will reject this conclusion, it is worth pondering whether those whose generosity allows them to store up for themselves a good foundation for the future might simply be securing potential assistance in this life through the reciprocal exchange of goods and services.

In fact, Tobit 4:5-11, which is often highlighted as a passage with intriguing thematic and linguistic parallels to 1 Timothy 6:17-19, may envision this very scenario. In a speech commissioning his son, Tobias, into the world, Tobit says:

> [5]Revere the Lord all your days, my son, and refuse to sin or to transgress his commandments. Live uprightly all the days of your life, and do not walk in the ways of wrongdoing; [6]for those who act in accordance with truth will prosper in all their activities. To all those who practice righteousness [7]give alms from your possessions, and do not let your eye begrudge the gift when you make it. Do not turn your face away from anyone who is poor, and the face of God will not be turned away from you. [8]If you have many possessions, make your gift from them in proportion; if few, do not be afraid to give according to the little you have. [9]*So you will be laying up a good treasure for yourself against the day of necessity.* [10]For almsgiving delivers from death and keeps you from going into the Darkness. [11]Indeed, almsgiving, for all who practice it, is an excellent offering in the presence of the Most High. (NRSV)[26]

It is possible that Tobit's statement in verse 9, that in giving alms "you will be laying up a good treasure for yourself against the day of necessity," refers simply to security against future fiscal disaster (cf. Sir. 29:12-13).[27] Even the following assertion, that "almsgiving delivers from death and keeps

---

26. LXX Tob. 4:9 reads: θέμα γὰρ ἀγαθὸν θησαυρίζεις σεαυτῷ εἰς ἡμέραν ἀνάγκης. The noun θέμα is a cognate of θεμέλιος in 1 Tim. 6:19, and the cognate verbs θησαυρίζω (Tob. 4:9) and ἀποθησαυρίζω (1 Tim. 6:19) are similarly employed. Moreover, both texts describe the action taken using a dative reflexive pronoun (σεαυτῷ/ἑαυτοῖς) followed by the preposition εἰς with reference to a future event (εἰς ἡμέραν ἀνάγκης/εἰς τὸ μέλλον). An allusion to LXX Tob. 4:9 in 1 Tim. 6:19 cannot be ruled out.

27. So Carey A. Moore, *Tobit*, AB 40A (Garden City, NY: Doubleday, 1996), p. 168; cf. Joseph Fitzmyer, *Tobit*, Commentaries on Early Jewish Literature (Berlin: De Gruyter, 2003), pp. 170-71.

you from going into the Darkness," need not refer to the afterlife, since it might be implied that the practice of ἐλεημοσύνη literally saves from physical death.

Moreover, although pagan authors in Greco-Roman antiquity do not promote the practice of almsgiving with the same frequency as Jewish and Christian writers, a common topos in Greek and Roman moral discourse is the notion that, given the insecurity of wealth, sharing one's resources with those in need can lead to reciprocity in the future of this life.[28] In the same way, Paul advises the Corinthians that they ought to contribute to a relief fund for believers in Jerusalem because, although the Corinthians are presently experiencing an abundance when compared with the need of Jerusalem, at some point in the future the situations might be reversed, with the abundance of the saints in Jerusalem supplying the needs of the Corinthians (2 Cor. 8:13-14).[29] Thus, we should not automatically assume that a reference to "storing up a good foundation for the future" necessarily denotes an eschatological reward from God.

For three reasons, however, it seems unlikely that 1 Timothy 6:17-19 refers to a this-worldly return on one's generous sharing with the needy. First, the instruction is specifically directed to "the rich in the present age" (τοῖς πλουσίοις ἐν τῷ νῦν αἰῶνι) in verse 17, a phrase that frames the injunction in the context of an eschatological dualism (cf. Gal. 1:4; 2 Tim. 4:10; Titus 2:12). Second, given the overlap between the language of "storing up a good foundation for the future" in verse 19 and Gospel traditions that employ similar terminology with reference to the storing up of heavenly treasure (Matt. 6:19-20; 19:21; Luke 12:21, 33-34), it is likely that the phrase εἰς τὸ μέλλον in verse 19 refers to the eschatological future. Third, although I shall argue below that the phrase τῆς ὄντως ζωῆς is not the equivalent of "eternal life" (cf. 1 Tim. 6:12), the phrase does appear to designate an eschatological reward of some sort (see below). On balance, the traditional eschatological reading of 1 Timothy 6:17-19 is still to be preferred, and therefore the dynamic between human action and divine recompense merits consideration.

---

28. See Aristotle, *Rhet.* 2.5.1383a; Seneca, *Marc.* 9.1; Ovid, *Tr.* 5.8.4-18; Abraham Malherbe, "Godliness, Self-Sufficiency, Greed, and the Enjoyment of Wealth: 1 Timothy 6:3-19 Part II," *NovT* 53 (2011): 73-96, esp. 78-88.

29. On the need to interpret 2 Cor. 8:13-14 as a reference to an exchange of material resources (instead of the spiritual and material reciprocity discussed in Rom. 15:26-27), see Downs, *Offering*, pp. 137-39.

What Kind of Eschatological Reward?

In a few brief but pointed comments on 1 Timothy 6:19 in an article on almsgiving in patristic literature, Christopher Hays criticizes the strategy, cited above, of "simplistically" drawing a distinction between "'earning heaven'" and "'demonstrating' godliness." Hays's primary reason for this claim is his conviction that the purpose clause of verse 19b (ἵνα ἐπιλάβωνται τῆς ὄντως ζωῆς) "indicates a more robust relationship between the generosity and the attainment of eternal life." According to Hays, "This passage clearly indicates that munificence will somehow be directly beneficial for attaining eternal life."[30]

I would like to suggest, however, that neither Hays's perspective nor the one he opposes quite accurately captures the significance of the purpose clause in 1 Timothy 6:19b. On one hand, the common suggestion that the text is not about "earning" but "demonstrating" one's salvation does fail to adequately account for both the economic language of verse 19a and the syntax of the ἵνα clause in verse 19b. On the other hand, Hays's supposition that the construction ἵνα ἐπιλάβωνται τῆς ὄντως ζωῆς in 1 Timothy 6:19b denotes eternal life, with the stated implication that generosity will somehow bear on the attainment of eternal life, also misses the mark. In short, my argument is that 1 Timothy 6:19 indicates that those who are rich in the present age are able to accumulate heavenly treasure through the generous sharing of material resources in this life (v. 19a), and this heavenly treasure allows them to take hold of reward, not salvation, in the next life (v. 19b).

The section opens with an indication of the intended recipients of the instruction: "to the rich in the present age" (v. 17). It is difficult to know how exactly these believers should be plotted on a scale of economic stratification. Likely these members of the audience are not imperial or even civic elites but rather Christians of (relatively) moderate surplus resources whose lives are not marked by subsistence-level existence, but whose economic level does not reach the highest 1-3 percent of the population.[31] The

---

30. Christopher M. Hays, "By Almsgiving and Faith Sins Are Purged? The Theological Underpinnings of Early Christian Care for the Poor," in *Engaging Economics: New Testament Scenarios and Early Christian Reception,* ed. Bruce W. Longenecker and Kelly D. Liebengood (Grand Rapids: Eerdmans, 2009), p. 275. Hays also writes, "To imply that the only alternative to 'demonstrating' is 'earning' evinces a lack of theological reflection on the manner in which works could be involved in attaining eternal life" (p. 275).

31. I am drawing on the important article of Steven J. Friesen, "Poverty in Pauline Studies: Beyond the So-Called New Consensus," *JSNT* 26 (2004): 323-61. Friesen excludes the

content of the mandate that Timothy is told to communicate to believers of means is spelled out in two negative infinitive clauses in verse 17: the first, with a verb that Paul seems to have coined on his own, μὴ ὑψηλοφρονεῖν, instructs believers not to be haughty; the second, μηδὲ ἠλπικέναι, charges them not to hope in the uncertainty of wealth but in God, "who richly grants to us all things for enjoyment."

That earthly possessions should be employed "for [the purpose of] enjoyment" (εἰς ἀπόλαυσιν) is often linked to Paul's anti-ascetic affirmation earlier in the letter that "everything created by God is good, and nothing is to be rejected, if it is received with thanksgiving, for it is made holy by God's word and prayer" (1 Tim. 4:4-5), a statement motivated by the rejection of marriage and the demand for abstinence from certain foods by false teachers (1 Tim. 4:3).[32] In this sense, ἀπόλαυσις is realized not in self-indulgence or in greedy consumption but in the humble acknowledgment that God is the one who richly grants all things for the purpose of enjoyment.

Abraham Malherbe has recently offered an exegetical perspective that clarifies our understanding of the means by which the rich in this world realize their enjoyment of the wealth that God has richly supplied them. Malherbe suggests that, while the prepositional phrase εἰς ἀπόλαυσιν might be absolute because it is not followed by a genitive or accusative noun specifying the object of enjoyment, "it is possible to read ἀγαθοεργεῖν as in apposition to and epexegetic of εἰς ἀπόλαυσιν, πλουτεῖν as epexegetic of ἀγαθοεργεῖν, and εἶναι as epexegetic of ἀγαθοεργεῖν."[33] That is, a string of epexegetical infinitives describes *how* wealth is to be enjoyed by listing three actions through which enjoyment of wealth is manifested: by doing good, by being rich in good works, and by being generous and sharing. As Malherbe comments on the significance of this reading:

> What is striking is that the purpose for the gift of wealth is not the proper use of it, which is attended by enjoyment; rather, the purpose is enjoyment, which is explicated by the three infinitives that follow. Whatever the local circumstances, if there were any that were responsible for this inversion, the author wishes the benevolent use of one's

---

Pastoral Epistles from consideration in his discussion of economic stratification and the Pauline churches, however (but cf. p. 348 n. 79).

32. So, e.g., Marshall, *Pastoral,* p. 672; Towner, *Letters,* p. 426; Luke Timothy Johnson, *The First and Second Letters to Timothy: A New Translation with Introduction and Commentary,* AB 35A (New York: Doubleday, 2001), p. 310.

33. Malherbe, "Godliness," p. 89.

wealth to be an expression or means of enjoyment rather than, say, something done out of duty or compulsion. The enjoyment in view is not centered on the self but is other-directed. . . . The reason for enjoyment is that this is what God intends in providing richly. What is required is not reflection but action.[34]

One's true enjoyment of wealth is found in the employment of material resources to perform good works, most specifically through the generous and charitable disposal of wealth. This "hedonistic" liberality, moreover, allows those who practice benevolent sharing to "[store] up for themselves a good foundation for the future, so that they may take hold of the life that is truly life" (v. 19). It seems entirely appropriate to speak of "meritorious almsgiving" in 1 Timothy 6:19 in the sense that acts of mercy and distributions of material assistance have the potential to secure merit for donors.[35] Here the metaphor is mixed, combining the economic and/or agricultural imagery of "storing up" or "treasuring up" goods (ἀποθησαυρίζω) with the architectural image of laying the foundation (θεμέλιος) of an edifice.[36] To borrow language from the anthropological literature on gift-exchange, this is "interested" giving, in the sense that givers are encouraged to anticipate some return, even if the reciprocity comes from God in the form of heavenly reward and not from the human recipients of the assistance.[37]

As noted above, however, it is the purpose clause ἵνα ἐπιλάβωνται τῆς ὄντως ζωῆς at the end of verse 19 that has caused the most difficulties. In what sense are the rich in the present age encouraged to engage in meritorious almsgiving so that, as a result, they may take hold of the life that is truly life? On one hand, the common distinction between earning and demonstrating salvation disregards the syntax of the text, for it is clear, as Hays rightly points out, that saving up heavenly treasure is advocated *for the purpose of* taking hold of true life. On the other hand, Hays's conten-

---

34. Malherbe, "Godliness," pp. 91-92.

35. I prefer to distinguish between "meritorious almsgiving" and "redemptive almsgiving." The former focuses on alms as a means of accumulating reward; the latter focuses on alms as a means of redeeming (or cleansing or canceling) human sin.

36. Jerome D. Quinn and William C. Wacker present an interesting argument that the term θεμέλιος "has a double meaning of the base for a building and a deposit of money that produces interest" (*The First and Second Letters to Timothy: A New Translation with Notes and Commentary,* Eerdmans Critical Commentary [Grand Rapids and Cambridge: Eerdmans, 2000], pp. 555-56).

37. See, e.g., Jacques T. Godbout and Alain Caillé, *The World of the Gift,* trans. Donald Winkler (Montreal: McGill-Queen's University Press, 1998).

tion that the text "clearly indicates that munificence will somehow be directly beneficial for attaining eternal life" falls short because verse 19 does not, in fact, speak of "eternal life." The phrase used instead is "life that is truly life." Hays, along with many other interpreters, appears to conflate the phrase ἐπιλάβωνται τῆς ὄντως ζωῆς in verse 19 with the earlier charge to Timothy in verse 12: "Take hold of the eternal life to which you were called and about which you confessed the good confession before many witnesses."[38] The instructions are similar — not least because both feature the verb ἐπιλαμβάνομαι — but they are not *identical*. For one thing, the wording is different, and it is significant that Paul did not write ἵνα ἐπιλάβωνται τῆς αἰωνίου ζωῆς in verse 19. Moreover, "eternal life" in verse 12 is a reality that Timothy is instructed to grasp in the present, "a goal to be achieved here and now in this world and not just at the end of the contest."[39] In verse 19, however, both the notion that the rich store up for themselves a heavenly foundation *for the future* (εἰς τὸ μέλλον) and the aorist subjunctive ἐπιλάβωνται indicate that, whatever it is, "life that is truly life" is not possessed by the rich in the present. Everything about verse 19 suggests that the object of the verb ἐπιλαμβάνομαι is a prize to be seized in the future, and this differs markedly from the charge to Timothy in verse 12.

Life That Is Truly Life and Divine Judgment

Much rests, then, on the precise meaning of the phrase τῆς ὄντως ζωῆς, a term that does not find a precise parallel in biblical literature. A statement in Philo of Alexandria's *De congressu eruditionis gratia* may offer some assistance, however. In this treatise, Philo offers an extended allegorical meditation on Genesis 16:1-6 in order to bolster the belief (held by Stoics but rejected by Cynics and Epicureans) that an encyclical education (i.e., a liberal arts curriculum) was a necessary precursor to the study of philosophy.[40] In discussing an individual's sojourns into the lands of Egypt, which

38. See, e.g., Merkel, *Pastoralbriefe*, p. 52; Quinn and Wacker, *Timothy*, p. 556; Towner, *Letters*, p. 428.

39. Marshall, *Pastoral*, p. 660.

40. See Alan Mendelson, *Secular Education in Philo of Alexandria* (Cincinnati: Hebrew Union College Press, 1982). In Philo's allegorical interpretation, heaven-born men like Abraham must "enter into" Hagar, who represents encyclical education, before passing on to Sarah, who stands for virtue.

is the symbol of the passions and associated with childhood, and Canaan, which is the symbol of wickedness and associated with youth, Philo cites Leviticus 18:1-5, a passage in which God tells the Israelites not to follow the statutes of the Egyptians or the Canaanites but to obey instead the Lord's commandments, for "the one who does them shall live in them" (*Congr.* 86).[41] Philo then provides commentary on the text:

> So then true life [ἡ πρὸς ἀλήθειαν ζωή] is walking in the judgments and commandments of God, so that the practices of the godless must be death. And what the practices of the godless are we have been told. They are the practices of passions and evils, from which spring the many multitudes of the impious and the workers of unholiness. (*Congr.* 87)

Philo's interpretation of Leviticus 18:1-5 here has generated much discussion, not least because of the role that Leviticus 18 plays in the soteriology of several Old Testament and Second Temple Jewish texts, including the Pauline Epistles.[42] The key point for our purposes is Philo's presentation of his concept of "true life," which he defines here rather precisely by means of a predicate participle: "true life is walking in the judgments and commandments of God" (περιπατοῦντός ἐστιν ἐν ταῖς τοῦ θεοῦ κρίσεσι καὶ προστάξεσιν).

Philo employs the concept of "true life" in a variety of ways in his many writings. Sometimes the phrase "true life" is used in a Platonic sense to denote a person's rational soul (i.e., the incorporeal and animating aspect of a person that results from God's life-giving breath; *Leg.* 1.32, 35), sometimes it describes authentic spiritual life in contrast to destruction and death (*Leg.* 3.52; *Migr.* 21; *QG* 1.70; cf. *Her.* 201; *Leg.* 3.35), and sometimes it serves as a general reference to wise or virtuous existence (*Leg.* 2.93; *Mut.* 213; *Her.* 53; cf. *Virt.* 17; *Somn.* 2.64).[43] In *Congr.* 87 and elsewhere in Philo's corpus, however, the phrase "true life" designates the *reward* that one receives from God for virtuous behavior. For example, in *QG* 4.238 "true life" is the "prize" (ἆθλον) for Jacob's discipline, in contrast to the death that results for the

---

41. Translations of *De congressu* are modified from Philo, *On Mating with the Preliminary Studies*, in *Philo*, vol. 4, trans. F. H. Colson and G. H. Whitaker, LCL (Cambridge, MA: Harvard University Press, 1932).

42. See especially Preston M. Sprinkle, *Law and Life: The Interpretation of Leviticus 18:5 in Early Judaism and in Paul*, WUNT 2:241 (Tübingen: Mohr Siebeck, 2008), pp. 101-14.

43. On this diversity, see Dieter Zeller, "The Life and Death of the Soul in Philo of Alexandria: The Use and Origin of a Metaphor," *SPhilo* 7 (1995): 19-55.

wicked and evil person, and in *QG* 4.46 "true life" is a reward denied to those who seek "low and base and earthly things," for they die with respect to "true life." Similarly, in *Post.* 45 "true life" (τὴν ἀληθῆ ζωὴν) is the promised outcome for a good person, as opposed to the individual who follows the example of Cain and dies with respect to virtue. As Preston Sprinkle observes, "[T]hese three passages show that 'true life' is a reward for the virtuous soul while death is the recompense for the wicked soul."[44] This reward can take the form of eternal life (*Spec.* 1.345), but it can also simply reflect God's favorable judgment — either in the present or the future — of one's virtue, often in contrast to divine punishment of impious behavior (*Post.* 12, 45; *QG* 1.16; cf. *Mut.* 216; *Gig.* 14).[45] In *Congr.* 87, for instance, "true life" entails both obedience to God's commandments and also, significantly, walking in the "judgments" of God. Interestingly, in his gloss on the text of LXX Leviticus 18:1-5, Philo substitutes the word κρίσεις for κρίμα (i.e., LXX Leviticus 18:4: κρίματά μου ποιήσετε), perhaps suggesting more strongly than his source text the theme of God's active judgment of human virtue or wickedness.[46] True life, according to Philo, involves not only obedience to God's statutes but also the positive judgment of one's behavior by God.[47]

Without positing any sort of literary relationship, I would suggest Paul in 1 Timothy 6:19 utilizes the phrase "life that is truly life" (τῆς ὄντως ζωῆς) in a manner that parallels Philo's notion of "true life" as a reward for honorable action in *Congr.* 87, although certainly Paul does not locate this concept in an allegorical narrative of the virtuous soul's journey to God. In short, to "take hold of the life that is truly life" in 1 Timothy 6:19 is to live in light of

44. Sprinkle, *Law*, p. 112.

45. On the complex and sometimes inconsistent dynamic of reward and punishment in Philo's writings, see Alan Mendelson, "Philo's Dialectic of Reward and Punishment," *SPhilo* 9 (1997): 104-25.

46. For another example of Philo's interpretation of a scriptural text that more strongly emphasizes divine judgment than its biblical antecedent, compare Num. 25:1-18 and 31:1-18 with *Virt.* 45 (cf. *Virt.* 174). This interpretative strategy is not exactly common in Philo, however, and elsewhere Philo appears to distance God from active punishment of the wicked; see Mendelson, "Dialectic," pp. 106-23.

47. In spite of the fact that his analysis of the concept of "true life" in Philo is very helpful, the theme of divine judgment is muted in Sprinkle's interpretation of *Congr.* 87. While Sprinkle initially follows Colson in translating the phrase ἐν ταῖς τοῦ θεοῦ κρίσεσι καὶ προστάξεσιν as "in the judgments and commandments of God," his summary statement and later translations omit reference to divine judgment: e.g., "Philo considers the key feature in Lev. 18:5 to be the 'true life' that consists in *walking in the commandments* of God" (p. 106); "true life is walking in the *statutes* and *ordinances* of God" (p. 110 n. 48, emphasis added).

the judgments and commandments of God in the sense that, through their generosity, the rich store up for themselves a heavenly treasure for the future *so that*, at the eschatological judgment, they can take hold of the heavenly reward that will be given to those who have lived in light of God's future judgment and in obedience to God's commands. One advantage of this proposal is that it coheres with Eubank's suggestion that "the commandment" in 1 Timothy 6:14 refers to care for the needy. Enjoyment of wealth — which is demonstrated in doing good, performing good works, and generously sharing one's possessions — leads to the accumulation of heavenly treasure, and from these funds believers are able to "purchase" not salvation but "true life," that is, the reward given to those who have obeyed God's commands, especially, in this context, the command to give alms.

A second advantage is that this reading of the phrase τῆς ὄντως ζωῆς is entirely compatible with the Pauline notion that, while the salvation of those in Christ is determined solely by divine grace and not on the basis of human merit or action, believers should anticipate a future eschatological judgment according to deeds (Rom. 2:6-10; 1 Cor. 3:12-15; 4:4-5; 2 Cor. 5:10; 1 Tim. 5:24-25; 2 Tim. 4:6-8, 14).[48] It is not "eternal life" that one obtains with the heavenly treasure accrued on the basis of obedience to God's commands but rather the prize of God's affirmative judgment at the final assize. In the conclusion to his commentary on 1 Timothy 6:19, Calvin offers a helpful summary:

> So far are we from rendering full payment, that, if God should call us to strict account, there is not one of us who would not be a bankrupt. But, after having reconciled us to himself by free grace, he accepts our services, such as they are, and bestows on them a reward which is not due. This recompense, therefore, does not depend on considerations of merit, but on God's gracious acceptance, and is so far from being inconsistent with the righteousness of faith, that it may be viewed as an appendage to it.[49]

48. See Kent L. Yinger, *Paul, Judaism, and Judgment according to Deeds,* SNTSMS 105 (Cambridge: Cambridge University Press, 1999); Michael F. Bird, *The Saving Righteousness of God: Studies on Paul, Justification, and the New Perspective* (Milton Keynes, UK: Paternoster, 2007), pp. 155-78; Kyoung-Shik Kim, *God Will Judge Each One according to Works: Judgment according to Works and Psalm 62 in Early Judaism and the New Testament,* BZNW 178 (Berlin: De Gruyter, 2010).

49. John Calvin, *Commentaries on the Epistles to Timothy, Titus, and Philemon,* trans. William Pringle (Grand Rapids: Eerdmans, 1948), pp. 172-73.

Because Calvin recognizes that 1 Timothy 6:19b promises a reward for good works, he does not force upon the text an artificial distinction between "earning" and "demonstrating" one's salvation. Yet Calvin also perceptively, if briefly, captures the complex dynamic of divine and human action at work in the economic exchange described in 1 Timothy 6. If 1 Timothy 6 does promote meritorious almsgiving in the sense that the rich in the present age are able to obtain future heavenly treasure through the generous sharing of material resources in the present (vv. 17-19), this exchange of possessions for heavenly reward must be located in a larger literary and theological context in which Paul insists that all things come from God.

Meritorious Almsgiving and the Divine Economy

Indeed, it is possible to unpack Calvin's theological interpretation with slightly more attention to the literary context of 1 Timothy 6:17-19. I have suggested that 1 Timothy 6:6-19 is a unified section on the proper employment of wealth and possessions. It is notable, therefore, that this discourse on wealth is also densely theocentric, prominently highlighting the character and action of God throughout.

First, the charge to Timothy in 6:11-14 emphasizes Timothy's service to God (v. 11), calling by God (v. 12), and God's dynamic identity as the one "who gives life to all things" (v. 13). The last of these three statements stresses God's role "as the creator of life and sustainer of the universe," a cosmological affirmation that anticipates the doxology in verses 15b-16.[50] Second, the doxological material that punctuates the charge to Timothy clearly echoes the exalted description of God earlier in the letter:

> 1:17: To the King of the ages, immortal, invisible, the only God, be honor and glory forever and ever. Amen.

> 6:15b-16: He who is the blessed and only Sovereign, the King of kings and the Lord of lords, who alone has immortality, who dwells in unapproachable light, whom no human has seen or is able to see; to him be honor and might forever. Amen.

These emphatic confessions of God's uniqueness, sovereignty, immortality, and glory at the beginning and end of 1 Timothy provide a properly

---

50. Towner, *Letters,* p. 413.

theological frame for the entire epistle.[51] Moreover, the doxology also grounds the teaching on wealth in the recognition of God's absolute authority and, significantly, in the *practice* of worship. That is, I understand the doxological section to represent not merely discourse *about God* but active worship and praise *of God,* a reminder that human reflection about the appropriate use of possessions is rightly understood as a liturgical activity, focused on the immortal and only God.[52] Third, and finally, the specific instruction to the rich in verses 17-19 begins with the pointed teaching that they should not place their hope in the uncertainty of wealth, but in God, "who richly grants to us all things for enjoyment" (v. 17). As in verse 13, where God is said to give life to "all things," here, too, God is declared to be the one who gives believers "all things richly" (πάντα πλουσίως). God is both the only suitable object of human hope and the one who lavishes "all things" upon those who place their trust in him.

As Calvin rightly intuited, the motif of God's creating, redeeming, and sustaining action in 1 Timothy 6:6-19 must be appreciated in order to obtain a properly theological perspective on the topic of human beneficence. With respect to the issue of meritorious almsgiving in 1 Timothy 6:17-19 in particular, those who secure the treasure of a good foundation in order to take hold of life that truly is life do so with funds they have already received from God, for all that they are and all that they have to share comes from God. Thus, even the human action of meritorious almsgiving is located in a larger divine economy in which God is proclaimed to be the source and provider of all things.

51. So Greg A. Couser, "God and Christian Existence in the Pastoral Epistles: Toward *Theo*logical Method and Meaning," *NovT* 42 (2000): 262-83; Vasile Mihoc, "The Final Admonition to Timothy (1 Tim 6,3-21)," in *1 Timothy Reconsidered,* ed. Karl P. Donfried, Colloquium Oecumenicum Paulinum 18 (Leuven: Peeters, 2008), pp. 135-52.

52. For this notion in Paul's comments about the Jerusalem collection, see Downs, *Offering,* pp. 120-60.

Jesus Christ, the End of the Law

Katherine Sonderegger

In a dissertation at once provocative and consoling, the German theologian Friedrich-Wilhelm Marquardt famously declared Barth's *Church Dogmatics* to be the "discovery of Judaism for Christian theology."[1] Marquardt — who later went on to provoke yet more people with his claim that Barth was a radical Marxist — focused in his dissertation on Barth's epic treatment of election in volume II/2. But I think we might well extend Marquardt's observation to Barth's christology more broadly. Barth's christology *is* the "discovery of Judaism for Christian theology," for it is in the life, death, and rising of this One Son of Israel that Barth's attention to the covenant people Israel is anchored and driven forward. As Barth puts this with characteristic boldness:

[T]here is one thing which we must emphasise especially. It is often overlooked in this context. It is not taken seriously or seriously enough.

1. Friedrich-Wilhelm Marquardt, *Die Entdeckung des Judentums für die christliche Theologie: Israel im Denken Karl Barths* (Munich: Kaiser Verlag, 1967); issued also as a dissertation (Berlin: Kirchlich Hochschule, 1966).

As readers familiar with Beverly Gaventa's exemplary and rich scholarship already know, the subject matter of this essay touches on several themes central to her work: the place of doctrine within the work of exegesis; the scriptural roots of the church's christology; the irreducible Jewishness of Jesus; and the sustained biblical theology of Karl Barth. Two works of Gaventa's I have found formative to my own thinking in this essay are her path-breaking essays in Beverly Roberts Gaventa and Richard B. Hays, eds., *Seeking the Identity of Jesus: A Pilgrimage* (Grand Rapids: Eerdmans, 2008) and the splendid *The Acts of the Apostles,* ANTC (Nashville: Abingdon, 2003). I am honored to be included in this collection in honor of Professor Gaventa; she is an honor to biblical theology and to the church.

Yet from this one thing everything else, and particularly what we have just stressed, acquires its contour and colour, its definiteness and necessity. The Word did not simply become any "flesh," any man humbled and suffering. It became Jewish flesh. The Church's whole doctrine of the incarnation and the atonement becomes abstract and valueless and meaningless to the extent that this comes to be regarded as something accidental and incidental. The New Testament witness to Jesus the Christ, the Son of God, stands on the soil of the Old Testament and cannot be separated from it. The pronouncements of New Testament Christology may have been shaped by a very non-Jewish environment. But they relate always to a man who is seen to be not a man in general, a neutral man, but the conclusion and sum of the history of God with the people of Israel, the One who fulfils the covenant made by God with this people. (*CD* IV/1, §59.1; ET: p. 166)

Now, to join christology to a renewed and restored relation to Judaism, as Barth does here, is to make the sort of counterintuitive claim that Barth himself — but not many others — often favored.

It is counterintuitive because christology, as Rosemary Radford Ruether said a generation ago, seems to be the root cause of all the troubles and terrors between Christians and Jews, Christianity and Judaism. Much work in the Christian theological reappraisal of Judaism, from Ruether to Paul van Buren, has dedicated itself to a reformulation of christology that would extract from its pith the sting of "absoluteness," of "realized eschatology," and thereby, they say, of anti-Judaism. Christology, it is often said, must be reconceived to ward off the central Christian "teaching of contempt" toward Judaism: that the church replaces — supersedes — Israel or Jews as the elect people of God. To find in christology, then, not the problem but rather the *promise* of a renewed place for Judaism within Christian theology is startling and, certainly, contrary to expectation. But it is just this provocative thesis Marquardt defends; and I believe he is right to do so.

Christology is the sum of the gospel; it is the power of God for salvation to everyone who has faith, to the Jew first and also to the Greek. But to say just how this is so is no small endeavor; it consumed Marquardt's whole dissertation and the Apostle Paul's whole Letter to the Romans. And, I should say, in a more personal confession, that I believe that seeking and setting out just how christology can be *good news* for Jews, as well as Greeks, after the tragic and terrible sins Christians have committed against

Jews and Judaism, is a task worthy of a whole life. It is, I believe, a chastening, and judging, and directing gift of the Spirit to the church in our day that we Christians should begin the repentance and renewal that awakens us to the people Israel and their unshakeable place in the covenant love of God. A reconsideration of Barth's christology in light of the irrevocable covenant between God and the people Israel is one small step, I hope, in this pilgrimage of repentance that the Spirit lays upon us this day.

For Barth, this theme of Christian repentance hardly surfaces explicitly in his christology proper, although he spoke out early against Nazi anti-Semitism and the terrible German-Christian "dream" of a Christianity without Jews. But Barth *does* devote himself explicitly to the *locus* of covenant in his doctrine of reconciliation, and he is decidedly firm in his rejection there of a broken or abandoned pact with Israel. Christology as the promise — no, the victory — of reconciliation between God and sinner, Barth says, centers on the one, true covenant between God and Israel, faithfully sustained and kept by God and sealed by the blood of Jesus Christ, the rejected and true king of Israel. Covenant shapes Barth's christology as a crystal structures precious metal: firm, multifaceted, brilliant. It is here we must turn to learn just how Barth's christology is a "discovery of Judaism" for the church.

It is no simple act to treat Karl Barth's christology, of course. To summarize it is to sum up the *Church Dogmatics* as a whole and, even more, the gospel of God's astonishing grace itself. But I think we might well dwell on a particular aspect of Barth's covenant christology that speaks for the whole: Jesus Christ as the *fulfillment* of the covenant.[2] Barth does not merely make use of covenant to give formal shape to his doctrine; although he does do this. Rather, Barth holds that Jesus Christ upholds the one covenant with Israel in such a radical, complete, and, in just this way, traditional form, that this ancient covenant is now fulfilled — brought to its goal — in him. The theme of covenant fulfilled is sounded at the head of Barth's massive treatment of reconciliation in the fourth volume of the *Church Dogmatics;* it sets the framework for all that follows. Indeed, in a famous aside, Eberhard Busch reports that Barth intended at first to title his christology as a whole, the doctrine of the covenant. Such a title promises a rich "discovery of Judaism for Christian theology." As I will develop a

---

2. We can see this theme echoed in Gaventa's overarching interpretation of the Acts of the Apostles: "Much of the characterization of Jesus in Acts concerns Jesus as the fulfillment of Israel's hopes" (*Acts,* p. 31).

bit later on, this discovery is not without its cost; but I want to begin, as is fitting for such a remarkable christology, with its real achievements for our topic today, the relation of Barth's dogmatic theology to Judaism.

Here is Barth on the *locus* of covenant:

> Jesus Christ is God, God as man, and therefore "God with us" [humanity], God in the work of reconciliation. But reconciliation is the fulfillment of the covenant between God and [humanity]. "Reconciliation" is the restitution, the resumption of a fellowship which once existed but was then threatened by dissolution. It is the maintaining, restoring and upholding of that fellowship in face of an element which disturbs and disrupts and breaks it. It is the realisation of the original purpose which underlay and controlled it in defiance and by the removal of this obstruction. The fellowship which originally existed between God and [humanity], which was then disturbed and jeopardised, the purpose of which is now fulfilled in Jesus Christ and in the work of reconciliation, we describe as the covenant. (*CD* IV/1, §57.2; ET: p. 22)

Now, as in all of the summary paragraphs in the *Church Dogmatics,* Barth digs deep in a compressed and compact space. We leave to one side for our purposes the pregnant phrase Barth uses to head this paragraph, Jesus Christ is God, *God as man;* a whole christology lies dormant there. But we focus now on the delicate relationship Barth sketches out between reconciliation and covenant. These two are not identical, Barth tells us; rather, reconciliation is perfect enactment or *fulfillment* of covenant. Central to Barth's christology is the notion that reconciliation — atonement, *Versöhnung* — rests upon a prior relationship God has established from the beginning with his creatures. This relationship, Barth insists, is the *presupposition* of atonement. Barth does not need to give a historical or temporal account of the relation between covenant and reconciliation, as do the older dogmaticians in their doctrines of Adam in his integrity, followed by Adam in the fallen state. Rather, Barth sets up a logical or conceptual relation between the two. Much as creation itself is the "outer basis" of covenant, and covenant the "inner basis" of creation, Barth knits together covenant and reconciliation as unity in distinction, an ordered and inseparable relation.

Barth also dispenses with the awkward worry that in the atonement God must change course, repent of an old direction, and repair a work somehow imperfect in its creation. We do not have in the doctrine of

Christ's saving work, Barth tells us, a *novum,* an utterly new work, shattering the structure and integrity of God's way with the world. Rather, Christ reconciles and saves through *realizing* a structure already ingredient in the relation of Creator and creature: he *fulfills* the covenant. In Barth's doctrine of God, then, a primordial decision underlies the incarnation: God wills to be "with us," to be Immanuel. So central is this decision to Barth's christology — a position associated with the medieval scholastic Duns Scotus — that Barth heads the fourth volume of the *Church Dogmatics* with this phrase, "God with us." There are dangers in this position — Barth is not averse to taking risks in theology, even grave ones — but there are also strengths. One strength vital to our topic is the priority such a relation between covenant and reconciliation gives to the pact between God and Israel, a pact that cannot be discarded by Christ's saving work but is rather honored, preserved, and restored by him.

Barth sums up this saving work in this way in the paragraph quoted above: reconciliation is the restitution, resumption, maintaining, restoring, upholding, and realizing of the original fellowship between God and humanity, the covenant. Note this string of participles! Barth tips his hand here on a reading of the covenant and of christology itself — the pact between God and humanity as *event* — that will occupy our attention at some length in a moment. But more to the point here, Barth, by these verb forms, shows us that Christ's personal work in reconciliation cannot be contained in a single act. Much more rests on this point than is sometimes imagined. It *is* true, as Eberhard Busch says, that Barth's christology in the fourth volume of the *Church Dogmatics* reworks the traditional motif of the *munus triplex,* the threefold office of the mediator, announced in Thomas's *Summa* but developed most fully by John Calvin in the *Institutes* and by the later Reformed scholastics. Barth's assumption and adaptation of this framework for christology give to his doctrine of reconciliation a variegated and rich content, exemplified in part by his elaboration of the atonement first as justice, then as ransom, then as sacrifice — the work of a king, a prophet, and a priest.[3]

Even more important than this, I believe, is Barth's insistence that Christ's astonishing and gracious work cannot be exhausted in *concepts.* Christ does not undertake and perfect a work on our behalf that can be identified with and summed up by a single notion. To put this in another,

---

3. Note the fine-grained handling of this Reformed motif in Gaventa's essay, "Learning and Relearning the Identity of Jesus from Luke-Acts," in *Identity,* pp. 148-65, esp. pp. 155-59.

perhaps more felicitous way: Christ does not just happen to be the one who carries out the one thing needful — as though the *act* were the important and essential element. No, Christ *himself,* his person, his life, his divine-human reality *is* the covenant fulfilled, the atonement, the reconciliation of a lost and sinful world. Barth signals this by his refusal to fully separate Christ's person and work. He elaborates it more daringly in the claim that christology is an *event,* a *history,* as Barth puts it in volume IV/2, or more conceptually, in volume IV/1, where he affirms that, since the "atonement is an act of divine sovereignty, we are forbidden to try to deduce it from anything else or to deduce anything else from it" (*CD* IV/1, §58.1; ET: p. 80). The atonement is a personal act, and a personal life; it is a name, the name of Jesus Christ. Just as a human life cannot be reduced to a single act or even less to a concept, so Jesus Christ cannot be simply a means to the end of atonement. Just so; but how much more! His work in fulfilling God's pact with Israel is manifold, and ultimately, inexhaustible, just as his divine person is infinitely rich, manifold, and perfect.

The atonement is a divine work, then: an upholding, sustaining, restoring, renewing, and realizing of the divine will to be with us, to be our atoner as Jesus Christ, the reconciler. In this divine person and work, the original covenant with Israel and, through it, to the whole world, is given its perfect and final form in Jesus Christ himself. He, this one son of Israel, is the *fulfillment* of the covenant. Now, this christological reality and act doubles back and sheds light on the nature of the covenant itself; it is here that we see the benefit, but also the cost, of Barth's "discovery of Judaism for Christian theology." Let us begin with the covenant itself.

Barth is surprisingly broad in his account of Israel's covenant with God. Although he will spend much of section 57 on the Protestant scholastics — Johannes Coccejus in particular — Barth displays his wide reading in the biblical theologians of his day by the attention he pays to the varying historical forms of covenant in Israel's history. Unlike some scholastics and many anti-Judaic Christian theologians, Barth knows that Israel's covenant includes and extends toward the world as a whole. Giving a nod toward the historical work on suzerain treaties in the Ancient Near East, Barth recognizes that Israel's pact with God does not rest on a full mutuality or equality of the partners — a *foedus dipleuron,* in scholastic terms — but rather on the Almighty Lord's free condescension to his creatures. The covenant is already an act of grace, and not a "covenant of works" or, even less, a covenant of "works righteousness." This gracious *pactum* begins with Israel and extends to embrace the whole created world. Barth knows, too, of the Noachide covenant, the covenant God declares between himself and Noah and every living thing, and Barth recognizes that this is not a piece of "natural theology" but rather an element of Israel's own history with God. Just as the covenant itself looks back to creation as its own proper starting point, so the covenant treaty with Israel begins with the promise to Noah that all living things upon the earth will never be swept away again by the waters of God's righteous wrath.

Barth knows as well that Israel's covenant includes *within* it and not beyond or against it a pact that encompasses the Gentiles, the nations of the earth. We might well pause a moment to take note of the significance of Barth's insight here, arrayed against the dominant forms of Protestant biblical theology of the day. Barth will have nothing of the favored Christian notion of "universality" by which Christians plumed themselves against a "nationalistic" or "carnal" Israel. Though he does not make this explicit, Barth quietly rejects the pattern set up by Hegel and Schleiermacher in which a limited, particular, and narrow Israelite preoccupation with its own kith and kin is replaced — *superseded* — by a broad, universal, and expansive Christian world community. Drawing together a catena of witnesses from Isaiah, Barth underscores the final destiny of the people Israel, to be a "light to the nations"; *that* is the "glory of the people Israel." Indeed, Barth is so intent on setting aside the old anti-Judaic pattern of Israel's darkness against the Christian light, that he *incorporates* the Suffering Servant songs *within* the prophetic covenant of Israel with all nations. These Isaianic prophecies, long a staple of the christological reading of the Old Testament, do not function for Barth, as they do for others, as a promise that God's redeeming work will in the fullness of time burst the borders of exclusivity to inaugurate a fresh reign of universalism. Rather, the Servant of God, painted in such somber hues within the book of Isaiah, demonstrates, Barth says, the universal reach of *Israel itself.* It is this people and its king or regent that hold the promise for the Gentiles: they will be reconciled by and engrafted into the one covenant with Israel, fulfilled in Jesus Christ.

Finally, Barth knows, as his contemporaries often did not, that Israel's covenant with God was a matter of the heart, and not just of deeds or outward acts. It was a staple of Christian anti-Judaism to assume Israel imagined that it could please almighty God through something these Christians called "externalism" or, in older sources, "carnal works." The Matthean woes against the Pharisees were effortlessly imported back into the Israelite covenant itself, so that ancient Israel focused its eyes on material forms of the divine promises — land, riches, and healthy families — and carried out its covenant duties by physical acts of observance — festivals, food rituals, circumcision, sacrifice. The prophetic denunciation of Israel's cultus — strongly overplayed in much nineteenth-century Protestant theology and set rigorously against the temple worship — was cited as a sign that the church would finally emerge as the true successors to the prophets and the true inheritors of the proper, spiritual, and inward worship of almighty God. Barth, for all the truly terrible things he can allow himself to say about ancient Israel and, even more, postbiblical Judaism, does not countenance such distortions of Israel's sacred pact. Rather, Barth carefully examines the witness of the prophets Ezekiel and Jeremiah, especially the famous prophecy in Jeremiah 31, and notes that the inwardness of Israel's covenant — God's words written on the heart, God's presence and recognition to all Israel, from the greatest to the least — is a form or "economy" of the one, true covenant of Israel's God with his people Israel. This covenant is not cast away or rejected or replaced by a "new and eternal covenant," an old, outer "covenant of works" replaced with a new, sublime "covenant of grace." No, as Barth says, "What happens to this covenant with the conclusion of a new and eternal covenant is rather — and the wider context of the passage points generally in this direction — that it is upheld, that is, lifted up to its true level, that it is given its proper form, and that far from being destroyed it is maintained and confirmed" (*CD* IV/1, §57.2; ET: p. 32).

In sum, Barth holds that there is a *single* covenant between God and humanity, a pact begun, then maintained, and fulfilled, between the God of Israel and his people. "I shall be your God; and you shall be my people" — that classic scriptural declaration of covenant is never set aside, broken, or repudiated. Rather, this declaration of grace from Creator to creature belongs from the beginning and *remains* until the end of days, Israel's own identity, promise, and glory. Even the one Son of Man, when he comes to do his Father's will, can only observe, restore, and complete this one covenant with the people Israel. He was, and because of the covenant, *must* be "Jewish flesh." And, although the history of the church is the tragedy of a Gentile mission indifferent to and distinct from Israel, the one covenant with Israel and the Jews remains intact, exclusively and permanently upheld as God's lordly grace to the world he has made. These are the foundation stones of Barth's "discovery of Judaism for Christian theology," and they constitute a permanent and, I believe, irreversible achievement for proper Christian dogmatics. But they come at a cost, a very high cost indeed.

We begin with a signature theme of Barth's dogmatic work: the covenant as *event* or *history*. Barth writes: "The covenant remains — and it is in this way and only in this way that it does remain — the event of a divine and human choice, just as God Himself *exists* to the very depths of His being, and is therefore a (personally) living, active, acting and speaking God, and just as His human partner, His Israel, is actual only in its history, in the doing of its good and evil deeds, in the acting and suffering of the [people] who compose it" (*CD* IV/1, §57.2; ET: p. 23). From this programmatic statement, Barth draws the conclusion that "there is no single and definitive narration of the original conclusion of this covenant" (*CD* IV/1, §57.2; ET: p. 23). He lists the various biblical *loci* that are customarily cited as covenant ceremonies, ratifying and sealing the divine-human *pactum,* ranging from Genesis, through Exodus and Joshua, to Kings and Nehemiah. None of these can be in fact what they are purported, *prima facie,* to be: records of the final acceptance and specification of the covenant between God and Israel. Now, it is rare that Barth allows formal and methodological considerations to shape and terminate a biblical debate, but he does so here, I believe. So strong and deep is his conviction that *history* is the proper category for divine and human being, that he allows the variegated nature of the scriptural witness to count *against* the reality and plain truth of its subject matter. These cannot be covenant ratification ceremonies because there are too many of them told in Scripture; this seems to be the rough and ready argument at work here. It does not carry much force, it seems to me, and comports rather poorly with his confidence, throughout the *Church Dogmatics,* that the sheer variety of scriptural testimony underscores its reliability and significance for Christian belief. Barth underscores his commitment to this actualist view of the covenant, however, by his own reading of the federal theologian, Johannes Coccejus.

Here is the famous verdict Barth passes on Coccejus: "The Federal theology was an advance on mediaeval Scholasticism, and the Protestant Scholasticism which preceded and surrounded it, in that (true to the century of the *baroque*) it tried to understand the work and Word of God attested in Holy Scripture dynamically and not statically, as an event and not as a system of objective and self-contained truths. When we read Coccejus — even as compared with Polan, Wolleb, and the Leidner Synopsis — we cannot escape the impression that the traditional dogmatics had started to move like a frozen stream of lava" (*CD* IV/1, §57.2; ET: p. 55). It really is a wonderful image! And it is followed up by a characteristically close and shrewd reading of Coccejus himself and the unwitting anticipations he and his school made of Enlightenment attacks on biblical and dogmatic confession. After all his detailed criticisms, however, the impression Barth leaves on the reader is that in Coccejus he has finally found a theologian "after his own heart." Here at last is a dogmatician who recognizes and takes with full seriousness that "Christian doctrine is a description of this movement . . . a history of God and [humanity] which unfolds itself from creation to the day of judgment" (*CD* IV/1, §57.2; ET: p. 55). The covenant is the name for this movement; and as such no ceremony or ritual or conclusion can stem its mighty, downward rush to history's end.

Now all this dynamism makes for exciting theology — I love Barth precisely for this! — but we have to note just what an actualist account of the covenant excludes: the giving of the law. It is striking and unmistakable that Barth's long and careful treatment of the covenant with Israel in volume IV/1 of the *Church Dogmatics* says almost nothing about Israel's law, the Torah of God. Indeed, the *Church Dogmatics* as a whole says remarkably little about law itself.[4] Even in Barth's account of the earthly Jesus, the Royal Man, there is little about Christ's teaching and observing and ratifying of Israel's law, despite Barth's obvious admiration for Bonhoeffer's repudiation of "cheap grace." There is much about "divine command," much about divine instruction and direction, much about Jesus' obedience to God's will, and much about the famous, living voice of God, the *Deus dixit*. And all these of course are *in the neighborhood* of Israel's Torah; but they are self-consciously event-oriented, dynamic versions of what Israel and Jews of all ages call the ordinances, statutes, and precepts of the divine covenant with his people.

But there is, for Israel and for Judaism, no covenant without the law. It is in the ratification ceremonies — the sealing of the covenant by the Lord's people — that the law is solemnly read and the people give their solemn assent. Deuteronomy — literally, the Second Law — retells the giving of the law at Sinai, Mount Horeb, and the reinterpretation of covenant law

---

4. This lacuna in Barth's christology seems to echo a pattern present already in Luke's Gospel, itself a strong influence on Barth's reading of the passion. Gaventa deftly sums this up — and much else in the freighted matter of anti-Judaism in the New Testament — this way: "Jesus himself cannot be understood apart from Israel's history. That connection between God and Israel does not necessarily signal a uniform endorsement of Jewish law, about which Luke's view is not exactly determined. . . . Th[e] pattern [of law observance in Acts] scarcely constitutes a ringing endorsement of the law; instead, the treatment of the law appears to serve other concerns. . . . In other words, the law in and of itself does not seem to be a central Lukan concern" (*Acts*, p. 46).

given there. The history of Israel, as of old and so now, is the recounting of this people's seeking to do the Lord's will; to follow in his paths; to meditate on his law, day and night; to honor his precepts, ordinances, and statutes; and to bind them before their eyes and write them on their hearts. It is in light of the whole Torah given and read out to the people that Moses declares in a solemn oath:

> I call heaven and earth to witness against you today that I have set before you life and death, blessings and curses. Choose life so that you and your descendants may live, loving the LORD your God, obeying him, and holding fast to him; for that means life to you and length of days, so that you may live in the land that the LORD swore to give to your ancestors, to Abraham, to Isaac and to Jacob. (Deut. 30:19-20)[5]

Without the ratification ceremonies, the sacred covenant between the LORD and Israel is reduced to the history of the obedience — and disobedience — of the people to its God: a living obedience and walking in his ways, to be sure, but a path without the markers, the record, the treaty law itself to guide, define, and sanctify this people for God's very own. And Israel without the law is not the Israel honored, remembered, and sustained by Jews and Judaism to this day, nor, I would say, the Israel Jesus Christ himself came to shepherd, obey, and fulfill in his own covenant righteousness. When Israel studies and loves the law, we Christians say, it takes up, possesses, and cherishes Jesus Christ himself, Jesus in his "objectivity" to the people Israel. For Christ was and is a *bar mitzvah*, a son of the commandment, or in the Apostle Paul's words, Christ is the τέλος νόμου, the goal and perfection of the law (Rom. 10:4).

I now turn to Barth's christology for a moment to flesh out the consequences, as I see them, of this marginalization of the Torah from Israel's covenant history. It is the very great achievement of Barth's section 59, "The Way of the Son of God into the Far Country," that the deity of Christ is strongly affirmed and anchored firmly in the humble obedience of this one Servant of the LORD. No one who has read even a syllable of Barth needs telling that the scope, innovation, mastery, and sublimity of Barth's christology in this volume are unmatched in modern theology; indeed few rival Barth's christology in the tradition as a whole. We would hardly be reading the same text were we to bring up quarrels and worries about

---

5. All of this essay's biblical quotations come from the NRSV.

Barth's treatment without pausing to admire and praise it in this way. Jesus Christ is LORD here, truly LORD. And the grace and victory that are his are honored, explored, and sustained throughout the *Church Dogmatics* and especially so here. But the quarrels and worries remain.

Throughout *Church Dogmatics* IV/1, Barth speaks of Jesus Christ as the "obedient One." He it is who comes to do the Father's will; he it is who suffers temptation and trial in this road of obedience; he it is who remains faithful while all betray and desert him; he it is who drinks the final cup, who goes his lonely way to the cross, an obedience unto death, even a death of curse and shame. He fulfills the covenant in just this way, by setting his face like flint toward Jerusalem, by setting out this *via crucis* directly in front of him and his disciples, and against all fears of the flesh — his own sinful, Adamic flesh — to hear his Father's voice and serve only him. This is the obedience without idolatry, without false neutrality or freedom over against God, without holding back or "making up his own mind," but rather with joyful, glad, ready willingness to walk before the LORD, to serve his covenant people, to bind up and heal and drive Satan far away, and to make their sin his own, to bear it for them and bear it away. This is the life history, the event of Jesus Christ, and in him the covenant as event is met, the "circle closed," as Barth puts it, and the atonement made, truly and perfectly made, for the sins of the whole world. This, for Barth, is the sum of christology, the sum of the gospel.

Once again, it is striking that this Son of the covenant, in Barth's treatment, rarely obeys specific and particular commandments, precepts, or ordinances of the divine law. Barth is wary even of finding in the Matthean giving and interpreting of the law — the Sermon on the Mount most notably — a specific guideline for Christian life and practice. There are "general lines," Barth says, "patterns" or indications that "cut through" the whole Gospel testimony; but we should not see in the Sermon on the Mount or other torah-like passages of Scripture a given commandment and rule that Christians must follow and endorse. Barth of course knows of the traditional doctrine that Christ merited his own justification through his perfect following of the law. He knows, too, and respects, the traditional Reformed emphasis upon the *tertius usus legis,* the third use of law, which guides Christians in their call to a holy life. Yet, Barth since the early days of his Romans commentary feared those structures, capacities, norms, and deposits he called "the given." Always the giver must be master over the gift.

Revelation can never become the "possession," he would say, of the recipient. This, in very short compass, is the famous problem of "objectivity" in Barth's thought, and it casts a long shadow over the whole *Church Dogmatics*. Now I will not pretend here to have said everything that should be said, and with the proper care, about this notoriously prickly subject in Barth studies. But I do think that while Barth recovered over the course of the *Church Dogmatics* a more proper sense for theological objectivity — particularly for the gracious and unsurpassed gift of God's becoming object to us and our thought — he nevertheless objected throughout his career, sometimes strenuously, to the notion that God's reality and speech could become document or statute or created grace or order of creation. To all these dangers Barth sounded the warning of the "static," the "lifeless and abstract," and the rigid and "frozen" repristination of doctrine. Again, I find in Barth's dynamic liberty and openness a congenial and persuasive account of Christian life before God. But it runs strongly counter to the Torah of Israel, a gift given on Sinai. And it runs counter to the portrait of Jesus Christ as the faithful observant Son and interpreter of this very particular, very concrete and specific torah.

Two consequences flow directly from Barth's insistence upon obedience "apart from the Law," to borrow Paul's language here: one, in the reading of Israel's history, and the other, in Christ's own atoning work. The first follows the pattern we observed with the formal decision to make covenant the presupposition to the atonement, and the atonement the fulfillment of the one covenant. Christology will follow the formal pattern of covenant but will also shape and shed light back on covenant. In our topic in view here — the free obedience of the Son of God to the living voice of the Father — we can see an ominous light cast back by these doctrinal decisions upon the history of the people Israel. Christ's obedience as fulfillment of covenant exposes and confirms the history of the people Israel as one of *disobedience*. Barth's treatment of the atonement in volume IV/1, and not merely the shocking caricature of "the Synagogue" in volume II/2, bristles with a portrait of Israel I can only call "Stephen-like."

In the Acts of the Apostles, the evangelist sets the stage for the great drama of the church as a Gentile mission under Paul by giving several programmatic addresses to early church leaders. Striking among these is the testimony given by the first Christian martyr, Stephen. Saint Luke shows his hand at sound historical portraiture by the careful way he distinguishes the speeches of Peter, which dominate the opening chapters of the book, from Stephen's, a prelude to his martyrdom. Stephen catalogues with merciless detail the idolatry and disobedience of Israel: the patriarchs abused

Joseph, fellow slaves taunted Moses, the wandering Israelites rejected him, they committed idolatry with the golden calf and Aaron's conniving, and Solomon built a house for the LORD who does not in truth dwell in houses made by human hands. Not enough in this catalogue to satisfy Stephen's drive to lay out Israel's sins before the people, he concludes with these famous and terrible words:

> You stiff-necked people, uncircumcised in heart and ears, you are forever opposing the Holy Spirit, just as your ancestors used to do. Which of the prophets did your ancestors not persecute? They killed those who foretold the coming of the Righteous One, and now you have become his betrayers and murderers. You are the ones that received the law as ordained by angels [perhaps we hear an echo of Paul's angry dismissing of the Law in Galatians; see Gal. 3:19], and yet you have not kept it. (Acts 7:51-53)

Little wonder that "[w]hen they heard these things, they became enraged and ground their teeth at Stephen" (Acts 7:54). Unlike the thousands of newly baptized who joined the Way after Peter and John spoke, only stoning followed Stephen's address — a stoning and an approval by the young, zealous Saul.[6]

Now, Barth *does* catalogue a terrible list of sins and disobedience and idolatry and self-will in the history of this covenant people Israel; his analysis in section 60.2, "The Pride of Man," of the Golden Calf, of the kingships of Saul and Ahab and the punishment of the prophet Jeremiah, is somber reading indeed. But I should hasten to add that Barth here aims to treat *sin* itself — little wonder the catalogue is a dark string of disloyalties and failure — and, even more, to use this biblical exegesis in service of his larger, more fundamental claim, that all humanity, all our wayward sinfulness, pride, and self-deception, are laid bare and summed up in the history

---

6. Gaventa devotes several careful pages to this somber address of Stephen's (see *Acts*, pp. 116-34, esp. pp. 119-30). She notes the striking move from the language of "our" to "you" and to the speech's "locat[ing of] Israel's present resistance to Christian proclamation solidly within the tradition of Israel's persistent rejection of God's messengers" (*Acts*, p. 117). Stephen articulates the emerging church's struggle over Israel's legacy: "Which group rightly identifies itself with the temple and its traditions?" (*Acts*, p. 119). Yet God's foreknowledge of Christ's passion and his election of his Son as the risen fulfillment of Israel's hopes make this rejection and resistance by the covenant people, Gaventa argues, a movement within the *Providentia Dei*, by which "[t]he God of Israel's history is also God of all the nations" (*Acts*, p. 134).

of the covenant people Israel. Just as there is no abstract knowledge of God, so there is no abstract diagnosis of sin. It is known only in the revelation of God's covenant with creatures, a covenant in the end of grace, of deliverance, and of victory over sin. All this is important, true, and vital in the proper interpretation of Barth's doctrine of sin and atonement. Yet it must be said that Barth's summary of Israel's history — just because it is the foil to Christ's own true obedience — can only stand in the shadow of apostasy, pride, and ingratitude.

Barth shows little conceptual room for an Israel that "*rejoices* in the law," and little place in his historical work for a covenant people that also *obeyed* the precepts and statutes Moses gave, followed in the traditions of the ancestors, kept holy the divine name, and taught their children, by the way, at their down-sitting and up-rising to call upon the name of the Lord and praise his mighty deeds toward his people Israel. David danced before the Lord when the ark entered Jerusalem, and all the people rejoice together in the psalms of exaltation about the gracious law of God. The Wisdom literature spills over with a near sensuous delight in the guidance given in the Torah; the law is sweeter than honey in the comb. God is faithful and gracious and ready with steadfast, covenant love: of course this is the great truth of Scripture. But the people Israel, too, love the Lord and assent to follow, teach, and rejoice in the law he has given. When the covenant is understood in light of the law, the instruction given to Israel, the way is opened, I believe, for Christians to affirm Israel's own loyalty, love, and gratitude toward this gift — amid, of course, the failures, betrayals, and sins to which Israel is heir too. Such a mixture of shadow and light, of sin but also of obedience and love and covenant faithfulness, conforms more fully, I believe, to Scripture itself, and points more faithfully to the identity of Christ himself.

For Jesus Christ is not merely the obedient Servant; although, to be sure, he is this. He is not merely the one who follows in humility and hears truly the Lord's voice; although he is this as well. He is not simply the living and dynamic fulfiller of the covenant, although again he is this as well. No, Jesus Christ most properly and fully is the *fulfillment of the law,* as the apostle says famously in Romans 10:4. He is *himself,* in his person as well as his work, the law, the instruction of Israel. He is not only giver but gift, the law given to his people and his disciples from his own hand. He is the life-giving Spirit, and in just this way he fulfills the aim, the *telos* of the law: to give life, that the people may flourish in the land. Much more of course would need to be said here about how this identity of Christ with the law

275

can be fleshed out in doctrines of atonement, providence, and covenant. But we should say here, at least in the briefest compass, that such an identity allows us to use the language of "natures" as well as "event," of statutes as well as acts of obedience, of ratification and assent to law as well as the steady unfolding of the Living LORD's life with his creatures. In my view, most potent of all, this christology is grounded not by finding a place for *obedience* within the life and being of God — a puzzling and very risky innovation in the doctrine of God — but rather by finding law, principle, and justice at the very heart and nature of God himself. These are strengths, I believe, that might well recommend a christology built up out of the gracious, covenant gifts of the law itself.

For our purposes here, I believe in the end that the great strength of such a torah-observant christology, if I may put it so, is that the promise Friedrich-Wilhelm Marquardt found in Barth a generation ago could be advanced, deepened, and secured. The gospel of Jesus Christ might be more fully recognized as a word of salvation to the Jew first, and also to the Greek, should the law of Israel, followed, loved, and studied by Jews then and now, be made visible, whole, honored, and perfected in Jesus Christ, the Son of the commandment, the Son of David, the Son of God. In the *Church Dogmatics,* Karl Barth has given us the great riches of his doctrine of reconciliation, grounded in the astonishing grace of the covenant with the people Israel. He drew our eyes to this people, beloved, preserved, and saved by almighty God; he made plain that our Savior belongs by nature, history, and observance to the one people, to "Jewish flesh." May we, with Barth, seek to enter ever more fully into this one Jew, Jesus Christ, for "in [him] are hidden all the treasures of wisdom and knowledge" (Col. 2:3), and in him we see confirmed the divine mystery, that "all Israel will be saved; as it is written, 'Out of Zion will come the Deliverer; he will banish ungodliness from Jacob.' 'And this is my covenant with them, when I take away their sins'" (Rom. 11:26-27).

Role Model — God's Image — Life-Giving Spirit: Who Is Jesus Christ for Us Today?

Michael Welker

Today, when we ask young people if they have a role model, they tend to point first to athletes, singers, or actors, and then often their parents. Friends and teachers also act as role models. Role models are people we identify with consciously or unconsciously. We copy their behavior (or at least try), and we use their lives as a model for our own. Can we place Jesus Christ into this group? Can Jesus Christ be a role model for us today?[1]

Jesus Christ as Role Model?

In Christian theology, "image christology" often has negative connotations.[2] Theology warns us that those who believe in Jesus Christ must never reduce him to the level of an ethical role model. And yet in contrast to this theological apprehensiveness we find a very different message in the Christian piety of the past and present. "Jesus still lead on," we sing, "'til our rest be won. And although the way be cheerless, we will follow calm and fearless; guide us by your hand, to our fatherland."[3] As with so many

1. The following is a small contribution of a systematic theologian to the great project: Beverly Roberts Gaventa and Richard B. Hays, eds., *Seeking the Identity of Jesus: A Pilgrimage* (Grand Rapids: Eerdmans, 2008); Beverly Roberts Gaventa and Richard B. Hays, "Seeking the Identity of Jesus: A Rejoinder," *JSNT* 32 (2010): 363-70.

2. Cf. Friedrich Schweitzer, "Vorbild I," *RGG*, vol. 8, col. 1207-8.

3. "Jesu, geh voran auf der Lebensbahn! Und wir wollen nicht verweilen, dir getreulich nachzueilen; führ uns an der Hand bis ins Vaterland," *Evangelisches Gesangbuch,* no. 391. See also no. 384: "Lasset uns mit Jesus ziehen, seinem Vorbild folgen nach" ("Let us ever walk with Jesus, follow his example pure").

of our spiritual songs, this early eighteenth-century hymn by Nikolaus Ludwig von Zinzendorf presents an image of Jesus that flickers between human role model and eschatological Savior, one who will lead his people into a heavenly "fatherland." In the verses that follow, Zinzendorf stresses the example given by Christ, who bears his own suffering as well as that of others. The message is clear: with patience and humility, and without complaint, we should follow the example of Jesus.

In 1896, Charles Monroe Sheldon (1857-1946), a pastor in Kansas and one of the leaders of the Social Gospel Movement, published a book *In His Steps,* with the subtitle: *What Would Jesus Do?*[4] The book became an enormous best seller, with 30 million copies sold. Even today, a number of paperback versions are still in circulation.[5] For a short time in March 1900, Sheldon became the publisher of the *Topeka Daily Capital* and introduced a new editorial principle: "Newspapers should be operated as Jesus Christ would operate them." The *Capital* saw its circulation numbers increase rapidly from 12,000 to 387,000 copies. A hundred years later, in the 1990s, the Michigan lay preacher Dan Seaborn picked up the slogan "What would Jesus do?" and organized an incredibly successful grassroots movement. Businesswoman Jamie Tinklenberg struck on the idea to create an armband with the initials "WWJD?" and sold over 50 million. Perhaps Jesus Christ was a super role model after all.

The philosopher Immanuel Kant developed the famous categorical imperative: "Act in such a way that the subjective rules by which you live could, at any time, become a universal law." In a way similar to this categorical imperative, "What would Jesus do?" became a moral appeal: act in such a way that the rules by which you live are oriented to the words and actions of Jesus. But does such a religio-moral "role-model christology" correspond to the life and work of Jesus, and is it even possible to live such a role-model christology?

At least some of the "historical Jesus specialists," whose research saw a strong revival at the end of the twentieth century, would say yes. In this group, we find John Dominic Crossan with his two U.S. best sellers *The Historical Jesus: The Life of a Mediterranean Jewish Peasant* and *Jesus: A Revolu-*

---

4. He appealed, among others, to the journalist William Thomas Stead (1849-1912) and his book *If Christ Came to Chicago: A Plea for the Union of All Who Love in the Service of All Who Suffer* (Chicago: Laird & Lee, 1894; reprint: BiblioLife, 2009).

5. E.g., Redford, VA: Wilder Publications, 2008; Grand Rapids: Zondervan, 1970; reprint 2010.

tionary Biography.[6] As Crossan points out, all extant early biblical and extrabiblical texts focused on the life and teachings of Jesus were written between 30 and 150 CE. He was particularly interested in the two oldest layers, from the years 30 to 60 and 60 to 80. Crossan also highlighted narratives about Jesus or references to him that appear repeatedly in unrelated texts. From the texts he examined, Crossan identified 522 "complexes" of Jesus material, finding that 42 have words or actions of Jesus that were recorded in three sources; and 33 references to Jesus were repeated even more than three times. Interestingly, one of these is Jesus' command "Let the little children come to me . . . for the kingdom of God belongs to such as these" (Mark 10:14 and pars.).[7] On the basis of this textual-archeological approach, Crossan offered an impressive image of Jesus.

Jesus was one who recognized the most elementary needs of the people — the need for healing, food, and community. In healing the sick and in open table fellowship, Jesus accepted others. But he did more than that: he launched a new social order. Old and young, women and men, unclean and clean, slaves and slaveowners grew together into a new community in the Jesus Movement. This led to a revolutionary, yet nonviolent, transformation of political and familial relationships of power.

The image of Jesus that Crossan offered us is not misleading. It certainly portrays features of the historical Jesus and his work, and it clearly emphasizes the nature of the life of Jesus as an ethical ideal. Yet, this image of Jesus obscures the deep structures of Jesus' proclamation, in the same way that it loses sight of those events that were so central to his person, life, and work: the events of the cross and resurrection. Remembering Jesus as an ethical role model who saw the basic human needs of others and strove to help them, and the "role-model christology" linked to such a view, distorts our understanding of the life and work of Jesus and our faith in him. One need not be a "pious Christian" to appreciate this problem.

Jesus Christ as God's Image?

There is an anecdote told about Charles-Maurice de Talleyrand-Périgord, the great yet enigmatic French politician from the period of the French Revolution. A contemporary of Talleyrand asked his advice about found-

---

6. San Francisco: Harper, 1992; San Francisco: Harper, 1995.

7. Unless indicated otherwise, all of this essay's biblical quotations come from the NIV.

ing a new religion. According to the story, Talleyrand leaned back in his chair and said: "Our Lord and Master Jesus Christ founded a new religion by being crucified and then rising from the dead after three days. In your matter, I would suggest that you try something similar." It is here at the cross and resurrection that we see the failure of reductionistic and simplistic "role-model christologies." When one looks at Jesus' journey to the cross, one can certainly highlight his exemplary and symbolic actions, such as the miraculous feeding of thousands and his nonviolent resistance against the Roman Empire. And for this reason, other heroes of nonviolent resistance, such as Mahatma Gandhi or Martin Luther King Jr., are often associated with the person and work of Jesus. Yet the incredible depth of Jesus' suffering really calls into question all talk of "Jesus as role model."

Jesus was nailed to the cross in the name of the Roman Empire, in the name of the Jewish religion (which stood in conflict with that Roman world power), in the name of two forms of law (Jewish and Roman), and in the name of public opinion ("'Crucify him!' they shouted" [Mark 15:13 and pars.]). Even his disciples left, abandoned, betrayed, and denied him.[8] The absolute, utter, and purposeful isolation of the crucified Jesus, against whom "the entire world" conspired, radicalizes powerlessness and the helplessness of excruciating suffering even under the most brutal of injustices — a condition Jesus has shared with the many martyrs and "victims of world history."

In the same way, talk of Jesus as our role model seems equally misleading when we consider the resurrection. Unfortunately, the resurrection of Jesus has repeatedly been equated with a simple physical resuscitation — which has in turn been the basis for much doubt and ridicule. In contrast, the biblical witnesses to the resurrection are far more subtle.[9] On one hand, they stress that when the disciples encountered the resurrected Jesus, he was *not* immediately recognized. This speaks against a physical resuscitation. They also highlight the way that Jesus suddenly withdrew, much like a vision. On the other hand, the narratives also stressed the continuity with Jesus' pre-Easter life, and the certainty that Jesus of Nazareth was present there with them in a new form. The story of Christ's appearance on the road to Emmaus is particularly revealing (Luke 24:13-35): on the road to Emmaus, two disciples encounter the risen Jesus but fail to recog-

8. Michael Welker, *What Happens in Holy Communion?* (Grand Rapids: Eerdmans, 2000), esp. pp. 46-48, 71-72.

9. Hans-Joachim Eckstein and Michael Welker, *Die Wirklichkeit der Auferstehung* (Neukirchen-Vluyn: Neukirchener, 2010).

nize him. He explains to them "in all the Scriptures" the mysteries concerning the Messiah (24:27). When they reach their destination, the disciples ask the stranger to stay with them: "Stay with us, for it is nearly evening; the day is almost over" (24:29). At the table, as he performs the rite of breaking bread, "their eyes were opened" (24:31). But then immediately in the same verse we read, "He disappeared from their sight." Rather than feeling horrified at having encountered a ghost, the disciples come to a realization: "Were not our hearts burning within us while he talked with us on the road and opened the Scriptures to us?" (24:32).

Other records of the resurrection also testify to the strange tension between the sensory presence of the resurrected Christ and his hiddenness. It is in this tension — between the vivid experience of God's revelation and strong doubt — that the resurrection reports present the post-Easter presence of Jesus Christ. Thus in the resurrection, what we are dealing with is not a re-creation of the biological, pre-Easter body of Jesus but rather with the presence and efficacy of the post-Easter body of the exalted Christ — a body that extends to his witnesses and is indeed composed by them. With their spiritual gifts, they constitute the church as the body of Christ, with different parts each aimed at serving the construction and expansion of the church as well as its proclamation.

The biblical witnesses tell us that the resurrected and exalted Christ is the "head" of this body, and that he guides and reigns over this body through his Spirit. Quite soon after Jesus' crucifixion and resurrection, we find the conviction that God had revealed himself in this person. He is God's image and, indeed, in the words of the Nicene Creed, "God from God, Light from Light." It is in the resurrected and exalted Christ that God reveals himself and brings people to share in the life of the Resurrected One, and thus in the divine life, in eternal life. Here, talk of Jesus Christ as a role model appears completely misleading. In some ways, the pre-Easter Jesus can stand as a role model. But to say that the resurrected and exalted Christ is a role model for us would be like claiming God himself as a role model for humanity. Jesus Christ is not an image that we can aspire to; he is God's image. Yet is this alternative formulation really the answer?

The "Presumptuous Image Theology" of the Bible?

In 2010, Helga Kuhlmann published a book titled *Fallible Role Models in the Bible, Christianity, and Church: From Angels, Prophets, and Saints to Popes and Bishops.*[10] In this book, Kuhlmann speaks of a "presumptuous image theology in the texts of the Bible."[11] She points to biblical texts that, as she says, apparently stand "in striking tension to that which, with regard to the so-called Fall, has been repeatedly handed down throughout Christian dogmatics right into the twenty-first century as the archetypal definition of true sinfulness: namely the desire to be like God (Gen. 3:5)."[12] The biblical texts she points to explicitly encourage us to seek to be like God. In the Old Testament, we read: "Be holy because I, the LORD your God, am holy" (Lev. 19:2). And even the Sermon on the Mount tells us: "Be perfect, therefore, as your heavenly Father is perfect" (Matt. 5:48). Paul instructs the Corinthians to imitate him, just as he imitates Christ (1 Cor. 11:1), and the entire New Testament canon is marked by just such an imitative discipleship ethic, which is unthinkable without a well-developed concept of exemplary "role models." The book of Acts encourages us to follow Jesus through suffering; and the sending of the disciples mirrors the example of the life of Jesus.

The life of the resurrected Christ is clearly tied back to the features and characteristics that made the earthly Jesus a role model for us, and keeps him a role model today. The body of Christ works through many acts of love and forgiveness, and especially through the welfare work of the church; in the church's great mission journey and in the spread of Christianity we see this expressed particularly clearly in the ongoing building of hospitals and schools. But can we bring these dimensions together without losing a connection to the earthly, human life of Jesus? The resurrected Christ is much more than a human role model. Indeed, he stands as the very image of God among humanity. He is the bearer of that divine revelation through which God makes himself known. To use Helga Kuhlmann's expression, this corresponds with a "presumptuous image theology" in the texts of the Old and New Testaments.

---

10. Helga Kuhlmann, ed., *Fehlbare Vorbilder in Bibel, Christentum und Kirchen: Von Engeln, Propheten und Heiligen bis zu Päpsten und Bischöfinnen,* Theologie in der Öffentlichkeit 2 (Münster: LIT, 2010).

11. "Christus — Vorbild? Grenzen und Chancen von Vorbildlichkeit aus theologischer Sicht," in *Fehlbare Vorbilder,* pp. 146-47: "[u]nbescheidene[n] Vorbildtheologie in Texten der Bibel."

12. Helga Kuhlmann, "Christus — Vorbild? Grenzen und Chancen von Vorbildlichkeit aus theologischer Sicht," in *Fehlbare Vorbilder,* p. 147: "in eklatanter Spannung [stehen] zu dem, was in der christlichen Dogmatik im Anschluss an die Erzählung vom sogenannten Sündenfall bis ins 21. Jahrhundert wiederholt als herausragende Bestimmung genuiner Sündigkeit tradiert wird: sein zu wollen wie Gott (Gen 3,5)."

To gain some clarity here, we need to recognize the great conceptual arc that spans biblical understandings of the human person. On one hand, the human person is created as the image of God. The Psalms tell us: "You have made them only a little lower than God himself" (8:5, paraphrased). Yet on the other hand we must accept that we are finite, transitory beings. "For dust you are and to dust you will return" (Gen. 3:19; cf. Job 10:9; Ps. 104:29). The human being, as man and woman, is designated by God to be God's own image (Gen. 1:27). Human beings should rule over and order the world, shaping this volatile and turbulent creation in line with God's love and God's wisdom.

Yet people fail at this task, and by looking to human role models we can never find our way back to God's path. For this reason, we find in Jesus Christ not only the image of the true human person but also the true image of God. Yet above all, through the power of Christ's Spirit and through the resurrection we are drawn into Christ's post-Easter body and his post-Easter life. The associated power and glory of the image of God transform and exalt us. The power of the divine Spirit at work here overcomes that separation and tension between the concepts of divine image and role model. Yet in the light of the cross and resurrection, this tension becomes even more dramatic.

When we acknowledge that the resurrected and exalted Christ is Lord, κύριος, the Son of God, and indeed "God from God, Light from Light," then we discover a far deeper dimension to the message of the cross. In the incredible cooperation of the powers of this world against that exemplary work of the pre-Easter Jesus, and in the terrific violence that was directed and brought against him, we see the vain attempts of this world, caught under the power of sin, to oppose the goodness of God. In the light of the resurrection we see revealed God's victorious and yet compassionate opposition against these combined forces of the world. In its concentration on the cross of Jesus Christ, the Christian faith gains the comforting knowledge that no matter how great our despair and fear may be, no matter how deep our suffering, no matter how difficult and threatening the conflicts are that face us, even beyond the limits of death God will be near us and will remain faithful to us. God seeks to save us out of the darkest depths of our suffering and despair and enfold us within his eternal life. This leads us away from the idea of a role model or from an image of God to the dimension of the life-giving spirit — a spirit made present in Jesus, and which takes on concrete form in the person of Jesus Christ.

Jesus Christ as "Life-Giving Spirit" and the Human Spirit

In 1 Corinthians 15, Paul notes: "'The first man Adam became a living being'; the last Adam, a life-giving spirit" (1 Cor. 15:45). Jesus Christ as life-giving spirit — this is hard to understand, and yet we must grasp this insight if we hope to understand the "presumptuous image theology" of the biblical texts, or if we want to understand why Jesus Christ is far more than a role model, even though in many ways he does act as a charismatic role model for us in our direct testimony about him, and in the lives of those who follow him and become, in various ways, his witnesses.

In order to grasp this concept, we need to unpack these difficult references about the spirit. In German, as in English, the word "spirit" is often related to an individual's personality ("Goethe was a great spirit of his age"). The word can also refer to ghostly apparitions ("After he began seeing spirits, they placed him in an institution"). Yet primarily, "spirit" tends to symbolize an authority, medium, or power that binds together and orients the thinking, action, and behavior of a group, institution, society, culture, or epoch ("the spirit of this community," "our school spirit," "the spirit of the age"). In German, the word *Geist* does double duty, referring also to the human mind.

To gain some clear insights into the human and divine spirit, it will be helpful to start with human beings, particularly our undisputed cognitive *(geistig)* abilities. Even something as supposedly simple as placing external objects into our memory and imagination is attributed to the human mind *(Geist)*. This act of "picturing" the external world within us is actually an incredibly nuanced activity. An object, or indeed a whole complex of objects, an entire environment with differing stimuli and signals can be stored in the human memory and imagination. Facts, natural events, and webs of experience can be "spiritualized." They exist then not only in physical reality, but also in a type of mental, spiritual form within our memory and imagination. These mental events can then be altered or combined in a broad variety of ways. And yet, these so-called "mental pictures" can be extremely deficient: they can lack focus, be fleeting, be accompanied by pain, or be tainted by disappointment. These images remain then, as we say, more or less "removed from reality." These spiritualized, mental constructions can lose contact with reality and can become oppressive and traumatizing. They begin to hinder normal life as well as our ability to experience life. They begin to undermine our mental and spiritual health.

Yet such boundaries and borderline cases of experience should not lead us to underestimate the great richness, cultural solidity, creative power, and varied blessings of the spirit and of our cognitive abilities. Not only are we able to store individual items and entire networks of objects and experience in memory and imagination, but we can release these contents into latent memory, storing and protecting them, and then recall them. These contents can be varied and recombined in an almost infinite number of ways. In our own imaginations and memories, we rule over an incredible "cognitive realm." These "spiritualized" realities can be used for our individual and communal entertainment and edification, they can aid our powers of persuasion and imagination, and they support our solid insights and offer orientation. In a person's memory and imagination, there is room for an entire ocean, indeed a whole world of mental impressions and sensations. Not only sights but also impressions from sounds and spoken words can be stored in all their richness, combined and contrasted, ordered and placed into association with a world of mentally pictured images and even series of images. Scents, sounds, melodies, and even mentally transposed tactile impressions all animate and enrich this "spiritual" world. Connected with them are often lasting impressions and powerful emotions.

Both the rich interplay of these objects and elements of the spirit, as well as a good selection and limitation of these elements, are vitally important. Both determine the quality, power, and extent of our mental operations. At different levels, religious rituals, literature, the fine arts, music, and especially today's electronic media all demonstrate the power of the spirit to process human experience, as well as the power of imagination. Abstract symbol systems and the use of symbols in mathematics, as well as formal logic and analytical thought, have helped us to discover in the natural and cognitive worlds a range of principles, rules, and correlations of order that allow us not only sensibly to systematize the richness of these mental impressions, but to unleash astonishing powers that enable us to control the world.

Our cognitive potentials allow us to reconstruct highly complex past situations and even entire worlds, and to imagine and anticipate (with some certainty) many future events, as well as their subsequent interconnections. They also allow us to communicate over vast distances, and to transfer and share not just information, or our thoughts and stories, but even complex impressions and infectious emotions.

We can coordinate extraordinarily multifaceted memories and expectations, producing the orienting and organizational power of a communal, cognitive world. On this basis, the human spirit not only achieves cognitive feats, but also brings about a real wealth of cognitive-material cultural achievements that intensify and accelerate their own processes of communication and formation. The machinery of science and education, of research and technological innovation, of political and cultural organization are all fruits of the human spirit. And yet despite all these reasons to be enthralled by the powers of the human spirit, we must be extremely careful not simply to glorify this spirit.

When we examine the phenomena of the spirit, we must take into account psychotic phenomena and also our many possibilities to use our cognitive powers (either consciously or unconsciously) for the severe detriment of others, of culture, and of nature. We throw a wealth of ideas and impulses into global circulation, broadcast them around the world, and these are not always helpful or healthy. Entire torrents of trivializing and banalizing ideas, forms of thought, and emotions also become cognitively transported and culturally ingrained. Fanaticizing, brutalizing, and destructive dispositions and views are placed into circulation via the power of this same spirit and gain incredibly binding and charismatic social and political power. Over long periods of time, and often unnoticed, brutal mentalities spread, destroying and impoverishing everything around them.[13]

As Paul Tillich warned us, countless manifestations of the spirit are highly ambiguous and ambivalent. In a highly dangerous way, numerous achievements of the spirit blind people, as well as entire societies, cultures, and epochs, creating naïve images of the world and committing us to aggressive ideologies. An "evil spirit" then begins to rule the people and uses many of our great mental abilities to destroy and corrupt the conditions of human and creaturely life. Therefore, it would be a dangerously negligent practice simply to connect this spiritual world from the outset with "goodness," "the promotion of life," "freedom," or even "the divine." This sobering and shocking insight reminds us of the need always to "test the spirits" (1 John 4:1) and orient ourselves to the creative, life-giving Spirit of God

---

13. Today, the poisoning of entire societies and epochs by deeply rooted racist, sexist, imperialist, and colonialist attitudes and their correlated use of force is undeniably and shockingly clear. Even into the 1960s one could read in academic textbooks and encyclopedias that water and air were "infinite resources" and thus did not need to be accounted for economically. Thus "in all innocence" ecological brutalism was cognitively propagated across the globe.

revealed in Jesus Christ. "[T]he last Adam [is] a life-giving spirit" — but what does this mean?

The Power of Jesus and His Spirit to Create Role Models

Without surrendering the many and diverse exemplary characteristics of his pre-Easter life, the resurrected and exalted Christ still meets us, not only in a personal encounter, but also in the efficacy of the Spirit, which the biblical traditions described with the image of the "outpouring of the Spirit." Already in the Old Testament we find passages describing how God will "pour out [his] Spirit on all people," men and women, old and young, and male and female slaves (Joel 2:28-29). The report of the Pentecost event in Acts 2 then picked up this language. The outpouring of the Spirit was revolutionary. In those patriarchal societies, where only men and the elderly had any say, and where the young were simply expected to obey, in those societies built upon slavery (as were all societies in antiquity), even the mere proclamation of this outpouring of the Spirit was revolutionary. A promise has now been given to society's marginalized and ostracized individuals and groups that they too will be able to testify to God's wonders and will be given access to God's truth and justice. Even the weak and excluded will be enabled to see the central forces of life and to share these with others, to set into motion cognitive, spiritual, and even material processes that will shape the world in accordance with God's desires.

It is Jesus Christ, the life-giving spirit, who offers us this divine, orienting power. In his great volume on Christian doctrine, the Reformer John Calvin (whose 500th birthday was celebrated around the world in 2009) offers us an exceptionally important double insight: Jesus Christ — upon whom the Spirit of God rests, the Spirit of justice, compassion, and the knowledge of God — pours this Spirit out upon those who belong to him.[14] In Calvin's main work, the *Institutes of the Christian Religion,* he is emphatic in his insistence that Christ, the Messiah, was anointed not with oil but with the Holy Spirit, so he could give those who belong to him a share in his power: "Therefore the anointing of the king is not with oil or aromatic unguents. Rather, he is called *'Anointed'* of God because 'the spirit

---

14. Cf. James D. G. Dunn, "Towards the Spirit of Christ: The Emergence of the Distinctive Features of Christian Pneumatology," in *The Work of the Spirit: Pneumatology and Pentecostalism,* ed. Michael Welker (Grand Rapids: Eerdmans, 2006), pp. 3-26.

of wisdom and understanding, the spirit of counsel and might . . . and of the fear of the Lord have rested upon *him*' [Isa. 11:2]. . . . [H]e did not enrich himself for his own sake [or 'privately,' *privatim*], but that he might pour out his abundance upon the hungry and thirsty."[15] Here Calvin stresses the so-called "baptism of the Spirit" through the one who was "anointed by the Spirit." This was a revolutionary spiritual experience for the early church, and in the twentieth century it came to stand as the center of the global Pentecostal movement and the charismatic revival.[16] The second key insight that Calvin gives us is: if we want "to know *the purpose for which* Christ was sent by the Father and *what* he has brought us, we must look above all at three things in him: *the prophetic office, kingship, and priesthood*."[17] The teaching of the "threefold office of Christ" *(munus triplex Christi)* has made its way today into all Christian confessions.

According to the biblical texts and the theologies based on them, Jesus Christ is the true king. This king is brother and friend, and yet simultaneously a poor and despised person. He revolutionizes the concepts and conditions of rule, placing them in the service of the church's welfare work (the service of our neighbor), in the service of love, acceptance, and forgiveness. He thus stands for us in various ways as a role model, across the entire spectrum of various human relationships. The passionate pursuit of a free and democratic life, as well as universal education and healthcare for all members of society, stands in this tradition.

Jesus Christ also stands in the prophetic tradition. Through his proclamations and through his suffering and death he reveals to us the evil spirits and powers that consciously and unconsciously oppose God's salvific presence. He is a role model for truth-seeking and justice-seeking communities, not only in the church but also in the sciences, law, and civil society. He is a role model for prophetic, nonviolent resistance against injustice and oppression.

Finally, he is also a priestly role model. By establishing the sacraments of baptism and holy communion (celebrating our change of lordship away

---

15. John Calvin, *Institutes of the Christian Religion* II.15.5 (ET: ed. John T. McNeill, trans. Ford Lewis Battles [Philadelphia: Westminster, 1960], pp. 499-500, emphasis added).

16. Frank Macchia, *Baptized in the Spirit: A Global Pentecostal Theology* (Grand Rapids: Zondervan, 2006).

17. Calvin, *Institutes* II.15; ET: p. 494, emphasis added. Cf. Michael Welker, "Rethinking Christocentric Theology," in *Transformations in Luther's Theology: Historical and Contemporary Reflections,* ed. Christine Helmer and Bo Kristian Holm, Arbeiten zur Kirchen- und Theologiegeschichte 32 (Leipzig: Evangelische Verlagsanstalt, 2011), pp. 179-92.

from the powers of this world to the power of God), in a continually renewed remembrance of his life, suffering, and death, and in anticipation of his perfect revelation in glory, the Resurrected One also gives orientation to our spiritual service — not only for ordained pastors but for the entire community of Jesus Christ and, potentially, the entire world.

It is in the power of the Spirit that all people have a share in this human as well as divine work. Here before our spiritual eyes we see an incredible polyphony of this role-model-creating work. Thankfully, we can perceive an incredible polyphony of this role-model-creating work in those real lives that orient themselves both consciously and unconsciously toward this person and role model.

Jesus Christ is much more than an individual, human role model. Indeed, when we reduce his image to that of an individual, human role model, it becomes distorted and destroyed. According to the biblical traditions, it was demons and unclean spirits who, after Jesus' first spectacular healings, announced: "You are the son of the highest, you are the Son of God!" As the Gospels tell us, Jesus reacted by swearing them to silence. (Already in Mark 1:34 we read that "he would not let the demons speak because they knew who he was.") His identity should not be made known before the resurrection, so that others will not reduce his work, seeing him simply in the role of great healer or great teacher, or taking him simply as a role model for the acceptance of others or for political resistance. In the cross and resurrection, Jesus seems to be utterly removed out of the hands of those seeking a role model or a corresponding life orientation. When we recognize in the resurrected and exalted Jesus Christ the presence of this life-giving spirit, in all continuity and discontinuity with his pre-Easter life, then we see that this life-giving spirit materializes and concretizes itself within his many witnesses. It is then that we regain Jesus as a role model, coming back to us almost explosively through the polyphony of the Spirit's work and in the charismatic power of his witnesses.

More precisely: as a "life-giving spirit," Jesus Christ calls countless people to follow and imitate him. He enables his disciples to live, in a multitude of ways, their own exemplary lives with their many different gifts and abilities — even by bearing witness through patience and suffering. From the perspective of the Christian faith, Jesus Christ, as the resurrected and exalted life-giving spirit, raises up countless people (even beyond the borders of the church) to be role models and to imitate him. That, too, is why today, and for all time, he remains far more than a human role model.

Bibliography

Adams, Edward. *Constructing the World: A Study in Paul's Cosmological Language.* Studies of the New Testament and Its World. Edinburgh: T. & T. Clark, 1999.

Agamben, Giorgio. *The Kingdom and the Glory: For a Theological Genealogy of Economy and Government.* Translated by Lorenzo Chiesa with Matteo Mandarini. Stanford: Stanford University Press, 2011.

Anderson, Gary A. *Sin: A History.* New Haven: Yale University Press, 2009.

Bader-Saye, Scott. *Church and Israel after Christendom: The Politics of Election.* Boulder: Westview, 1999.

Badiou, Alain. *Saint Paul: The Foundation of Universalism.* Translated by Ray Brassier. Stanford: Stanford University Press, 2003.

Bakhtin, Mikhail. *Rabelais and His World.* Translated by H. Iswolsky. Bloomington: Indiana University Press, 1984.

Barclay, John M. G. "'I Will Have Mercy on Whom I Have Mercy': The Golden Calf and Divine Mercy in Romans 9–11 and Second Temple Judaism." *Early Christianity* 1 (2010): 82-106.

———. *Pauline Churches and Diaspora Jews.* Wissenschaftliche Untersuchungen zum Neuen Testament 275. Tübingen: Mohr Siebeck, 2011.

Barr, James. *Biblical Words for Time.* Studies in Biblical Theology 33. London: SCM, 1962.

Barrett, C. K. *A Critical and Exegetical Commentary on the Acts of the Apostles.* 2 vols. International Critical Commentary. Edinburgh: T. & T. Clark, 1994-1998.

———. *The First Epistle to the Corinthians.* New York: Harper & Row, 1968.

———. *Freedom and Obligation: A Study of the Epistle to the Galatians.* Philadelphia: Westminster, 1985.

Barth, Karl. *Church Dogmatics II/2: The Election of the Community.* Translated by Geoffrey W. Bromiley et al. Edinburgh: T. & T. Clark, 1957.

———. *The Epistle to the Romans.* Translated from the 6th edition by E. C. Hoskyns. Oxford: Oxford University Press, 1968.

Beker, J. Christiaan. *Paul the Apostle: The Triumph of God in Life and Thought.* Philadelphia: Fortress, 1980.

Belleville, Linda L. *Reflections of Glory: Paul's Polemical Use of the Moses-Doxa Tradition in 2 Corinthians 3.1-18.* Journal for the Study of the New Testament: Supplement Series 52. Sheffield: Sheffield Academic Press, 1991.

Bénétreau, Samuel. "La richesse selon 1 Timothée 6,6-10 et 6,17-19." *Etudes théologiques et religieuses* 83 (2008): 49-60.

Benjamin, Walter. "Theses on the Philosophy of History." In *Illuminations: Essays and Reflections,* translated by Harry Zohn, edited by Hannah Arendt, pp. 253-64. New York: Schocken Books, 1969.

Berger, Klaus. *Identity and Experience in the New Testament.* Minneapolis: Fortress, 2003.

Berkhof, Hendrikus. *Christ and the Powers.* Translated by John Howard Yoder. 2nd edition. Scottdale, PA: Herald, 1977.

Berlin, Adele, and Maxine Grossman, eds. "Covering of the Head." Page 192 in *The Oxford Dictionary of the Jewish Religion.* 2nd edition. Oxford: Oxford University Press, 2011.

Betz, Hans Dieter. *Galatians: A Commentary on Paul's Letter to the Galatians.* Hermeneia. Philadelphia: Fortress, 1979.

———. "The Literary Composition and Function of Paul's Letter to the Galatians." *New Testament Studies* 21 (1975): 353-79.

Bird, Michael F. *The Saving Righteousness of God: Studies on Paul, Justification, and the New Perspective.* Milton Keynes, UK: Paternoster, 2007.

Blinzler, Josef. "Lexikalisches zu dem Terminus *Ta stoicheia tou kosmou* bei Paulus." Pages 429-43 in volume 2 of *Studiorum Paulinorum Congressus Internationalis Catholicus 1961.* Rome: Pontifical Biblical Institute, 1963.

Bockmuehl, Markus N. A. *Revelation and Mystery in Ancient Judaism and Pauline Christianity.* Grand Rapids: Eerdmans, 1997.

The Book of Common Prayer. New York: Church Publishing, 1979.

Booth, Wayne C. *The Rhetoric of Fiction.* 2nd edition. Chicago: University of Chicago Press, 1983.

Bovon, François. *Luke 1: A Commentary on the Gospel of Luke 1:1–9:50.* Hermeneia. Minneapolis: Fortress, 2002.

———. *Luke the Theologian: Thirty-Three Years of Research (1950-1983).* Translated by Ken McKinney. Princeton Theological Monograph Series 12. Allison Park, PA: Pickwick, 1987.

Bowen, Nancy. *Ezekiel.* Abingdon Old Testament Commentaries. Nashville: Abingdon, 2010.

Bråten, Stein, ed. *On Being Moved: From Mirror Neurons to Empathy.* Advances in Consciousness Research 68. Amsterdam/Philadelphia: John Benjamins, 2007.

Bretherton, Luke. *Christianity and Contemporary Politics.* Malden, MA: Wiley-Blackwell, 2010.

Britt, Brian. "Concealment, Revelation, and Gender: The Veil of Moses in the Bible and in Christian Art." *Religion and the Arts* 7 (2003): 227-73.

Brown, Raymond E. *The Birth of the Messiah: A Commentary on the Infancy Narratives in the Gospels of Matthew and Luke*. Revised edition. New York: Doubleday, 1993.

Bruce, F. F. *1 and 2 Corinthians*. New Century Bible. London: Oliphants, 1971.

———. *The Acts of the Apostles: Greek Text with Introduction and Commentary*. 3rd edition. Grand Rapids: Eerdmans, 1990.

———. *The Epistle to the Galatians: A Commentary on the Greek Text*. New International Greek Testament Commentary. Grand Rapids: Eerdmans, 1982.

———. "The Holy Spirit in the Acts of the Apostles." *Interpretation* 27 (1973): 166-83.

———. "Luke's Presentation of the Spirit in Acts." *Criswell Theological Review* 5 (1990): 146-53.

Bullinger, E. W. *Figures of Speech Used in the Bible: Explained and Illustrated*. Reprint, Grand Rapids: Baker, 1968 [1898].

Bultmann, Rudolf. *Exegetica: Aufsätze zur Erforschung des Neuen Testaments*. Edited by Erich Dinkler. Tübingen: Mohr Siebeck, 1967.

Burns, J. Patout, with Constantine Newman, eds. and trans. *Romans: Interpreted by Early Christian Commentators*. Grand Rapids: Eerdmans, 2012.

Burton, Ernest DeWitt. *A Critical and Exegetical Commentary on the Epistle to the Galatians*. International Critical Commentary. Edinburgh: T. & T. Clark, 1921.

Cairns, Douglas L. "The Meaning of the Veil in Ancient Greek Culture." In *Women's Dress in the Ancient Greek World*, edited by Lloyd Llewellyn-Jones, pp. 73-93. London: Duckworth; Swansea: Classical Press of Wales; Oakville, CT: Distributor in the United States of America, David Brown Book Co., 2002.

Calvin, John. *Commentaries on the Epistles to Timothy, Titus, and Philemon*. Translated by William Pringle. Grand Rapids: Eerdmans, 1948.

———. *The Epistles of Paul to the Romans and to the Thessalonians*. Translated by Ross Mackenzie. Calvin's Commentaries 8. Grand Rapids: Eerdmans, 1960.

———. *Institutes of the Christian Religion*. Edited by John T. McNeill. Translated by Ford Lewis Battles. 2 volumes. Philadelphia: Westminster, 1960.

Campbell, Douglas A. *The Deliverance of God: An Apocalyptic Rereading of Justification in Paul*. Grand Rapids: Eerdmans, 2009.

Campbell, William Sanger. "Unity." In *The New Interpreter's Dictionary of the Bible*, edited by Katharine Doob Sakenfeld et al., volume 5, p. 713. Nashville: Abingdon, 2009.

Carr, David M. *Writing on the Tablet of the Heart: Origins of Scripture and Literature*. New York: Oxford University Press, 2005.

Carson, David A. "Pauline Inconsistency: Reflections on 1 Corinthians 9.19-23 and Galatians 2.11-14." *Churchman* 100 (1986): 6-45.

Cavanaugh, William T. *Migrations of the Holy: God, State, and the Political Meaning of the Church*. Grand Rapids: Eerdmans, 2011.

Chatman, Seymour. *Coming to Terms: The Rhetoric of Narrative in Fiction and Film*. Ithaca: Cornell University Press, 1990.

Childs, Brevard S. *Isaiah*. Old Testament Library. Louisville: Westminster John Knox, 2001.

Clark, Andy. *Supersizing the Mind: Embodiment, Action, and Cognitive Extension.* Oxford: Oxford University Press, 2008.

Coakley, Sarah. "The Eschatological Body: Gender, Transformation, and God." *Modern Theology* 16 (2000): 61-73.

Coleridge, Mark. *The Birth of the Lukan Narrative: Narrative as Christology in Luke 1–2.* Journal for the Study of the New Testament: Supplement Series 88. Sheffield: Sheffield Academic Press, 1993.

Conzelmann, Hans. *Acts of the Apostles: A Commentary on the Acts of the Apostles.* Translated by James Limburg, A. Thomas Kraabel, and Donald H. Juel. Hermeneia. Philadelphia: Fortress, 1987.

————. *The Theology of St. Luke.* Translated by Geoffrey Buswell. Philadelphia: Fortress, 1961.

Couser, Greg A. "God and Christian Existence in the Pastoral Epistles: Toward *Theolog*ical Method and Meaning." *Novum Testamentum* 42 (2000): 262-83.

Cranfield, C. E. B. *A Critical and Exegetical Commentary on the Epistle to the Romans.* 2 volumes. International Critical Commentary. Edinburgh: T. & T. Clark, 1975-1979.

Crossan, John Dominic. *The Historical Jesus: The Life of a Mediterranean Jewish Peasant.* San Francisco: Harper, 1992.

————. *Jesus: A Revolutionary Biography.* San Francisco: Harper, 1995.

Cullmann, Oscar. *Christ and Time: The Primitive Christian Conception of Time and History.* Translated by Floyd V. Filson. Revised edition. London: SCM, 1962.

D'Angelo, Mary Rose. "Veils, Virgins and the Tongues of Men and Angels: Women's Heads in Early Christianity." In *Off with Her Head: The Denial of Women's Identity in Myth, Religion and Culture,* edited by Wendy Doniger and Howard Eilberg-Schwartz, pp. 131-64. Berkeley and Los Angeles: University of California Press, 1995.

Das, A. Andrew. "Another Look at ἐὰν μή in Galatians 2:16." *Journal of Biblical Literature* 119 (2000): 529-39.

————. *Paul and the Jews.* Library of Pauline Studies. Peabody, MA: Hendrickson, 2003.

Davis, Carl Judson. *The Name and Way of the Lord: Old Testament Themes, New Testament Christology.* Journal for the Study of the New Testament: Supplement Series 129. Sheffield: Sheffield Academic Press, 1996.

de Boer, Martinus C. *The Defeat of Death: Apocalyptic Eschatology in 1 Corinthians 15 and Romans 5.* Journal for the Study of the New Testament: Supplement Series 22. Sheffield: Sheffield Academic Press, 1988.

————. *Galatians.* New Testament Library. Louisville: Westminster John Knox, 2011.

————. "The Meaning of the Phrase τὰ στοιχεῖα τοῦ κόσμου in Galatians." *New Testament Studies* 53 (2007): 204-24.

————. "The New Preachers in Galatia: Their Identity, Message, Aims, and Impact." In *Jesus, Paul, and Early Christianity: Studies in Honour of Henk Jan de Jonge,* edited by Rieuwerd Buitenwerf, Harm W. Hollander, and Johannes Tromp, pp. 39-60. Supplements to Novum Testamentum 130. Leiden: Brill, 2008.

Dibelius, Martin, and Hans Conzelmann. *The Pastoral Epistles: A Commentary on the*

Pastoral Epistles. Translated by Philip Buttolph and Adela Yarbro. Hermeneia. Philadelphia: Fortress, 1972.

Dobbs-Allsopp, F. W., and Tod Linafelt. "The Rape of Zion in Thr 1,10." *Zeitschrift für die Alttestamentliche Wissenschaft* 113 (2001): 77-81.

Downs, David J. "Faith(fulness) in Christ Jesus in 2 Timothy 3:15." *Journal of Biblical Literature* 131 (2012): 143-60.

———. *The Offering of the Gentiles: Paul's Collection for Jerusalem in Its Chronological, Cultural, and Cultic Contexts*. Wissenschaftliche Untersuchungen zum Neuen Testament 2:248. Tübingen: Mohr Siebeck, 2008.

———. "Redemptive Almsgiving and Economic Stratification in 2 *Clement*." *Journal of Early Christian Studies* 19 (2011): 493-517.

Dschulnigg, Peter. "Warnung vor Reichtum und Ermahnung der Reichen: 1 Tim 6,6–10.17-19 im Rahmen des Schlußteils 6,3-21." *Biblische Zeitschrift* 37 (1993): 60-77.

Dunn, James D. G. "The Incident at Antioch (Gal 2:11-18)." *Journal for the Study of the New Testament* 18 (1983): 3-57.

———. *Jesus and the Spirit: A Study of the Religious and Charismatic Experience of Jesus and the First Christians as Reflected in the New Testament*. Philadelphia: Westminster, 1975.

———. "'Neither Circumcision nor Uncircumcision, but . . .' (Gal. 5.2-12; 6.12-16; cf. 1 Cor. 7.7-20)." In *The New Perspective on Paul*. Revised edition, pp. 313-37. Grand Rapids: Eerdmans, 2008.

———. "The New Perspective on Paul." *Bulletin of the John Rylands University Library of Manchester* 65 (1983): 95-122.

———. *The New Perspective on Paul*. Revised edition. Wissenschaftliche Untersuchungen Neuen Testament 185. Tübingen: Mohr Siebeck, 2005.

———. "The Theology of Galatians: The Issue of Covenantal Nomism." In *Pauline Theology*, volume 1: *Thessalonians, Philippians, Galatians, Philemon*, edited by Jouette M. Bassler, pp. 125-46. Minneapolis: Fortress, 1991.

———. *The Theology of Paul's Letter to the Galatians*. Cambridge: Cambridge University Press, 1993.

———. "Towards the Spirit of Christ: The Emergence of the Distinctive Features of Christian Pneumatology." In *The Work of the Spirit: Pneumatology and Pentecostalism*, edited by Michael Welker, pp. 3-26. Grand Rapids: Eerdmans, 2006.

———. "Works of the Law and the Curse of the Law (Galatians 3.10-14)." *New Testament Studies* 31 (1985): 523-42.

Dupont, Jacques. "Le Chrétien, miroir de la gloire divine d'après II Cor., III, 18." *Revue Biblique* 56 (1949): 392-411.

Eckstein, Hans-Joachim, and Michael Welker. *Die Wirklichkeit der Auferstehung*. Neukirchen-Vluyn: Neukirchener, 2010.

Elliott, Neil. *The Arrogance of Nations: Reading Romans in the Shadow of Empire*. Paul in Critical Contexts. Minneapolis: Fortress, 2008.

Elliott, Neil, and Mark Reasoner, eds. *Documents and Images for the Study of Paul*. Minneapolis: Fortress, 2011.

Endres, John C. *Biblical Interpretation in the Book of Jubilees*. Catholic Biblical Quarterly Monograph Series 18. Washington, DC: Catholic Biblical Association of America, 1987.

Eubank, Nathan. "Almsgiving Is 'the Commandment': A Note on 1 Timothy 6.6-19." *New Testament Studies* 58 (2012): 144-50.

Evans, Vyvyan, and Melanie Green. *Cognitive Linguistics: An Introduction*. Edinburgh: Edinburgh University Press, 2006.

Fee, Gordon. "Freedom and the Life of Obedience (Galatians 5:1–6:18)." *Review and Expositor* 91 (1994): 201-17.

Feldman, Jerome A. *From Molecule to Metaphor: A Neural Theory of Language*. Cambridge, MA: MIT Press, 2006.

Feuillet, A. "La dignité et le rôle de la femme d'aprìs quelques textes pauliniens: Camparaison avec l'Ancien Testament." *New Testament Studies* 21 (1975): 157-91.

Finn, Thomas M. *From Death to Rebirth: Ritual and Conversion in Antiquity*. New York: Paulist, 1997.

Fitzmyer, Joseph A. *The Acts of the Apostles*. Anchor Bible 31. New York: Doubleday, 1998.

———. *The Gospel according to Luke I–IX*. Anchor Bible 28. New York: Doubleday, 1970.

———. *Tobit*. Commentaries on Early Jewish Literature. Berlin: De Gruyter, 2003.

Fortna, Robert T., and Beverly R. Gaventa, eds. *The Conversation Continues: Studies in John and Paul in Honor of J. Louis Martyn*. Nashville: Abingdon, 1990.

Franklin, Eric. *Christ the Lord: A Study in the Purpose and Theology of Luke-Acts*. Philadelphia: Westminster, 1975.

Freedman, Harry, and Maurice Simon, eds. *The Midrash Rabbah, Leviticus 4*. Translated by J. Isaelstram. London: Soncino, 1961.

Friesen, Steven J. "Poverty in Pauline Studies: Beyond the So-Called New Consensus." *Journal for the Study of the New Testament* 26 (2004): 323-61.

Fuller, Michael E. *The Restoration of Israel: Israel's Re-gathering and the Fate of the Nations in Early Jewish Literature and Luke-Acts*. Beihefte zur Zeitschrift für die neutestamentliche Wissenschaft 138. Berlin: De Gruyter, 2006.

Furnish, Victor Paul. *II Corinthians*. Anchor Bible 32A. Garden City, NY: Doubleday, 1984.

Gager, John G. *Reinventing Paul*. New York: Oxford University Press, 2000.

Galambush, Julie. *Jerusalem in the Book of Ezekiel: The City as Yahweh's Wife*. Society of Biblical Literature Dissertation Series 130. Atlanta: Scholars Press, 1992.

Gallagher, Shaun. *How the Body Shapes the Mind*. Oxford: Oxford University Press, 2005.

Garber, David F., Jr. "A Vocabulary of Trauma in the Exilic Writings." In *Interpreting Exile: Displacement and Deportation in Biblical and Modern Contexts*, edited by Brad E. Kelle, Frank Ritchel Ames, and Jacob L. Wright, pp. 309-22. Society of Biblical Literature Ancient Israel and Its Literature 10. Atlanta: Society of Biblical Literature, 2011.

Gaston, Loyd. *Paul and the Torah*. Vancouver: University of British Columbia Press, 1987.

Gathercole, Simon. "Sin in God's Economy: Agencies in Romans 1 and 7." In *Divine and Human Agency in Paul and His Cultural Environment,* edited by John M. G. Barclay and Simon J. Gathercole, pp. 158-72. London: T. & T. Clark, 2008.

Gaventa, Beverly Roberts. *The Acts of the Apostles.* Abingdon New Testament Commentaries. Nashville: Abingdon, 2003.

———. "The Cosmic Power of Sin in Paul's Letter to the Romans: Toward a Widescreen Edition." *Interpretation* 58 (2004): 229-40.

———. *From Darkness to Light: Aspects of Conversion in the New Testament.* Overtures in Biblical Theology 20. Philadelphia: Fortress, 1986.

———. "From Toxic Speech to the Redemption of Doxology in Paul's Letter to the Romans." In *The Word Leaps the Gap: Essays on Scripture and Theology in Honor of Richard B. Hays,* edited by J. Ross Wagner, C. Kavin Rowe, and A. Katherine Grieb, pp. 392-408. Grand Rapids: Eerdmans, 2008.

———. "Galatians 1 and 2: Autobiography as Paradigm." *Novum Testamentum* 28 (1986): 309-26.

———. "God Handed Them Over: Reading Romans 1:18-32 Apocalyptically." *Australian Biblical Review* 53 (2005): 42-53.

———. "The Mission of God in Paul's Letter to the Romans." In *Paul as Missionary: Identity, Activity, Theology, and Practice,* edited by Trevor J. Burke and Brian S. Rosner, pp. 65-75. Library of New Testament Studies 420. London: T. & T. Clark, 2011.

———. "Neither Height nor Depth: Discerning the Cosmology of Romans." *Scottish Journal of Theology* 64 (2011): 265-78.

———. "On the Calling into Being of Israel: Romans 9:6-29." In *Between Gospel and Election: Explorations in the Interpretation of Romans 9–11,* edited by Florian Wilk and J. Ross Wagner, pp. 255-69. Wissenschaftliche Untersuchungen zum Neuen Testament 257. Tübingen: Mohr Siebeck, 2010.

———. *Our Mother Saint Paul.* Louisville: Westminster John Knox, 2007.

———. "Paul and the Roman Believers." In *The Blackwell Companion to Paul,* edited by Stephen Westerholm, pp. 93-107. Oxford and Malden, MA: Wiley-Blackwell, 2011.

———. "The Singularity of the Gospel: A Reading of Galatians." In *Pauline Theology,* volume 1: *Thessalonians, Philippians, Galatians, Philemon,* edited by Jouette M. Bassler, pp. 147-59. Minneapolis: Fortress, 1991.

———. "The Singularity of the Gospel Revisited: Exegetical Reflections on Galatians 1 and 2." Paper presented at the St. Andrews Conference on Scripture and Christian Theology: Paul's Letter to the Galatians and Christian Theology, St. Andrews, Scotland, 11 July 2012.

———. "Toward a Theology of Acts: Reading and Rereading." *Interpretation* 42 (1988): 146-57.

Gaventa, Beverly Roberts, and Richard B. Hays, eds. *Seeking the Identity of Jesus: A Pilgrimage.* Grand Rapids: Eerdmans, 2008.

———. "Seeking the Identity of Jesus: A Rejoinder." *Journal for the Study of the New Testament* 32 (2010): 363-70.

Genette, Gérard. *Narrative Discourse: An Essay in Method.* Translated by Jane E. Lewin. Ithaca: Cornell University Press, 1980.

Georgi, Dieter. *The Opponents of Paul in Second Corinthians.* Philadelphia: Fortress, 1986.

Godbout, Jacques T., and Alain Caillé. *The World of the Gift.* Translated by Donald Winkler. Montreal: McGill-Queen's University Press, 1998.

Gordon, T. David. "The Problem at Galatia." *Interpretation* 41 (1987): 32-43.

Green, Joel B. *The Gospel of Luke.* New International Commentary on the New Testament. Grand Rapids: Eerdmans, 1997.

———. *The Theology of the Gospel of Luke.* New Testament Theology. Cambridge: Cambridge University Press, 1995.

Griffiths, Paul J. "The Cross as the Fulcrum of Politics: Expropriating Agamben on Paul." In *Paul, Philosophy, and the Theopolitical Vision: Critical Engagements with Agamben, Badiou, Žižek and Others,* edited by Douglas Harink, pp. 179-97. Eugene, OR: Cascade, 2010.

Grumm, Meinert H. "Another Look at Acts." *Expository Times* 96 (1985): 333-37.

Guillaumont, A., et al. *The Gospel according to Thomas: Coptic Text with Translations into French, German and English.* New York: Harper & Row, 1959.

Gundry-Volf, Judith M. "Gender and Creation in 1 Corinthians 11:2-16: A Study in Paul's Theological Method." In *Evangelium, Schriftauslegung, Kirche: Festschrift für Peter Stuhlmacher zum 65. Geburtstag,* edited by Jostein Ådna et al., pp. 151-71. Göttingen: Vandenhoeck & Ruprecht, 1997.

Haacker, Klaus. *Der Brief des Paulus an die Römer.* Theologischer Handkommentar zum Neuen Testament 6. Leipzig: Evangelische Verlagsanstalt, 2006.

Hafemann, Scott J. *Paul, Moses, and the History of Israel: The Letter/Spirit Contrast and the Argument from Scripture in 2 Corinthians 3.* Wissenschaftliche Untersuchungen zum Neuen Testament 81. Tübingen: J. C. B. Mohr (Paul Siebeck), 1995.

———. *Suffering and Ministry in the Spirit: Paul's Defense of His Ministry in II Corinthians 2:14–3:3.* Grand Rapids: Eerdmans, 1990.

Hamerton-Kelly, Robert G. "Sacred Violence and 'Works of the Law': 'Is Christ Then an Agent of Sin?' (Galatians 2:17)." *Catholic Biblical Quarterly* 52 (1990): 55-75.

Harink, Douglas. *Paul among the Postliberals: Pauline Theology beyond Christendom and Modernity.* Grand Rapids: Brazos, 2003.

Harink, Douglas, ed. *Paul, Philosophy, and the Theopolitical Vision: Critical Engagements with Agamben, Badiou, Žižek and Others.* Theopolitical Visions 7. Eugene, OR: Cascade, 2010.

Hartman, Lars. *'Into the Name of the Lord Jesus': Baptism in the Early Church.* Studies of the New Testament and Its World. Edinburgh: T. & T. Clark, 1997.

Hauerwas, Stanley, and Romand Coles, *Christianity, Democracy, and the Radical Ordinary: Conversations between a Radical Democrat and a Christian.* Eugene, OR: Cascade, 2008.

———. *War and the American Difference: Theological Reflections on Violence and National Identity.* Grand Rapids: Baker Academic, 2011.

Haugeland, John. *Having Thought: Essays in the Metaphysics of Mind*. Cambridge, MA: Harvard University Press, 1998.

Hays, Christopher M. "By Almsgiving and Faith Sins Are Purged? The Theological Underpinnings of Early Christian Care for the Poor." In *Engaging Economics: New Testament Scenarios and Early Christian Reception*, edited by Bruce W. Longenecker and Kelly D. Liebengood, pp. 260-80. Grand Rapids: Eerdmans, 2009.

Hays, Richard B. "Christology and Ethics in Galatians: The Law of Christ." *Catholic Biblical Quarterly* 49 (1987): 268-90.

———. *The Conversion of the Imagination: Paul as Interpreter of Israel's Scripture*. Grand Rapids: Eerdmans, 2005.

———. *Echoes of Scripture in the Letters of Paul*. New Haven: Yale University Press, 1989.

———. *The Faith of Jesus Christ: The Narrative Substructure of Galatians 3:1–4:11*. 2nd edition. Grand Rapids: Eerdmans, 2002.

Helfmeyer, F. J. "הלך." In *Theological Dictionary of the Old Testament*, edited by G. Johannes Botterweck and Helmer Ringgren, translated by John T. Willis, Geoffrey W. Bromiley, and David E. Green, volume 3, pp. 388-403. Grand Rapids: Eerdmans, 1978.

Hinton, J., and L. L. V. Matthews. "Veiled or Unveiled? Plut. *Quaest. Rom.* 267B-C." *Classical Quarterly* 58 (2008): 336-42.

Hooker, Morna. "Authority on Her Head: An Examination of 1 Cor 11:10." *New Testament Studies* 10 (1964): 410-17.

Hopkins, Gerard Manley. *Poems and Prose*. London: Penguin, 1953.

Horrell, David G. "Disciplining Performance and 'Placing' the Church: Widows, Elders, and Slaves in the Household of God (1 Tim 5,1-6,2)." In *1 Timothy Reconsidered*, edited by Karl P. Donfried, pp. 109-34. Colloquium Oecumenicum Paulinum 18. Leuven: Peeters, 2008.

———. *The Social Ethos of the Corinthian Correspondence: Interests and Ideology from 1 Corinthians to 1 Clement*. Studies of the New Testament and Its World. Edinburgh: T. & T. Clark, 1996.

Hurley, Susan, and Nick Chater, eds. *Imitation, Human Development, and Culture*. Volume 2 of *Perspectives on Imitation: From Neuroscience to Social Science*. Cambridge, MA: MIT Press, 2005.

Immanuel, Babu. *Repent and Turn to God: Recounting Acts*. Perth, Australia: HIM International Ministries, 2004.

Jervis, L. Ann. "Accepting Affliction: Paul's Preaching on Suffering." In *Character and Scripture: Moral Formation, Community, and Biblical Interpretation*, edited by William P. Brown, pp. 290-316. Grand Rapids: Eerdmans, 2002.

———. *At the Heart of the Gospel: Suffering in the Earliest Christian Message*. Grand Rapids: Eerdmans, 2007.

———. "'The Commandment Which Is for Life' (Romans 7.10): Sin's Use of the Obedience of Faith." *Journal for the Study of the New Testament* 27 (2004): 193-216.

Jewett, Robert. *Romans: A Commentary*. Hermeneia. Minneapolis: Fortress, 2007.

Johnson, E. Elizabeth. "Romans 9–11: The Faithfulness and Impartiality of God." In

Pauline Theology, volume 3: *Romans,* edited by David M. Hay and E. Elizabeth Johnson, pp. 211-39. Minneapolis: Fortress, 1995.

―――. *The First and Second Letters to Timothy: A New Translation with Introduction and Commentary.* Anchor Bible 35A. New York: Doubleday, 2001.

Johnson, Luke Timothy. *The Acts of the Apostles.* Sacra pagina 5. Collegeville, MN: Liturgical Press, 1992.

―――. *The First and Second Letters to Timothy: A New Translation with Introduction and Commentary.* Anchor Bible 35A. New York: Doubleday, 2001.

―――. *Scripture and Discernment: Decision Making in the Church.* Nashville: Abingdon, 1996.

Joyce, Paul M. *Ezekiel: A Commentary.* Library of Hebrew Bible/Old Testament Studies 482. New York; London: T. & T. Clark, 2007.

Kahn, Paul W. *Political Theology: Four New Chapters on the Concept of Sovereignty.* New York: Columbia University Press, 2011.

Käsemann, Ernst. *Commentary on Romans.* Translated and edited by Geoffrey W. Bromiley. Grand Rapids: Eerdmans, 1980.

―――. "Das Formular einer neutestamentlichen Ordinationsparänese." In *Neutestamentliche Studien für Rudolf Bultmann: Zu seinem siebzigsten Geburtstag,* edited by Walther Eltester, pp. 261-68. Beihefte zur Zeitschrift für die neutestamentliche Wissenschaft 21. Berlin: De Gruyter, 1954.

―――. "On Paul's Anthropology." In *Perspectives on Paul,* translated by Margaret Kohl, pp. 1-31. London: SCM, 1971.

Kayser, Wolfgang. *The Grotesque in Art and Literature.* Translated by U. Weisstein. Bloomington: Indiana University Press, 1963.

Keck, Leander E. *Romans.* Abingdon New Testament Commentaries. Nashville: Abingdon, 2005.

Kennedy, George A. *New Testament Interpretation through Rhetorical Criticism.* Chapel Hill: University of North Carolina Press, 1984.

Kermode, Frank. *The Genesis of Secrecy: On the Interpretation of Narrative.* Cambridge, MA: Harvard University Press, 1979.

Kim, Kyoung-Shik. *God Will Judge Each One according to Works: Judgment according to Works and Psalm 62 in Early Judaism and the New Testament.* Beihefte zur Zeitschrift für die neutestamentliche Wissenschaft 178. Berlin: De Gruyter, 2010.

Kim-Rauchholz, Mihamm. *Umkehr bei Lukas: Zu Wesel und Bedeutung der Metanoia in der Theologie des dritten Evangelisten.* Neukirchen-Vluyn: Neukirchener, 2008.

Kodell, Jerome. "'The Word of God Grew': The Ecclesial Tendency of Λόγος in Acts 6,7; 12,24; 19,20." *Biblica* 55 (1974): 505-19.

Kroeker, P. Travis. "Recent Continental Philosophy." In *The Blackwell Companion to Paul,* edited by Stephen Westerholm, pp. 440-54. Oxford and Malden, MA: Wiley-Blackwell, 2011.

Kuhlmann, Helga. "Christus — Vorbild? Grenzen und Chancen von Vorbildlichkeit aus theologischer Sicht." In *Fehlbare Vorbilder in Bibel, Christentum und Kirchen: Von Engeln, Propheten und Heiligen bis zu Päpsten und Bischöfinnen,* edited by

Helga Kuhlmann, pp. 143-59. Theologie in der Öffentlichkeit 2. Münster: LIT, 2010.

Kuhlmann, Helga, ed. *Fehlbare Vorbilder in Bibel, Christentum und Kirchen: Von Engeln, Propheten und Heiligen bis zu Päpsten und Bischöfinnen.* Theologie in der Öffentlichkeit 2. Münster: LIT, 2010.

Lakoff, George, and Mark Turner. *More Than Cool Reason: A Field Guide to Poetic Metaphor.* Chicago: University of Chicago Press, 1989.

Lambrecht, Jan. "Transgressor by Nullifying God's Grace: A Study of Gal 2,18-21." *Biblica* 72 (1991): 217-36.

Lampe, G. W. H. "The Holy Spirit in the Writings of St. Luke." In *Studies in the Gospels: Essays in Memory of R. H. Lightfoot,* edited by D. E. Nineham, pp. 159-200. Oxford: Basil Blackwell, 1955.

Lapsley, Jacqueline E. "Body Piercings: The Priestly Body and the 'Body' of the Temple in Ezekiel." *Hebrew Bible and Ancient Israel* 1 (2012): 231-45.

——. "Doors Thrown Open and Waters Gushing Forth: Mark, Ezekiel, and the Architecture of Hope." In *The Ending of Mark and the Ends of God: Essays in Honor of Donald Harrisville Juel,* edited by Beverly Roberts Gaventa and Patrick D. Miller, pp. 139-54. Louisville: Westminster John Knox, 2005.

Larsson, Göran. *Bound for Freedom: The Book of Exodus in Jewish and Christian Traditions.* Peabody, MA: Hendrickson, 1999.

Lategan, Bernard C. "Is Paul Defending His Apostleship in Galatians? The Function of Galatians 1.11-12 and 2.19-20 in the Development of Paul's Argument." *New Testament Studies* 34 (1988): 426-30.

Lee, Spike W. S., and Norberto Schwarz. "Dirty Hands and Dirty Mouths: Embodiment of the Moral-Purity Metaphor Is Specific to the Motor Modality Involved in Moral Transgression." *Psychological Science* 21 (2010): 1423-25.

——. "Washing Away Postdecisional Dissonance." *Science* 328 (2010): 709.

——. "Wiping the Slate Clean: Psychological Consequences of Physical Cleansing." *Current Directions in Psychological Science* 20 (2011): 307-11.

Leisegang, H. *Pneuma Hagion: Der Ursprung des Geistesbegriffs der synoptischen Evangelien aus der grieschen Mystik.* Leipzig: Hinrichs, 1922.

Levenson, Jon D. *Theology of the Program of Restoration of Ezekiel 40–48.* Harvard Semitic Monographs 10. Missoula, MT: Scholars, 1976.

Levison, John R. *Filled with the Spirit.* Grand Rapids: Eerdmans, 2009.

Lieberman, Saul. "Two Lexicographical Notes." *Journal of Biblical Literature* 65 (1946): 67-72.

Lightfoot, J. B. *The Epistle of St. Paul to the Galatians.* 10th edition. London: Macmillan, 1890; reprint, 1900.

——. *Saint Paul's Epistle to the Galatians: A Revised Text with Introduction, Notes and Dissertations.* London and New York: Macmillan, 1887.

Liljenquist, Katie, Chen-Bo Zhong, and Adam D. Galinsky. "The Smell of Virtue: Clean Scents Promote Reciprocity and Charity." *Psychological Science* 21 (2010): 381-83.

Longenecker, Bruce W. *Remember the Poor: Paul, Poverty, and the Greco-Roman World.* Grand Rapids: Eerdmans, 2010.

Longenecker, Richard N. *Galatians*. Word Biblical Commentary 41. Dallas: Word, 1990.

Lund, Øystein. *Way Metaphors and Ways Topics in Isaiah 40–55*. Forschungen zum Alten Testament 2/28. Tübingen: Mohr Siebeck, 2007.

Luther, Martin. "Preface to the Epistle of St. Paul to the Romans." In *Word and Sacrament*, edited by E. Theodore Bachmann. Volume 35 of *Luther's Works*. Philadelphia: Fortress, 1960.

Macchia, Frank. *Baptized in the Spirit: A Global Pentecostal Theology*. Grand Rapids: Zondervan, 2006.

MacMullen, Ramsay. "Women in Public in the Roman Empire." *Historia* 29 (1980): 208-18.

Maddox, Robert. *The Purpose of Luke-Acts*. Studies of the New Testament in Its World. Edinburgh: T. & T. Clark, 1982.

Malherbe, Abraham. "Godliness, Self-Sufficiency, Greed, and the Enjoyment of Wealth: 1 Timothy 6:3-19 Part II." *Novum Testamentum* 53 (2011): 73-96.

Marcus, Joel. "The *Testaments of the Twelve Patriarchs* and the *Didascalia Apostolorum*: A Common Jewish Christian Milieu?" *Journal of Theological Studies* 61 (2010): 596-626.

Marguerat, Daniel. *The First Christian Historian: Writing the 'Acts of the Apostles.'* Translated by Ken McKinney, Gregory J. Laughery, and Richard Bauckham. Society for New Testament Studies Monograph Series 121. Cambridge: Cambridge University Press, 2002.

Marquardt, Friedrich-Wilhelm. *Die Entdeckung des Judentums für die christliche Theologie: Israel im Denken Karl Barths*. Berlin: Kirchlich Hochschule, 1966. Reprint, Munich: Kaiser Verlag, 1967.

Marshall, I. Howard. *A Critical and Exegetical Commentary on the Pastoral Epistles*. International Critical Commentary. London: T. & T. Clark, 1999.

———. *The Gospel of Luke: A Commentary on the Greek Text*. New International Greek Testament Commentary. Grand Rapids: Eerdmans, 1978.

Martin, Dale B. *The Corinthian Body*. New Haven: Yale University Press, 1995.

Martyn, J. Louis. "Apocalyptic Antinomies in Paul's Letter to the Galatians." *New Testament Studies* 31 (1985): 410-24.

———. *Galatians: A New Translation with Introduction and Commentary*. Anchor Bible 33A. New York: Doubleday, 1997.

———. "*NOMOS* Plus Genitive Noun in Paul: The History of God's Law." In *Early Christianity and Classical Culture: Comparative Essays in Honor of Abraham J. Malherbe*, edited by John T. Fitzgerald, Thomas H. Olbricht, and L. Michael White, pp. 575-87. Novum Testamentum Supplements 110. Leiden: Brill, 2003.

———. *Theological Issues in the Letters of Paul*. Nashville: Abingdon, 1997.

Mauser, Ulrich W. *Christ in the Wilderness: The Wilderness Theme in the Second Gospel and Its Basis in the Biblical Tradition*. Studies in Biblical Theology 39. London: SCM, 1963.

Meeks, Wayne A. "Image of the Androgyne: Some Uses of a Symbol in Earliest Christianity." *History of Religions* 13 (1974): 165-208.

Mendelson, Alan. "Philo's Dialectic of Reward and Punishment." *Studia Philonica* 9 (1997): 104-25.

———. *Secular Education in Philo of Alexandria.* Cincinnati: Hebrew Union College Press, 1982.

Méndez-Moratalla, Fernando. *The Paradigm of Conversion in Luke.* Journal for the Study of the New Testament: Supplement Series 252. London: T. & T. Clark, 2004.

Menzies, Robert. *The Development of Early Christian Pneumatology: With Special Reference to Luke-Acts.* Journal for the Study of the New Testament: Supplement Series 54. Sheffield: Sheffield Academic Press, 1991.

———. *Empowered for Witness: The Spirit in Luke-Acts.* Journal of Pentecostal Theology: Supplemental Series 6. Sheffield: Sheffield Academic Press, 1994.

———. "Spirit and Power in Luke-Acts: A Response to Max Turner." *Journal for the Study of the New Testament* 49 (1993): 11-20.

Merkel, Helmut. *Die Pastoralbriefe.* Das Neue Testament Deutsch 9/1. Göttingen: Vandenhoeck & Ruprecht, 1991.

Merrill, Eugene H. "הלך." In volume 1 of *New International Dictionary of Old Testament Theology and Exegesis,* edited by Willem A. VanGemeren, pp. 1032-35. Grand Rapids: Zondervan, 1997.

Meyer, Paul W. "Pauline Theology: A Proposal for a Pause in Its Pursuit." In *Pauline Theology,* volume 4: *Looking Back, Pressing On,* edited by E. Elizabeth Johnson and David M. Hay, pp. 140-60. Atlanta: Scholars Press, 1997.

———. "The Worm at the Core of the Apple: Exegetical Reflections on Romans 7." In *The Conversation Continues: Studies in Paul and John in Honor of J. Louis Martyn,* edited by Robert T. Fortna and Beverly R. Gaventa, pp. 62-84. Nashville: Abingdon, 1990. Reprint in *The Word in This World: Essays in New Testament Exegesis and Theology,* edited by John T. Carroll, pp. 57-77. New Testament Library. Louisville: Westminster John Knox, 2004.

Middleton, J. Richard, and Michael J. Gorman. "Salvation." In *The New Interpreter's Dictionary of the Bible,* edited by Katharine Doob Sakenfeld et al., volume 5, pp. 45-61. Nashville: Abingdon, 2009.

Mihoc, Vasile. "The Final Admonition to Timothy (1 Tim 6,3-21)." In *1 Timothy Reconsidered,* edited by Karl P. Donfried, pp. 135-52. Colloquium Oecumenicum Paulinum 18. Leuven: Peeters, 2008.

Milbank, John, Slavoj Žižek, and Creston Davis. *Paul's New Moment: Continental Philosophy and the Future of Christian Theology.* Grand Rapids: Brazos, 2010.

Miller, James David. *The Pastoral Letters as Composite Documents.* Society for New Testament Studies Monograph Series 93. Cambridge: Cambridge University Press, 1997.

Miller, John B. F. *Convinced That God Had Called Us: Dreams, Visions, and the Perception of God's Will in Luke-Acts.* Biblical Interpretation Series 85. Leiden: Brill, 2007.

Minear, Paul S. "Luke's Use of the Birth Stories." In *Studies in Luke-Acts: Essays Presented in Honor of Paul Schubert,* edited by Leander E. Keck and J. Louis Martyn, pp. 111-30. Philadelphia: Fortress, 1980.

Moore, Carey A. *Tobit.* Anchor Bible 40A. Garden City, NY: Doubleday, 1996.

Motyer, J. Alec. *Isaiah: An Introduction and Commentary.* Tyndale Old Testament Commentaries 18. Downers Grove, IL: InterVarsity, 1999.

Moule, C. F. D. *An Idiom Book of New Testament Greek.* Cambridge: Cambridge University Press, 1959.

Mounce, William D. *Pastoral Epistles.* Word Biblical Commentary 46. Nashville: Thomas Nelson, 2000.

Najman, Hindy. "Towards a Study of the Uses of the Concept of Wilderness in Ancient Judaism." *Dead Sea Discoveries* 13 (2006): 99-113.

Nanos, Mark D. *The Mystery of Romans: The Jewish Context of Paul's Letter.* Minneapolis: Fortress, 1996.

————. "What Was at Stake in Peter's 'Eating with Gentiles' at Antioch?" In *The Galatians Debate: Contemporary Issues in Rhetorical and Historical Interpretation.* Edited by Mark D. Nanos, pp. 282-320. Peabody, MA: Hendrickson, 2002.

Nave, Guy D., Jr. "Conversion." In *The New Interpreter's Dictionary of the Bible,* edited by Katharine Doob Sakenfeld et al., volume 1, pp. 728-29. Nashville: Abingdon, 2009.

————. *The Role and Function of Repentance in Luke-Acts.* Academia Biblica 4. Atlanta: Society of Biblical Literature, 2002.

Noy, David. *Jewish Inscriptions of Western Europe,* volume 2: *The City of Rome.* Cambridge: Cambridge University Press, 1995.

Oakes, Peter. *Reading Romans in Pompeii: Paul's Letter at Ground Level.* Minneapolis: Fortress, 2009.

Odell, Margaret S. *Ezekiel.* Smyth & Helwys Bible Commentary 16. Macon, GA: Smyth & Helwys, 2005.

O'Neill, J. C. "The Connection between Baptism and the Gift of the Spirit in Acts." *Journal for the Study of the New Testament* 63 (1996): 87-103.

O'Reilly, Leo. *Word and Sign in the Acts of the Apostles: A Study in Lucan Theology.* Analecta Gregoriana 243; Series Facultatis Theologiae, Sectio B, 82. Rome: Editrice Pontificia Università Gregoriana, 1987.

Pagels, Elaine H. "Paul and Women: A Response to Recent Discussion." *Journal of the American Academy of Religion* 42 (1974): 538-49.

Pahl, Michael W. *Discerning the 'Word of the Lord': The 'Word of the Lord' in 1 Thessalonians 4:15.* Library of New Testament Studies 389. London: T. & T. Clark, 2009.

Pao, David W. *Acts and the Isaianic New Exodus.* Wissenschaftliche Untersuchungen zum Alten und Neuen Testament 2:130. Tübingen: Mohr Siebeck, 2000. Reprint, Grand Rapids: Baker Academic, 2002.

Pecknold, C. C. *Christianity and Politics: A Brief Guide to the History.* Eugene, OR: Cascade, 2010.

Penney, John Michael. *The Missionary Emphasis of Lukan Pneumatology.* Journal of Pentecostal Theology: Supplemental Series 12. Sheffield: Sheffield Academic Press, 1997.

Pervo, Richard I. *Acts: A Commentary.* Hermeneia. Minneapolis: Fortress, 2009.

Posner, Michael J., and Marcus E. Raichle. *Images of Mind.* New York: W. H. Freeman, 1997.

Preuss, Horst Dietrich. *Old Testament Theology.* Volume 2. Old Testament Library. Louisville: Westminster John Knox, 1996.

Quinn, Jerome D., and William C. Wacker. *The First and Second Letters to Timothy: A New Translation with Notes and Commentary.* Eerdmans Critical Commentary. Grand Rapids and Cambridge: Eerdmans, 2000.

Räisänen, Heikki. "Galatians 2.16 and Paul's Break with Judaism." *New Testament Studies* 31 (1985): 543-53.

Richardson, Neil. *Paul's Language about God.* Journal for the Study of the New Testament: Supplement Series 99. Sheffield: Sheffield Academic Press, 1994.

Rizzolatti, Giacomo, and Corrado Sinigaglia. *Mirrors in the Brain: How Our Minds Share Actions and Emotions.* Translated by Frances Anderson. Oxford: Oxford University Press, 2008.

Robertson, A. T. *A Grammar of the Greek New Testament in the Light of Historical Research.* New York: George H. Doran, 1914.

————. *A Grammar of the Greek New Testament in the Light of Historical Research.* 4th edition. New York: Hodder & Stoughton, 1923.

Roloff, Jürgen. *Der Erste Brief an Timotheus.* Evangelisch-katholischer Kommentar zum Neuen Testament 15. Zürich and Neukirchen-Vluyn: Benziger and Neukirchener, 1988.

Rose, Gillian. *The Broken Middle: Out of Our Ancient Society.* Hoboken, NJ: Wiley-Blackwell, 1992.

Rosner, Brian S. "The Progress of the Word." In *Witness to the Gospel: The Theology of Acts,* edited by I. Howard Marshall and David Peterson, pp. 215-33. Grand Rapids: Eerdmans, 1998.

Rowe, C. Kavin. "The Grammar of Life: The Areopagus Speech and Pagan Tradition." *New Testament Studies* 57 (2011): 31-50.

————. *World Upside Down: Reading Acts in the Graeco-Roman Age.* Oxford and New York: Oxford University Press, 2009.

Rusam, Dietrich. "Neue Belege zu dem *Stoicheia tou kosmou* (Gal 4,3.9; Kol 2,8.20)." *Zeitschrift für die neutestamentliche Wissenschaft und die Kunde der älteren Kirche* 83 (1992): 119-25.

Sampley, J. Paul. *Walking between the Times: Paul's Moral Reasoning.* Minneapolis: Fortress, 1991.

Sanders, E. P. "Jewish Association with Gentiles and Galatians 2:11-14." In *The Conversation Continues: Studies in Paul and John in Honor of J. Louis Martyn,* edited by Robert T. Fortna and Beverly R. Gaventa, pp. 170-88. Nashville: Abingdon, 1990.

————. *Paul and Palestinian Judaism: A Comparison of Patterns of Religion.* London: SCM, and Philadelphia: Fortress, 1977.

Satlow, Michael L. "'Fruit and the Fruit of Fruit': Charity and Piety among Jews in Late Antique Palestine." *Jewish Quarterly Review* 100 (2010): 244-77.

Schlier, Heinrich. *Der Römerbrief.* Herders Theologischer Kommentar zum Neuen Testament 6. Freiburg, Basel, and Vienna: Herder, 1979.

Schmitt, Carl. *Political Theology: Four Chapters on the Concept of Sovereignty.* Translated by George Schwab. Chicago: University of Chicago Press, 2005.

Schnall, Simone, Jennifer Benton, and Sophie Harvey. "With a Clean Conscience: Cleanliness Reduces the Severity of Moral Judgments." *Psychological Science* 19 (2008): 1219-22.

Schnall, Simone, Jonathan Haida, Gerald L. Clore, and Alexander H. Jordan. "Disgust as Embodied Moral Judgment." *Personality and Social Psychology Bulletin* 34 (2008): 1096-1109.

Schofield, Alison. "Wilderness." In *The Eerdmans Dictionary of Early Judaism,* edited John J. Collins and Daniel C. Harlow, pp. 1336-37. Grand Rapids: Eerdmans, 2010.

Schürer, Emil. *The History of the Jewish People in the Age of Jesus Christ.* Revised and edited by Geza Vermes, Fergus Millar, and Matthew Black. 2 volumes. Edinburgh: T. & T. Clark, 1979.

Schüssler Fiorenza, Elisabeth. *In Memory of Her: A Feminist Theological Reconstruction of Christian Origins.* New York: Crossroad, 1983.

Schweizer, Eduard. "Slaves of the Elements and Worshipers of Angels: Gal 4:3, 9 and Col 2:8, 18, 20." *Journal of Biblical Literature* 107 (1988): 455-68.

Scott, Ian W. *Paul's Way of Knowing: Story, Experience, and the Spirit.* Grand Rapids: Baker Academic, 2009.

Scroggs, Robin. "Paul and the Eschatological Woman." *Journal of the American Academy of Religion* 40 (1972): 283-303.

————. "Paul and the Eschatological Woman: Revisited." *Journal of the American Academy of Religion* 42 (1974): 532-37.

Shapiro, Lawrence. *Embodied Cognition.* New York: Routledge, 2010.

Sheldon, Charles Monroe. *In His Steps: What Would Jesus Do?* Redford, VA: Wilder Publications, 2008.

Shepherd, William H., Jr. *The Narrative Function of the Holy Spirit as a Character in Luke-Acts.* Society of Biblical Literature Dissertation Series 147. Atlanta: Scholars Press, 1994.

Sider, J. Alexander. *To See History Doxologically: History and Holiness in John Howard Yoder's Ecclesiology.* Grand Rapids: Eerdmans, 2011.

Silver, Kenneth E. *Chaos and Classicism: Art in France, Italy, and Germany, 1918-1936.* New York: Solomon R. Guggenheim Foundation, 2010.

Skinner, Matthew L. "Acts." In *Theological Bible Commentary,* edited by Gail R. O'Day and David L. Petersen, pp. 359-71. Louisville: Westminster John Knox, 2009.

Smith-Christopher, Daniel. *A Biblical Theology of Exile.* Minneapolis: Fortress, 2002.

Soards, Marion L. "Seeking (Zētein) and Sinning (Hamartōlos & Hamartia) according to Galatians 2.17." In *Apocalyptic and the New Testament: Essays in Honor of J. Louis Martyn,* edited by Joel Marcus and Marion L. Soards, pp. 237-54. Journal for the Study of the New Testament: Supplemental Series 24. Sheffield: Sheffield Academic Press, 1989.

Sprinkle, Preston M. *Law and Life: The Interpretation of Leviticus 18:5 in Early Judaism and in Paul.* Wissenschaftliche Untersuchungen zum Neuen Testament 2:241. Tübingen: Mohr Siebeck, 2008.

Stead, William Thomas. *If Christ Came to Chicago: A Plea for the Union of All Who Love in the Service of All Who Suffer.* Chicago: Laird & Lee, 1894. Reprint, BiblioLife, 2009.

Steiner, George. *Grammars of Creation.* New Haven: Yale University Press, 2001.

Stendahl, Krister. *Paul among Jews and Gentiles.* Philadelphia: Fortress, 1976.

Stockhausen, Carol Kern. *Moses' Veil and the Glory of the New Covenant: The Exegetical Substructure of II Cor. 3,1–4,6.* Analecta biblica 116. Rome: Pontificio Instituto Biblica, 1989.

Talbert, Charles H. *Reading Luke-Acts in Its Mediterranean Milieu.* Novum Testamentum Supplements 107. Leiden: Brill, 2003.

Talmon, Shemaryahu. "The 'Desert Motif' in the Bible and in Qumran Literature." In *Biblical Motifs: Origins and Transformation,* edited by Alexander Altman, pp. 31-63. Cambridge, MA: Harvard University Press, 1966.

Tannehill, Robert C. *Luke.* Abingdon New Testament Commentaries. Nashville: Abingdon, 1996.

—————. *The Narrative Unity of Luke-Acts: A Literary Interpretation.* 2 volumes. Philadelphia and Minneapolis: Fortress, 1986-1990.

—————. "Repentance in the Context of Lukan Soteriology." In *God's Word for Our World,* volume 2: *Theological and Cultural Studies in Honor of Simon J. De Vries,* edited by J. Harold Ellens, pp. 199-215. Journal for the Study of the Old Testament 389. London: T. & T. Clark, 2004.

Taubes, Jacob. *The Political Theology of Paul.* Translated by Dana Hollander. Stanford: Stanford University Press, 2004.

Taylor, Nicholas H. "The Social Nature of Conversion in the Early Christian World." In *Modelling Early Christianity: Social-Scientific Studies of the New Testament in Its Context,* edited by Philip F. Esler, pp. 128-36. London: Routledge, 1995.

Thiselton, Anthony C. *The First Epistle to the Corinthians.* New International Greek Testament Commentary. Grand Rapids: Eerdmans, 2000.

Thompson, Alan J. *One Lord, One People: The Unity of the Church in Acts in Its Literary Setting.* Library of New Testament Studies 359. London: T. & T. Clark, 2008.

Thompson, Cynthia L. "Hairstyles, Head-coverings, and St. Paul: Portraits from Roman Corinth." *Biblical Archaeologist* 51 (1988): 99-115.

Thompson, Richard P. *Keeping the Church in Its Place: The Church as Narrative Character in Acts.* New York: T. & T. Clark, 2006.

Thweatt-Bates, Jennifer. "On Creation, New Creation and the Natural Order: A Theological Reading of 1 Corinthians 11.2-16." *Leaven* 16 (2008): 86-90.

Torrance, T. F. *Space, Time and Resurrection.* Edinburgh: Handsel Press, 1976.

Towner, Philip H. *The Letters to Timothy and Titus.* New International Commentary on the New Testament. Grand Rapids: Eerdmans, 2006.

Tuell, Steven. *Ezekiel.* New International Biblical Commentary 15. Peabody, MA: Hendrickson, 2009.

Turner, Max. *Power from on High: The Spirit in Israel's Restoration and Witness in Luke-Acts.* Journal of Pentecostal Theology: Supplemental Series 9. Sheffield: Sheffield Academic Press, 1996.

—————. "The Work of the Holy Spirit in Luke-Acts." *Word and World* 23 (2003): 146-53.

Twelftree, Graham H. *People of the Spirit: Exploring Luke's View of the Church.* London: SPCK, 2009. Reprint, Grand Rapids: Baker Academic, 2009.

VanderKam, James C. "The Judean Desert and the Community of the Dead Sea Scrolls." In *Antikes Judentum und Frühes Christentum: Festschrift für Hartmut Stegemann zum 65. Geburtstag,* edited by Bernd Kollmann et al., pp. 159-71. Beihefte zur Zeitschrift für die neutestamentliche Wissenschaft 97. Berlin: De Gruyter, 1998.

van Gennep, Arnold. *The Rites of Passage.* Chicago: University of Chicago Press, 1961 [1909].

van Unnik, W. C. "'With Unveiled Face': An Exegesis of 2 Corinthians iii 12-18." *Novum Testamentum* 6 (1963): 153-69.

Wagner, Ross. *Heralds of the Good News: Isaiah and Paul "in Concert" in the Letter to the Romans.* Novum Testamentum Supplements 101. Leiden: Brill, 2002.

Wall, Robert W. "The Acts of the Apostles: Introduction, Commentary, and Reflections." In *The New Interpreter's Bible,* edited by Leander E. Keck, volume 10, pp. 1-368. Nashville: Abingdon, 2002.

Wan, Sze-kar. *Power in Weakness: Conflict and Rhetoric in Paul's Second Letter to the Corinthians.* The New Testament in Context. Harrisburg, PA: Trinity Press International, 2000.

Watson, Francis. "The Authority of the Voice: A Theological Reading of 1 Cor 11:2-16." *New Testament Studies* 46 (2000): 520-36.

———. *Paul and the Hermeneutics of Faith.* London and New York: T. & T. Clark, 2004.

———. *Paul, Judaism, and the Gentiles: Beyond the New Perspective.* Revised edition. Grand Rapids: Eerdmans, 2007.

———. "Scripture in Pauline Theology: How Far Down Does It Go?" *Journal of Theological Interpretation* 2 (2008): 181-92.

Watts, John D. W. *Isaiah 34–66.* Revised edition. Word Biblical Commentary 25. Waco, TX: Thomas Nelson, 2005.

Watts, Rikki E. "Consolation or Confrontation? Isaiah 40–55 and the Delay of the New Exodus." *Tyndale Bulletin* 41 (1990): 31-59.

———. "Exodus." In *New Dictionary of Biblical Theology,* edited by T. D. Alexander and Brian S. Rosner, pp. 478-87. Downers Grove, IL: InterVarsity, 2000.

Weaver, John B. *Plots of Epiphany: Prison-Escape in Acts of the Apostles.* Beihefte zur Zeitschrift für die neutestamentliche Wissenschaft 131. Berlin: De Gruyter, 2004.

Weima, Jeffrey A. D. "Gal 6:11-18: A Hermeneutical Key to the Galatian Letter." *Calvin Theological Journal* 28 (1993): 90-107.

Welker, Michael. "Rethinking Christocentric Theology." In *Transformations in Luther's Theology: Historical and Contemporary Reflections,* edited by Christine Helmer and Bo Kristian Holm, pp. 179-92. Arbeiten zur Kirchen- und Theologiegeschichte 32. Leipzig: Evangelische Verlagsanstalt, 2011.

———. *What Happens in Holy Communion?* Grand Rapids: Eerdmans, 2000.

Wilckens, Ulrich. *Der Brief an die Römer.* Evangelisch-katholischer Kommentar zum Neuen Testament. 3 volumes. Zurich/Neukirchen: Benziger, 1978-82.

Winger, Michael. *By What Law? The Meaning of Νόμος in the Letters of Paul.* Society of Biblical Literature Dissertation Series 128. Atlanta: Scholars Press, 1992.

Wink, Walter. *Engaging the Powers: Discernment and Resistance in a World of Domination.* Minneapolis: Fortress, 1992.

———. *Naming the Powers: The Language of Power in the New Testament.* Philadelphia: Fortress, 1984.

———. *Unmasking the Powers: The Invisible Forces That Determine Human Existence.* Philadelphia: Fortress, 1986.

Wire, Antoinette Clark. *The Corinthian Women Prophets: A Reconstruction through Paul's Rhetoric.* Minneapolis: Fortress, 1990.

Wright, N. T. *The Climax of the Covenant: Christ and the Law in Pauline Theology.* Edinburgh: T. & T. Clark, 1991.

———. *Jesus and the Victory of God.* Christian Origins and the Question of God 2. Minneapolis: Fortress, 1996.

———. "Paul and Empire." In *The Blackwell Companion to Paul,* edited by Stephen Westerholm, pp. 285-97. Oxford and Malden, MA: Wiley-Blackwell, 2011.

———. "Reflected Glory: 2 Corinthians 3:18." In *The Glory of Christ in the New Testament: Studies in Christology in Memory of George Bradford Caird,* edited by L. D. Hurst and N. T. Wright, pp. 139-50. Oxford: Clarendon, 1987.

Yamazaki-Ransom, Kazuhiko. *The Roman Empire in Luke's Narrative.* Library of New Testament Studies 404. London: T. & T. Clark, 2010.

Yinger, Kent L. *Paul, Judaism, and Judgment according to Deeds.* Society for New Testament Studies Monograph Series 105. Cambridge: Cambridge University Press, 1999.

Yoder, John Howard. *The Politics of Jesus: Vicit Agnus Noster.* 2nd edition. Grand Rapids: Eerdmans, 1994.

———. *The Priestly Kingdom: Social Ethics as Gospel.* Notre Dame: University of Notre Dame Press, 1984.

Yu, Ning. "Metaphor from Body and Culture." In *The Cambridge Handbook of Metaphor and Thought,* edited by Raymond W. Gibbs Jr., pp. 247-61. Cambridge: Cambridge University Press, 2010.

Zeller, Dieter. "The Life and Death of the Soul in Philo of Alexandria: The Use and Origin of a Metaphor." *Studia Philonica* 7 (1995): 19-55.

Zhong, Chen-Bo, and Katie Liljenquist. "Washing Away Your Sins: Threatened Morality and Physical Cleansing." *Science* 313 (2006): 1451-52.

Zimmerli, Walther. *Ezekiel 1.* Translated by Ronald E. Clements. Hermeneia. Philadelphia: Fortress, 1979.

Zwiep, Arie W. *Christ, the Spirit and the Community of God: Essays on the Acts of the Apostles.* Wissenschaftliche Untersuchungen zum Alten und Neuen Testament 2:293. Tübingen: Mohr Siebeck, 2010.

Index of Modern Authors

Adams, Edward, 132n33, 216n14
Anderson, Gary, 245

Badiou, Alain, 154-55, 188n33, 193
Bakhtin, Mikhail, 1n1
Barclay, John M. G., 150n1, 156n9, 172-73
Barr, James, 142n11
Barrett, C. K., 66n16
Barth, Karl, 113n16, 155, 187, 192n43, 261-76, 270n4
Beker, J. Christiaan, 140n5, 230n16
Benton, Jennifer, 31n38
Berger, Klaus, 36
Betz, Hans Dieter, 226-27, 235n33, 237n41
Blinzler, Josef, 217n21
Bockmuehl, Markus N. A., 133nn35-36
Booth, Wayne C., 52n39
Bovon, François, 66n20
Bowen, Nancy, 13n27
Brown, Raymond E., 51n34
Bruce, F. F., 43n6, 44n11, 48n26, 56n50, 231n22, 232n25, 237n40

Calvin, John, 113n16, 156-57, 157n10, 258-60, 287-88
Campbell, Douglas A., 105n5
Carr, David M., 9n23
Carson, David A., 233n26
Chatman, Seymour, 52n39

Childs, Brevard, 28
Clore, Gerald L., 31n38
Coakley, Sarah, 174-75
Coleridge, Mark, 51
Conzelmann, Hans, 61
Cranfield, C. E. B., 108n10
Crossan, John Dominic, 278-79
Cullmann, Oscar, 142n11

Das, A. Andrew, 232n25
de Boer, Martinus C., 146, 229n15, 230n17
Dobbs-Allsopp, F. W., 8
Downs, David J., 248n21
Dschulnigg, Peter, 243n4
Dunn, James D. G., 44n12, 103n2, 229, 232n25, 233, 233nn26-27, 234n28, 235, 239

Eubank, Nathan, 244-47

Fee, Gordon, 239
Finn, Thomas M., 15
Fitzmyer, Joseph A., 43n8, 47n19, 48n27, 63n10, 66n16
Franklin, Eric, 60n2
Friesen, Steven J., 252n31
Fuller, Michael E., 18

Galambush, Julie, 7n14, 8

Index of Scripture References and Other Ancient Sources